Praise for

*From Binge to Blackout*

"I recommend this book to parents, students, and anyone interested in the current alcohol culture in which many of today's young people have become so entrenched. The dangerous attitudes and behaviors toward alcohol that many are exhibiting are a threat to the future of our children. I admire the courage it took Toren to recognize and overcome the devastation that alcohol was having on his life before it was too late. We challenge each of you to be aware of alcohol abuse and to educate yourselves and your children about the potential deadly consequences. It cost our family the ultimate, as our daughter, Samantha, died in September 2004 of acute alcohol poisoning. Our goal is to prevent another family from having to endure the pain of losing a child in such a senseless and preventable manner."

—Patty Spady, mother of nineteen-year-old Samantha Spady,
a student who died of alcohol poisoning at Colorado State University

"This is an important candid book by a mother and son who had to reconstruct all the warning signals they missed as alcohol and drugs invaded the perfect American family. I urge parents and their teenage children to read it together so they avoid the same fate."

—David Rosenbloom, Ph.D., director of Join Together and
Youth Alcohol Prevention Center, professor of public
health, Boston University

"There are many books written about drinking problems and alcoholism, but it's always someone else's family. Chris and Toren bring us inside a family as if it were our own. The struggles, denial, confrontations, lying, and eventually hope are all there as they attempt to reach other families. This book teaches and touches the reader. I recommend it to everyone who wants help for their family and to those who help families everywhere."

—Robert J. Ackerman, Ph.D., coauthor of
*Chicken Soup for the Recovering Soul*

"An important book for every parent of a teenager. This fearless and searching diary brings the reality home that alcohol does not care who it conquers. *From Binge to Blackout* offers honesty, hope, and hands-on guidance for parents and teens to make empowering choices."

—Marci Shimoff, coauthor of *Chicken Soup for the Woman's Soul*

"Having lost a husband to the ravages of alcoholism and drug addiction, Toren's gut-wrenching descriptions of hangovers, blackouts, attitudes, and withdrawals were incredibly touching, honest, and real to me. The torment of a loved one around the disease, as shared in Chris's open and honest writings, is equally on-target. *From Binge to Blackout* gives a rock-honest snapshot of feelings and symptoms of the disease of alcoholism that can be trusted to open people's eyes and, in all hopes, reach our youth and families in time to restore relationships and save lives."        —Susie Vanderlip, author of *52 Ways to Protect Your Teen*

"*From Binge to Blackout* . . . underscores why it is so important to address underage drinking issues with our children at a very early age . . . a candid, often heartbreaking revelation of what the 'perfect' family experiences when coping with an alcoholic adolescent. . . . The Volkmann family is to be commended for giving us such an honest and sometimes heartbreaking glimpse into their lives."

—Mikey L. Hoeven, first lady of North Dakota,
member of Leadership to Keep Children Alcohol Free,
the governors' spouses initiative

"This book is a treasure of education, insight, and experience about alcoholism. The authors have captured the essence of the struggle millions of families go through to get out of the alcoholic system and into recovery. Reading this book will open your brain, your guts, and your heart to an effective way of processing this diabolical disease."

—C. J. Kirk, LICSW, senior alcohol and drug consultant to
Peace Corps Office Medical Services (1984–2004)

"A profoundly honest and real story that all families could benefit from. The back-and-forth dialogue between parent and child about the pain, fear, and destructive consequences makes it feel like you have witnessed a ten-round boxing match."

—Stephen Bogan, MA, chemical dependency professional<br>division of substance abuse, State of Washington<br>nationally certified addiction counselor, youth treatment lead

"There aren't many books written in this style. Families, particularly parents, will find this book a helpful tool to understand addiction. This book will help move our society toward acceptance, which in turn will open doors for higher-quality treatment and decrease the tendency to look at the disease as a moral issue. I will definitely recommend this book to my patients!"

—Katie Revenaugh, BS, CDP, chemical dependency professional

"Because college is such a life-changing experience and drinking such a big part of it, [this book] will have an impact on campuses everywhere. I learned a lot, I cried, and the honesty was touching."

—Susan Fiksdal, Ph.D., Evergreen State College

---

As a national goal, the U.S. Surgeon General has established a 50 percent reduction in college binge drinking by the year 2010.

# FROM BINGE TO BLACKOUT

## A MOTHER AND SON STRUGGLE WITH TEEN DRINKING

## CHRIS VOLKMANN
### AND TOREN VOLKMANN

Foreword by Cardwell C. Nuckols, PhD
Introduction by Reverend Edward A. Malloy

**A Revised and Updated Edition of *Our Drink***

 NEW AMERICAN LIBRARY

New American Library
Published by New American Library, a division of
Penguin Group (USA) Inc., 375 Hudson Street,
New York, New York 10014, USA
Penguin Group (Canada), 90 Eglinton Avenue East, Suite 700, Toronto,
Ontario M4P 2Y3, Canada (a division of Pearson Penguin Canada Inc.)
Penguin Books Ltd., 80 Strand, London WC2R 0RL, England
Penguin Ireland, 25 St. Stephen's Green, Dublin 2,
Ireland (a division of Penguin Books Ltd.)
Penguin Group (Australia), 250 Camberwell Road, Camberwell, Victoria 3124,
Australia (a division of Pearson Australia Group Pty. Ltd.)
Penguin Books India Pvt. Ltd., 11 Community Centre, Panchsheel Park,
New Delhi - 110 017, India
Penguin Group (NZ), cnr Airborne and Rosedale Roads, Albany,
Auckland 1310, New Zealand (a division of Pearson New Zealand Ltd.)
Penguin Books (South Africa) (Pty.) Ltd., 24 Sturdee Avenue,
Rosebank, Johannesburg 2196, South Africa

Penguin Books Ltd., Registered Offices:
80 Strand, London WC2R 0RL, England

Published by New American Library, a division of Penguin Group (USA) Inc. Previously published in a different
version under the title *Our Drink*.

First Printing (Revised Edition), August 2006
10  9  8  7  6  5  4  3  2  1

Copyright © Chris Volkmann and Toren Volkmann, 2004, 2006
Foreword copyright © Cardwell C. Nuckols, Ph.D., 2006
Introduction copyright © Reverend Edward A. Malloy, 2006
Art on pages 90 and 126 by Virginia Norey
All rights reserved

*(For publisher's note and author permissions and copyrights see page 411.)*

REGISTERED TRADEMARK — MARCA REGISTRADA

LIBRARY OF CONGRESS CATALOGING-IN-PUBLICATION DATA:

Volkmann, Chris.
　　From binge to blackout: a mother and son struggle with teen drinking/Chris Volkmann and Toren
Volkmann.
　　　　p.  cm.
　　Includes bibliographical references and index.
　　ISBN 0-451-21909-0 (trade pbk.)
　　　　1. Volkmann, Toren.　2. Volkmann, Chris.　3. Alcoholics—United States—Biography.
4. Alcoholics—United States—Family relationships.　5. Teenage boys—Alcohol use—United States—Case
studies.　6. College students—Alcohol use—United States—Case studies.　7. Binge drinking.
　I. Volkmann, Toren.　II. Title.
　　HV5293.V65V64   2006
　　616.86'1092—dc22　　　　　2006001495

Set in Granjon
Designed by Ginger Legato

Printed in the United States of America

*For Don, Tanler, Tyson*

# CONTENTS

# ACKNOWLEDGMENTS

*Thank you to Stephen Bogan for inspiration and long-standing* belief in our work. Thank you to Nancy Harper for insight and wisdom. Accolades for all that you do.

Deep gratitude forever to C. J. Kirk and Larry Perez.

Thank you to our devoted first readers: Susan Fiksdal, Tara Ivey, Peg Ludwick, Chris Maxwell, Dan Murphy, Charles Smith, Sean Walsh.

From the first stirrings of this book, we are grateful for the support of Father Malloy and the gentle loyalty of C. C. Nuckols.

For dogged persistence and attention to every detail, thank you, Adam Chromy. We are indebted to Mark Chait, Kara Welsh, and the exceptional professionals at New American Library.

Toren thanks all of his friends throughout the years, and Peace Corps Paraguay (G-11).

Thank you to our steadfast friends and family for continuing love and support, especially Ken and Marguerite Shamberger, Walt Volkmann, Dave Volkmann, Paul Volkmann, Pam Selby, Linda Larson, Jay and Carla Quine, Elaine Shamberger and Neil Smith, Cheryl Selby, Kaye and Jerry Smith.

The spirit of this book belongs to Ric Volkmann, Montana Donini, and Nadia Melinkovich.

# INTRODUCTION

*It is often on residential college and university campuses where* young adults live on their own for the first time. This is where the peer culture is primed for having a good time, especially on the weekends, and alcohol use and misuse becomes the preoccupation of faculty, administrators, dorm staff, community neighbors, and government officials. It is not just the behavior of the isolated abuser. Rather, it is the whole peer culture that validates and sustains such activity, which is a matter of profound concern.

In the course of my professional career I have participated in, and chaired, a number of studies that have examined at the local, regional, and national level the extent of adolescent and young adult use and abuse of alcohol and other drugs, as well as the most effective strategies for combating the problem and for providing therapeutic assistance to those who suffer from unhealthy or addictive patterns of involvement.

This timely and important book combines a sustained mother/son narrative of one family's discovery of alcoholism and all the ramifications of this reality on the family dynamics. Included in the book are summaries of the best scientific perspectives on the nature of addiction and steps that can be taken by parents, teachers, counselors, and concerned adults to effectively intervene in this negative pattern. As Alcoholics Anonymous and other therapeutic groups have discovered, one person's (or family's) story of dysfunction and return to health can evoke the attention of other persons (or families) in order for their story to emerge.

*From Binge to Blackout* can serve as an excellent primer for those unfamiliar with the literature of teenage and young adult substance abuse. It is very practical and user-friendly in structure and orientation. I recommend it for those who, like the Volkmann family, need to make a fresh start from binges and blackouts to health and happiness.

—Reverend Edward A. Malloy, President Emeritus of Notre Dame, Board Member, the National Center on Addiction and Substance Abuse

*Most readers prefer to read an autobiography full of unexpected* events, tragic downfalls, and victories won at a great cost. We want to be taken on a journey that allows us to glean the character of the individuals involved, and, in the process, learn something about our lives as we reflect on others' struggles. I think it is also true that we readers prefer the miraculous to the commonplace. We look for those moments that are self-defining. It is those moments of conflict and resolution that teach us not only about the characters of the story but about our personal resolve and resources.

*From Binge to Blackout* is such an autobiography. In the length of time it takes to leave a voice message, a family is thrown into the abyss. Toren's call to his family telling them of his transfer back to the States to undergo alcoholism rehabilitation shatters the illusion of a "perfect" American family. It could happen to your family and it can happen to mine. That is one reason this book is vital. We can always learn from others' conflicts. We can derive hope from their courage. We can understand that we are not alone and that help is available.

I wish this chronicle of rapid addiction and binge drinking were an uncommon story. Unfortunately, it is not. This fact—exemplified in the story of Toren Volkmann's drinking life—is what makes this book so significant. Toren, the youngest of three sons, shared everything—

including fake IDs—with his brothers. One thing they did not share was Toren's proclivity for addiction. Not even science can predict with great accuracy who will develop alcoholism. We can only hope that supporting prevention initiatives will, in the future, help minimize this risk. And for those who love an alcoholic, we can learn to be prepared. *From Binge to Blackout* spells out such action on multiple levels. It teaches that although love and honesty are critical, it is apposite, expedient action that can save the day and maybe a life. In Toren's case, his incredible potential—in recovery—serves as a gift to the world.

The story of Toren Volkmann and his mother, Chris, is a story of hope and courage. Every family has its secrets. Maybe it is true that love is blind. How could an adolescent-turned-young-man have kept the symptoms of binge drinking from discovery by two intelligent, accomplished parents? The answer is easy! It happens all the time. The little episodes involving alcohol and drugs are seen as isolated events. What family wants to admit that their child has a problem?

There is an awakening in the twenty-twenty hindsight of life experience. Like any mosaic, the pieces were always there. Maybe the greatest gift of *From Binge to Blackout* is that it teaches families to be more aware of the details. In the business of life, the most important thing we do is raise our children. We revel in their success and obsess over their failures. Unfortunately, our desire for their success sometimes clouds our vision.

The story you are about to read will burn through the fog. You may be confronted with an understanding that, at times, may be a little too close to home and more than a little uncomfortable. Use this clarity to define your character. Whether a mother, father, brother, sister, friend, educator, or member of the clergy, we need to understand that to save lives and families there are times that call for fortitude in action. *From Binge to Blackout* calls us all out. After you read this moving story of love and pain, you will never be able to close your eyes or turn your back on the small and great symptoms and pleas for help from those suffering from this devastating disease.

Please understand that the alcoholic will not often come forward professing distress. Theirs is an illness that precludes clarity. It is up to us—the people who love them and understand their great potential—to take action. Do not be angered and confused by the alcoholic's abhorrent behavior. As Toren's story reveals, there is a beautiful human being full of potential and hope waiting to make a positive mark on this world.

Alcoholism is a lonely place. Alcoholics are hard to get close to. They protect their precious drink with denial, lies, and rationalizations. Had Chris rejected her son and withdrawn love and commitment, Toren might still be drinking today. On the other hand, there is a particular strength that Toren possesses called self-directedness. Often the level of self-directedness at the beginning of treatment predicts the degree of improvement. Self-directedness involves a sense of responsibility, purposefulness, resourcefulness, self-acceptance, and hopefulness. These traits are found in Toren.

*From Binge to Blackout* is an uncommon story of alcoholism and the family. It is one that ends in sobriety bringing a family closer together. So often alcoholism and addiction tears families apart or, at best, leaves long-lasting scars. In fact, a crisis such as alcoholism will never leave those involved the same. It either destroys or strengthens relationships. *From Binge to Blackout* is a recipe or road map for empowering bonds between loved ones. Not only does it strengthen bonds, but it shapes the character of those involved.

I well remember the first time I met Chris and Toren. We were in West Yellowstone at an alcohol and drug treatment conference. As I walked down a hallway, both Chris and Toren were sitting on the left. They were promoting their book *Our Drink: Detoxing the Perfect Family*. Although Toren was reserved, Chris's love for her son and enthusiasm about their mutual project was infectious. I guess I caught that infection.

It is easy to see myself and my family in this moving story. Toren's drinking history ranged from age fourteen to twenty-four. At twenty-four he seems to have found contentment in a lasting sobriety. Part of his recovery involves "giving it away to keep it." In other words, he and his mother take the message of hope and recovery to high schools, universities, and conferences of many varieties.

I used alcohol and other drugs during the same age range. The last thirty-five years of my life have been spent teaching others about alcoholism and drug addiction. My son is fifteen years old and comes from a family with a long history of alcoholism and depressive disorders. If we are faced with the same family problem of alcoholism, I hope that the outcome brings us closer together, as in the case of Chris and Toren.

Just about every family can feel kinship to the Volkmanns. Just about every family member of an alcoholic knows the pain and disillusionment brought on by addiction. Just about every family can find valuable lessons in *From Binge to Blackout*. Maybe the greatest lesson is that love and personal involvement are the greatest medicine.

—Cardwell C. Nuckols, M.A., Ph.D.

# ONE

# A PERFECT START

 **Friends and acquaintances joked about our family,** how they couldn't stand us. Our successful suburban household included three athletic boys with a strong work ethic and sensitivity; my husband, Don, with killer abs and two medical specialty degrees; and me, the mom who was a Renaissance woman, a former classroom teacher who had abandoned the public schools to lead her family to the pinnacle of fulfillment.

Yup. Our family did it all: kids turning out for three varsity sports each year, music lessons, community volunteering, snow skiing, summer jobs; Mom founding a public-school art docent program while running marathons and playing viola in the local symphony; Dr. Dad coaching soccer and coordinating team sports efforts between on-call jags. Our boys had supportive grandparents and aunts and uncles; dinner together in the family home; household chores; and a pet beagle—a true nuclear family myth.

All our sons graduated from college with solid grades. We could breathe a sigh of relief. We could stick out our chests and proclaim that, indeed, our way of raising kids worked. We had done it the right way. Backpacking as a family throughout the Pacific Northwest built the boys' character and persistence. They seemed to temper a healthy rebellious-

1

ness with good manners and positive intent. College admissions committees everywhere could look to our family for the "how-to" manual on successfully raising children.

Even though we had achieved a comfortable lifestyle, we stressed to our sons that they must be responsible for their own futures. Neither my husband nor I had come from privileged backgrounds. My husband's father worked for a trucking company and cultivated a small orchard, while his mother held down a secretarial job; my own parents served as educators in the public schools. Both of us took our educations seriously, fueled by defined goals and strong family ties. We applied these principles to the raising of our children.

Were there bumps in the road? Sure. Did we dwell on them? As little as possible. Did we hang out the dirty laundry? Seldom. Boys will be boys, after all. They weren't saints. They had energetic, adventurous spirits that sometimes got them in trouble. But better that than always safe and boring. After all, their mom and dad lived pretty adventurous lives too!

Our family did have its ups and downs. The boys gave us our share of sleepless nights. They were naughty on the playground in grade school, acted out in class at times, slipped out at night and experimented with alcohol and drugs in high school. In fact, if you added up their infractions over the years, we'd have a ledgerful. There were imposed penalties and restrictions, along with some MIPs (Minor in Possession, the charge for underage kids who are caught drinking by the law). My husband and I intervened as best we could; we even purchased a Breathalyzer and checked the boys when they came home on their high school curfew. But most people advised us not to worry about such missteps. They were part of growing up. Everyone had them in their youth.

During college, the brothers returned home for breaks and we were concerned they partied too much. They stayed out too late. Drank excessively. And we suspected that at times they had smoked cigarettes and sampled other social drugs. But my husband and I tried to be understanding because we had done the same things in the '60s and '70s. We'd experimented, but we handled it. And we had talked with our kids about moderation, about binge drinking, about setting goals, about not closing doors by taking thoughtless risks. We had been up front with them. Our family weathered those challenges, and believed we were on to better times. After all, our kids had graduated college. Their youthful indiscretions were history. We had successfully hatched, nurtured, and educated them for the larger world. Now we could sit back and watch them take their places. Or so we thought. . . .

Until that phone call.

It was the call from our then-twenty-four-year-old son, the youngest, the call telling us that he was considering committing himself to a rehab program for alcoholism.

Becoming an alcoholic couldn't have been that sudden for our son. There had been clues about what might happen, *about what was happening.* But until we filled in the scattered, morphed shapes on our paint-by-number child-rearing tableau, until we stepped back, we couldn't see. It was difficult for us to recognize our youngest son among the stricken slashes of color and pattern, and tough to make out his two brothers camouflaged there as well. Then, identifying *ourselves* took even more scrutiny. Through this painful process, I realized that the story of our family needed to be told.

The problem isn't just *too much to drink*; it is the fact that alcohol addiction happens before our very eyes, even under the conditions of success. And we don't recognize it. That's what is scary. Our son was killing himself in our presence, over several years' time, and we didn't see it. If the statistics about binge drinking in schools and colleges are true, then there must be more families like ours in the United States—and around the world.

"When did this happen?" we asked our son. A college graduate for hardly a year at that point, Toren confessed not only to having drunk alcohol since early high school but to have been binge drinking since that time. He said that's where it started. And we discovered that even though our son had graduated from the D.A.R.E. program (Drug Abuse Resistance Education, a drug and alcohol education program offered in the public schools), and was accepted into high school Honors Society, he had outsmarted us and even himself when it came to the deception of alcohol abuse.

Many kids these days talk casually about drinking or getting wasted, or binge drinking and blacking out. It's like mentioning going to a latte stand, as commonplace as snacking on popcorn at a movie. Binge drinking is not only a social custom among youth, it is an epidemic. In fact, binge drinking is the most widespread health problem in the United States on college campuses.[1] A 2003 multicampus study at Wake Forest University School of Medicine found that 63 percent of students under age twenty-one drink, and that 20 percent of the drinkers usually have seven or more drinks. More than half (54 percent) of the drinkers said they get drunk at least weekly.[2] Getting drunk is cited as the primary reason for consuming alcohol by 47 percent of students who drink.[3] The U.S. Surgeon General has established a goal of a 50 percent reduction in college binge drinking by the year 2010.[4]

After Toren's call, I searched the Web, thinking I might find books about teen drinking from the viewpoint of the family. There were some that discussed bingeing and others that presented information about alcohol and addiction, but missing was a matter-of-fact dialogue for families, one that addressed current practices of alcohol consumption in our cul-de-sacs and on our campuses.

Particularly absent from current literature was the bruised authenticity delivered by Toren when he sent us a journal entry revealing how his alcohol abuse had brought him to the point of desperation while he was volunteering in the Peace Corps in South America. It seemed Toren had slid overnight from a position of responsibility and respect into the depths of alcoholism. He faced immediate inpatient admittance to a rehabilitation facility. But Toren's severe problem with alcohol did not originate on a Peace Corps assignment in a foreign country. It began perhaps even before he was born. It marched with him through his youth and we missed all the signs. It trod through his adolescence and we thought it merely a flirtation. Now this alcohol calamity has shredded the veneer of our family. It has stomped on all that we provided for Toren and his brothers and kicked it in our faces.

When Toren called with the news of his alcoholism, I thought it was the end. So we'll start there—the end at the beginning.

# TWO
## *THE END AT THE BEGINNING*

**[CHRIS]** *September 22, 2003. When I got the message on* my answering machine, I was in shock. It was in three languages: English, Guarani, and Spanish. How do you understand a revelation like that even in one language?

Toren greeted us in Guarani, an indigenous dialect of Paraguay, where he had been working for the past seven months in a tiny village. *"Mba'éichapa,"* he said. The greeting means "How are you?"

"Don't worry," he went on in Spanish. And that began a month of worrying like hell for me, like I had never worried before. I worried about him immediately. I worried about his future. I worried about his past, about all the mistakes we might have made in our family.

"Mom and Dad, it's Toren. *Estoy en* Washington, D.C., *no se preocupen.* I'll call you later. *Todo está bien. Bueno. Chao."* All is well. Don't worry.

Right. I'm not worrying. I don't know what's wrong, why he called. He's supposed to be in South America. Now he's suddenly in the United States, calling me in the middle of hauling groceries in from the garage. I just came home to this, the mystery announcement. I don't even know what it is that I shouldn't be worrying about, *in any language.*

I imagine all the things possible: he's very ill; he got into legal trouble trying to cross a border; he contracted malaria. Do they have malaria in the Chaco of South America? I run for a map. I look up the emergency number in the parents' Peace Corps manual, *On the Home Front: A Handbook for the Families of Volunteers*. The corps's offices are in Washington, D.C., and I'm in Washington State on the other side of the country, three time zones away. It tells me not to bother them unless it's very important. This must be important, but Toren said he would call back. I shouldn't overreact. He's twenty-four. He'll call. I put the rest of the groceries away. I weed our autumn garden, ripping out tired alyssum. I want to phone someone, but whom? And the next three hours stumble by.

When he finally calls again early that evening, the first thing he tells me is that his phone card might run out any second.

"Talk," I command him.

So he does. He asks what version I want. "You see, I've been real honest here and there's stuff going down. Or should I not tell you?"

"Tell me."

And he does. "It's alcohol."

Alcoholism? It's only alcohol, I reassure myself. Not a really serious drug, like crack or heroin or cocaine.

"Mom," he warns me, "I'm sending you some of my writing. Stuff I wrote down in South America last May titled 'My Drink.' It's pretty blunt. You'll read some things about what I did in college. How I wasted it. I'm sorry. It sounds bad. And I suppose it is. I could've worked a lot harder. But I still appreciate all you did and I know college was at least partially a good experience. I hate to have you read this, but I have to be truthful about myself." He pauses. "It's time."

I'm standing in my kitchen on our state-of-the-art slate floors leaning on honed granite to keep from falling over in shock. Solid rock is the only material capable of holding me up. The phone card could expire any second. "When did this happen?" I blurt out. "It's so sudden!"

"No, it's been happening. You'll see. I wrote about it in my journal last May. And now it's September. But I couldn't take it anymore. I realized something was very wrong. I've been having bad side effects for a while now, and recently they're really horrible. I'm afraid."

"What side effects? Tell me." I can hardly breathe.

"It's gotten worse and worse every time I drink. I get the shakes, I can't sleep, I'm losing my memory; I have leg cramps," he explains.

"But how did you decide to get help?" I ask. I really want to know more, like how often he'd been feeling that way, how much he'd drunk, what he was drinking, why he was drinking, and how this could be happening.

"I went to the capital city for interim training. All the volunteers were there. We'd had a lot of workshops, and I couldn't make it through one without the shakes. So I'd go out and buy some *caña* [local liquor] to calm myself, and I hated the feelings that were coming over me. It was getting bad."

"Oh, Toren."

"And so I went to see the nurse. Remember when you told me once about Dustin?"

I remembered. It had been one of those whispered conversations between two mothers bumping into each other a year or two after their kids had graduated high school, after huddling along the sidelines of football games, after the worries of steroids, drugs, alcohol, and all the fearsome temptations of adolescence. Dustin's mother confided in me, asking me not to tell anyone whatsoever. She said they'd had to pick Dustin up from college because he was having seizures, alcohol problems. But I hadn't kept my word, because, soon after, I heard my boys talking about Dustin at a party of reunited high school chums over holiday vacation, how Dustin was out of control. So I told my boys what Dustin's mother had confided. It had scared me. And I knew they saw Dustin occasionally, had played sports with him in the past. I thought it might make an impression on them.

"Well," Toren continues, "I always remembered what you told me about Dustin. How serious it was, and I got to thinking, I'm having some of the same problems. So I confessed to the Peace Corps, to get some help."

In Paraguay, Toren had lived in a tiny whitewashed house with a tin-

and-straw roof and an outhouse in back. He'd formed friendships with people in his village, planted a garden, and was preparing to work with them on a mutual project. Toren adored his assignment and the South American villagers. The Peace Corps allowed him the opportunity to learn languages, to interact in a new culture, and, hopefully, to better others' lives. It was Toren's aspiration after college, and he had planned to use the experience as a springboard for graduate work in psychology. I pictured him in Paraguay picking corn, digging roots for his dinner, plucking chickens.

"And what did the nurse say?" I ask him.

"She had to turn me in, and a lot happened that I'll tell you later, but they medevaced me outta there. Now I'm here in D.C. getting evaluated."

"Are you okay?"

"Well, I had people with me for three days straight in Paraguay, helping me detox. They gave me Valium. It's my last day of it."

"Valium?!" I almost yell. "Are you sure?" Valium, the drug of the 1960s and '70s, for my son. I'm holding my breath now. I don't think I can inhale one more time. I need a drink myself.

"It helps me down. Otherwise it's horrible. They didn't leave me alone. Someone was with me twenty-four hours a day."

Alone. It's my fault. I left him alone in that far-flung tangle. And now he's still alone in D.C., all messed up. But then I realize all his dreams are shattered—all that effort to apply to the Peace Corps, interview, train, his preparation for grad school—all down the drain, the hours of instruction in Spanish and Guarani. Shipped home from the jungles of South America, where he was working with people he could help, people who were supposed to be worse off than he.

"But don't worry, Mom. We're working out a plan. I've got a counselor here and we're figuring it all out. I've gotta get back to my village fast—as soon as we get this thing settled. I don't crave alcohol, really. It's just a problem when I drink; I react badly. There's some sorta abnormality there. I think they overreacted when they flew me out, but it's just Peace Corps protocol. The thing they do."

"Yeah," I say as offhandedly as I can. Are there any cheap flights to D.C. from Seattle, I ask myself. After all, I haven't seen him since nine months ago, when he left our hometown of Olympia. Not that I could change a thing. But just to hug him. To say it will be okay. That's what I need.

"I've gotta go, Mom," he slurs. "I have homework. The counselor wants to see my journal writing. I'm typing it out for him. And I'll e-mail you a copy. Right away. I'll call you tomorrow. I love you."

When I left for the market earlier that day, my son was living in Paraguay working for the Peace Corps. By the time I returned home to put the groceries away, he'd become an alcoholic headed for rehab. So what happened between the produce aisle and my driveway? Toren's father, Don, is at work. He needs to know. I could call him at the hospital. I could e-mail him, since he picks up messages in the OR between cases. The subject line could be "Sit Down." There's no granite counter in the operating room.

So do I start at the end or the beginning when I tell him? It's hard to know just where we are.

**As far as my husband and I could tell, Toren had** completed the requisite Peace Corps training in the first months of 2003, embraced his assignment, and was adapting to life in Paraguay. He told us funny stories on the phone and related that he was very involved with his village family, just "living" and following people around, helping them with whatever tasks they were doing. He felt extremely busy each day. He said that one day, for example, he'd gone with a twenty-year-old guy into a cornfield. They picked corn, husked it, cut off the kernels, mashed the kernels, then made some smushy, sweet corn cakes, cooked them, and ate them. He also caught some chickens, killed them, plucked them, and ate them with the family. "I'm like another kid in the family," he said. "They don't think I can do anything. The first time I whistled, they were astounded. 'Look! He already knows how to whistle.' The children think that I'm not only stupid, but blind because I wear glasses. The little *niña* comes up to me and holds three fingers in front of my face really close, and says, 'How many?' And when I answer with a bad accent or slowly, she yells, 'See, I told you he can't see!'" Toren wanted to tell the family that he does actually know some things, but he couldn't speak clearly in the indigenous language.

"It's hopeless." He sighed. He survived by just playing along. He said if he picked up an orange, they'd rip it out of his hand and explain how to peel an orange to him. They believed he needed extra help because they hadn't seen many people his age who talked so poorly. Toren originally thought that he would move to his own place sooner, but he understood that there were a lot of skills he needed to acquire in order to function, including using the language. So living with a helpful family had been ideal at the beginning.

Though frustrated by his language skills, Toren was very positive about his situation and happy to immerse himself in his new life there. He laughed when we talked about visiting him sometime in 2004—he couldn't imagine us in that environment. He felt that 99 percent of the people he knew in the United States wouldn't be stimulated by his lifestyle or living circumstances. Toren found himself supported by the people around him. With so much to learn, he was satisfied to concentrate on day-to-day life. He had recently moved into his own house and was cultivating a garden. That was all we knew about his life.

When he left for the Peace Corps in January of 2003, Toren took two books along with him, *The Complete Works of Shakespeare* and a book of Spanish verbs. He lamented over leaving his drum set behind, but purchased a guitar as soon as possible after arriving in South America. He'd used his own money from his summer employment to pay for three months of intensive Spanish-language training in southern Mexico prior to his induction into the Peace Corps.

Immediately after college graduation and prior to leaving for the Peace Corps, Toren had chosen to live on his own in Seattle, close to his summertime landscaping job. He shared living expenses with friends. (Our family policy with all three boys was that once they finished college, they supported themselves, which included paying for their own health and auto insurance, their food, and their housing.) In September, Toren moved to Las Vegas to live with his two brothers for a few weeks prior to attending the language school in Mexico. Our extended family, with all the grandparents, aunts, uncles, and cousins, planned to spend Christmas in Mazatlán, so Toren joined us directly after his studies and travel. There he spent the week reading stories to his young cousins and talking with grandparents and aunts. And partying at night with his brothers.

When the rest of the family departed for home after Christmas, Toren returned to Las Vegas and San Diego—where he had graduated college six months ago—to pick up his personal belongings, then flew to Olympia to stay with Don and me the final week before his Peace Corps departure. There were last-minute arrangements to finalize and supplies to purchase. Toren faced decisions about gear that needed to last two years and three months, his assigned term of service.

Even though he came home from San Diego looking rather bedraggled, we accomplished a lot during our final week together. I remember being perturbed with Toren's lack of physical and mental preparation, but I thought it was because he was having difficulty coping with the length of his impending absence, that he needed to say farewell to all his friends and brothers in grand style. I tried to overlook his spaciness, figuring he was young and insecure. Don and I drove him to the airport and felt a real ache as he strode down the jetway to begin his training.

After Toren's January arrival in South America, we didn't communicate often. The mail service was sporadic. Over fifteen letters mailed from the United States never reached him, and his e-mail connection was over an hour's walk from his village. Our best means of communication was by phone, so Toren usually had us call him about once every six weeks.

I noticed by July that Toren's already infrequent e-mails had become even more sporadic. He lacked enthusiasm when we spoke with him on the phone. He seemed scattered. I asked his brothers if they heard from Toren often, if they thought he was okay. No one suspected problems. But I sensed that Toren was avoiding returning my e-mails and I worried that something was brooding under the surface.

In August, I wrote him a rather terse letter in which I requested he respond to us, and I pointed out that he had yet to send us even one letter!

I felt guilty for doing this because the Peace Corps had warned parents about expecting too much during the first year, while the volunteer is in a big adjustment phase.

When Don and I called Paraguay in late August to talk with Toren about scheduling a visit in May 2004, Toren was vague about when we should come and seemed less than welcoming. This was not the cheerful Toren I remembered.

The part of Toren's life we knew very little about was what he had now confessed to me on the kitchen phone—and what he subsequently e-mailed to us from his journal, "My Drink"—the longtime alcohol abuse. This was the other side of Toren, the aspect that sent me into a frenzied state of misery.

My first reaction to Toren's announcement was shock. I began sifting through memories of the recent past, wondering what clues I had missed. Then, my angst mounted. The days following Toren's initial phone call were filled with intense agitation and despair. I moped and tearfully told myself this wasn't about me, it was about Toren. But in my heart and soul I knew how connected we were, and that whatever affected Toren also became a part of me and a part of our family. At the same time, I knew Toren's strength and will, and I knew his optimism. He definitely had a challenge before him, perhaps a lifelong one, and if he could formulate a consistent plan, I was positive he would triumph.

Had I known more about alcoholism, I may not have been so optimistic at this point. I'd had a few friends go through rehab, and I remembered that their recovery involved permanent changes of behavior. I hoped Toren could do that.

Don and I took this stumble very hard and we took it together. Actually, it was more than a stumble, it was a downslide into a chasm, causing us to look at our own lifestyle and at how much our social interactions needlessly revolved around alcohol. Suddenly it seemed that everything we did involved meeting for a beer or having a glass of wine. We spent time discussing how this alcohol problem fit into the puzzle of our family. I tried to think of it as Toren's gift to us, the chance to reflect and to talk with our other boys about substance abuse.

We checked out both the Alcoholics Anonymous (AA) and the Al-Anon Web sites in our search for information. AA is an organization well known throughout the world. Its members' primary purpose is to stay sober and help other alcoholics achieve sobriety. I also found a group called Narcotics Anonymous (NA), which employs AA principles but was founded for those who suffer from drug addiction. NA maintains that alcohol is a drug, no different from heroin, cocaine, or other drugs or addictive substances. And to help the families of alcoholics, Al-Anon and Alateen were also founded. I glanced at the Twelve Steps and figured I ought to learn more about them if Toren would be studying them, too. The Steps seemed foreign to me, yet reasonable. I found it hard to imagine attending an Al-Anon meeting.

Toren's life suddenly seemed out of our control. And out of Toren's control. Decisions were being made about his future while I was home grinding coffee beans and vacuuming car mats. There was nothing I could do about it. It was frustrating having no means to communicate with Toren. We didn't even know his phone number. We were dependent upon his calls from Washington, D.C., calls telling us of the drastic decisions being made about his life by total strangers. I hoped that this team of competent professionals could help him deal with his problem.

It was all the more painful for us being unable to talk with anyone else about this sudden news. Toren had asked us not to divulge this incident to anyone, and we were abiding by that. He wanted people to think he was still in South America. He said there was still hope that he could go back and no one would know any different. So we kept it all to ourselves. Don and I had a large support system in our town that we were unable to utilize. We truly leaned on one another at this point.

Sleepless nights haunted me. I wondered how Toren was doing, where he was in Washington, D.C., what he was deciding. I wondered how I could have let this happen. My pacing often led me to the boys' shared upstairs bedroom, where I would bury myself on their couch, wrapped in an afghan, weeping at what had become of our family.

I made a List of Worries:

 1. That I will lose a child.
 2. That I can't help my child.
 3. That my child has gone astray.
 4. That my child is hopeless.
 5. That my child is paralyzed.
 6. That I can't make him better.
 7. That my child is making bad choices.
 8. That my child is in pain.
 9. That my child feels alone.
10. That I don't know where he is.
11. That I can't concentrate.
12. That I feel despair.
13. That I threw everything into raising my child, but it didn't help.
14. That my child doesn't see his own potential.
15. That I am judging my success by my child's deeds.
16. That I thought he'd be "launched" by now.
17. That my child is closing doors on himself.
18. That I failed to recognize my child's needs.
19. That I didn't provide necessary structure for:
    ✓ fiscal judgment
    ✓ self-esteem
    ✓ ability to execute a plan
    ✓ avoidance of substance abuse
20. That I don't know what to do next.

I read my list to Don the next morning. He put his arm around me and advised, "Chris, you can't be the poor devastated mother-victim. Pull yourself out of this. No one is going to feel sorry for you. No one wants to hear about it."

"But I *am* a failure. I totally screwed up," I sobbed to him. The Breathalyzer, the nights waiting up for them in high school, the family projects, the discussions. It was as if our efforts to raise a solid family had never happened. It was like the boys ran out and immediately did everything we advised them not to do. If one son was an alcoholic, maybe they all were. I probably hadn't found out about the rest of them yet. "I feel like a CEO who spends her whole life building up a corporation to find out no one she's trained is capable." Where is my crying couch?

"You can't be the poor devastated mother, Chris," my husband repeated. He looked as miserable as I.

"Just imagine how you would feel," I said, "if, after all these years of practicing medicine, suddenly one-third of all your healthy patients either died or had life-threatening complications while in the OR, even though you were practicing the best medicine possible and doing everything in your power to have successful outcomes. Wouldn't you feel personally responsible? It's been your career to manage them well, to help them! Moreover, what if the remaining two-thirds were also in jeopardy? Suddenly you may have all your patients at risk of death or lifelong problems. How do you feel now? So let me mourn," I told my husband. "Let me have my bad times here in the privacy of my home." He hugged me and smiled, his own eyes tearing.

And he let me be. For the next two weeks I hovered close to home, refusing to answer the phone, reading and writing, practicing the viola, thinking and thinking and wondering what the hell had happened. My lack of composure made me avoid most of my friends. I was afraid they would see how upset I was. People always say that a parent isn't to blame for what a child does, but when this parent has purposely elected to stay home in order to raise and nurture a child, a poor outcome is relatively incriminating. To me the cause of the problem was not clear at all, except that it had to be something that took place in our home. The crying couch got a lot of use for a few days. I just couldn't help it.

I admit I was selfish to fixate on this problem. On the overall scale of global misery, the dilemma of my alcoholic son was relatively low. But to me, it was catastrophic. Owning up to having raised an alcoholic child would be devastating to any mother, regardless of whether she was a stay-at-home mom or career-oriented. All parents, mothers or fathers, would feel the stigma and pain of acknowledging their own addicted child. But now I needed to make sure my focus was looking forward, not backward.

During my wake of our family's innocence, Toren called twice more. The very next day, he answered more of our questions about his final days in Paraguay. The majority of his drinking, he said, had been with fellow volunteers, when they would meet on occasional weekends. The drinking occurred at a social level outside the jurisdiction of Peace Corps work. Toren described to us how medical supervisors from the Peace Corps helped him detox, then how a few days later they drove him on dirt roads in an SUV to his village, where he packed his things and locked his house.

"Did you get all your stuff?" I asked him.

"No. There's still some there. It was so rushed. I felt sick, it was confusing, it was hell. I couldn't say a proper good-bye to anyone in my village because I returned there so suddenly. I packed, then . . . I just left in that car."

"Did anyone in your village know about this?"

"No. I didn't really drink that much there; I only got really drunk a few times. I didn't have that many problems there because I drank mainly in Asunción with other volunteers. I told my Paraguayan mom that I had a family emergency. I gave her my keys. I had to leave all my ideas for projects, my new family, my friends. I had to leave my life there."

"Will anyone go back for your belongings?"

"I haven't given up on that yet. I want to go back. I know I can."

"But Toren, it sounds like they want you to go into treatment. Isn't that what you've told us?"

"The Peace Corps tricked me into leaving. I wouldn't have gone to the nurse if I'd thought they would make me leave South America. So they have to let me return. It's just that I react badly to alcohol. They need to tell me how to fix the problem so I can go back. I know I have a problem, but I can handle it. I have to get back to Paraguay. I didn't get to say good-bye."

**Paraguay, May 21, 2003. A long night of drinking** used to make me tired . . . now it makes me stay up and shake. I'm an alcoholic. I guess drinking like an alcoholic for about eight or nine years was part of the problem. Luckily, it was fun as hell.

Now what? Cocaine? How can I find a new identity when I used to drink mine by the fluid ounce and then turn around and juggle reality?

I thought the problem with being an alcoholic was you just drank a lot. I did that just fine and things were great. No one ever said, "Dude, you're gonna start losing your money, your memory and, above all, your longevity and tolerance . . . ," as if just being shit-faced and happy every night weren't enough, ". . . and when you stop a mean bender you're going to be a fevering, shaky, paranoid halfwit for a day or two who can't think, sleep, relax, or even eat until withdrawals are over. . . ." That page of my D.A.R.E. book must have been ripped out, right after the one part I do remember that said the bad guys always had fun and got all the chicks.

I used to be able to handle the worst of hangovers, wear it like a soldier wore a uniform, or drink it off. I could deal with hellacious sleeplessness from drinking for a day or through the night, maybe ending up in some random bed and still charging through class, ball practice, or family happenings like the dark angel that I was . . . even the torrential blackouts that would be reported or random acts of split personality. My friends and I always gave ourselves alternate drinking names (mine was Poren), as a joke, saying, "So and so did that, not *me*." It was nothing to be ashamed of in the glory days. Things are changing, and what I once thirsted for and sucked on with the finest appreciation, shared with the warmest of friends in the best and most fucked-up times, is beginning to scare me.

The problem isn't controlling my urge to drink; it's what happens to me now when I drink. (Twenty-four pack, where are you?) What was once all benefit and reward—raging parties, boring conversation turned into passionate arguments, blaring music and endless cigarettes, slurring exchanges of understanding (or even unfaithful or unwarranted kisses)—now seems to be packaged with much more unpredictability. I now have a harder time controlling how much I drink and how drunk I get.

Even more disturbing are the terrible physical reactions, depending on the amount of alcohol I consumed and my eventual detox. This is the big problem. During detox, inside the unsettled body, a nervous and sometimes nauseous sense begins . . . an anxiety and almost a fear, like being too alone. You see yourself and everything differently. Like a sudden collapse of the stock market in your brain and every single nerve ending throughout your body wants to turn inside out and puke out some unidentifiable pain or itch. You sweat, and you sweat increasingly when you let unreasonable thoughts trick you into feeling like whatever you are thinking must be true, like for example, "this is normal," "this will never end," "I deserve this," or "hhhhmm . . . maybe another drink will solve the problem."

Each summer, I returned from college in San Diego to my home in Olympia, to live with my folks and work by day as a groundskeeper. But really, I lived for the weekends, and everything worked out perfectly that way. I would go up to Seattle and rock all weekend, hardly eating and just shooting the shit (loving it always), cracking beers from the early morning and turning over what was remaining from the previous night. The weekends were endless parties, fiascos, adventures. And always intoxicating.

That last summer at home, I grew to dread Monday mornings at work, and sometimes Tuesdays, too. It wasn't due to a headache or hating the job. I liked being outside and listening to all the jack-offs on talk radio with their big opinions and constant advertising. But more and more, I would feel exhausted. Sunday or Monday nights I would find myself in bed at nine or ten p.m., knowing that I may not get to sleep until four, five, or six a.m. My legs would cramp sometimes, or ache, depending on how bad it was, or how much I had drunk. I'd have sweaty, sudden convulsions just as my body began to relax or fall asleep. I would be scared to fall asleep and would lie awake frightened, having no clue what to do, in total dread until it would finally subside enough to let me sleep. *Hell.* I tried to think it was normal, but I knew something was up. Little did I know it was the start of what I would slowly come to realize was part of my reality. It was my penance after coming off another celebratory binge. Starting out subtly as uneasiness, anxiousness, and sleeplessness, these reactions slowly progressed over the last two years of college.

The first time I ever noticed that I had the shakes and didn't attribute it to lack of food was in 2000, my sophomore year of college . . . I was not even twenty-one years old. I was trying to fix a tangled cassette. Unfortunately, my hand was vibrating, so I gave myself some wine and was able to enjoy the tape along with the rest of the wine, after both problems were fixed. Buzzed and horrified, I called my brother and recounted to him what had happened, as if I'd just had my first wet dream or some other eventual rite of passage to manhood. He was unsurprised, if I remember correctly, and I think he more or less welcomed me to the club or alluded to the idea of "Where have you been?" That made me feel better, as did the rest of the boxed wine.

I made it through college just fine and, from what I remember, it was the time of my life. I have a lot of really screwed-up pictures, a black book, and valuable friendships to prove it. I became very disheartened with my difficult routine by the end, though. My senior year was awfully tough. Getting blitzed every weekend was amazing, and returning to the dorms on campus, backpedaling, was always a challenge . . . to say the least.

I used to tell people, the few who understood, how my ridiculous schedule went:

**Schizophrenic Monday**: Inferior to myself, self-worth plummeting, no schoolwork, too preoccupied and on edge . . . easily startled by common things, vulnerable, and self-esteem at negative ten.

**Worry Tuesday**: Still fevering, blankly staring at TV, wondering how I am gonna magically execute all that reading, classes, papers, exams (brilliantly done in the end, I must add).

**Whatever Wednesday**: How much I really drank last weekend = how I function this day.

**Productive Thursday**: Back on track and kicking ass, do it all, I *am* school.

**Fucking Friday**: Sense of humor fully restored, all energy and in gear . . . just in time to start the cycle all over again . . . pattern here?????????????

This gave me about two or three days of productivity. So on Fridays I would delve into bliss, oblivion, carelessness, and a state of being that defied concern. One that was mostly impossible for the average student or peer. Satisfactorily saturated, self-sufficient, and in need of nothing more than my friends and my cheap booze (211, forties, ice beers, or maybe some other high-class malt liquor), I was set. I would drink the half-empty leftover beers (wounded soldiers) and I'd wonder about the party-goers who had gone home early, "What was their problem?" Well, whatever those people did, they didn't seem to catch *my* disease. It must be something toward the bottom of the drink that did it. Anyway, I had the best of times. Simplicity—lots of rocking music, companionship, and drinking games (Quarters, Keg Stands, Beirut, Kings, and Dr.

Kilabrew). Done deal. No bars or girl chasing, just laughs, craziness, and comfort. Where was the problem? (See Schizophrenic Monday.)

At this point in my life, I wasn't sure if this was a disease or not (they say it is). I chose it and loved it. Now if I choose to drink like I did before, the symptoms that ensue are surely my fault. I am simply struggling with the aftermath of the next good time that I want to have. Why does detox have to exist and be sooooo painful, making me struggle to talk, and even lose my sense of humor? These are the functions alcohol usually eases for people, but now the results are the opposite. It has me totally puzzled and unsure how to explain it, mainly to the ones I care about, and also the ones who may be alcoholics, as well.

After I graduated college in the summer of 2002, I moved up to Seattle to live with some old friends from high school. To save words, I again put into action what I did best. I drank—almost every day. No more school, a bad job market, and man, it was perfect. Even better, there were World Cup soccer matches on TV every night to keep me wasted until five in the morning. *Gooaaallll!!!!!*

Eventually I started landscaping, and I still went hard every night, partying. It didn't seem to matter. I woke up with vigor and readiness. I packed my lunch, and then would get stuck in traffic with my music and a cigarette, knowing that I could work, get money, and go home to good friends and drinks. And those were my summer week*days*. The weekends were ten times better, with girls and parties, concerts, or occasional visits to Olympia. There wasn't a care in the world, and I never had to come down.

Sometimes I would start to come down—maybe I didn't drink much the night before or had an appointment or family dinner. I snuck by without drinking or even nursing a few down, and I'd start slipping into alcohol withdrawal. In these moments, with a wet and hot/cold forehead, I'd find it difficult to focus on the task at hand, like remembering that I was supposed to bring something to the car or not knowing what I had just talked about with someone for ten minutes. My inability to recall details was very annoying, and the further into withdrawal I would get, the more frustrations turned into fears, anxieties, loss of confidence and purpose, and even worse, a disappearing sense of humor. This is the shit that makes up your personality, and when it suddenly starts to change or disintegrate, it is freaky and no fun. It seems totally beyond control—purely physical.

The summer ended with the whole crew of friends seeming to have graduated, changed locations, or split up to travel or whatever. I had signed myself up to go with the U.S. government for two years, hopefully to South America. It was not to fight in the armed forces but to serve as a volunteer in the Peace Corps. This gave me several months to kill, and I would almost literally do this.

I spent the better part of September and October of 2002 in Las Vegas, and at times on road trips to the coast—mainly to touch base with all my study buddies, right? My biggest plan was to spend time with my two brothers, who worked in Vegas, and visit friends from school in San Diego. I have tried to recount and distinguish the nights and different trips to San Diego, and it is almost impossible. Invariably we had a blast and I was losing great chunks of each night, either corresponding to (1) how much fun we had, or (2) how much of a jackass I (Poren) may have been.

I drank every night in Vegas, too. It was great. We raged through the casinos, walked down the crowded strip with our sleazy malt liquors and cheap half racks, almost rubbing in the fact that we could do such a thing in front of such "classy" gambling folks. On our better nights, we would then find ourselves at the trashy Gold Spike Casino, giggling and doing penny slots super early in the morning. Luckily, we knew gambling was another issue we didn't need. Besides, every time you give the 7-Eleven cashier ninety-nine cents, you know you get a twenty-four-ounce can of Steel Reserve malt liquor that'll get you just that much more wasted. Where's the gamble in that?

Soon after, I went to Oaxaca, Mexico, to study Spanish in preparation for my upcoming service in South America. En route, on a layover in Houston one morning, I took desperate measures to put off the impending withdrawal that I knew would be coming after five months of continuous drinking. I made a quick stop at the airport bar to down three screwdrivers (orange juice and vodka). It was worth the twenty-dollar bar tab because it bought me some time before the madness of my detox would set in. It helped me get through the air travel to Mexico City, and later a bus trip to Oaxaca without sweats, memory breakdowns, and the general ineptness that occur during withdrawal. Not that I wanted to see this as a problem or anything.

Upon arrival in Mexico, I was met with the harshest of withdrawals, which magnified everything I have previously described. I spent two solid nights in a hotel, clawing at bedsheets, taking cold showers, and only going out to find water and a banana (hoping not to be noticed or to have to talk while aiming to remember where my room was with all my stuff). After those two days I proceeded to "recover," and basically stayed away from alcohol all but two or three times in the following weeks. The clarity was quick in coming, comforting, and surprisingly easy. I knew my reality was scary.

From this point on, I think something hit me and began telling me "I can never, at least physically, go back to the way I was." I knew that, not just financially, but physically, I would pay for every drink or intoxicatingly good time I would have. Meeting my family for Christmas in Mexico after eight weeks of language class (and some travel, with a few slipups, we'll say) was perfect—a chance to say good-bye before leaving for the Peace Corps for two years. I showed up sober and beyond any chance of withdrawal. My bros pulled in from Vegas with carry-on bags under their eyes and the scent of a great night on their breath. I was amazed and jealous at the same time. But they didn't seem in too bad shape. How? I couldn't have done that.

The first two days or so with the family were great. I remember sitting with one of my brothers at a table at sunset, watching my uncle and cousins surf-fishing in the shallow waves. We were talking, smiling, sharing a beer, and savoring a perfect moment. How things should be.

How could the situation change?

"Paging Dr. Toren Volkmann. Please report to your own personal disaster called alcoholism—the tremors, sweats, and antisocial symptoms will be right with you." All I needed to do was start drinking.

Sure enough, after a few hard drinks (tequila that tasted like it had been made in a bathtub), the process began to start. Eventually, the paranoid, confused, intoxicated *me* showed up, teetering on the edge of withdrawal. This side of detox is the one that turns a regular conversation into a task. Even if it is with the closest of friends, it doesn't matter. Although they might not notice, inside me is another whole world of pain. The anxiety and difficulty that exists depends on the alcohol levels in my body—either previously consumed or in deficit.

After Mexico, I had one last stint in San Diego before my final goodbye with my brothers in Las Vegas. I don't remember shit for the most part, and even skipped out on seeing some of my most important friends because I was too gone to really care or make an effort to contact some of them. As it turned out, thanks to a stolen disposable camera and Satan himself, some pictures revealed that I did actually see a few of them. Silly ol' me.

That last morning in San Diego I found myself driving to Vegas in a borrowed car with a gal I didn't know too well. We stopped once, and talked about the same number of times. Although sleepless, I knew that my good old withdrawals wouldn't let me relax, so I was confident I would not fall asleep at the wheel. I even let the same CD repeat over and over because I felt too sick and stupid to suggest that we put in another.

The more days in a row I would drink, the more easily these symptoms would surface, and the more intensely they hindered my normal relaxed style of thinking and way of interacting with others. It really started to steal my enthusiasm, my aura, and my soul. I probably could have looked into a mirror and seen the back wall at times, things seemed so bad. This was not the life I'd ordered.

During my final Las Vegas days, I kept a steady supply in me and generally had a good time. The previous months studying in Mexico had made me realize that my drinking situation was worse than I thought. Drinking now emerged as both my problem and my solution. In opportune moments I think I tried to hint to both my brothers that I was bothered by some of the shit that it was doing to me. (They knew what "it" was and what I was talking about. They're my fucking brothers! But maybe they didn't.) What I was trying to tell them surely didn't come out clearly. In fact, nothing came out conclusively because I didn't want to say it. If the first step to beating the problem is admitting it or accepting it, I guess I just didn't want to beat anything quite yet. Why the hell did it have to be so bad all of a sudden?

Leaving Las Vegas was maybe the low point to this day, in my new "dialogue" with alcohol [things got much lower after writing this]. On the floor that last morning, I woke up all too early—which often happens when the body starts losing its normal equilibrium of alcohol—lying next to a girl I really cared for. We may have actually had sex the previous night (if I could only piece together a few simple clues with some certainty). The fact is that I totally slept with her. I was leaving for two years and I knew we should talk about it. Experiencing withdrawals, uncomfortable and unable to sleep, I tried to act asleep to avoid the whole situation, which should have been a memorable good-bye. I didn't know what the hell to say and I felt like crap. It only made me feel worse hiding my problem from her and sweating out the hours that should have been shared between friends.

With few hours left in Vegas, my problem was worsening without drinks (I didn't want to reek of alcohol when my mom picked me up at the airport), and I had to tear down whatever I wanted from our tastelessly covered walls and pack for my departure and upcoming disappearance. My brothers did half of the work for me, I was so worthless. Good-byes are always difficult, but what ensued was terrible. I look back on it with sadness and regret. I tried but couldn't even smile or appreciate our final moments, or express the joy, the love I had for my brothers and my friends. I was too lost in fevers, trembles, and general ineptness, and I felt like they all could see right through it. I was out of my mind. I was scared to leave, scared of what was happening inside me. It was killing me and was all wrong for no reason. My life was supposed to be great.

Eventually, I boarded a plane home to Seattle, my body in pain, shaking, and my legs aching. Behind me, all the way, a baby shrieked as if to express my exact state of being while magnifying it at the same time. I could barely tolerate to sit, stand, think—to live. My mom picked me up at the airport and I played it off legit. It was a tough ride home, trying to read letters about my Peace Corps assignment in South America, making normal conversation that made no sense to me, only wanting to disappear.

I had two days to "relax" and a night of nonsleep, like so many previous nights during those wild Seattle summers, before the symptoms slowly subsided. I didn't even try to start packing for South America, knowing any brainless attempt would just provoke sweaty confusion and stress. I was worthless. I could barely explain photos of my language school and travels in Mexico to my parents, because I was still so affected by the recovery from that latest binge I had put myself through. Why was it suddenly so hard?

In my hometown in early January 2003, with a bit more time before leaving, I wiggled my way out of seeing most of my old high school friends and drinking buddies. I wanted to be sane in my final days before departing for the Peace Corps in order to prepare myself. Yes, by then I had learned what happens when I drink, but it wasn't over yet. Being sober, I was able to find myself and deal with fears of leaving the country for two years with logic and confidence in myself. But departing to another continent by no means left my problem behind.

The question is: What do I do now? How can I make this work? What I can't help but wonder is whether all those famous (dead) rock stars, winos on the streets, or some of my best friends have experienced these same types of things or are experiencing them now? Maybe they just never said so or aren't admitting it. Maybe what I experience is much different from others. But I can't imagine anyone bearing the internal hell that I feel as a result of hard drinking and continuing on without letting others know. How did I not ever hear about this side of alcohol and withdrawal? For me, the silence is over and it is time to start looking for answers. I am also looking for the right cliché to end this—bottoms up!!

# FIVE

# BREWING A PLAN

*She knew what it was like to fall back into the inner darkness*
*of the self. To implode nights and come to every*
*morning like reconstituted misery. Come crawling back in*
*the day cell of the puny withering body. She knew*
*all about the black holes of the self.*

Thom Jones, Cold Snap[1]

**September 23, 2003. For the first time I open** Toren's "My Drink" e-mail, forewarned about the content. I sit at my computer, staring at tough words describing our son's struggling and alienation. Even greater is my grief at his silent suffering, his grappling with learning how to detox himself on his own. I recall the times he splayed uselessly on our couch, peering through his own sweat at nature videos. Over and over. And I now realize my ignorance. I feel foolish and inept. I undergo such inner remorse that I cannot move away from the tangle of his words. So I read them again.

A sudden visceral reaction causes me to detest alcohol. I wish to remove it all from our house. At the same time, I want to pour myself the largest glass of scotch in the world and gulp it down as fast as I can. I hate what alcohol has done to our family. And I worry about Toren's brothers, if they may be in the same gurgling boat.

The next day, by the time Don returns home, Toren calls again from Washington, D.C. He is trying to make a decision about his treatment and wants us to talk to Carl, a counselor assigned to him by the Peace Corps. Carl connects us for a telephone conference with Toren. We're talking together as if we are executives making a touchy policy decision. With our boys' grinning pictures splashed on desktops and shelves, my

31

husband and I speak on separate phones in our home while we decide where our youngest should be sent. Carl tells us the team has been assessing Toren's level of disease and informs us that Toren has been classified as an alcoholic.

"Of course, you knew he was an alcoholic," Carl states.

Did we? I want to say, no, no, we didn't. We're shocked. But Carl has already moved on. Doesn't Carl know we have hardly lived under the same roof with our son for five years? How could we "know"? Maybe we did. I'm trying to defend myself and be agreeable all at once. There isn't time to decide whether I knew or not. I must have known. He's my son, isn't he?

And then Carl emphasizes, "If ever Toren is to return to the Peace Corps as a recovering alcoholic, he must first stay sober for three years." In a matter of seconds, Toren has evolved from slick college-grad volunteer to a failing alcoholic, and now suddenly Carl is calling Toren a *recovering* alcoholic. It's like a miracle. Toren's *already* recovering before I even perceived he *was* an alcoholic!

Three years. It sounds like an eternity to not drink alcohol. Don and I drink it several times a week. I picture Toren going three years without it and I can't imagine it. This Carl must have high hopes. And before I can catch my breath, he goes on to say that Toren is eligible for inpatient therapy (with a success rate of 80 percent after one year), or he could do outpatient therapy (with a 20 percent success rate after one year). Carl maintains that Toren is ahead of the game because he already acknowledges that he's an alcoholic. He is motivated, he turned himself in. Most of Carl's clients, he says, have to be hauled into rehab kicking and screaming. I don't hear any sounds from Toren. Maybe he's sitting there tied up. It's just Don, me, and Carl talking about Toren as though he were a hunk of concrete. We go on to discuss the rehab facility recommended by Carl, which Carl says is not a lockup facility—it's spiritually based and twelve-step-oriented, and there's a Family Education Program. Such amenities. I'm thinking all this time, *What am I going to tell my mother?* And did Toren have a window or an aisle seat on his plane flight out of South

America? For some reason I don't feel like cooperating. If I don't, maybe Carl will go away and I won't have to hear all this wrenching news. Carl won't want to work with me. He and Toren can figure it out without me. It's hard to concentrate on all this information.

Carl tells us that Toren thinks he's at a nine-out-of-ten level of awareness in understanding his alcohol problem, whereas Carl maintains Toren is actually at a level four out of ten. Toren listens to all this as we yak about him, and I wonder if he wants to add anything. Maybe he's still on Valium. I strain to hear his breathing. He must be amazed at how, just two days ago, he was digging roots in South America, and now is in D.C. talking on the phone to his parents and an addiction expert. Carl has been doing this sort of thing for fifteen years, and tells us he "puts away" about twenty-five people a year. He has about one person every three years who turns himself in, like Toren; the rest have to be wrestled in.

Carl is very professional, and I can tell he's trying to let us down easy when he breaks the news that, most likely, Toren will be discharged from the Peace Corps. But here Toren cuts in, "Wait a minute. I'll do the rehab, but let's not close the doors on returning to South America!" He sounds agitated, determined.

But Carl retorts that they've already tried sending people back to the Peace Corps in the past. It has never worked because the job is too isolating and there's not enough support for recovery. "Recovery"—there's that word again—is such an optimistic term. I wonder how Carl can throw it out there so easily, before our son has even started. I'm barely used to the fact that Toren's an alcoholic. How can I even begin thinking of his recovery? But maybe Toren's recovery is already starting, now that he's sought help. I try to be optimistic. I want to cooperate with Carl.

"Liquor in South America's too cheap and too available. Toren would plummet," Carl warns. He says not to count on Toren going back before three years of sobriety.

Toren asserts that he still wants to return to his project. He maintains that just because the Peace Corps has tried returning people unsuccessfully in prior years doesn't mean it won't work with him. He's positive that he will succeed. It's quiet a few seconds before Toren says, "Okay, I'll go into inpatient therapy. But I want to have a discussion *afterward* about returning to Paraguay."

Carl responds to us and to Toren by saying, "I don't want Toren going into rehab focusing on returning to South America. Instead, Toren needs to focus on alcohol addiction and his disease and learning what to do about it. He needs to meditate, to gain spirituality." Carl won't budge.

From my end of the phone connection I can tell that Toren is fuming about abandoning Paraguay but is resigned for the present. "I don't have a choice at this point," Toren concedes. "I'm going to rehab." He chuckles and I wonder what could possibly be amusing.

Toren agrees to sign a contract saying that if he decides to quit the program, he will contact Carl first. Carl will make the final recommendation on Toren's status after the twenty-eight-day program, and reminds us again that if Toren can stay sober for three years, he could have a chance to reenter the Peace Corps one day. He wants Toren to begin the rehab program on Thursday, September twenty-fifth. Tomorrow. Carl feels we shouldn't waste any time. Toren will be driven there. We won't hear from him for over one week. If Toren has problems, he'll call Carl. The first week is very hard, apparently.

What could be hard about one week in comparison to the last nine months of hell that Toren went through?

Don and I hang up and rush to one another. It's worse than we'd thought. We had no idea. Or did we? How could we have missed it?

"I'm not going to drink while Toren's in rehab," I announce to Don. "I want to support him."

"Okay. I'll do it, too," Don says. And suddenly we both recognize that there'll be no wine with dinner this evening. No gin and tonic on the end of the dock at sunset. Even though it's Wednesday and we don't drink during the week, maybe tonight we would have, since it was such a stressful day. But we've made the decision. And that's final. If we can't do this for twenty-eight days, how do we expect our son to do it the next three years?

I have symphony rehearsal anyway. And wouldn't you know, after rehearsal, a friend invites me out for a beer. She and I have performed in the viola section for twenty years. We're string player nerds, but usually we go out once every six weeks. I tell her yes, and when we sit at the bar and I order a soft drink, she asks me, "Chris, are you okay?"

And now I understand how the next twenty-eight days will go. I want to say, "Yes, I'm fine. I'm not drinking because I'm supporting my son in rehab."

But I remember that Toren has asked us to keep this news in the family; he wants only his brothers and us to know about it. "Because," he conjectures, "maybe when I finish rehab, I'll go back to South America and no one will know I left."

I blunder through my fizzy non-mood-altering drink. Yet my fellow musician senses my malaise. She knows me too well. I steer all conversation away from our family, hoping she won't ask how Toren's doing. We talk about her kids, her classroom where she teaches, the music for the upcoming concert. Soon it's time to leave. I wonder how I will ever survive twenty-eight days of deceit with my friends. I will be forced to lie.

The next month cannot pass too quickly for me. On Saturday it's eighty degrees, most unusual for late September in the Pacific Northwest. Our bay waters are a sublime blue and Don is out in the early morning setting crab traps for our dinner. We will eat alone on our beach before a fire and talk about Toren, our family, and our life in this intimate universe of missteps and giant leaps.

How can all these footprints, one after another, have led to this? I remember as a child I often played Mother, May I? in the backyard with my sisters and neighbors. There were many kinds of maneuvers we invented to get to the finish line: banana steps, scissor steps, baby steps, giant steps. And sometimes we tried to cheat, to get away with something if we thought we could. If we made it across the line before anyone else, we won. Somehow, we got there. It was a game of chance, of contortion. Of surviving the best way we could.

Don and I call Toren's brothers. Toren has asked us to let them know. Even though he wants to call them himself, his phone calls are limited. "Your brother isn't in South America," we begin. And we spit it out about Toren's alcoholism.

"Are you sure there isn't a mistake?" one brother asks from Alabama, where he's in grad school. Twenty-six years old, he had visited his younger brother in his Paraguayan village just two months prior. Certainly he would have sensed this overwhelming problem. We tell him it was Toren's own idea to confess. He listens to us and doesn't say much, realizing that what's happening will not be changed by a brother's opinion. After the next call, to the oldest, our twenty-seven-year-old son, who lives in Nevada, we are finished informing . . . for the time being.

Each of us must learn the news and sort through the facts of Toren's disease for ourselves. Toren has decided to go into an inpatient rehab program, and none of us has lived in his skin. We cannot tell him whether it is right or wrong. Both brothers will soon read Toren's "My Drink" composition on an e-mail attachment. I want to ask them what they think about Toren's pleas, the time he said he had hinted to them about his distress. But we're raw now. We can't talk about this yet. All of us are waiting for more information, waiting to examine ourselves more closely. And it looks like what Toren has set in motion will pull us right along with him. We're brewing up our own plans for rehab.

# SIX

# YOU'RE ALL IN DENIAL

**What the hell am I doing in rehab? I think I've** always been a pretty levelheaded guy, but I had a lot coming at me in my first days back from my interrupted venture in South America. Things had certainly changed since the good old days. Being a part of the student body at my university had given me license to party and get as messed up as I wanted—as long as I held up my end of the deal: objective, measurable results (grades) that justified the absurd weekends, the ones that washed all that hearty education right out of my brain.

Who cares? I certainly didn't, and there wasn't anyone else who would intervene, because most of my drinking (scary enough) seemed normal, as long as you remember that any good drunk will surround himself with people who can party like rock stars as well. So what's the problem? I was a great student, from a great family, and I became a damn good volunteer. And don't question my motives in South America, because, by signing up, I wasn't avoiding my drinking, the real world, or the crap-ass job market. I entered the Peace Corps for other reasons.

I've worked hard to paint such a bad-boy image of myself. I wasn't always this way. My decision to go into the Peace Corps stems from visions I'd had since I was young. I'd traveled with my family and experienced the beauty and cultural diversity offered in the world. As a child, I always dreamt of being a professional athlete, musician, and artist all in one lifetime—and a sensitive, fun-loving, and adventurous person, as well. I never envisioned I'd be the "I Told You So" poster boy for the D.A.R.E. program.

When it came time to start making postcollege plans and decisions, the Peace Corps seemed like a worthy option. Although I realized I'd have to sacrifice countless familiarities, my cultural identity, my passion for the music scene, and everything else that rocked about being young in the good old United States of America, I felt I had a chance to learn another way of living, become a part of something bigger, and to potentially give back to a life that had given me everything. I might have been trying to maintain the course of my childhood dreams, but as a result of my drinking, all that I had ever envisioned hit the skids. Somewhere muddled up in my adolescence, "alcohol" and "ism" intermixed and my disease began to reveal itself.

So how did I land in rehab?

After being assessed by a professional in Washington, D.C., as a result of my desperate honesty (something new for me), I was told that I was an alcoholic and would need to go to an inpatient rehabilitation facility to learn about my disease and how to live with it. Screw that. Give me some therapy and some ways to deal with or control my drinking and put me on a plane back to South America. That's what I thought. With some tears and more negotiation, I figured I'd hold up my end of the deal, and after I was out of rehab and the doctors found out how great I was, how different, they'd just send me back to my wonderful life down in the hinterland. I am an exception, and always have been, right? *Denial.*

My first day in group therapy, I told everyone my story, what brought me to rehab, how I always drank to get drunk, and that I felt that my withdrawal symptoms were getting so bad and unbearable that I'd asked for help. I was okay because I had known something was wrong and sought help of my own accord, right? I wasn't in denial. Besides, I looked around the place and saw all these crazy people with outrageous stories—addicts, lowlifes, winos—and I knew that I wasn't like them. I was fine.

This center was full of people in pain, with damaged marriages or devastated families, pending charges and court orders, and all kinds of shame, guilt, and depression. These people were extremely sick.

When I was done and had shared my story, I felt pretty good about my situation and my honesty. We switched to some other people in the group and talked about some of their drinking, destructive habits, and behaviors. It was amazing how their denial completely disallowed them from seeing their own lives and drinking objectively and how their actions drastically affected other people. I thought it was insane. These guys had carted vodka into the office, had drunk on the way home from rehabs and detox centers, had countless DUIs or other offenses, had lost interest in their hobbies, and had destroyed many personal relationships. How could they not know they were alcoholics, that they had lost control, and that they were powerless over their substance? Their defenses were strong and they were in complete denial.

I wasn't in denial because I had asked for help and I came to rehab willingly. My story seemed so much better than most, and so clear to me. Since my blackouts and withdrawals were worsening, I was tired of it. So I figured rehab was necessary for the proper "adjustments." It felt good to finally talk about what had been bothering me for some time and it was easy for me to describe what worried me about my drinking. I didn't have any shame, guilt, or real consequences from my consumption. I drank purely for recreation, and whether I used alcohol to escape or not, well, who cares? The point is, I was doing it with all my good friends and we seemed to be just where we wanted to be.

Socially, alcohol had really seemed like a blessing to me, and the fact that I was in rehab angered me. I may have been able to use some help, but this was lame. I was able to shrug it off as another part of my story, and thought it would be a good learning experience.

"Hi, my name is Toren, and I'm an alcoholic." The first time I'd ever said that was in an AA meeting. I was nineteen and had just finished my freshman year of college. It really meant nothing to me in 1999. I said it with no ownership. I was there only because I was forced to be. I said it because everyone else said it, but it didn't apply to me at the time (so I thought). In 1999, at the end of my freshman year of college, my loving campus residence director (RD) told me that in order to be able to return to school the following fall, I would have to attend ten AA meetings and learn about the consequences of drinking and evaluate the seriousness of my problem. He told me, "Toren, I think you have a problem with alcohol." What the fuck did he know?

My freshman year had been one big celebration in a bottle, can, pill, pipe, or whatever seemed to fit or make itself available on that given Wednesday, Friday night, Sunday afternoon, or what have you. College life was a great chance to capitalize on everything that I had begun to excel at by the end of high school: having fun and not adhering to the rules or circumstances that applied to everyone else.

My first night in the dorms, before most people arrived, I unpacked and got settled in with blaring music and guzzled down about seven or eight ice beers, like any normal person would do. I was at home. The first time I met my residence assistant (RA), I was drinking beer out of a coffee mug. I mistook him for a regular student and kept drinking in front of him, until I realized who he was. He didn't catch me that time.

Obviously, I hadn't planned to follow the rules from the start . . . definitely not when it came to drinking. Coincidentally, I was put in a dorm with kids that shared my love for partying. In college? No kidding. We had a blast. Put a bunch of inventive college guys together and the outcome is almost a guarantee. I was in a single room and had no one to blame for all the behavioral issues that were to follow.

I lived in a dry part of campus, with all freshmen, but by the way I was drinking you wouldn't have guessed it. I was written up the first week for having alcohol in the dorm. By week four, I had been written up three different times for alcohol violations. I was penalized with fines that could be reduced by donating canned food. To pay my last fine, I came back to campus with two suitcases full of canned soups, vegetables, chili and beans. We joked that the RAs and RDs just sat around and ate it all themselves.

The second time I was caught, I was forced to go to a "second of-fenders meeting" with a few other kids who had also been caught twice. It was early in the year, so the counselors asked why we were getting caught like we did, and what would help us stay out of trouble. They asked why we drank so much, and wondered if alcohol-free student ac-tivities were lacking on campus, as if maybe that was part of the problem. To me, the problem was that I kept getting caught. I decided to ensure that it didn't happen again.

My third offense was a week later, proving all my efforts were in vain. I was the first freshman to have a "third offenders meeting," and at-tended it alone with only counselors. I no longer thought it was funny. For different reasons, the counselors thought it was pretty serious, too. But screw them all. The rules were too strict. The RAs weren't fair and were going after or picking on certain people. I just had bad luck. I'd be damned if I was going to mellow out—this was college, for God's sake.

With my new buddies, I made frequent trips to a big grocery store and got kicks out of sneaking cheap handles of vodka, forties, tall cans of malt liquor, and glorious half racks of shitty ice beers back into the dorms. Always giddy and excited, we exercised our freedom to celebrate or abuse every chance we got, and that was often. Excessive drinking led to plenty of random acts of chaos, the occasional trash-can fire or petty vandalism, or general insanity. It was all fun and games and no one got hurt. With more and more write-ups on our floor, and empties collecting outside our entryway, ours became a marked building.

The unpredictable fire drills we set off required the whole building to evacuate in the middle of the night. Watching tired and unprepared students file out was icing on the cake. It was a joke to us. I guess no one else enjoyed it on as many levels as we did. The staff surely didn't. Their attempts to control us seemed to make us wilder and more rebellious, and we ate it up. It was an exciting time for a bunch of "serious" students.

Of course, I didn't divulge any real information about my behaviors to the counselors or other residential-life staff. I maintained innocence, and I continued to play the bad-luck card. Even though I had already tallied my third offense, they still wanted to believe me. I was fine. I cited my good grades as proof. It seemed convincing.

As a result of my third offense, I had several meetings with the RAs and RD. My drinking was assessed in a confidential meeting. I met with a counselor one-on-one and was asked about my drinking style and the choices I was making for myself. I suppose this was all part of my intervention process, but I didn't give it a fair chance. For the most part I knew that certain behaviors would indicate risky drinking or problem drinking, so I toned down my answers and shaved the numbers regarding how much and how often when talking about my drinking habits. I wasn't into the whole honesty thing.

The staff on campus wanted me to take a look at my drinking. They said it was serious. All I wanted was for them to lay off me, and for me to be able to do what I wanted. Was that so much to ask?

My grades were outstanding that fall, as were my party achievements. Although crazy and belligerent for the most part, I managed my time well. I played hard, but I studied hard, too. I even made the dean's list. But by spring, my standing on campus had gotten pretty ugly. I couldn't stay out of trouble. I was a victim of unwanted and what I perceived as unfair attention by the campus police. After being relocated away from most of my friends and moved up onto the main campus, I was given fair warning. No more violations or setting foot on the lower portion of campus, or I was out.

Still, I had only bad things to say about all the snooty people on the campus and the nothing-better-to-do Public Safety Team. They patrolled past my door constantly, and, on weekends, even checked the balcony with a spotlight in order to make sure there were no shenanigans happening after hours. I was pretty fed up at this point with all these authority figures on their high horses telling me what to do and singling me out. I wasn't the only minor drinking, on or off campus, and I sure as hell didn't need my hand held during my adjustment to college life—my grades were fine.

I continued to push buttons, bend rules, and enjoy my first year of college as I pleased. I managed to remain on campus, although barely, the entire year. While my grades began to suffer a bit that spring, I was also working part-time for dining services setting up snacks and drink bars for big-money conferences and helping to cater special events on campus. The occasional complimentary wine was nice and made me less resentful of the weak-ass paychecks. In my last meeting with the RD, we had a serious chat. The cumulative behavior and damage was enough, I guess. He understood in some way that a lot of people have problems adjusting to college and that maybe it would be good for me to reevaluate my motivation for being in school.

My motivation? I was there to have fun, party, meet new people, and, of course, to get that pricey degree—in four years or under.

My parents were paying for my education, not for my exploitation of college life, and it was my job to perform in school in order to stay. I was walking a fine line and my parents were always at the other end with their radar, questions, concerns, and, thankfully, their support and unconditional love. It was tough to satisfy my own expectations, my parents' expectations, and all those people catching my slipups. No one from the college contacted my parents or informed them what I'd been up to.

The RD told me that in order for me to return, there had to be some major changes in my attitude. My current behavior would not be allowed. What he couldn't understand was how I could seem like such a reasonable person during the day, yet get caught twice publicly urinating in the same spot—the second time out of drunken spite. Why was it like dealing with an angel in our face-to-face meetings and like dealing with the devil at night when I was confronted by Public Safety? My answer was simple: those bastards were always following us around, trying to catch or control us, and we just wanted to do what normal college kids are doing everywhere. Therefore, I didn't like Public Safety, and I let them know it at certain times.

Surprisingly, this brilliant answer didn't really cut it. I would not be allowed to live on campus the following year. The RD said it was a shame that sometimes some of the brightest kids with the most potential seemed to cause the most trouble and find themselves with the most problems. I thought it was a shame that he was a forty-year-old man living in the dorms, babysitting a bunch of college kids and penalizing them for their basic right to have fun. I felt that we students were completely justified in raging and spending our youth and invincibility while we had it. He also told me to go to those AA meetings. What a joker. He didn't know who I was.

This attitude of mine did not crop up overnight. I had always felt indestructible, and reacted pretty sarcastically to the whole notion of being an alcoholic. Even back in high school, I remember being sixteen or seventeen, drinking beers with a couple of friends and mockingly reading through one of those typical self-help pamphlets. We were checking the one or more drinking behaviors that applied to us (in my case, there were many more). If I remember right, exhibiting only a few of those behaviors signified that you were probably an alcoholic. I remember laughing, as we were pounding beers, because one of the questions asked if we ever "drank faster in certain situations or thought that we took bigger than average gulps at times." Our response was, of course, "Hell yeah we do, how else would we do it?" That was the only way we did it. I proudly exhibited pretty much every indicator. But I felt like I was doing most of them intentionally. I drank to get drunk. I thought it was hilarious, and never once considered that someday that kind of drinking might not be a choice. In short, that is how I landed in rehab.

Sometime after my momentous freshman year of college, I bought a cheesy greeting card on a whim because it caught my eye, and sent it to my brother. Along with this last-minute card I probably sent a letter, or some pictures or newspaper clippings. On the front of the card was a big bottle of champagne with celebratory glasses and colorful balloons splashed with confetti going everywhere. Right over the top, in fancy writing, it read *"Congratulations!"* Inside, the card was blank. But what I wrote there typified my attitude and glorification of drunkenness at the time: *"You're a Flaming Alcoholic!"* I thought it was the funniest thing in the world and sent it off to my brother.

*Sure.* My bothers and I took pride in drinking like alcoholics. I guess in some ways, I shouldn't have been so surprised to find myself in rehab, after all.

While I was in treatment, that same brother sent me a letter, doing his best to be supportive and sensitive. It's too bad he didn't include that same card with his letter. It would have been so much more appropriate for me. "Congratulations! *You're* a Flaming Alcoholic!" I wonder if the idea ever crossed his mind.

# SEVEN
## BINGEDRINKING . . . BINGEDRINKN . . . BINGINGDRUNK . . . ING BIGDRUNKMINGBLMGDG

*Don't just give me a beer. I've never done one beer.*
*Give me all the beer.*

—Toren Volkmann, 2003

**[CHRIS]**

**When our boys were adolescents, I posted a chart** about binge drinking in their bathroom. I hoped not only that the brothers would read it, but that all their friends who trooped in and out of our house would notice it as well. It would advertise that I was aware of alcohol abuse and tip them off that they weren't concealing drinking behaviors from me. It might cause them to think. It might also cause them to avoid me, but it seemed worth the risk. The chart, printed on sea green paper, stated salient facts from an American Medical Association survey. It defined binge drinking as the consumption of five or more drinks in a row (four for women), one or more times during a two-week period: drinking to get drunk. I talked with (or at) our boys about bingeing, and mostly they just stared back at me. But at least I had done my job. I had dared to bring it up.

The green list still hangs in the bathroom when I check for it after our conference call with Toren's addiction counselor, Carl, in Washington, D.C. I see that the chart also points out that lifelong patterns of alcohol abuse are established in high school. It says that on average boys usually try alcohol for the first time at age eleven; girls at age thirteen.[1] After Carl's sobering call, I untape the list and stick it inside a drawer with some extra towels. It hasn't done any good anyway.

Drinking these days is full of glamour. It seems everyone does it. The alcohol industry targets its marketing to every one of us: it will make us beautiful in those long, slinky black velvet dresses; it will make us healthier if we have a glass of wine with our evening meal; it will make us feel young and playful as we munch pizza with our friends while watching football games; it will heighten romance and encourage intimacy. Not only is alcohol visible in creative advertising (croaking frogs in beer commercials or referees blowing the whistle between feuding brands), but in most movies watched by teens alcohol is represented by clips of actual brand names, another form of lobbying.

Drinking alcohol is a legal and socially acceptable activity. Society tells us all we have to do is drink *responsibly*. There's never any mention of how alcoholism is a progressive, addictive disease, how it sneaks up on you. Drinking alcohol is not presented as a dirty, dangerous activity in the same way as smoking cigarettes is. A few stiff ones won't pollute the environment or burn out our lungs. And remember, when you're young, you're indestructible! My son doesn't relate to that pathetic guy with gray stubble lying in the gutter at two a.m. That bum's old and scarred, someone who shouldn't have been drinking in the first place, someone who obviously couldn't control himself. My son knows he couldn't become such a hopeless loser.

Imbibing spirits has a sophisticated social history dating back through the centuries, with nomenclature and boorish wine-tasting sommelier traditions, *n'est-ce pas?* We caution our children to wait until they're *ready* for alcohol, say at age twenty-one. Then we hold our breath as they crash through the starting gates. Some of them launch earlier than others.

Adult drinking is quite different from adolescent drinking (an adolescent is a person twelve to twenty years old). It takes five to ten years for some adults to become alcoholic from the time of their first drink. But because the adolescent brain is still developing, *it may take only five to fifteen months to become alcoholic once an adolescent begins heavy drinking*. Parents can suddenly find their perfectly normal kid transformed into a robot controlled by the disease of alcoholism in less than a year's time.[2] Research confirms that the adolescent brain is more vulnerable to the neurotoxic effects of alcohol than the adult brain.[3] For a young woman, the brain does not finish developing until she is around age twenty, and for young men, it often takes until age twenty-three or twenty-four. (This could explain why Toren took his adolescent behavior into his twenties.) Heavy drinking during the teen years may be especially damaging to the hippocampus, a brain region important for taking in new information. The frontal lobe, one of the last regions to mature, is needed for such functions as making judgments and the ability to plan. A young teen's brain appears to be highly susceptible to the effects of alcohol, especially on learning and memory function. Data indicates that people in their twenties who have been alcoholics as teens have smaller hippocampal volumes. These studies provide a strong warning against teen drinking.[4]

Statistics show that young people who binge drink may risk serious damage to their brains and suffer memory loss later during adulthood. For an adolescent, even binge drinking one single time can cause irreparable harm.[5] Not only is there concern about the immediate effects of heavy, chronic drinking, but also concerns about the long-lasting consequences of this abuse.[6] Experiments on heavy drinking at Duke University showed impaired activity to brain receptors responsible for memory and learning. Males are more alcohol-dependent and experience more alcohol-related problems than females. And the highest rates of problems are among young adults ages eighteen to twenty-nine.[7]

Sometimes we parents learn about the way our kids party whether we like it or not. Don and I accidentally landed at one of our son's parties when he was a junior in college. Since we knew many of his guests, fellow soccer players, we strolled outside onto the deck to talk with them. There I saw a large funnel lurking in the shadows. It was the kind of funnel used to fill the gas tank of a lawn mower, one you'd commonly have in your garage. Kids use funnels to make beer bongs, a way to drink large quantities of alcohol as quickly as possible, as if in a competition. I figured that the kids had been bingeing. The party attendees were mostly over twenty-one years old, were at a quiet private residence, and were breaking no laws. So what was my beef? Hadn't I ever been to college? I pulled my son aside and asked him why he had that funnel. Immediately I was "Oh, Mom'd!" out of the party. I could tell our son was very perturbed by my presence.

Through the ensuing years, I had found myself removing all colors and sizes of funnels from our kids' car trunks as we unexpectedly opened them to pack or unpack for various events. They didn't argue with me, because they knew if I saw a funnel, it would be confiscated. Don't any other parents find these? Why has no one ever talked about it? Other parents probably figure, just as I did, that this binge drinking is a passing phase, harmless and short-lived. Besides, my boys were just transporting these funnels to *other* kids' parties; it is *other* parents' kids who binge drink, not my own.

Much of the data about binge drinking originates on college campuses; this is natural, because the collegiate arena is ideal for adolescent studies. Even though research is oriented toward users on the campus, problems exist wherever youth are drinking. Many kids drink during middle school and high school and continue drinking afterward, college or not.

Including *all young people* (not just college kids):

- More than 10 million current drinkers in the United States are between the ages of twelve and twenty, and of these young drinkers, 20 percent engage in binge drinking and 6 percent are heavy drinkers.[8]
- Nearly one in every five teenagers has experienced blackouts, after which they could not remember what happened the previous evening.[9]

How do rates of binge drinking compare between college students and similarly aged youth who choose not to attend college? A study released in March 2005 addresses this question. It found that nineteen- to twenty-one-year-olds who attended college drank more alcohol on a weekly, monthly, and yearly basis, but that nonstudents of that same age were more likely to drink alcohol every day. The conclusion was that college students do not appear to be at greater risk than their non-college-attending peers for problems associated with alcohol dependence.[10] While college campuses are breeding colonies for high-level alcohol addiction and abuse, kids who do not attend college are drinking at high levels as well. The reality is, parents of *all* teens, not just parents of college-bound teens, need to be aware of drinking habits.

One of our boys once arrived home from college sporting a contraption of valves, tubes, and funnels. It was aptly and affectionately named the Triceptatrough, after some sort of prehistoric reptile, and I could see it was a tool used for beer bonging. It wasn't Toren who brought it home, but one of his older brothers. He was proud of the craftsmanship, how he and his buddies had invented it. I told him to get it out of the house, and he did. The boys knew how I felt about beer bongs.

Even back in the 1960s, I sensed that binge drinking was dangerous. A guy I knew in college used to chug whole pitchers of beer after rugby matches. I was apprehensive, because I thought it discharged too much alcohol into the system too fast. Many college guys in those days chugged beer to show off, but I don't remember it being an every-weekend occurrence. Now bingeing appears to be more commonplace. That's why I had made it a point to talk with our boys about binge drinking. Since then, I've found out that such bingeing is even *more* serious than I ever realized: Binge and heavy use rates for college students were at 43 percent in 2004.[11]

Researchers have determined that teens are introduced to the heavy drinking culture while they are in high school, and that we parents have a huge influence. How are we unknowingly influencing our kids' drinking choices? One in five American adults binged on alcohol recently (had five or more drinks in one sitting or drank to get drunk).[12] Teens report a relative lack of parental concern about drinking and feel that their parents regard alcohol as a benign substance. They also notice and perceive heavy parental drinking.[13] Approximately 14 million people in the United States—one in every thirteen adults—abuses alcohol or is alcoholic.

Of course, we know that adults' brains are also affected by heavy drinking. Repeated drinking kills the cells in specific brain areas. Grown-ups who quit drinking after many years of alcohol abuse may still have significant memory deficits. Even adult social drinkers who drink heavily on the weekends can acquire these deficits, as can young people in high school, college, and in the working world.[14] The most up-to-date studies show that heavy social-drinking adults who are not in treatment but function relatively well in the community exhibit the same patterns of brain damage as seen in hospitalized alcoholics. Brain scans show enough damage to impair day-to-day functioning in balance and reading. Apparently, to fall into this category men must consume an average of one hundred drinks per month and women must consume an average of eighty per month.[15]

In his "My Drink" e-mail, Toren talks about not being able to remember chunks of time when drinking. What he is describing is a blackout. I had always thought if you were blacked out, you were on the floor, totally passed out. But no, blacking out is completely different from passing out. I found in my research that *during an alcohol-induced blackout, a person can be conscious but form no memory of the event*. This blackout period allows the person to be actively engaged in behaviors (for example, walking or talking), but the brain is unable to form new memories of the events, leaving the person unable to recall what happened once he or she is no longer intoxicated.[16] It is because the hippocampus, the deep part of the brain associated with memory, shuts down.

Blackouts may happen when a person is in a drinking setting but may or may not appear intoxicated. Dr. Aaron White at Duke University Medical Center has researched this phenomenon.[17] He found that during blackouts students engage in all kinds of potentially dangerous activities, such as driving cars, vandalizing property, engaging in unprotected sex, or spending large amounts of money. And the next day, they have no memory of it. This is a warning sign of damage being done to the brain. Blackouts can occur even among nonalcoholics.

Though blackouts and passing out are different, because blackouts tend to occur at quite high blood alcohol levels or after rapid consumption of alcohol, a person often experiences a blackout prior to passing out.

Individuals who experience blackouts frequently sober up unaware of where they are or how they arrived there. Half of college students interviewed (more females than males) report that they were frightened by a recent blackout experience. In the College Alcohol Study, one out of every four students who drank reported having forgotten where they were or what they did while drinking at some time during the school year. The incidence of blackout was 54 percent among frequent binge drinkers. The average alcohol intake of females who blacked out was five drinks per occasion, while with males it was nine drinks per occasion.[18] Although blackouts can occur in normal, healthy drinkers who have overindulged, blackouts are unquestionably a warning sign of problematic drinking.[19]

When we first caught Toren drinking in high school in 1995, we did not know that he had been binge drinking or blacking out. At that time, he confessed to drinking alcohol. But never did we parents know the extent. If we had, we should have been alarmed because *kids who binge drink are more likely to have problems with alcohol addiction further down the road*. Chances for a male becoming addicted to alcohol increase tremendously if he consumes more than three or four drinks per day. For females, it's about three drinks per day. Brain damage due to heavy drinking occurs sooner than scientists thought possible. Lab animals that were allowed to binge drink around the clock for four days showed immediate damage.

I cringed when I learned about the damage caused to the brain by binge drinking, that tissue shrinks and dies and cannot be replaced, thinking my own son may now face these deficits. How can this have happened? I read that the discrepancies may disappear as time passes, but

## Five Areas of Mental Ability Compromised by Chronic Alcohol Abuse or Binge Drinking[20]

As many as 70 percent of people who seek treatment for alcohol-related problems suffer significant impairment of these abilities:

1. **Memory formation**
   Heavy drinkers become unable to form new memories. An individual will recall what he learned earlier in life, but not what he ate for lunch two hours ago.

2. **Abstract thinking**
   One way to measure abstract thinking is to show someone a group of objects and have her group the objects according to shared characteristics. Binge drinkers will consistently group things based on concrete characteristics (such as size, color, shape) rather than on abstract characteristics (such as what they are used for, what kinds of things they are).

3. **Problem solving**
   Persons who are chronic drinkers often have difficulty here. They get stuck in one mode, take longer to find a solution. The executive functions of the frontal lobes appear damaged.

4. **Attention and concentration**
   It is difficult for chronic drinkers to focus attention, especially visual attention (like reading an instruction manual, driving a car).

5. **Perception of emotion**
   It appears that binge drinkers have difficulty perceiving emotion in people's language, especially hearing the tone and cadence of language. This can cause difficulty in social relationships.

there is evidence that even after seven years, many chronic drinkers retain significant memory deficits.

Binge drinking oftentimes begins in middle and high school, as Toren demonstrates. Statistics say that if a student binges in high school, she will be three times as likely to binge in college. Over half the binge drinkers (almost one in four students) are frequent binge drinkers—that is, they binge three or more times in a two-week period. (One in five students abstains from alcohol.)[21]

College presidents agree that *binge drinking is the most serious problem on campus*. So why aren't more parents talking about this? Is it because we send the kids away and don't have to watch what's happening? Why do we see news reports of drunken campus fiascos and it's always someone else's kids? According to the 1999 College Alcohol Survey, 40 percent of all students are binge drinkers. They must be *someone's* kids.

When you really think about it, binge drinking seems like an odd thing to do, pouring vast quantities of specialty poison down your throat that can make you sick, act stupid, and black out. It's especially strange for grown-ups to contemplate. According to research, here's why kids binge drink: *peer pressure and the status of drinking*.[22]

I tried to figure out what influenced our own boys so heavily. Certainly our kids saw alcohol at parties hosted by Don and me, and perhaps they found the allure too enticing. Even though we did not consider our use of alcohol excessive as they were growing up, when we did consume it, we had the house decorated with candles and fine food, and we socialized with laughing and happy people. The image of alcohol as a necessary and fun party enhancer was certainly reinforced in our household, even though we didn't have funnels hooked onto our belt loops.

Presently, alcohol reigns *big* in American society. And it has been *king* for years. Don interned at Harlem Hospital in New York City in the 1970s, a time when everyone was concerned about heroin and cocaine. But what he saw was that alcohol was by far the most common cause of ruin, heartache, and health problems to the people he treated. It hasn't changed all that much in his present-day practice in Olympia, Washington, thirty years later. Alcohol still drives medical and social problems. "The recurrence of binge drinking at the adolescent and college levels has reestablished the tradition of heavy drinking by our American ancestors. And, as a nation, we are consuming more alcohol each year."[23]

Literature about alcoholism maintains that people who are addicted to alcohol are often abusers of other substances, such as nicotine, marijuana, and cocaine, and even eating disorders are a variety of such addictions. Alcohol was Toren's drug of choice, but during his foray, he admits that he also experimented with plenty of other drugs and smoked cigarettes. Although he abandoned them along the way, some alcoholics are unable to do so. Or perhaps when they kick alcohol, they turn to other addictions to replace it.

In the 1999 College Alcohol Survey, less than 1 percent of students reported using crack, heroin, or LSD; less than 2 percent used barbiturates; and only about 5 percent reported using any illicit drugs ever. About 27 percent smoked marijuana, and 29 percent smoked cigarettes. *But 68 percent of students drank alcohol, and 44 percent binged.* In 2004, the rates were similar, but a new increase was reflected by 6 percent of youth aged twelve to twenty-one using nonmedical prescription drugs. Yet 69.8 percent of this aged youth were still drinking the beverage of choice: alcohol.[24] Even though alcohol surpasses all other drug use on college campuses and causes more damage and expense, the federal government excludes alcohol from its war on drugs. This exclusion exists because the alcohol industry lobbied for it, which reinforces the idea that alcohol is benign and subtly promotes underage alcohol use.[25]

Alcohol *is* a drug. Alcohol abuse causes not only devastation to the brain but carries risks of cancer, liver and digestive failure, heart disease, problems with the pancreas, colon and esophagus, and high blood pressure, not to mention social risks of divorce and domestic violence. With a history of ongoing alcohol-related problems such as these, you'd think there would have been more of an enlightenment by now. But recent studies indicate that alcohol is *the* drug of choice by educated partiers. And they're serious about it. They continue to drink and drink, even when it causes death. In 2002, the *British Medical Journal* reported that death rates for young adults and middle-aged women increased with the amount of alcohol they consumed, even when it was as little as one drink per week.[26] Alcohol is the preferred legal tool for both intoxication and mortality. We just seem to love it to death. How could we blame our kids for loving it, too?

Maybe you'd think our family did little to stop our alcohol-crazed boys. But it's not true. We tried several ideas, one of which was using a Breathalyzer. The Breathalyzer idea came about after we'd dined out with some of our closest adult friends one night in Tacoma. Having finished three hours of reminiscing and dining, each couple would be driving home to Olympia or Seattle. Some of us had consumed martinis prior to dinner, and all of us had drunk wine with dinner. Two people had cognac after dessert. One of my friends said she was to be the designated driver, because her husband had imbibed both martinis and cognac.

Upon arriving at our cars in the parking lot, one of the guys proposed that all of us blow on a Breathalyzer; he had just purchased one and it was inside his car. We were curious, so we all tried it out. To our surprise, several of us were over or near Washington State's 0.08 percent blood alcohol level, a legal definition of drunk, including the aforementioned designated driver (who had only consumed wine with her dinner). Her husband, on the other hand, was well below the limit, even with a martini, wine, and cognac. "It's because he ate bread," his wife insisted. As a result of our parking lot Breathalyzer test, we adjusted drivers and proceeded home. (Perhaps every car should come equipped with a Breathalyzer.)

After this, Don and I bought one as well, to use on ourselves and on our kids. More than once, it proved a reliable measure of consumption. We made use of it sporadically to test our boys when they returned home from social events.

I wished I could ask Toren more about his early drinking. During his first week of rehab, we didn't hear from him because the first days of his program did not allow outside contact. So I called his brothers. We talked frankly about binge drinking for the first time. Even though I'd posted the green list during their high school and college years, it had been *me* talking, not *them*. Now they were able to tell me about it more easily. Yes, there'd been bingeing. It's like tap water in college.

Even kids who didn't attend college but lived on their own participated in bingeing. The boys didn't think it was necessarily a problem, just something a young person needed to be aware of.

A study from 2002 shows that 31 percent of college students meet clinical criteria for the misuse of alcohol.[27] One in ten college men under age twenty-four meets the twelve-month diagnosis of alcohol dependence. So our Toren fits into the one in ten. How could we have identified him sooner?

---

### The CAGE Test[28]

✓ Have you ever felt you should **C**ut down on your drinking?
✓ Have people **A**nnoyed you by criticizing your drinking?
✓ Have you ever felt bad or **G**uilty about your drinking?
✓ Have you ever had a drink first thing in the morning to steady your nerves or to get rid of a hangover (**E**ye opener)?

**CAGE** is what it spells, and it indicates a possible alcohol problem. With one "yes" it is possible that a problem exists; more than one, it is highly likely a problem exists.

---

*As if* our kids would have been honest with us about the CAGE questions! Or that they would have taken them seriously. What's more, some studies have shown that females tend to feel guilty about their drinking no matter how much they consume, so they frequently reply "yes" to the G question. While the CAGE test is one tool, it may not be totally reliable. There are many other tests that bring forth differing results.

So what's a binge drinker to do but keep on bingeing?

Toren's drinking certainly disturbed his own life, but what about all those other students on campus? When a drinking student is disruptive, it affects not only the drinker but everyone around the drinker, an effect commonly referred to as secondhand drinking. Roommates, security personnel, teachers, and even strangers are affected by intoxicated behaviors

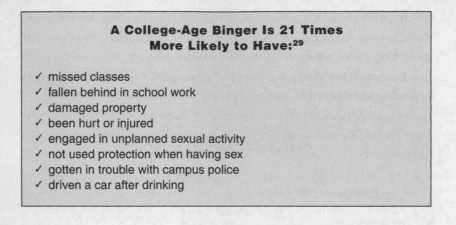

**A College-Age Binger Is 21 Times
More Likely to Have:**[29]

✓ missed classes
✓ fallen behind in school work
✓ damaged property
✓ been hurt or injured
✓ engaged in unplanned sexual activity
✓ not used protection when having sex
✓ gotten in trouble with campus police
✓ driven a car after drinking

and the consequences of heavy drinking. Some students are weary of these dangerous inconveniences (as in disrupted sleep, humiliation, or assault) and are lobbying for change. With 47 percent of college students who consume alcohol drinking to get drunk, campuses are experiencing myriad social problems related to alcohol.

In a 2004 interview with *USA Today* where undergraduates talk about campus drinking, one of their suggestions is to involve students in decision making about campus alcohol problems. More students are sensing the need for reform and supporting tougher penalties for those who violate campus alcohol policies.[30]

Evidently, neither my green list in the drawer nor the D.A.R.E. program offered by our schools seemed to impact Toren's drinking decisions in college. In fact, one of Toren's friends recently commented to me that it was the D.A.R.E. program that first informed him about and heightened his interest in substances. He did not feel it was an effective tool. (This program is typically taught to ten- and eleven-year-old students in grades five and six by police officers. It aims to inform students about alcohol and other drugs and to teach social and decision-making skills to help students resist their use.) Studies have found that D.A.R.E. essentially has no impact on alcohol use.[31]

So in lieu of successful alcohol education for my son, clever media ads and peer influence seem to have triumphed. The more I learn about the behavior of binge drinkers and the effects of this national pastime, the more thankful I am that Toren was able to graduate from college. My brain is overflowing with the facts I've uncovered. I wonder how parents or *anyone* could possibly change this trend.

---

### College Drinking Facts[32]

- 73 percent of fraternity and 57 percent of sorority members are binge drinkers.
- 58 percent of male athletes and 47 percent of female athletes are binge drinkers.
- Frequent binge drinkers constitute less than one-quarter of all students (23 percent) but consume three-quarters (72 percent) of all the alcohol college students drink.
- A ring of bars and liquor stores surrounds most colleges. At one college, 185 outlets were located within two miles of campus.

# EIGHT
## WHAT I FORGOT TO REMEMBER

 **Getting into trouble on campus wasn't my fault.** Throughout most of my freshman year of college, I did things my way. I managed to shrug off monetary fines and attributed the various punitive measures to external forces and the stupidity of a system developed by a bunch of people who couldn't take a joke. Besides, it wasn't reality. It was a little happy bubble of a campus. In the real world, I would blend in better.

I was extremely good at seeing the faults of others and shutting out anyone who wasn't conducive to my path of self-destruction. I was also really successful at twisting a story to justify the outcome and consequences of my behavior. "No, Mom and Dad, you see, this happened, that happened, and then *they* did this . . . or actually . . ." In reality, I was just trying to protect them and myself. I wasn't proud of some of the things that happened. But I wasn't necessarily ashamed, either. Still, I could never let my parents know that my first year away at school was defined by chaos, crazy consumption of alcohol, and disregard for anyone in the way of my fun. One long binge, more or less. What an awesome year.

I went to two of the ten AA meetings required by my RD the summer after my freshman year, and I realized:

1. That I wasn't an alcoholic (the Twelve Steps weren't for me).
2. That the folks who mandated it would never find out that I didn't actually go to ten meetings.

I was right about the latter.

I told my parents that I was going to the meetings for a class—over the summer? They had damn well better believe it. *I* was actually beginning to believe some of the things I told them, as well as some of the things I told myself. My sophomore year I would choose to live off campus because, well, because it was closer. To what? The liquor store, I guess. Either way, I was very careful to let only some of the truth show—just enough for my parents to get the idea that there was an occasional brush with the law or an incident with the campus police, and that it was just another learning experience for their sparkling college boy.

I generally look back on the summers in between college as great times in my life when many of the various parties or weekend outings have blurred together—for obvious reasons. However, there is one blackout that was especially alarming. It must have been after my freshman year in college, I am guessing. Not that it matters really, but it surely was tough to ignore. Maybe it was because it coincided with a conversation I had with my mother right around then, or maybe it was the fact that my friend had a video camera. Sometime before I actually had the pleasure of seeing my friend's video, my mom told me about going to her most recent high school class reunion. Basically, she explained how strange and sad it was that every five years or so, at each new reunion, there would be a new "alcoholic" who got way too drunk and somehow inevitably made a fool out of himself. Some of the classic examples are falling on the dance floor, inappropriately hitting on people, or sharing too much information about all the problems or wreckage from the most recent divorce. The kicker was when she said that these drunks often had been the most adored, charming, or fun kids in high school. I remember thinking, *Damn, Mom, that sucks.* But that was about it.

This particular blackout didn't have that one moment where everything disappeared. Rather, I started out by drinking slowly and constantly throughout most of the day. It was a graduation party out at the cabin of a special family with whom our family had grown up and shared many memories. In more recent years, I had also lost a lot of memories while hanging out with the three sons in that family. Either way, this occasion was a sizable pig roast with many of our families, the brothers, and our friends all celebrating together. I remember how surprised the adults were at how fast we kids dusted off all the kegs without even seeming that buzzed. We had also brought reinforcements in our car trunks, and we went to the nearby store and stocked up as supplies got low.

In typical fashion, most of the adults left the party, and the real drinking started—for me anyway. My last memories are of sunrise the next morning, and from what I remember, I still really had it going on. I can remember stashing my beers in the basement of the cabin a little later, because we were running low again, then drinking out by the fire pit with random people and lighting off bottle rockets (always a good thing). My final memory was of shooting hoops with a couple of friends who had also survived until the wee hours of the morning. That really was it. I faintly remember shooting baskets with a girl and a few other people. After that, who knows? Of course things were blurry, but it was pretty straightforward. Dot dot dot.

And then I saw the video. I was completely astonished. Sure thing, it showed all of us out on the basketball court . . . right during those last moments that I could barely remember. Except it was so much different from what my memory had apparently cut and pasted or just plain reconstructed. What I saw on the video was me basically splayed out on the court under the basket. Although I was barely able to talk, one of the girls was giving me the ball and I was throwing it at the hoop, hardly coming close at all. One time I actually made it, I think, and clearly everyone else thought it was great. I don't believe I even noticed. I showed no coordination and looked completely clueless. At best I was pathetic. It was horrifying to see.

While viewing the video with my friends, I didn't make a big deal about it. I tried to laugh it off and pretend like it was funny, or that it didn't bother me. It would be one thing if I had remembered the scenario that way, and could say, "I can't believe how shit-faced I was, I couldn't even stand up . . . that was ridiculous." But it wasn't like that. I had no clue how out of it I had been, or that people were basically humoring me as the way-too-drunk guy.

Even scarier was thinking back to previous occasions when I had blacked out. It had happened so many different times. I have no clue on which nights I turned into the blithering, slobbering idiot who should have been put to bed. This made me reflect a little harder about the classic drunk at the high school reunion. *Maybe I am destined to be that guy*, I thought.

But I wasn't that guy yet, and that was still what mattered. Things didn't get any better for me over my sophomore year of college. If anything, you could say that I had some of my first bouts with control. If there was anything beneficial besides fun, maybe I gained a little bit of self-awareness. But let me be clear, at age twenty my objective was still having a good time. And "problem" was not a word in my vocabulary.

The fall of my sophomore year I juggled eighteen units of class along with my abusive lifestyle. I probably peaked in my experimental drug use, claiming that I should at least try every drug once. I began to dabble in harder drugs, sampling acid, heroin, crack, and crystal meth. Ecstasy and cocaine became commonplace on weekends, accompanied by large quantities of alcohol. Always alcohol.

The fall and winter of 1999 saw me continuing my pattern of drug and alcohol abuse in a variety of settings. I spent the greater part of that Thanksgiving Day in the Santa Barbara County Jail (away from my parents' scrutiny). But at the turn of the year 2000, I vowed before my brothers to quit smoking. I felt good about that decision and was ready to stick by it. Over winter break, I took a monthlong intersession course with three hours of class per day. It was an interesting course on ethics and the media. Many students were away at the time, and I did a lot of drinking with a few select friends. The lack of structure seemed to just ask for it. I turned my term paper in a week early and skipped out of town for the last week of class, spending the end of January in Arizona, hanging out with friends and destroying my brain.

During that week in Arizona, I managed to go through a generous supply of painkillers made available by a friend. For the better part of seven days, I accompanied the painkillers with constant drinking, a few nights of heavy ecstasy dosing, and a bunch of cocaine to finish it all off. All the while I impressed myself by abstaining from smoking cigarettes. This made me feel in control. In control of smoking. But on that Greyhound bus ride back to San Diego, my nose was bloody, my mind was numb, my mouth was dry, my heart felt weak, and my soul felt sick.

My brain hurt. I decided it was time for a new semester, time for a new start. I decided I'd do February sober. I would not only show I didn't need to smoke, but I'd prove that I didn't need *any* substance. I referred to the month as Sobruary.

Excluding the fact that February is the shortest month in the year, I was delighted to demonstrate that although I had previously been "drug and alco crazy," I did not really need to use anything. I was good to go. I could not only control my intake, I could abstain.

The second weekend in Sobruary, my friend purchased a forty, and I a gallon of nonfat milk. I tried to drink it fast, like a substitute for malt liquor. I drank as much as I could and tried to finish it in under an hour. But milk didn't flow through me like malt liquor did, so I spent a few minutes laughing and retching nonfat dairy whiteness over our balcony. No. I didn't need alcohol.

The next weekend some good mushrooms were made available to that same friend. After thinking hard about the definition of Sobruary and the goals I had set, I decided to classify the hallucinogens under the "horizon-broadening" category. This psychedelic endeavor was more of a spiritual venture than a break in my sobriety. Besides, there was no other way I could explain my attempts to ice skate a golf course, make farm animal sounds from the trees, and play with tracers under melting stars, all the while strengthening my connection to the universe. It was just mental exercise, an exception. A special occasion. That was it.

On my way up to Santa Barbara for the next weekend, I still considered myself sober, and planned on completing my monthlong vow. It was not to prove that I wasn't an alcoholic. I had no worries about that. I did it because it was fun to be sober, and this state of being contrasted with my normal extreme drinking and drug use. This experiment was something different. It was a challenge. I took pride in my strong will and my self-control.

I did fine not drinking for the first night in Santa Barbara. I could watch people drink and party while taking it all in. It was easy for me not to drink. Other times before I'd had to take one for the team and be the designated driver.

The second night out, at my brother's house, we threw a good-sized kegger. This was a typical off-campus house party, where half of the people trickled in from a densely populated college area, with lots of pedestrian traffic. The rest of the party was made up of our friends. In order to celebrate in style and fully showcase my bold abstinence, I bought myself a six-pack of O'Doul's premium nonalcoholic beer.

The party raged on with people trampling through the house, in and out from the front and backyard. I drank each little green bottle, emptying it down into my stomach, fast. And I got no buzz. I was sober. I was having a good time, and I finished my last nonalcoholic beer, participating just like everyone else.

Eventually another keg arrived. Maybe I needed something else to drink. Maybe I forgot what I was supposed to remember about my sober mission. Maybe I rationalized that I'd already demonstrated enough self-control. Besides, it *was* the *end* of February. Who was counting, anyway? Maybe things just got to be too boring. After all, it took a lot of work to act drunk, play along, and never feel any buzz at all. Or maybe I just wanted to get drunk.

One way or another, I began to fill up my O'Doul's bottles with regular keg beer and continued to drink. I secretly maintained the illusion to everyone (and myself) that I was still sober and only drinking nonalcoholic beers. But that couldn't last long.

Eventually I disclosed my fall off the wagon to those who were still paying attention, and joined my drinking partners in full force. Within a few hours I blended right in with the rest of the crew, and it would have been impossible for anyone to believe that I had been drinking nonalcoholic beer, no matter what bottle I was still toting around. I got hammered with a vengeance, and blacked out within another hour or two. After not having drunk alcohol for one month, I got down to business and remained good and sloshed the rest of the three-day weekend.

In other words, my monthlong sober streak was not a success. But I did not view Sobruary as a failure either. I just didn't think about it. I had still managed not to smoke a single cigarette and *most* of the month I *had* stayed sober. I decided to give myself partial credit and reveled in the novelty of my Sobruary. The mushroom trip and the Santa Barbara bash only demonstrated my wild streak. I knew how to have fun.

A month and a half later, I made it through a spring break outing still not having smoked a cigarette. On a four-day road trip to Las Vegas and through Zion and Bryce Canyon National Parks, a few of my friends and I decided to obtain as many different drugs as we possibly could—and do them all during this time. We laced long drives, various day hikes, and moonlight excursions with plenty of marijuana, beer, cocaine, mushrooms, opium, and a few bottles of Robitussin.

At one point I was so poisoned with mushrooms that I was convinced we were lost. Within the snow-covered depths of red and orange rock formations and intertwining ravines, the sun went down. I thought I was going to freeze up and die, tripping out of my mind in some endless canyon. I swore off drugs at that moment. (This was not the last time I regretted my drug intake and pleaded for my sanity back.) Even though I had freaked out, I eventually regained some control over my thoughts and enjoyed the rest of the shroom trip. Then I drank myself back down. I did all of this without a single cigarette. I wasn't addicted after all, right?

I had control. A few times, I even held a cigarette up to my mouth and faked a drag. I held the power. Nothing owned me.

About a month later I hosted a bunch of out-of-town visitors at my apartment. By this time, I was drinking as heavily as ever, and once again smoking liberally. Extreme amounts of noise, broken bottles, and an indoor barbecue all contributed to getting me evicted. Madness. Because of this event, I spent the final month of my sophomore year on friends' couches, getting by like the homeless man I felt like on the inside. To satisfy my parents, I explained on the phone that there had been a problem at my apartment and that I'd had to move out early. I called them as frequently as I could from wherever I landed to keep up the semblance of routine. I had nowhere to go until I returned home for the summer.

The whole second semester of my sophomore college year seemed like a long alcoholic blackout laced with one drug or another. Somehow, I knew it would all work out, though. I hoped to be studying abroad that next fall, anyway. I could start fresh.

# NINE

## PUT ON YOUR BEER GOGGLES
## AND DON'T ASK WHY

**[CHRIS]** *He asked me how to wash a pillow. One of our* sons called me in September of his freshman year after a rugby hazing. It didn't take much probing to discover that he had trashed his pillow being sick after the rugby club team had initiated all the freshman athletes.

"I told them I didn't want to drink that much, but that I'd try. But it wasn't enough for them," our son lamented.

Upperclassmen had tied one-gallon trash bags around the necks of the freshmen and commanded them to drink a beer for every year of their lives—that would be eighteen or nineteen sixteen-ounce beers. The freshmen began puking into the bags at the same time they were required to finish their quotas. Eventually, our son said, he dumped most of the drinks down his chin. He was so ill an upperclassman had to drive him back to his dorm. There he stayed in bed for two days. Now his bedding was filthy. His newly assigned college roommate had tried to help him, but he didn't know our son well and did not realize his desperate state. He left him on the top bunk in the dorm room for two days of misery.

A scholarship student, our son took his studies seriously and did not relish missing classes. When I hung up the phone, it hit me how he'd changed. His voice, once so enthusiastic, sounded weak and confused. I tried to be calm when I told him how to launder the pillow, mattress pad, and the sheets. I didn't want to sound like an overprotective, crazed mother. But it broke my heart because I remembered how excitedly he had talked to his father and me about selecting a club sport, the fun of rugby practices, his success on the team, the thrill of meeting guys from all over the country. He was a strong athlete and I knew how much he desired to fit in and be accepted. I saw his quandary at "getting through the initiation" so that he could continue to play. Not only did it cause me sadness, but it infuriated me.

Alcohol poisoning had not been listed as a prerequisite in the catalogue of this expensive, private Eastern university. I wanted to call the administration to tell them so. Here we were paying tuition (not to mention buying new bedding), and our son calls home telling us of team-enforced alcohol abuse. But isn't this a long-standing tradition in American higher education? Complacent parents pay money to enroll their outstanding offspring in this cycle of abuse and seeding of addiction.

When I talked more about the hazing to our son, he agreed with me that it was dangerous for neophyte drinkers, that indeed he had been seriously affected. But he said if word got back that his mother had complained, he wouldn't be safe on campus. The rugby players had told him he'd get used to the drinking, that everyone had to go through it because drinking after rugby games is part of the tradition. After that, our son played two more games, then quit the team. At the next postgame celebration, he had not been forced to drink, but felt extremely uncomfortable. It just wasn't worth it. He later transferred to a different university. It wasn't that he didn't drink alcohol during his freshman year; the problem was being forced to drink more than he knew was safe.

After the fact, we realized our family could have asked questions about this campus's alcohol policies before our son had enrolled. Knowing about hazing policies and campus attitudes toward risky drinking is essential. By inquiring about such regulations, we communicate to schools the importance of campus drinking practices in selecting a university. There are many other questions parents can ask a potential college. Even knowing whether a campus holds classes on Friday is telling.

Some students call Thursday "Thirsty Thursday" or just plain "Thirst-day," implying a party atmosphere on Thursday nights that would pre-clude serious class work on Fridays. In fact, the number of Friday classes has decreased on many campuses over the past years. (There are 50 per-cent fewer classes on Fridays at Arizona State University and the Univer-sity of California, Irvine.) Some students use Fridays for studying or part-time jobs, "but for many, Friday is a day in recovery, spent sleeping past noon." Charles Reed, the chancellor of the twenty-three-campus California State University system, explains the pattern as he sees it: "Stu-dents don't think they have to study or prep, then it's off to party on Thursday night, then sleep it off on Friday, then do it again Friday night, go to the game Saturday and do it again Saturday night. This is not a healthy atmosphere."[1] A habitual three-day weekend would be appealing to students who love partying.

---

### Questions to Ask *When Choosing a College*[2]

- Include inquiries about campus alcohol policies
- During campus visits, ask for clear terms of drinking prevention, no-tification procedures, available counseling services, and follow-up on students who exhibit alcohol abuse behaviors
- Inquire about substance-free housing
- Ask if campus housing employs RAs or dorm monitors
- Inquire about the influence of fraternities or sororities on campus
- Ask what percent of classes are held on Fridays (no class leads to an early start in partying)
- Find out the average number of years it takes to graduate from the college/school
- Determine the emphasis placed on athletics and tailgating
- Find out the number of liquor law violations and alcohol-related injuries/deaths in recent years
- Consider the college/school location, and social atmosphere
- Look at the school newspaper (ads for parties, local bars, security incidents listed?)

Binge drinking and hangovers go hand in hand on college campuses. Even mild hangovers are a threat to a student's academic standing.[3] Approximately 159,000 first-year college students drop out of school for alcohol- or drug-related reasons.[4] No wonder, because a hangover is unpleasant and few students care to go to class feeling under the weather. Hangovers are caused by a number of things. Ethanol has a dehydrating effect, which causes headaches, dry mouth, and lethargy. It is also a metabolic poison, and its impact on the stomach lining probably accounts for the nausea. Noise and light sensitivity during a hangover are most likely caused by removal of the depressive effect of alcohol in the brain. The amount of tannin and the presence of alcoholic by-products from fermentation may also exaggerate the symptoms.

Withdrawal from alcohol presents many of the symptoms described by Toren —sleeplessness, shakes, sweats, muscle cramps, headaches, and anxiety. This is also called acute abstinence syndrome. A more severe type of withdrawal is called delirium tremens, or DTs. This is a life-threatening condition; about 20 percent of sufferers die from it if it is left untreated. DTs involve delusions (loss of contact with reality, such as a schizophrenic may experience), hallucinations, vivid confusion, and severe nervous-system hyperactivity. DTs usually begin more than forty-eight hours after the last drink, and occur in the later stages of alcoholism.

The Doors performed a popular song in the late '60s about getting to the next whiskey bar on time.[5] Back in the good ol' days, we sang it over and over, requesting that someone show us the way to the next whiskey bar, then chanting, "Oh, don't ask why." The conclusion of the song is that if you don't find the whiskey bar in time, you could die. Whether or not kids are finding their way to the next whiskey bar or not, they *are* finding a way to die.

Getting to the next whiskey bar is not such a worry anymore, because the alcohol outlet density—bars and liquor stores—within two miles of most campuses is increasing. The Harvard School of Public Health College Alcohol Study confirmed strong correlations between the saturation of alcohol outlets and risky drinking behavior among college students.[6]

The swilling of alcohol on college campuses is being examined in several studies. One study uncovered the fact that *underage students* (as was our rugby-playing son) *drink approximately half of all the alcohol* college students report consuming.[7] This includes schools with graduate populations and older students. During fall alcohol promotions, alcohol prices are low, as cheap as twenty-five cents per beer. The drinking lifestyle is a well-advertised and low-budget form of entertainment on college campuses, according to Henry Wechsler, Ph.D., the principal investigator of the College Alcohol Study. "Our study confirms that the lower the prices and the more extensive the specials, the more heavy the drinking. What this means for programs to protect college students from destructive drinking and its consequences is clear: they have an uphill battle."[8]

"Most college presidents are afraid to take on the problem of alcohol abuse on their campus. They think it will hurt enrollment and offend alumni who have fond memories of the haze of alcohol," states Robert Carothers, the president of the University of Rhode Island. He goes on to say, "I tell them that I found just the opposite. I have very strong support in terms of enrollment patterns, support from parents and from 95 percent of the alumni. Taking a principled and intelligent stand on these issues brings good things to the president."[9] In 2004, the University of Oklahoma mandated campus-wide reform after the death of a freshman from alcohol poisoning. The campus has completely banned drinking in the school's frat houses and residence halls. "These policies send a strong signal that alcohol abuse will not be tolerated at the University of Oklahoma," President David Boren said.[10]

Adolescent binge drinking is not a phenomenon limited only to the United States; other governments are also researching the problem. *Because half of the world's people are under the age of twenty-five, this is a far-reaching dilemma.*[11] The fact that other nations are investigating chronic heavy drinking signifies international concern about the problem. Western European countries are experiencing the effects of drinking adolescents. The BBC's Margaret Gilmore reports that "there is an increasing culture of intoxication." British researchers are finding that the binge-drinking period that was once confined to the late teens now often runs from age sixteen to twenty-four. English ministers published strategies in 2004 for tackling binge drinking and other alcohol-related problems. Lord Victor Adebowale, the chief executive of the charity Turning Point, told the BBC, "We are talking about families dissolving in a sea of alcohol." The chief executive of the British Beer and Pub Association, Rob Hayward, stated, "We also need to get to the root causes of what motivates a significant number of people who think it is acceptable to go out on a Friday or Saturday night, drink to excess and indulge in anti-social behaviour."[12]

The current discussion about binge drinking in the United States includes those who say that if we lowered the legal drinking age to eighteen, there would be less glamour in drinking and that kids would stop sneaking alcohol in fast and furious quantities. This may not prove true; European countries with lower drinking ages are also having the same problems. A study in November 2005 maintains that European teenagers drink more alcohol and get drunk more frequently than their American counterparts. "The claim that Europeans learn to drink moderately and safely in a family setting has been used by many in the United States to argue for lowering the drinking age," says Joel Grube, "but our research shows that premise is a myth. Easy access to alcohol seems to allow young people to drink heavily and in a risky fashion, whether in Europe or the United States."[13]

European countries usually have a lower drinking age (sixteen in France, for example) or even no minimum age. Yet the age for obtaining a driver's license is older in these same countries. Rather than focusing on keeping alcohol away from youth, Europeans emphasize highway safety and strict enforcement of drunk driving policies, including immediate license suspension with little recourse. Even with this structure, one-quarter of the forty thousand people killed each year in the European

Union are killed in alcohol-related crashes. With this additional fact in mind, lowering the U.S. drinking age is not currently supported by most professionals or law enforcement.

"Binge drinking is rising all across Europe," said Berteletti Kemp of Eurocare. "It's the alcopop culture (wine cooler and hard lemonade). Adults don't drink these things—it's the young people." The World Health Organization has now agreed to launch an international study on how to prevent excessive drinking and alcohol-related problems, according to Reuters. This research could lead to a global campaign against alcohol misuse.[14]

Are U.S. kids drinking earlier than other nations' youth? A recent study compared international alcohol consumption among fifteen-year-olds considered to be drinkers: 96 percent in Denmark; 77 percent in France; 94 percent in Greece; 87 percent in Russia.[15] Compare this to the United States, where 80 percent of kids have drunk alcohol by the time of high school graduation, at age seventeen or eighteen.[16] The study points out that while some countries have wet cultures where alcohol is integrated into daily life and often consumed with meals, other cultures, such as in the United States, Canada, and Scandinavia, are considered dry, where alcohol consumption is not common during everyday activities. This makes it difficult to compare alcohol cultures.[17]

Even in France, a country steeped in drinking tradition, where one in ten people is considered an alcoholic, the alcohol culture faces remodeling. The French Health Ministry is currently at odds with the Bordeaux Wine Trade Council about proposed labels on wine bottles that would warn pregnant women not to drink. The ministry would like to show people that alcohol is a drug, whereas the trade council professes that such labels will "create an atmosphere of fear."[18]

Europe and the United States are not alone in agonizing about alcohol. A study of two thousand teenagers in Australia found that one in twelve teens developed symptoms of alcohol dependence during the ten-year period of the study. Professor George Patton, the director of Australia's Centre for Adolescent Health, stated, "We don't have much experience (with young alcohol dependents). Nobody really knows what happens to somebody who is alcohol-dependent at the age of twenty-five."[19] And in New Zealand, after lowering the legal drinking age from twenty to eighteen in 1999, lawmakers are currently considering raising it back to age twenty after rising hospital admissions and addiction problems.

China has now joined the high-risk drinking fray. *USA Today* reports that alcoholism is surging in the more prosperous urban areas. The average Chinese person drinks four times as much alcohol per year as they did in 1978.[20] "Alcohol is now a global problem," states Catherine Le Galès-Camus, the World Health Organization's assistant director general for noncommunicable diseases and mental health. Binge drinking is a major issue and "alcohol has become one of the most important risks to health globally."[21]

How does this information affect my family in the United States? After looking at drinking regulations internationally and comparing them to policies in this country, I have come to the conclusion that arbitrary rules about alcohol consumption don't make a whole lot of sense, period. Kids will try alcohol when they decide to do so. The real guidelines for drinking practices need to be strong preparation and up-to-date information about the social and physical costs of drinking for *both* kids and parents. This brings about a better understanding of the responsibilities that accompany drinking and why it is important never to abuse alcohol. It's not necessarily drinking that is wrong, but drinking abusively. The bottom line is taking responsibility for oneself, and looking out for our adolescents' brains and well-being, instead of relying on prohibitive laws for protection. No matter what the legal age for drinking, there will always be someone who ignores it.

After Toren's high school experiences with alcohol, we worried he might go crazy with it in college. Our gut suspicions, it turns out, were correct. But Toren was a great actor, able to camouflage his alcohol abuse. When we visited him during the fall of his freshman year, he seemed to be adjusting well. He did appear moderately stressed about his studies, particularly about an upper-level Shakespeare class he had talked his way into. He loved the class but worried obsessively about achieving satisfactory understanding of the material and his grade. We had seen his brothers struggle in their adjustments to college during previous years and figured Toren would also learn to manage. His grades came through at a high level, even earning him a place on the dean's list, and we assumed he had found his niche.

But late in the spring Toren confessed to us that he wasn't living in the same dorm anymore because there had been an "incident." He'd been kicked out and was relocated. According to Toren, the situation had involved a bunch of guys on his floor drinking and being disrespectful. It was hard to dig out the whole story. But Toren said he'd recently found a roommate for his upcoming sophomore year and planned to live in some apartments close to campus. We did not like this, but it wasn't the first time we'd disapproved of our sons' living choices while they were in college. You could say that we were somewhat battered down by this time. Once again, we crossed our fingers and talked and talked with Toren about his choices. He moved into the apartment his sophomore year, and while we held our breath, things seemed to be going well; at least that's what *we* thought.

Why weren't we more suspicious of Toren during his sophomore year? We visited him in California while he lived in the apartment. Did we notice anything out of the ordinary? No. The apartment looked clean and organized, Toren's friends were very cordial to us, and we sighed in relief that our son seemed to be getting along so well.

Years later, when I talked with counselors at Toren's rehab, they listed characteristics of addicts. One trait was dishonesty, because addicts typically will lie to obtain their substance or hide the use. Of course Toren hid his use from us, because Don and I would have been appalled to learn the truth about it. "Did your loved one ever lie to you?" the counselor had asked. Even then, as I sat in that room, I reassured myself, "My son Toren doesn't lie. He maybe stretches the truth or fibs a bit. But not dishonesty—not from my son." Don and I *wanted* to believe that Toren was doing well. If his apartment was clean, his grades good, and his treatment of us loving, then what more could we have asked as parents?

Toren's substance abuse only got worse and we continued to be oblivious from two states away. As exhibited already by Toren and his social network, *one-third of college students have alcohol disorders and 6 percent meet clinical criteria for dependency.*[22] Studies stress that students who drink heavily are at high risk for mental disorders, and these same findings maintain that prevention programs are needed at colleges. I wonder how alcohol prevention programs would be able to attract kids such as our son and the guys on his dorm floor, or the ones who partied with him at his apartment his sophomore year. I wonder what could be done to influence a change in their drinking patterns. In Toren's case, we parents were not notified of his alcohol abuse (because that was the school's policy at the time), even though we were the people paying his tuition. When the infractions occurred, our son was under the legal drinking age.

What can parents do to stay involved while their kids are away at college? Knowing the school's protocol for substance-abuse violations and carefully monitoring a student's adaptation to college life can be key.

A current concern in the United States is the challenge of reaching

---

### Staying Involved with Your College Freshman[23]

**Before your student leaves for college, use these for conversation starters:**
How will you decide whether or not to drink at college?
What will you do if your roommate wants to have alcohol in your residence hall room?
What will you do if your roommate only wants to drink and party?
What will you do if you find a student passed out?
How will you handle it if you are asked to babysit someone who is very drunk?

*(continued)*

**After your student is at college:**

- Pay special attention to your son's or daughter's experiences and activities during the crucial first six weeks on campus. With a great deal of free time, many students initiate heavy drinking during these early days of college, and the potential exists for excessive alcohol consumption to interfere with successful adaptation to campus life. About one-third of first-year college students fail to enroll for their second year.
- Find out if there is a program during orientation that educates students about campus policies related to alcohol use. If there is one, attend with your son or daughter, or at least be familiar with the name of the person who is responsible for campus counseling programs.
- Inquire about and make certain you understand the college's "parental notification" policy.
- Call your son or daughter frequently during the first six weeks of college.
- Inquire about their roommates, the roommates' behavior, and how disagreements are settled or disruptive behavior dealt with.
- Make sure that your son or daughter understands the penalties for underage drinking, public drunkenness, using a fake ID, driving under the influence, assault, and other alcohol-related offenses. Indicate to them that you have asked the college/university to keep you informed of infractions to school alcohol policies. [For alcohol policies on college campuses, see www.collegedrinkingprevention. gov/policies.]
- Make certain that you and your son or daughter understand how alcohol use can lead to date rape, violence, and academic failure.

Hispanic and Latino youth, both in the college population and the larger community. These teens face serious and disturbing consequences of alcohol abuse. Latino youth represent a large portion of our population, since, according to a 2004 report, one of every seven people in the United States is Hispanic.[24] The prevalence and consequences of underage drinking among Hispanic youth are noteworthy. A recent report from the Center on Alcohol Marketing and Youth (CAMY) finds that underage Hispanic youth are being significantly overexposed to the alcohol industry's advertising, often to an even greater extent than underage youth in general.[25] If Hispanic youth and their parents perceive binge drinking as normal, then the pattern of abuse will continue. Alcohol problems cross all ethnic, social, and economic sectors.

---

### Hispanic Youth and Alcohol Use

- Hispanic young people are more likely to drink and to get drunk at an earlier age than non-Hispanic white or African-American young people.
- Mexican and Cuban twelve–seventeen-year-olds are more likely to "binge" drink than the general population in that age group.
- Alcohol use contributes to the three leading causes of death among Hispanic twelve–twenty-year-olds: unintentional injuries (including car crashes), homicide, and suicide.

---

Because alcohol doesn't have the negative stigma of tobacco, and the product is legal, it is justified and glamorous. There's research out there about problems with alcohol, but the public hasn't absorbed it. Obviously the college rugby team thinks it's a manhood enhancer, and dorm buddies bond in a lather of suds. Fraternities and sororities commonly embrace drinking and underage consumption of alcohol as status quo, often as an alluring supplement for membership and initiation. Sports teams look the other way. College apartment dwellers revel in off-campus freedom. Binge drinking looks fun and blurs the reality of what really happens when thousands of kids drink way too much.

And all the while, we parents are blind. Maybe that's because we're busy sipping wine as we bid at fund-raisers, or we're knocking back a few tall cold ones at our alumni tailgate parties, or maybe we're out to a two-martini dinner with intimate friends while our successful kids are tucked away on campuses where fun can't be categorized as dangerous. Or progressive. Or addictive.

So, in the perfectly balanced family's college history, one son passes up a rugby team because of alcohol peer pressure, and another epitomizes the need for programs to manage campus drinking. We worried about Toren as he made his way through college, but we wanted to give him a chance to make decisions for himself. He appeared to be succeeding as he made new friends, found a part-time job on campus, kept up his grades, and worked through his own problems. We thought he should begin to learn his own way.

To the next whiskey bar.

"We ought to give him some space," we said.

Space to die. To kill himself.

Oh, don't ask why.

# TEN

# I DON'T GIVE A RAT'S ASS

**During the fall semester of 2000 (my junior year** of college), I had the chance of a lifetime to study abroad on the Semester at Sea program. I put a lot of effort into getting the nod of approval from my parents, and worked hard to stay out of trouble so I wouldn't lose the opportunity beforehand.

This voyage of discovery embarked from Vancouver, B.C., in September, first docking in Japan, then continuing south and west through Asia, to Africa, to South America, to Cuba, and finally home in December. I realized that this circumnavigation of the globe was an incredible opportunity, and I made it my goal to complete it without any unwanted infractions, tickets, visits to jails, or dangerous situations.

Aboard ship, alcohol was served nightly (during happy hour and later in the evenings), and numerous occasions arose for drinking on- and offshore. At the beginning, I tried to stay out of the alcohol scene, but as I got to better know the other students on the ship, I slowly came into my own as the lush that I normally was. I didn't have any severe withdrawal symptoms at this point, and, for the most part, my extra precautionary measures kept me out of trouble in port cities, at least at the beginning.

By the end of the semester-long voyage, although I was drinking heavily, I had not joined the club of notorious drinkers banned from *any* alcohol on or off the ship. (Enough problems with alcohol arose for certain people that they were forced to attend meetings and were no longer allowed the privilege to consume alcohol, at the threat of being sent home.) I somehow slid under that radar, despite plenty of heavy drinking, which increased as I became comfortable with the people, the ship, and the constant change of locales. I got caught extremely intoxicated on board one time and was issued a warning for the infraction, but nothing serious came of it.

Even while still participating in classes and cultural activities during the last half of the voyage, I drank with a higher frequency than I ever had in college. For the final month, I rarely missed a happy hour at the bar, and then drank again later in the evenings. Being confined on board, the bar seemed like the best place to be (when the smuggled booze supply from various ports ran low in our cabins), and that is where most of my socializing took place. On top of drinking, there was no shortage of sea-sickness medication like Dramamine, or other pills like Adderall, Lariam, or Vicodin to keep me going to bed with some sort of buzz every night. My body definitely got used to consistent intoxication, rather than the weekend binges I normally endured early in college.

Although I drank heavily on the ship, I valued my time in port and tried to counterbalance the drinking by being productive. I didn't squander away all my opportunities. With the chance to experience new adventures in different port cities, I learned about the ancient religion Shinto in Japan, and hiked in awe along the Great Wall of China. I contemplated the meaning of war memorials in Vietnam, visited the jungles and tea plantations of Malaysia, and participated in a homestay with a working-class family in India. In Kenya, I had an incredible chance to visit missionary friends of our family and joined them on a safari in a game park. While in South Africa, I contrasted the wineries in the countryside to the townships of Cape Town. In Salvador, Brazil, I played music and games with orphans. All of these cultural exchanges fascinated me, and I absorbed and relished each one. Fortunately, my partying at night did not extinguish my curiosity and compassion. I felt that I had the best of both worlds—of *all* worlds.

But in the last few port cities, I began taking risks and had some solid blackouts as well. Whether I deserved a break or not, I experienced no severe consequences and never caught the attention of any authorities. While traveling, I took in everything I could during daylight, then went all out with my friends at night. In the last moments before we departed Kenya, some fellow students and I scored a bunch of Special K (pure ketamine) in a pharmacy. On board, we either shot it with syringes or dried it out with a hair dryer and cut it into lines. In our cabins, each dosing sent us deep into a dream state, and we lost all concept of reality and time. As the drug kicked in, a warm drip started at the top of my brain and overcame my whole body in a dizzying, melting high, accompanied by all kinds of visual hallucinations. It is a wonder we were not caught wandering the ship with our hands gripping the walls and feet floating down the hallways. What seemed like hours would turn out afterward to be only minutes. While the intense high lasted, reality was nowhere to be found.

In South Africa, Brazil, and Cuba I sought out ecstasy and cocaine with various friends and spent many nights drinking anything and smoking everything. Long conversations, good buzzes, and wild scenarios became my late-night pursuit in the final ports. With cheap foreign cigarettes, local liquors, beach cabanas, plenty of sun, and an array of new friends, it turned into one extended spring break.

We scored more Special K in Cuba. These were my first experiences with this drug, and I ultimately used it a total of five or six times. One night, before going out to a bar, I injected myself with a good dose. Then, later at a club, I made another run to do more in the bathroom. I still had plenty in my system. I took a rolled-up bill and snorted a bunch out of the corner of the bag I had brought with me. I sucked it up my nose too hard and ingested way more than I had intended. As soon as I'd done it, I knew I had taken too much. Most of what had been in the bag was now gone. Whoops. The drug was pure, strong, and its effects were impossible to control.

I left the bathroom before it began to kick in, and anchored myself down. My heart raced. I sat in a chair and clung to a pole in the middle of the club as lights, all kinds of colors, and scenery danced, rotating around me. All the while I spun in and out of conversations with various people who may or may not have been there. I blindly nodded at them whether or not they were even looking at me, and clenched my jaw as tight as I could. Finally I confessed to some girl what was wrong, and she looked after me for who knows how long. It seemed like an eternity. Eventually I wanted to leave, and she escorted me to the door so I could get out of there. It was chaos and I could barely take it.

Slowly, I walked myself back to the ship. My legs felt wiry and robotic and my machinelike feet clomped along the pier the entire way, I was so out of it. Once again, I had overshot myself to the point of vowing that I would never do drugs again. At best, I figured this was another example of my bad judgment. I didn't have a drug problem. I had just gotten too high, that was it. Besides, the drug was really strong and pure. So it took me for a ride. All I wanted was for my drug trip to end, and I would behave myself. And only drink. That would be it from there on out. Reality finally came back, and I decided to mellow out. Eventually everything worked out okay.

We returned stateside in late December, and sometime after the New Year I received a Christmas card in the mail printed with something generic, like "Happy Holidays," and below someone had written, "Hey Toren, I don't know if you remember me, but I helped you back to the ship the last night in Cuba. I hope you are well. Seasons Greetings and take care."

No. I didn't know who it was. I could not recall the student whose name I saw signed on the note. (And after looking through several books of student pictures, I still didn't know.) I felt horrified, embarrassed, and confused when I received the greeting. I'm not even sure if I realized I had blacked out, as a matter of fact. I knew I had drunk hard that last night or two, even after overdoing it with the Special K, but I didn't know it had gotten *that* bad. I had been more out of control than I thought. I

never responded and eventually threw the card away, because it was an ir-
ritating reminder that I couldn't remember squat and I still didn't know
who had helped me that night. So I guess I didn't have any "incidents" at
sea, but really I had just barely floated by.

At times my behavior while on Semester at Sea didn't quite seem to
add up. As if I were some conflicted individual, a contradiction between
my drug use and other interests continued to grow. Extreme drugging, to
me, was a very reasonable thing to be doing. Someone might ask why I
would want to waste a voyage around the world by ingesting drugs and
bingeing on alcohol. To me, that would have been a stupid question.

As a twenty-one-year-old, new experiences (drug experimentation
included) and pleasure were my top priorities, and taking risks just added
flavor. I sought to enjoy my experiences and get the most out of everything. Although I may have seemed reckless or careless, another part of
me attempted to learn and gain a better understanding of the world that
engulfed me. I had a hard time differentiating between the two. Drugs
and alcohol continued to alter my perception of normalcy and to impair
my judgment, because drinking and trying new drugs were my motivation for everything. Consequently, I did drugs like an addict and drank
like an alcoholic, while still maintaining the illusion that it was all choice
and always would be.

Had other drugs been cheaper, more available, and more practical to
ingest in social situations, like drinking was, I'm sure I would have been
addicted to more than just alcohol by the end. I was hooked before I
knew it, and at times my decisions became skewed because of it. My
abuse drove a wedge between my desires and my intentions. I lost sight of
the person I may have once wanted to become, and became a person who
simply wanted. Period. I wanted everything and anything and lots of it. I
wanted all things pleasurable, and I became the ultimate life junky, although self-destructive by nature. A contradiction.

Physically, my drinking (or drug use) never seemed to take a huge
toll on me in the beginning. In high school and at the start of college, I
could drink super hard for a weekend and then turn around and sleep it

off immediately. On top of that, I rarely faced the excruciating hangovers that many normal drinkers seemed to complain about. Mine were usually mild, if I had one at all, and rarely debilitating. Yes, I did wake up dehydrated and feeling like shit sometimes, and sure, I did wake up still tipsy from time to time, but of course I didn't really mind that. The fact that I was so resilient to hangovers and certain effects of alcohol (with an increasing tolerance) may have suggested I wasn't a normal drinker. But these were warning signs I preferred to ignore. And I clearly wasn't *that* concerned about my blackouts.

It seems like my physical dependence only started to grab hold my junior year, after I returned from Semester at Sea and was again allowed to live on campus. After all the problems I had caused on campus my freshman year, it seemed impossible that I would ever be allowed to move back again. Luckily, I had disappeared sophomore year by living off campus in an apartment. Along with traveling abroad on Semester at Sea, this three-semester time lapse seemed to keep me away long enough to be forgotten. With few problems, I moved into my new dorm room. During this second phase of on-campus living, as an upperclassman, I managed to navigate between the cracks with very little trouble and only a few visits from the Public Safety officers. I survived the remainder of my junior year and into my senior year. It wasn't until the last month of my senior year that I had my final run-in with the head RD.

Reports of a broken car window led straight back to me after a long weekend and a wild party. Some things were allegedly thrown from our third-story balcony. I stepped forward and took the blame I deserved when I realized enough evidence had piled up against me. I ended up funding the windshield replacement. The RD didn't know which question to ask first: "How is it that you are living on campus?," and "How have I not known about it?," and "How have you managed to stay out of trouble?," and finally, "What happened here?" After we got past all this, he made me promise that no more problems would occur, emphasizing that I wasn't even technically allowed to live on campus, and that I was so close to graduating and moving on. I had almost made it, and I think that idea thrilled him as much as (or more than) me. He attended graduation, and the moment finally came when I "walked," and he knew that it was over. I think we were both pretty pleased.

One reason I didn't get into much trouble on campus my senior year was because I spent a good part of the weekends off campus, partying elsewhere. I may have been getting ready to join the real world, but my alcoholism was progressing rapidly at this point and affecting my studies dramatically.

In hopes of better preparing myself for graduate school and to get a taste of something more specific in the field of psychology, I had the opportunity to assist with research at one of the nearby state schools during my final semester of college. Coincidentally, the research I helped out with investigated the effects of alcohol on rats' behaviors and learning capacities. Using rats as models, the project studied how exposure to alcohol impaired physical development in the brain and central nervous system, as well as behaviorally in regard to learning. The researchers were looking for treatments that could be administered to abate or counteract fetal alcohol damage. I observed how the studies were designed and run, helped out entering data, and helped to run some of the very basic pilot studies being developed for future research.

The rats' abilities to learn were measured through behavioral tests, such as swimming, climbing, and navigating mazes, while another test measured the regularity or irregularity of their movements in a box designed to quantify such activity. It was hypothesized that rats exposed to various levels of alcohol would perform differently and demonstrate less learning aptitude, and, therefore, less improvement from previous testing.

I learned that some research indicates one of the most damaging effects on the rats' brains occurs during the withdrawal period. Usually I worked on Mondays, Wednesdays, and Fridays. Interestingly, I found that *I* was able to perform *my* tasks better on Wednesday and Friday depending on how much alcohol I had exposed *myself* to during the previous weekend. Some Mondays I felt like I was experiencing worse withdrawal symptoms than the alcohol-saturated lab rats. (Sometimes I had not even made it home to campus before going straight to my internship—having slept somewhere else—to begin my always difficult Monday, usually feeling sick, feverish, and bracing for withdrawals.) I dreaded going to work at the lab, because the ideas underlying our research were being rubbed in my face. It was obvious that my memory was failing as a direct result of my drinking. Still, I was not willing to acknowledge my drinking problem.

Although I only helped out with pilot studies, my own alcohol consumption did not allow me to effectively contribute to the academic research, which was attempting to tackle the root of my problem—abuse of alcohol. I refused to reconsider my self-destruction, even though the research revealed to me various negative effects of drinking on a scary level. My weekend binges were in direct conflict with my work there, but there wasn't a moment when I wanted to step back and identify this contradiction or question my drinking. I guess I had to conduct my own research on the weekends to find out what really constitutes a problem, and what it really takes to be an alcoholic.

(The results are in.)

"Hi, my name is Toren, and I'm an alcoholic." This time when I said it, in the fall of 2003, I had just turned twenty-four and was in rehab, so things were a little bit different. But still, I was saying it as a way of taking the path of least resistance. I didn't want to challenge the idea, because that would have required me to examine the problem and see why I was really there. As it turns out, I didn't know what being an alcoholic meant. I knew it carried a bunch of colorful stigmas, but it was always one of those things you heard about, and, unless it directly affected you, you could pass through life ignoring it.

I have found that you can be an alcoholic and still disregard it. Being in rehab, seeing other examples, you can learn to ignore it. You can stay in denial until it drags you to your grave and devastates everything in your path.

But I was an expert on my drinking and didn't see what there was to be fixed in my therapy. In this particular rehab, each patient was given a specific treatment plan and requested to take steps in understanding his addiction and the disease. These steps would allow me to evaluate how it has affected myself and others, and what I need to do in order to get control of my life to escape physical, mental, and spiritual deterioration. Sounds pretty deep for rehab, huh? Well, it is.

For me, I thought it'd be easy. I wasn't really an addict. I'd only craved alcohol more recently, and that was only once I'd started drinking. I didn't drink daily, and sobriety was good to me when I needed to be sober. Shit, I didn't have a disease. I *chose* to drink and party in high school and college, and it was always great for me. My use didn't affect anyone else. Most people had no idea how much I drank, and when I blacked out I wasn't losing their memory, only mine. And finally, I had control over my life—well, for the most part, anyway.

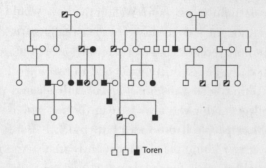

Toren

**[CHRIS]**

*September 24, 2003. As soon as Don and I find* out the name of the rehab facility where Toren is assigned, we jump onto the Internet. The treatment Web site looks encouraging and upbeat. I suddenly have hope.

Toren's rehabilitation program offers more information about alcohol and drug addiction than I can comprehend. Definitions, charts, slide shows, resources, photos of staff and grounds, philosophy, the "contact us" portion—it's all there. But this friendly site identifies the Dysfunctional Family as one cause of an adolescent's demise. "The family is being neglected," the slide show states. It goes on to say how families aren't sitting down to dinner together anymore, how families lack control and structure. It emphasizes that family education is a tool of recovery. I agree that some families are dysfunctional. But not ours.

To me, the cause for our family's dilemma is elusive. Yet everywhere we look, fingers point and the world screams back: Dysfunctional!! I put on my armor and rush out to combat this hated term. How dare they name-call in our direction! This mother is ready to ride into battle. Maybe I need something to get mad at. I'm weary of being so damned understanding and loving. It's time to bring out my defensive reinforcements.

Let's start with sitting down as a family for dinner. If you challenged any one of our sons about the Volkmann dinner hour, they would laugh in your face. We sat down to a nutritious dinner at six o'clock whether anyone wanted to or not.

And as for structure, well, there again, the boys would ridicule this premise right off the Web site. Who was known as the strictest mother in middle school? Probably me. Perhaps . . . just maybe, this is what drove my son to drink.

"So get over it," my husband says. "Just because you consider yourself the perfect mother doesn't mean you have the perfect son."

(Believe me, many fine drunks are nurtured in families who sit down jointly for dinner every night, read excellent literature together, make and enforce strict ground rules, and emphasize ethics and morals. In fact, the quality of alcoholics produced in such a family is outstanding. I'm here to prove it. Actual results may vary.)

Let's find another category to pick apart this family. We're laying out all the reasons for an alcoholic's downfall, and, as yet, we've skipped a vital category: genetics. Hello, deep and scary skeletons of the Volkmann past. And greetings to the fanatical Shamberger DNA pool. I usually tell people that the defects of our family fall to my husband's side. It isn't really true, but it counters the sting of the dysfunctional dinnertime accusation. I feel better already.

It's a statistical reality that if a person has a close relative (like a parent, grandparent, or an aunt or uncle) who is an alcoholic, he has four times the chance of becoming an alcoholic. According to the NIAAA (National Institute on Alcohol Abuse and Alcoholism), researchers have uncovered a genetic factor that could predispose certain youths to binge drink.[1] College-aged kids with a particular variant of the serotonin transporter gene (5-HTT) drink more alcohol per occasion, drink more often just to get drunk, and are more likely to engage in binge drinking than students without the variant. This new evidence provides important information about the risk of developing a maladaptive pattern of alcohol consumption influenced by genetics.[2]

On my desk sits a stack of brochures and papers from the rehab institute. We have to fill out a form requested by Toren's therapist, Gretchen. She has such a grounded name; I know she will straighten him out. Gretchen has sent us a big packet of papers telling us about the twenty-eight-day program and the Family Education Program, and she asks that we fill in data about our family alcohol history. It's called a Family Assessment, which sounds scary. I don't know if I want to send this private stuff across the country to be scrutinized by complete strangers. But then I remember we're desperate. Our son is in crisis. He's asking for help. I don't have to cover up for him now, because he's totally admitted he messed up. What a relief. Still, I'm smarting on the inside. This isn't just a survey to summarize our family hobbies or avocations. It's a serious confession about the way we raised our son, about our values and family experiences, and we are requested to spell out the exact times where we fell short. I have to be honest.

The form mostly focuses on Toren's history (as I perceive it, which most likely could be, and is, different from how he perceives it). In fact, not until some time after Toren's rehab do I learn the full extent of his other drug usage. Filling out this survey from my uninformed vantage point is like a cursory glance into the crater of a volcano. I have no idea what really exists beneath the crust. I am in the dark about Toren's other drug use. It asks what chemicals I think Toren is using or has used, when he started, and any negative behaviors I have encountered concerning his chemical use. It sounds pretty benign at that point, until I start listing nine years of drinking consequences on four inches of paper—and that's only the ones I know about. There's hardly sufficient room. I become sweaty. Should I lie? Maybe delete a few screwups? I don't. I'm a perfect mother, remember? I write it as I saw it. And it hurts.

The assessment also asks about each family member's usage of drugs and alcohol, like what drugs, how much, how often. I begin to feel guilty when I have to write the word "dope"—but they call it weed now—and I can't remember how to spell "marijuana." There are a lot of reasons I'm slowing down on my responses, because all of a sudden I'm thinking about thirty years ago. At that time I had no idea some rehab center would be asking me these questions. You don't think of that sort of thing in your twenties. You just do it. As I think back on it, we didn't use marijuana that often; only for a few years in the '70s. You can't complete medical school, an internship, two different residencies, teach a classroom, play in a symphony, and be pregnant and nursing three times while stoned on marijuana. It doesn't work. Earning a living and being productive were always high priorities for Don and me, as well as carrying and nourishing my babies drug- and alcohol-free. And it was scary to buy an illegal substance. Even though we wore tie-dyed shirts and bell-bottoms, we were lightweights. But I still feel a twinge of guilt as I fill in the form. It whispers to me, "No wonder your son's in trouble. . . ."

On the next part of the questionnaire, our alcohol consumption falls into the heavier-than-normal category, I speculate. I'm starting to become more aware of this, as we are not drinking during Toren's treatment. It sticks out, and now I realize we could cut back. So I fill in that portion, too.

The next section asks about our families' generational alcoholism/drug usage. There is about a half inch allowed for the response. That's easy. My family has been Anabaptist, pacifist, and nondrinking for generations. It would have been impossible to have an alcoholic there. (Luckily the document doesn't ask for other addictions, such as shopping, marathon running, or Bible reading.) But now Don is home and hands me a letter he has written to Toren. I realize immediately that we're going to need several attached pages. As I said, it's *his* side of the family. Here's how Don describes it:

*Hi Toren,*

*The other day I was reading one doc's discussion on the causes of alcoholism. His opinion is that 60 percent is genetic and 40 percent environmental. I know this is hotly debated and you are learning all about that now. Regardless, you figured it out and that is what is saving you. Congratulations!*

*But just to give you a better understanding of your genetic background for whatever it may mean to you, I will recount some of my family's history of alcoholism.*

## The Volkmann Hall of Alcoholics (Those We Know)

**NANA'S SIDE ALCOHOLICS (paternal grandmother):**

Two of Nana's brothers, Bert and Greg.

*—She had six brothers and they were all terribly color-blind, so they probably didn't even know if they were drinking light rum or dark rum and I am sure they didn't care, especially Greg. Bert, I think, conquered it okay. Greg died miserably from it, leaving a few pissed-off wives, but one sober kid.*

Nana's sister's daughter, Beth.

*—(my first cousin)—She has been through lots, and possibly more than one rehab program. She has turned her life around more than once, if you know what I mean. Nearly four years ago, in her late forties, she apparently turned her life around again and, in fact, has been sober since. She's instrumental in counseling and supporting other alcoholics.*

**VOLKMANN SIDE ALCOHOLICS (paternal grandfather):**

Great-granddad, Tom.

*—For his times, your great-granddad had a bit of a wild streak. There were rumors of cases of Old Crow in the cellar. And he was known to fall asleep on the back of his wagon after a time in town. Fortunately, his sober horses were more on the wagon than he was and always returned him home safely.*

Granddad's younger brother, Bill.

*—Abandoned Lutheranism for Catholicism to marry wife Jane (also an alcoholic). Bill died twenty-some years ago from diabetes*

*and other complications of lifelong alcohol poisoning. Some considered him a closet drinker. It appeared to me that the whole world was his closet.*

**Bill and Jane's oldest daughter, Kathy.**

*—(my first cousin)—followed both her parents' alcoholic habits. Kathy's mother's family history (my Aunt Jane) is littered with stories of rehab attempts and alcoholic tragedy, nearly too much to recount. Alcohol conquered Kathy at age forty-eight after a lifelong battle. She died of cirrhosis and bleeding to death from a predictable complication of her destroyed liver.*

**Bill and Jane's son, Grant.**

*—(my first cousin, who took over his dad's orchard and bad habits)— He was the first person I knew who installed a keg in a refrigerator with the tap out the side! Yeah, baby! To his credit, he is nearly ten years sober now after losing one marriage to the disease. His son, Todd (in his twenties), has already been through a rehab program.*

**Bill and Jane's three other children.**

*—(my first cousins)—As far as I know, two of these three siblings also may have had problems with addiction.*

**Granddad's older brother Glenn's son, Tim.**

*—(my first cousin)—I remember him commenting several years ago, "I don't drink." I found out he recently celebrated fourteen years of sobriety. Prior to sobering up, he helped union workers deal with alcohol-related problems by getting them into rehab so they could return to their jobs. One day he realized that he was drinking more than those he tried to help, so he signed himself up for a program. He would be a good resource for you if you wish to talk with another family member.*

**My dad, your granddad.**

*—Has admitted to drinking way too much when in the military (what else could you do?) in his thirties. He has never had a "prob-*

*lem" and handles his "beer time" successfully for an eighty-eight-year-old.*

**My brother, your uncle Ric.**

*—He started drinking at an even earlier age than you, and smoking, and then doing drugs of all sorts. But, ultimately, alcohol was his favorite, although any high probably worked. They say that he died of snorting heroin, probably combined with too much alcohol—two huge depressants. He stopped breathing. Ric's typical booze-binge alone or the heroin alone would probably not have done him in that night, but at age thirty-one and with his history, it's hard to imagine anything but a tragic end to his life. According to those who were close to him at the time (I was just starting to get to know him better), he was in the process of cleaning up his act. I would think cleaning up the Hanford Nuclear Site would have been easier.*

**Me, your dad.**

*—Although I am not admitting to being an alcoholic (yet), I have not ruled it out. As a seven-year-old, I would pop open beer bottles for my dad and take a swig, but didn't like it. Never drank in high school except for one time. I didn't drink again until my freshman year in college, where, after Hell Week in our fraternity (halfway through my freshman year), I had a sip of beer just because eighty-five people were about to kill me if I didn't (most of them are probably alcoholics). Slowly through college, I learned to drink a bit, occasionally getting drunk. Did some weed. The next few years, the same, sometimes overdoing it, but pretty controlled. Nothing regular. Never affected studies. Then med school, residencies, practice, the same.*

*A master of titration I became. Both with the anesthetic drugs I administered to my patients and the booze that slithered down my throat. The past ten-plus years, having a drink after work and wine with dinner became a routine. Your mom and I have frequently* talked about drinking less. So we made the rule: no weekday drinking, and, of course, the unspoken five o'clock rule. Well, unless friends came over or there was another event, etc. And summer— one long weekend. Geez, sounds worse when I write it down. There have been some bad day-afters, feeling some hangover and a little shaky for an hour or so, making me think that it probably wasn't healthy. I have not had really bad reactions or trouble sleeping. I have looked forward to the weekend drink but have not felt a craving exactly. It has never affected my work, but I can recall twice going to work thinking that I wish I didn't feel the way I did.

Probably ten years ago, your grandma said she was concerned that I was drinking more than I should. She asked, "When was the last time you went a week without drinking?" I informed her that I was on call lots so it had occurred. She was reassured. I was left wondering.

Today marks one week for me without drinking. I don't remember when that last happened. So, how am I doing after a week? Well, frankly, I missed having a drink out on the boat last evening and wonder how severe I need to be with myself. I don't want to give up drinking. But I don't want it to be a focus, a need, a crutch, or a problem. I will not be drinking for the duration of your program and will be assessing my situation throughout that time. After that, I will see how I feel and decide if I should moderate or quit.

So, Toren, that's one hell of a 60 percent for you to deal with. I thought you would want to know where you fit into the Family Hall. I'm counting on you being on the side with the happy, successful survivors. You can forever be an inspiration to the rest of our poor, genetically challenged family members, like me. Thanks for helping me look at me.

Love,
Your Dad

Don will send his letter to Toren at rehab, and also mail a copy to Gretchen. His letter reveals a cumbersome appendage to our family, one that neither of us had previously acknowledged. Nor had we ever really sat down with our children and discussed it. His data makes my green binge drinking chart look anemic. I realize that we totally missed the boat here. Our kids needed to know this important family history, and we slipped up by not forewarning them.

When Toren went to Mexico to study Spanish, he arrived shortly before *Día de los Muertos*, the Celebration of the Dead. It is a colorful fiesta to honor deceased family members. *Día de los Muertos* has a purpose. The Mexicans understand that there's a reason to celebrate with ancestors, to know them, to remember how they were. Our relatives' lives may help us recognize ourselves. Too often, we Americans just set them aside (a memorial service and a burial and *voilà!*) without understanding the impact. The history of our ancestors will, in fact, become our legacy, and we will carry parts of them forward with us. Sometimes unwillingly. All the better to know what we've got.

Don and I failed to recognize the predisposition of our children to alcoholism. Now we have a crisis in our family, an addiction to deal with, whatever the cause. I find myself demoralized thinking about Toren's recovery from alcoholism, a disease that seems even more complicated than I thought.

We receive e-mail correspondence from a fellow Peace Corps volunteer in Paraguay, a person we've never met before, one who is enthusiastic about having Toren return to his post there. She suggests people we might contact to help Toren's cause. I write back that I cannot interfere with the decisions being made. In my heart, I'm thinking that Toren is not yet ready to decide whether he should return. While I'm gratified that this fellow volunteer feels Toren's work was of high quality, pushing him back up the hill will not help any of us. Maybe I, too, am moving along, because I now realize that protecting Toren will no longer serve him. His life is his own to create. I recall the term "codependent," so I toss out to her that I don't want to be a codependent. It sounds knowledgeable,

though I'm not exactly sure what it means. I seem to remember that being a codependent is not a good thing. All this addiction talk is new to
me. I make a mental note to look it up.

I remember how Don and I once placed M&Ms along the trail for
Toren during our first family backpacking trips. The candy encouraged
him to continue on; it kept him content. And it made the hike easier for
us. How young are patterns of codependency fostered?

No matter how we're labeled, we are a family bound by our love for
one another. We function now as five grown people, separate, yet attached
by years spent learning from one another. Some of our tendencies reach
behind awareness, to places our grandparents traveled. Even though we
weren't there, we know about it. Who said we are dysfunctional? Our
family swills success as we kneel down for a deserved smack in the head.

# TWELVE

# THE START OF (WHICH?) GOD'S NIGHTMARE

### LUCK

I was nine years old.
I had been around liquor
all my life. My friends
drank too, but they could handle it.
We'd take cigarettes, beer,
a couple of girls
and go out to the fort.
We'd act silly.
Sometimes you'd pretend
to pass out so the girls
could examine you.
They'd put their hands
down your pants while
you lay there trying
not to laugh, or else
they would lean back,
close their eyes, and
let you feel them all over.
Once at a party my dad

came to the back porch
to take a leak.
We could hear voices
over the record player,
see people standing around
laughing and drinking.
When my dad finished
he zipped up, stared a while
at the starry sky—it was
always starry then
on summer nights—
and went back inside.
The girls had to go home.
I slept all night in the fort
with my best friend.
We kissed on the lips
and touched each other.
I saw the stars fade
toward morning.
I saw a woman sleeping
on our lawn.
I looked up her dress,
then I had a beer
and a cigarette.
Friends, I thought this
was living.
Indoors, someone
had put out a cigarette
in a jar of mustard.
I had a straight shot
from the bottle, then
a drink of warm collins mix,
then another whisky.

And though I went from room
to room, no one was home.
What luck, I thought.
Years later,
I still wanted to give up
friends, love, starry skies,
for a house where no one
was home, no one coming back,
and all I could drink.

Raymond Carver[1]

**Toren built a fort during his high school days. He** and a couple of friends constructed it on the vacant lot across from our house. It was nestled amidst cedar and fir trees, well designed, and the boys even used a blueprint drawing. Because we suspected they might be partying there, we forced them to tear it down. We told Toren it was his good luck to have parents who cared. He said it didn't seem like good luck to him.

Toren gave us the sense that he wasn't lucky at all. He said he always got caught. We believed him at the time, but now I realize it wasn't the truth. The number of times we caught him was minuscule. When we didn't catch him, sometimes someone else did. During his freshman year of high school, Toren attended a party (without our permission) at a river not far from our house, one of those potential situations you read about in the newspapers where someone drowns from drinking too much. But that didn't happen. Instead he got busted by the police (along with other more inexperienced kids who were also "unlucky"). One of his brothers was with him and also got caught. Toren swore to us it was his first high school party with alcohol and that he had not been drinking, just attending. But we decided to hand him a tough sentence. We penalized both Toren and his brother. Don and I wanted them to know that we took this offense seriously, and we tried to construct consequences that would reinforce better use of their time. Due to the arrest, they also had to go through legal steps for kids with MIPs and were required to do community service.

Still in our files is the list we provided to the court that enumerated the consequences we had levied. (Each son had his own list.) We wished to prove to the court that our family did not take underage drinking lightly:

## Toren's Consequences

Toren is a high school freshman, has a 3.79 accumulative GPA, is a select year-round soccer player, lettered in swimming and starts on the JV soccer team.

### Toren's Penalties from April 16 to May 16, 1995:
1. Toren removed from high school JV soccer team.
2. Write letter of apology to asst. principal and high school soccer coach.
3. No going out for *one month*. Come straight home from school. No friends over.
4. No phone calls the first weekend. Afterward, no phone calls after 8:00 p.m. for one month.
5. Urinalysis drug screen at local laboratory, April 18, 1995. *(Negative results.)*
6. Give away Nintendo. Out of house until further notice, perhaps forever.
7. Work out at community athletic club one hour per day.
8. Maximum two hours of TV per week, two hours per weekend.
9. Improvement of attitude to be measured at end of one month. Keep room picked up, take care of lawns, extra household chores each weekend (painting, weeding, upkeep).

10. Visit grandparents out of town with family one weekend.

11. Spend evening with all house guests, visiting at dinner table, etc.

12. Loss of prized Beastie Boys tickets for May 29, 1995. Not allowed to attend concert.

13. Community service: ✓ Crop Walk, collect $25 ✓ three hours work at Neighborhood Beach ✓ Arrange to assist coaching throughout summer in youth soccer league (to begin first of June, several nights per week through August)

14. Meeting with parents of other boys involved in episode. Common ground rules set, information and phone numbers exchanged. Agreement to mutually support one another and one another's sons.

**Toren's Guidelines from May 16 until end of summer:**

1. Allowed to go out one night per weekend until 11:00 p.m., midnight if arranged ahead.

2. Limited viewing of TV: one program per night except Wednesdays.

3. Anticipation of all A grades and one Pass in college prep courses for grades in June 1995.

4. Part-time summer job at cessation of school; save three-fourths of earnings for college.

5. Assist on youth soccer team (community service).

6. Mow lawn every week.

7. Pay any increases in car insurance and/or court costs out of own funds.

8. Announce whereabouts to parents when leaving house.

There were about fifteen boys netted in that swoop. The above consequences established us as the strictest parents in the area. (At the parents' meeting, one mother advised me that we shouldn't be too hard on our boys, that they were just kids.) We didn't care because we felt it important to take a swift and immediate stand in regards to underage drinking.

This was the first time Toren was kicked off a high school sports team for violating high school drug and alcohol policy. But not the last. If you could joke about it, Toren turned out for three different varsity sports each year during high school; did that not increase the odds? It seemed that every year he was kicked off one or another team in accordance with the high school's no-tolerance alcohol and smoking code. Each time we found Toren teamless, one of the hardest parts for our family was what Toren would do with his unscheduled time. We insisted he continue working out, we imposed consequences at home, and we always hoped it would never happen again.

In reality, suspensions are supposed to be a learning process to remind a student to change undesirable conduct and to protect other students from risky behaviors. When dismissal happens from any high school activity (such as cheering, music, drill team, sports), it presents a timely opportunity to help struggling kids in a real way. Merely expelling youths from teams or activities without providing structure for changing a behavior is ineffective. While Don and I attempted to remedy the problem at home, support by coaches and school counselors or treatment specialists would have increased our chances for success. Young students like Toren experiencing their first screwups offer a superb prospect for school personnel to intercede early enough to make a difference. As in Toren's case, young athletes are motivated to stay on the team, to please their coaches and fellow players. The consequence of a meaningful suspension could offer kids not only a real-life consequence, but tools for future social skills.

If I could recommend a revised structure for high school code violations, it would definitely include being suspended from the team or activity, but also packaged with this consequence would be drug or alcohol intervention or counseling, not only for the student but for the family. Perhaps coupled with the counseling would be the chance to continue turning out for team practices (if compliant), and participating in specified games or activities after sanctions are meaningfully fulfilled. Schools across the nation could make an impact by providing such help, and even insisting upon it, for substance-abusing students instead of casting them aside. Pulling in the family allows for straightforward communication about expectations.

But aren't schools already being asked to do too much? How can they be expected to take over for every substance-abuse issue? Here again, with so many adolescents corralled into the school system, it is an ideal time and location to begin treatment and intervention. Because schools are already overburdened in meeting all students' needs, and teen substance abuse is essentially a family problem, perhaps state or county departments of substance abuse could partner with schools to intervene, providing both the teen and his or her family with expertise and guidance. By offering programs that interface directly with substance-abusing youth and their families, schools and communities may seize the opening to impact kids at the earliest point. This creates a win-win for schools, students, families, and community.

Both Don and I worked closely with the coaches and parent groups at the high school. We had a good rapport with them. When we went to conferences about Toren's transgressions, all of us felt extremely chagrined. Interestingly, our conferences usually included a coach and a vice principal, but never a school counselor. It never even occurred to us that we should seek out a counselor. Of course we always believed that this particular meeting in the office would be our last, because surely Toren didn't really have a problem, he was just at a "difficult stage." Late in Toren's high school career, the mother of one of Toren's best friends would call to forewarn me to put on my power scarf and power lipstick, because she and I were frequently called to attend these unpleasant debriefings together. We hoped Toren would "get it" soon. It bothered me that he apologized so readily, spoke to us sincerely about his missteps, performed his penalties, and yet would make repeated infractions. Each time, we thought Toren had finally wised up.

As I thought I remembered, Toren did well with his penalties after the river mishap. In fact, it wasn't until Toren's rehab that I put two and two together, figuring out that *he did not do well*. Not at all. I had to go back to my 1995 journal to dredge up the next incident. Surprisingly, it occurred just a few months after the river episode, subsequent to the severe restrictions we had thought would be so effective. And even more revealing is how much I had forgotten or minimized that experience. The next story has more details than I remember, but only because I wrote them down in my journal. I will relay the story as I interpreted it then, nine years before Toren would be enrolled in rehab. Little did I know that my rhetorical beginning would ultimately manifest itself.

## July 16, 1995—Chris's Journal Entry

*The power of helplessness. It can overtake. Knowing that all you've done for fifteen years wasn't enough preparation for a few hours of bad decisions. And knowing there remains a whole lifetime to do more damage, more destruction to oneself. That is helplessness. Many parents face it and give up. You think adolescence is the time of life to let go of your child, to allow the young person to turn the corner and carry his own weight. Ultimately, he'll bring along a sound mind and body, one that could function well in the world. Or the dreaded opposite, he will carry wreckage and damaged goods. A few hours can undo all the love and nurturing a parent has offered. Totally. It leads one to believe in helplessness. And that's where we are.*

*It began when Don and I were returning home from Seattle after attending a chamber music concert, an evening of Mozart and Schumann. We spotted Toren walking along North Street holding hands with a waify girl, accompanied by someone on a bicycle at 11:30 p.m. (Summer curfew at midnight.) I suggested we go over and let Toren know we were back, make sure he'd be in on time. Don said, "Let him be. It looks innocent enough." So we drove on home without bothering him.*

*At 12:10 a.m. he still wasn't in. His oldest brother had come in and gone to bed. It was a Wednesday night; both the older brothers had to get up by 6:30 a.m. for their summer jobs the next day. The second brother would be in by 12:30.*

*I checked downstairs and thought it smelled like someone had smoked a cigarette, but found no evidence of partying. Then I went to our back entrance, where I found Toren "resting" on our landscaped hill-side, the approach to our daylight basement. I called, "Toren, get in here!" and he said okay. He came upstairs into the great room, tripping as he entered. For a fifteen-year-old, stumbling is not highly unusual. But I watched him closely. He sprawled across the couch when I asked him to sit down, almost flopping. "Where have you been?"*

*He looked at me, glazed, and began mumbling things like, "We were walked then together mubuymumble." He stopped.*

*"What?"*

*"The others. We walked." He drooled.*

*"Oh, my God." I ran to get Don, who was in bed watching TV, looking like he was about ready to fall asleep. "Don, Toren can hardly talk or walk. Get up here!"*

*He hurried along with me and had Toren stand up. "What have you had? Were you sniffing something? Drinking?" Don asked in his ER triage voice.*

*Toren didn't make sense—he sputtered meaningless words until he garbled something like, "I've never drunk before. The first time."*

*"Where's your bicycle?" I asked him. I knew it was at the neighbor's, but Toren said it was at another friend's. I couldn't really smell alcohol on Toren, which scared me all the more. I wondered if he was high on something worse.*

*Toren muttered something else and Don asked again, "What did you drink?"*

*"From a cup."*

*"What?" He didn't know.*

*"Okay," Toren challenged us, "test me!"*

*Because we had previously tested his urine at a lab after the river* party, Toren was ready to do it again. This idea seemed absurd because Toren could hardly sway to the bathroom. He tilted himself into the wall, and then couldn't give a specimen. Then he wobbled back to the great room and slumped onto the tile floor and began burping. I knew Toren would soon be sick, which relieved me, because it now looked like the culprit was alcohol rather than other drugs.

We questioned Toren further, me in my blue bathrobe and flip-flops, Don in his T-shirt and shorts. It was the standard, "Where were you? What were you doing? Who were you with? Why are you doing this?" inquisition. With little cooperation and a slur of jumbled denials, Toren swore he wasn't with anyone. But we had seen him on the street with two people. Absent was the thoughtful, gracious, and cheerful kid we'd raised. I wished we had not gone to the concert. Then he began throwing up. I smelled alcohol for sure.

Don got out the video camera and filmed Toren trying to swagger down our hallway, trying to answer my questions as I perched at our kitchen table looking extremely perturbed. He made Toren stand and asked him questions to which Toren could hardly respond. He filmed Toren retching. "Toren'll never remember this," Don told me. [I couldn't believe it. How could anyone forget a thing like this? It shows how naïve I was.]

I couldn't get through to Toren. It was as though he wasn't inside his body. He had no soul. Just spitting and syllables. He didn't seem to have any idea what he was doing.

To solve the riddle of what had happened, I called a girl, Hillary, whom I suspected had been with Toren on the street that night. She claimed she had not been with him. I told her we were worried about Toren and needed to know what he had ingested. It crossed my mind that Toren could get worse, might lose consciousness. She said she'd call around to find out.

Meanwhile, Toren wanted to lie down. We were worried because he was so out of it. Hillary called back and said she'd talked to some people who were with Toren and that he'd had seven beers, best estimate.

*We were shocked. Hillary seemed guarded with her information, but I sensed that she wanted to help us. I knew better than to ask more.*

*Toren asked us to leave him alone so he could sleep. Don explained that it would be irresponsible for us to let him fall into a deep sleep because of the potential for vomiting or aspiration.* [An anesthesiologist, he specializes in rendering people senseless, and he recognized when someone was in potential jeopardy. He also knew the risks of overdoses and alcohol poisoning.] *So we had Toren sleep on the floor of our bedroom beside our bed, and we took watchful care of him that night.*

*Toren woke up frequently, spitting up all over our bedroom carpet. I tried to give him a drink of water, holding up his head, but he spit into the glass. It's the only time Don and I laughed. Toren looked pathetic. As he lay there I thought about him willfully chugging down seven beers. It was disgusting to me. I felt so bad for him and wondered why he would do it. A 3.79 GPA, friends galore, nice house, summer job. Why?*

*The next morning, Toren did not remember a thing, did not seem to have a hangover, and wondered why he was in our bedroom. He walked calmly to his own room, where we allowed him to sleep a few more hours.*

*When he awoke the second time later that morning, we asked Toren what he had done the night before, and he said, "I went to Lakefair."* [Lakefair is a summer festival in Olympia.] *He had no memory of being sick, sleeping in our bedroom, or our conversations. In fact, he appeared incredulous that we would invent such a story. He only remembers waking up the next morning and being tired.*

*Then we showed him the video. "I never want to see that again," he told us.*

*After over twenty-four hours of phone calls and discussions, a story finally came through. Toren told us that he'd bought the beer at the Safeway grocery store. We still weren't sure that his brother didn't buy it for him and that Toren wasn't trying to protect him. It turns out that Toren and four other boys had partied at our house and at a tree farm near our house. Another girl, named Sara, and one of Toren's friends were not walking with Toren innocently as we had thought, but literally holding him up like a Gumby doll and helping him vomit on the way home. Had Don and I stopped by, I think we would have noticed. It's amazing Toren made it home at all.*

*Toren admits to having had friends and girls over and drinking two beers, but after that, who knows? He acts like he is being forthright with us, even though there must be more to the story.*

*Don and I have decided not to let Toren get his driver's license until six months after his sixteenth birthday. That will be soon enough. And that's only if we have no more incidents.*

The previous admission describes how I felt at the time of Toren's drunken debut: helpless and devastated. It's "lucky" none of us knew what we would yet go through.

We did a few things right. We went over Toren's behavior; we thought he had given us a mostly truthful story. We emphasized to him the risks in drinking so much. Don had the foresight to videotape Toren in his blacked-out state. But as we talk with Toren now, he tells us that he barely remembers seeing the tape! How can this be possible? It's because he was still too inebriated the next day to recall what he was doing. If Don and I had realized this, we would have waited several days to show him the video, when his brain function had restored itself. The impact of our video would have been stronger. It wasn't until Toren was out of rehab nine years later that we reviewed this event with him and realized the ineffectiveness of our efforts! That's what caused me to dig out my journal, and then, to my dismay, review what I *thought* had happened. At the time of the incident, though, Don and I believed we'd made an impact and that Toren would long remember this dismal experience.

While talking to Toren later that day, I cried and told him that it had caused me great sadness to see him abusing himself that way when I had been so careful during my pregnancies not to drink alcohol. I could not understand why he would drink so heavily. He seemed too young and too talented for such destruction. We levied consequences and hoped that Toren would respond well to them. He was a good sport, apologized, and said he was sorry. He did not make excuses for his bad behavior. The start of our nightmare.

Research shows that those kids who have a supportive tie with a parent or guardian will have more protection from alcohol-related problems. But bringing up the subject of alcohol with teens can be tough. When a parent does this, the teen may feel immediately that the parent has no trust. For example, at our house, Toren usually denied that he used alcohol or drugs and tried to change the subject. Experts say this is a normal behavior, and that parents must expect to have this discussion many, many times. It's a good idea to bring up the subject of alcohol before problems arise, before the discussion can be seen as an accusation. (No kidding, I'd give back that scene in our kitchen if I could!) Since the average teen first drinks at around age eleven to thirteen, this interchange should take place early. In fact, the first casual conversations about alcohol can begin when a child is a toddler. It is unrealistic to cover every fact about alcohol at once. Having a number of talks about drinking throughout childhood creates the most impact. One could think of this discussion as part of an ongoing conversation.

To boost the chances for a productive conversation during adolescent years, it is recommended that parents take some time to think through the issues they want to discuss *before* talking with their teens. Also, it is important to anticipate how a child might react and consider ways to respond to a teen's questions and feelings. Choosing a time to talk when both parent and teen feel relaxed can be helpful. In our family, drives in the car often provided opportunities for conversation (and no method for escape).

Obviously, it wasn't enough to simply tell Toren that he should avoid alcohol. As I now know, specific language may have better helped him figure out how. For example, what can your daughter say when she goes to a party and a friend offers her a beer? Or what should your son do if he finds himself in a home where kids are passing around a bottle of wine and parents are nowhere in sight? What should her response be if she is offered a ride home with an older friend who has been drinking? Experts suggest brainstorming with a teen for ways that she might handle these and other difficult situations, and make clear how parents are willing to support her. Another example: "If you find yourself at a home where kids are drinking, call me and I'll pick you up—and there will be no scolding or punishment." The more prepared a child is, the better able he or she will be to handle high-pressure situations that involve drinking. Toren's preparation could have been better scripted by our family.

In a discussion about drugs or alcohol, kids often want to know what parents did when they were teens. This is the question many parents dread. Don and I tried to be honest about our past drinking choices with our kids. The reality is that many parents did drink before they were old enough to legally do so. So how can we be honest with a child without sounding like hypocrites who advise, "Do as I say, not as I did"? This is a judgment call. Some parents may choose not to share prior drug or alcohol history. Another approach is to admit that we did do some drinking as teenagers, but that it was a mistake—and give our teen an example of an embarrassing or painful moment that occurred because of our drinking. This is also a chance to bring up family history and genetic risks without pointing fingers. Realistic talk about addiction struggles within our extended family or other families allows the subject to be broached without blame. A combination of this information may help our child better understand that youthful alcohol use has negative consequences.

In talking about this serious subject of underage drinking, no matter what is said, it seems most important that we told Toren we loved him and that we were worried. It is vital that we told him alcohol could have serious consequences. (It did.) We were there to listen to him. (Sometimes we didn't like what he said.) We wanted him to be part of the solution. (Eventually, he was.) We told him what we would do to help him. (We stayed by his side.)

Every teen is unique, and parents are forced to trust their own par-

### Tips for Communicating to Teens About Alcohol[2]

**Establish open communication**. Make it easy for your teen to talk honestly with you. Show you care. Even though young teens may not always show it, they still need to know they are important to their parents.

#### Some ways to begin:

*Encourage your child to talk about whatever interests him or her. Listen without interruption and give your child a chance to teach you something new. Your active listening to your child's enthusiasm paves the way for conversations about topics that concern you.*

*Ask open-ended questions. Encourage your teen to tell you how he or she thinks and feels about the issue you're discussing. Avoid questions that have a simple "yes" or "no" answer.*

*Control your emotions. If you hear something you don't like, try not to respond with anger. Instead, take a few deep breaths and acknowledge your feelings in a constructive way.*

*Make every conversation a "win-win" experience. Don't lecture or try to "score points" on your teen by showing how he or she is wrong. If you show respect for your child's viewpoint, he or she will be more likely to listen to and respect yours.*

**Make it a point** to regularly spend one-on-one time with your teen—time when you can give him or her your loving, undivided attention. Some activities to share: a walk, a bike ride, a quiet dinner out, or a cookie-baking session.

**Draw the line**. Set clear, realistic expectations for your teen's behavior. Establish appropriate consequences for breaking rules and consistently enforce them.

**Offer acceptance.** Make sure your teen knows that you appreciate his or her efforts as well as accomplishments. Avoid hurtful teasing or criticism.

**Understand** that your teen is growing up. This doesn't mean a hands-off attitude. But as you guide your child's behavior, also make an effort to respect his or her growing need for independence and privacy.

*(continued)*

**Quick tips**

| | |
|---|---|
| Be available— | Parents can't communicate if they're not there |
| Listen and Hear— | Pay attention to what a child is saying and feeling |
| Stay calm— | Get hold of emotions before talking |
| Encourage and accept— | Accept the person if not always the action |
| No mixed messages— | There is a time to correct and a time to praise |
| Deal with today— | What happened in the past is not always pertinent to today |
| No attacking— | Sarcasm and hostility have no place in mature communication |
| No nagging— | It takes two to communicate |
| No preaching or moralizing— | It won't get parents anywhere |

## Language to Use When Communicating to Teens About Alcohol

**Ask Your Child's Views about Alcohol**
Ask your teen what he or she knows about alcohol and what he or she thinks about teen drinking.

Ask your teen why he or she thinks kids drink.

*Listen carefully without interrupting.* Not only will this approach help your teen to feel heard and respected, but it can serve as a natural lead-in to discussing alcohol topics.

**Important Facts to Share About Alcohol**
Although many kids believe they already know everything about alcohol, myths and misinformation abound.

- Alcohol is a powerful drug that slows down the body and mind. It impairs coordination; slows reaction time; and impairs vision, clear thinking, and judgment.

*(continued)*

- Beer and wine are not "safer" than hard liquor. A 12-ounce can of beer, a 5-ounce glass of wine, and 1.5 ounces of hard liquor all contain the same amount of alcohol and have the same effects on the body and mind.
- On average, it takes two to three hours for a single drink to leave the body's system. Nothing can speed up this process, including drinking coffee, taking a cold shower, or "walking it off."
- People tend to be very bad at judging how seriously alcohol has affected them. That means many individuals who drive after drinking think they can control a car—but actually cannot.
- Anyone can develop a serious alcohol problem, especially a teenager.

**Media and Alcohol**
The media's glamorous portrayal of alcohol encourages many teens to believe that drinking will make them popular, attractive, happy, and "cool." Research shows that teens who expect such positive effects are more likely to drink at early ages. You can help to combat these myths by watching TV shows and movies with your child and discussing how alcohol is portrayed in them.

**Six Ways to Say "NO" to a Drink**
At some point, your child will be offered alcohol. To resist such pressure, teens say they prefer quick "one-liners" that allow them to dodge a drink without making a big scene. It will probably work best for your teen to take the lead in thinking up comebacks to drink offers so that he or she will feel comfortable saying them. But to get the brainstorming started, here are some simple pressure-busters—

1. No thanks.
2. I don't feel like it—do you have any soda?
3. Alcohol's not my thing.
4. Thanks, but I'm driving.
5. I don't drink.
6. Why do you keep pressuring me when I've said no?

enting instincts when setting up strategies. Although our penalties and guidelines did not seem to stop Toren from drinking, they were a necessary foundation for setting limits and accountability. Whereas Toren was well aware of our position on underage drinking and our expectations for him, he still chose to ignore us; other teens may be more receptive.

## Prevention Strategies for Parents[3]

**Monitor Alcohol Use in Your Home.** If you keep alcohol in your home, keep track of the supply. Make clear to your child that you don't allow unchaperoned parties or other teen gatherings in your home. If possible, however, encourage him or her to invite friends over when you are at home.

In a recent national survey, 71 percent of eighth-graders said alcohol was "fairly easy" or "very easy" to get. The message is clear: Young teens still need plenty of adult supervision.

**Connect with Other Parents.** You're likely to find out that you're not the only adult who wants to prevent teen alcohol use—many other parents share your concern.

**Keep Track of Your Teen's Activities.** Be aware of your teen's plans and whereabouts.

**Develop Family Rules about Teen Drinking.** When parents establish clear "no alcohol" rules and expectations, their children are less likely to begin drinking. Some possible family rules about drinking are:

- Kids will not drink alcohol until they are twenty-one.
- Older siblings will not encourage younger brothers or sisters to drink and will not give them alcohol.
- Kids will not stay at teen parties where alcohol is served.
- Kids will not ride in a car with a driver who has been drinking.

Once you have chosen rules for your family, you will need to establish appropriate consequences for breaking those rules. Be sure to choose a

*(continued)*

penalty that you are willing to carry out. A possible consequence might be temporary restrictions on your child's socializing, such as revoking driving privileges.

Finally, you must be prepared to consistently enforce the consequences you have established.

**Set a Good Example**. Parents and guardians are important role models for their children. Studies indicate that if a parent uses alcohol, his or her children are more likely to drink. But even if you use alcohol, there may be ways to lessen the likelihood that your child will drink.

- Use alcohol moderately.
- Don't communicate to your child that alcohol is a good way to handle problems. For example, don't come home from work and say, "I had a rotten day. I need a drink."
- Let your child see that you have other, healthier ways to cope with stress, such as exercise, listening to music, or talking things over with your spouse, partner, or friend.
- Don't tell your kids stories about your own drinking in a way that conveys the message that alcohol use is funny or glamorous.
- Never drink and drive or ride in a car with a driver who has been drinking.
- When you entertain other adults, make available alcohol-free beverages and plenty of food. If anyone drinks too much at your party, make arrangements for them to get home safely.

**Don't Support Teen Drinking**. Avoid making jokes about underage drinking or drunkenness, or showing acceptance of teen alcohol use. In addition, never serve alcohol to your child's underage friends.

**Help Your Child Build Healthy Friendships.**

There is a huge gray area surrounding whether parents are too strict or not strict enough when supervising teens. Experts stress that teens need lots of adult supervision. In my mind, I go over Toren's early years to look for the first clues of his tendency to abuse substances. Could it have started with his sneaky escapades to the corner candy store in second grade? I realize that Toren navigated grade school on a narrow margin of charm. His charisma and antics could crack up any well-behaved group of kids so that they turned into uncontrollable goons. You could say teachers kept a close eye on him. Maybe that was a sign he would become addicted to alcohol, but it was never on his report card. Toren was considered the kid to talk to, the one who had all sorts of classmates calling him for advice and consolation, even though he was also considered mischievous by his teachers.

Middle school saw him beginning to smell like teen spirit, influenced by Kurt Cobain and Nirvana. He still kept up his grades, played select soccer, and talked openly to us about his life. Lots of friends came to the house, and there were girls in and out.

High school didn't seem as innocent. Toren continued to joke with our family, contribute around the house, and hold summer jobs. He did everything a parent could ask and had a great attitude. Toren was fun to be around. When it came to the weekends, however, we were always suspicious that something was going on. A sort of mischief followed Toren, always with a grin and a wink. We attempted to be aware of what he was doing and with whom, as parents of early teens try to do, but in hindsight, I'm afraid we were often in the dark.

Some people would tell me that the reason Toren became addicted to alcohol was because we didn't have God on our side. Of course, they mean their brand of God. We didn't attend the correct church, hadn't done what good Christians would do in educating our children. I wonder if other Gods would have liked to help us? Okay, I'm calling them out. Step up to the plate, all available Gods! Whichever one will help, I'll take.

I know several religious drunks, even some ministers who have been through rehab. (They must not have had God on their side, either.) Which God gets the credit for this? Our God-fearing country has difficulty grappling with this disease called alcoholism, even with a president who is a recovering alcoholic. We would rather ignore it or point fingers. The moral high road to addiction is a lofty one. It would be much easier to carry some sort of religious banner for deflecting criticism and the silent looks of condemnation that I anticipate from our extended family, especially the devout branch. I dread telling them about Toren. Luckily, I don't have to—yet.

Toren has been at his inpatient rehab now for a week. Don and I wonder how he's doing, how he's dealing with what they are teaching him. The twelve-step program's Higher Power will certainly be emphasized. Which Higher Power is best for the battle? We wonder how Toren will handle this part of his program, since he does not embrace any particular religion. Then we receive his first letter, where he talks about this very struggle:

> *My biggest problem so far is dealing with GOD. This is a twelve-step program and God is the source and reason for every single testimony and story of recovery. As if there is no way around it, the foundation of it all. The initial step is admitting powerlessness over a substance and turning it over to an "acknowledged" Higher Power as we understand it. So on day two, I had a session with my journal and decided to give myself a working definition of "God" or my Higher Power so I wouldn't cringe through every prayer said over the next four weeks. I decided that the combination of family, friends, nature—both perfect and imperfect—and music create a resource of power, an inspiration, and a will greater than me that I could equate with God. And that will provide me the strength to do what I need to in order to get through this. This allows me to invest my energy into this program without feeling like I'm selling myself out.*

At the same time Toren is working on his spiritual orientation, a group of Tibetan monks is visiting Olympia to create a mandala, a circular pattern that represents the world in its divine form. These enlightened monks travel throughout the world to promote healing and peace by constructing a beautiful design composed of colored sand. It takes over thirty hours to complete the intricate design, and when it's finished, they sweep the five-foot-by-five-foot pattern away as a manifestation of *life's imper-manence*, how nothing is ever the same or lasts forever. Both the creation and the destruction of the mandala are meaningful expressions of lessons in life. Don and I check in on the monks during the week to watch them meditate and build the mandala. We are pleased to see them because they remind us of our travels in the Spiti area of northern India.

On Tuesday night, the monks perform traditional dances, chants, and blessings in a sacred celebration. Don and I join the candlelit parade as the grains of sand are carried to Puget Sound at high tide. The monks' bright orange robes are illuminated by a full moon across inky waters. Through crisp air dotted by points of flame, long brass horns plead. There the monks toss multicolored grains into the mirrored liquid. We are given one small vial of sand to pass on to Toren, a poignant symbol for his healing and the impermanence of his struggle. Don and I are hopeful that Toren will conquer this addiction. We embrace the monks' energy so that we can integrate it into our family, to honor the steps Toren is taking. During the ceremony, we hold hands as we march to the dock, determined that the symbolic act of setting the sands free will also release our son.

There is no way to tell Toren what we have done because we cannot contact him during his rehab. The small container of sand stays on top of my dresser until I can deliver it to Toren later. I will write him a letter ex-plaining the meaning.

Each day during Toren's rehab, I send a card, an old photo, some-thing to remind him of his family, his center. I want him to think about the different phases of his life, to reflect on how he evolved to his present situation. One day, I send him a description his paternal grandmother wrote about eating Jell-O molded in the snow banks of Nebraska in 1929, describing how thrilling it was because Jell-O was a novelty, how you could only have it in the winter when the snow would set it up. I want Toren to understand that even the simplest things can be startling and beautiful—fresh. The rehab facility has told us not to send food or books or magazines. Toren is supposed to be concentrating on twelve-step literature and his recovery. I wonder if making Jell-O during a snowstorm fits in, but it doesn't seem to matter.

In the past, Toren has always been diligent about tackling goals. He seems to have decided on the course of his recovery with the same absolute determination. I do not sense him faltering, even though he did not want to leave South America. But it's early; I can't believe he's only been in the program one week. To me, it seems like ten years already. It is still difficult for me to go out in public, even though I have errands to do. I go to the bank but forget which account I'm accessing; I leave my car keys on top of the gas pump; I forget why I am walking into a store. When I even start to think of my best friends, it makes me tearful, because I don't want to talk about my family to them. I wish I could scream out what has happened; it's difficult to maintain composure. I neglect to return phone calls. Certainly, I must be making too much of this. Our son's life isn't that hopeless. But to me, seeing his dreams shattered is overwhelming. I feel guilty for having participated in it.

On the same day that the packet arrives from the rehabilitation facility with the alcohol history form, Toren's therapist calls us. She says that she will be calling weekly. Gretchen assures us that Toren is very motivated, very young, and very naïve about his problem. He is doing well and will be able to call us later this week. Toren will be allowed two ten-minute calls every week. If he doesn't have visitors on Sunday, he can have an additional call that day, too. Visitors must be approved, and anyone who "used" with him is not allowed. (Are we allowed? I wonder what "using" means.)

Gretchen questions me about alcoholism in our family and our level of support for Toren. I inquire about the packet that has arrived in the mail, and I tell her we will attach a family alcohol history for her information. We talk about Toren's work in South America, and she says no way will Toren be allowed to return. I ask her if perhaps there is room to reconsider at the end of his rehab, and she says no. She explains that the counselors do not tell Toren at the beginning about the impossibility of him returning. It's because he has to come to that realization by himself. Toren needs to be the one to say that he's not capable on his own. My heart sinks when I hear this. Gretchen tells me that Toren will be released in about twenty-eight days, on Monday, October 27, if all goes well.

# THIRTEEN
## PARTY MY FACE OFF

*We're gonna bury ourselves in cans,*
*Duct tape bottles to our hands,*
*And when there's nothing else to do*
*The keg's gonna make our plans.*

—Toren Volkmann, from "Alcohology"[1]

**October 6, 2003. My therapist gave me the first** steps of my treatment plan, which said, "Toren lacks understanding of addiction, evidenced by his statement that he did this to himself and he deserves it . . . Toren will internalize the disease process and identify the severity of his disease."

After my original shock, amazed that she was bold enough to say that I lacked an understanding, I tried to relax and let the professional do her work. Through some assigned readings, I learned a bit more about alcoholism, the role of genetic inheritance, and how it is chronic, progressive, and potentially fatal. Basically, plenty of time-tested evidence suggests that alcoholism is passed on genetically and is a disease. In more blunt terms, it is a brain disorder that doesn't go away; it only gets worse and will kill you if not properly treated and arrested. Maybe I should keep reading.

The process of breaking down denial doesn't happen in one day. It took me at least another week or two of exposure and kicking my own ass at rehab for me to be able to say, "I'm an alcoholic," and know what it meant. But did I understand it or believe it? It is pretty hard to know whether or not you're being honest with yourself.

A good visual way of understanding the progression of my disease was by looking at an alcohol dependency model called the Jellinek Curve.[2] Along this curve the symptoms that one experiences are exhibited throughout the progression of addiction. Everyone experiences it differently, but it seemed that my physical dependence and withdrawal symptoms progressed rapidly for my age.

I was told to identify all the symptoms listed throughout the early, middle, and late stages of alcoholism. I related to many of the subtle increments that are indicators: *blackouts increase, inability to discuss problem, neglect of food, tremors and early morning drinks and loss of ordinary willpower*. On top of those there are obvious behaviors that are genuinely alcoholic, like never leaving a drink unfinished (whether it was mine or not), or my tendency to always be out partying or drinking but be able to come up with endless reasons not to go to dry events or hang with people who didn't drink. Little things like this, traits that always seemed normal to me, appear in the early stages of alcoholism, but at that time there was no reason to examine them as warning signs. For me, in fact, these were all just choices, and they didn't seem like problems. I was a pretty typical alcoholic and related to most of the progression on the Jellinek Curve.

As the curve moved into the middle stage (for example, *the effort to control drinking but failing repeatedly*), I was even more typical because I was hesitant to identify certain things that I couldn't relate to, since "I wasn't *that* bad." *Denial*. Luckily, my therapist was there to point out lots of those other characteristics for me.

I was a drunk from the time I started. While it never seemed wrong in the party atmosphere, it was my way of thinking that there was no point in drinking just one or two drinks. I always drank to get hammered. A lot of people do, but not all go down the same path, I guess. Most learned drunks will agree that one is too many and a thousand is never enough.

Although I drank more than the average person in terms of quantity and frequency, there were and are no definite telltale signs of alcoholism in the earliest stages. This is what was so devastating to me and would be to any alcoholic. What happens is a complete deception and twisting of

# ADDICTION AND RECOVERY / THE JELLINEK CURVE

**Crucial Phase**

**Chronic Phase**

**Rehabilitation**

Occasional Relief Drinking

Constant Relief Drinking Commences

Increase in Alcohol Tolerance

Onset of Memory Blackouts

Increasing Dependence on Alcohol

Surreptitious Drinking

Urgency of First Drinks

Feelings of Guilt

Unable to Discuss Problem

Memory Blackouts Increase

Decrease of Ability to Stop Drinking When Others Do So

Drinking Bolstered with Excuses

Grandiose and Aggressive Behavior

Efforts to Control Fail Repeatedly

Persistent Remorse

Tries Geographical Escapes

Promises and Resolutions Fail

Family and Friends Avoided

Loss of Other Interests

Unreasonable Resentments

Work and Money Troubles

Loss of Ordinary Willpower

Neglect of Food

Decrease in Alcohol Tolerance

Tremors and Early Morning Drinks

Onset of Lengthy Intoxicants

Physical Deterioration

Impaired Thinking

Moral Deterioration

Indefinable Fears

Drinking with Chronic Users

Obsession with Drinking

Unable to Initiate Action

All Alibis Exhausted

Vague Spiritual Desires

Complete Defeat Admitted

Obsessive Drinking Continues in Vicious Circles

Learns Alcoholism Is an Illness

Stops Taking Alcohol

Personal Stocktaking

Assisted in Making

Spiritual Needs Examined

Onset of New Hope

Appreciation of Possibilities of New Way of Life

Regular Nourishment Taken

Realistic Thinking

Natural Rest and Sleep

Family and Friends Appreciate Efforts

New Circle of Stable Friends

Facts Faced with Courage

Increase of Emotional Control

First Steps Toward Economic Stability

Care of Personal Appearance

Rationalizations Recognized

Group Therapy and Mutual Help Continue

Enlightened and Interesting Way of Life Opens Up with Road Ahead to Higher Levels Than Ever Before

Increasing Tolerance

Contentment in Sobriety

Confidence of Employers

Application of Real Values

Rebirth of Ideals

New Interests Develop

Adjustment to Family Needs

Desire to Escape Goes

Return of Self-Esteem

Diminishing Fears of the Unknown Future

Start of Group Therapy

Physical Overhaul by Doctor

Right Thinking Begins

Meets Former Addicts Normal and Happy

Told Addiction Can Be Arrested

Honest Desire for Help

one's perception through time. I fell in love with the wonder drink because it made an already awesome life so much damn better. It made things so great that, even if it partially interfered with other aspects of my life, I could let them be compromised or justified in order to keep the party alive. That is what it's about, right? Being flexible and having a good time? Maybe so, but that doesn't have to entail being blind to pain, problems, and potential disaster.

Alcohol was my answer to teen boredom on the weekends, a way of filling downtime. It turned the average night into a lively evening. With just a few drinks or a heavy buzz, socializing became easier and stress disappeared. I felt free. Life was easier with alcohol. When I drank, pleasure became my focus and reality shifted to the periphery. Parties were no more of an event than a mentality. I learned to rely on drinking to have fun, and became socially dependent on alcohol sometime in high school. (The actual physical symptoms of my drinking dependence began to show up in college.)

In hindsight, or maybe from the parents' eyes, some warning signs are a bit more obvious. But to a high schooler who is just cracking his first beers and getting a taste of a new life of _____ (fill in the blank with parents' worst nightmares), these alleged warning signs are more fittingly seen as validation, battle scars, a rite of passage or any other of youth's skewed misinterpretation. Besides, I seemed to be very good at finding myself at the wrong place at the wrong time. Whenever I was caught, it was bad luck and not my fault for doing what everyone else did, too.

At the beginning of high school in 1995, with my favorite group of friends, we were pretty open to trying anything, and I certainly thought we were on the forefront of exploration. What started as simple experimentation with marijuana and drinking resulted in our new way of socializing every weekend. This was nothing abnormal (or so I thought), and it became our way of life. Whether someone's parents were out of town, or whether we congregated at a park, in deeper wooded areas or private undeveloped areas, we'd always go out boozing or getting high.

From that point, it didn't really matter what we did, whether it be in a car picking up fast food, at someone's house, or at a more formal party. We were content with our recreational use, often too wasted or stoned to really care to figure out what other normal people did. As far as we were concerned, we *were* it, and I'm not sure I can argue. We loved getting messed up, making asses out of ourselves, and being kids. On the other hand, most of the guys in my group of friends were above-average athletes, reasonable students, and participated normally in school activities. We just had more fun. It wasn't our fault.

I started out my high school freshman football season with high hopes. Within a week or two I felt a bit indifferent, maybe too cool or too wimpy, but either way, I quit. Unfortunately, a pattern of me not being able to complete an entire season began to surface by the end of my sophomore year. The second, third, and fourth times I didn't finish an athletic season had nothing to do with deciding to quit: I was kicked off. I racked up two MIPs for alcohol—that got me kicked off the JV soccer team my freshman season and the varsity team my sophomore season. I was kicked off the football team for smoking cigarettes on campus my sophomore year, and those were just the times I got caught.

It would be wrong of me to leave out that in 1998, my senior year, I was also suspended from school for two weeks. After drinking, I was involved in verbally instigating a fight in the stands at a basketball game. I didn't physically participate, but the tussle got out of hand. Intoxicated and attempting to avoid trouble, I nearly hit the vice principal with my car as I tried to leave the school campus. My bad. Even though I was a more-than-proud cocaptain of the swim team, the faculty wasn't impressed. Therefore, I wasn't able to speak at or even attend our final banquet. Guess how much of an impact that had on me? Jack shit.

The problem of my repeated removal from sports teams wasn't enough for me to reevaluate my behavior as a whole. Instead I worked on modifying my use or activity at certain times during specific situations or seasons, to avoid getting caught or punished. I always felt terribly guilty for what I put my parents through. They had such high expectations for me. I knew that in their eyes, I was closing doors, missing out on great experiences, and really just suffering from my bad decision making. I still chose A over B again and again. And again. The sick part is, I still don't regret it. I loved sports, but, ya know.

One could say that these were warning signs of alcoholism . . . but one could also shut the hell up. Back then, I wasn't going to listen to anybody, and they could stick their expertise up their own. . . . As it turns out, they would have had a good hypothetical point, but I wasn't ready. I was young, ready to rock, and didn't need advice. Besides, rather than chalk all that up to alcoholism or saying that my disease made me do it, I think it's pretty clear that I wasn't the best decision maker. The argument that I'm a risk taker and a bit impulsive may hold water to this day. But the disease was always with me, and several times red flags arose, alerting the whole family that something wasn't normal in the Volkmann household.

There were two occasions during high school, both extremely ugly, where I was discovered by my parents in more than poor form. The first such alarming incident happened one evening after my freshman year in high school, when my parents had gone up to Seattle for a chamber music festival. Bad move—always. About ten to twelve of us, including one of my brothers and some of his friends, started the evening off pounding ice beers. We did our thing for a while, and, still able to make decisions, we cleaned up and left before the folks got home. Then we headed out to a nearby tree farm to finish the job. Scene missing.

Eventually, when I was torn up as all hell, I guess my good buddy walked me home and dumped me off at my house, hardly able to talk. My parents met their obliterated son, who was unable to say what'd happened to him. I barely enunciated to them, "I drank whatever's in the cup." That was my blacked-out attempt to rid myself of the blame. Pretty good for someone operating at a two-year-old brain level.

In the morning, I woke up confused and hazy with a glass of water beside my bed that I didn't remember getting. I was "invited" to watch a video by Mom and Dad. Oh, shit, it was over now. There I was dry heaving and trying to fend off questions I was incapable of answering. I barely remember watching the video, I was still so trashed. But I know I was pretty surprised and embarrassed. I felt horrible about all the shock, disappointment, and concern I could see in my parents. It hurt. Damn. That wasn't part of the plan.

My brothers must have thought I was stupid to get so ridiculously drunk and come home like that, at age fifteen. I didn't mean to. Later my mom cried, telling me how sad it was to see her baby destroy himself like that after all the effort, sacrifice, and care she'd put into raising me. I felt like the biggest pile of shit, *but not big enough to change*. That afternoon, I went to soccer practice and still smelled like alcohol. Other than negotiating the usual social restrictions, we didn't talk about it too much after the fact. I'd grow out of it, right?

The second incident occurred during the spring of my junior year in 1997, when another good friend and I were dating two senior cheerleaders. Yeah, that's right, whoopee. I'll laugh with you. But this meant, of course, that we would get to double-date to prom, and stay out and reap the benefits of being with the older and more socially advanced seniors. It was soccer season and our team kicked ass, and I was under a super-close eye because of my two-year history of breaking code [a no-tolerance drug and alcohol policy for athletics]. I tried to make a deal with my parents that, if I didn't drink, I could stay out all night and do what all the seniors were doing. Mom and Dad didn't agree with me, and I didn't see it their way.

So I came home at midnight, as expected, proud and sober, and declared that I'd be returning to the festivities. I hadn't been drinking, everything was cool, and I'd earned it. I woke up in the morning in a hotel with my girlfriend, still sober. No big deal. I had done what I was supposed to, in my eyes. I held up my end of the deal while everyone else got shit-faced. (I assume they did. I don't know. That's what I would've done.) Then I marched straight over to the heaps of leftover hard alcohol from the night before (a drink that I usually didn't have a chance to sample) and poured myself a nice congratulatory drink. Cheers.

No more than a few hours later, I was ridiculously drunk, out of control and out of line. What I had thought would be just a few harmless drinks got me beyond wasted. And fast. I was pretty much blacked out and on my own little agenda the rest of that Sunday afternoon. Apparently I had a lot of unwanted opinions, and things were coming out of me completely uncensored and unwarranted. I refused to let anyone else drive. (The next time I got into the car, I was surprised at how loud I had cranked up the music.)

That evening I woke up, or came to, after "napping," still in a haze, and began arguing with my parents . . . still totally in denial that I had gotten *that* drunk. I was pissed because I had gloated about how responsible my conduct had been, and then I had completely eclipsed it all with that jackass maneuver. I was raging. Even when my mom tried to hug me, I felt so disgusted, angry, and closed off that I actually pushed her. I acted completely out of character and it felt terrible. I still remember that feeling today, and it was just wrong.

I'm not sure what type of punishment ensued after this outburst. I'm sure it sucked. My parents' punishments were notoriously the worst of anyone we knew. They were more severe in the amount or types of social privileges revoked, as well as duration. Being grounded in the Volkmann household was never taken lightly and was always irreversible. There was no such thing as being out on good behavior, either, for plenty of reasons. This particular time was a big deal to me and I'm sure it was damaging to my parents, maybe more so to their trust in me.

The red flags were once again up. What was wrong with me? Nothing, I thought. I chalked it up as a symptom of the good life, brushed it off, and moved on. Besides, it happened under the legal/school radar, so you're damn straight I completed the varsity soccer season.

As our glorious high school days were coming to a close in 1998, all of us seniors had our eyes on the horizon, and I toured several colleges. These were my first glimpses of what college life could be like. I visited a family friend at a Seattle school first. Then I took a weekend in San Diego to preview the school I would head to next fall. Following that I planned to visit my brother on the East Coast to see what it was all about for him.

Being a young visitor to a college campus is a privilege, an exciting time for a high schooler. It was obvious on my visits that I was inexperienced and eager to be away. Up in Seattle, in all the excitement, I got extremely trashed, and I blacked out in someone's dorm room. I turned a mellow movie night for all of them into an intoxicating show as I was transformed from innocent and well mannered to a vomiting, needy, and just out-of-line drunk. So I heard. The next weekend in San Diego, I heard I was lucky to make it back across the border from Tijuana and woke up with gum in my hair. Whatever. So it goes.

On my visit to my brother's East Coast campus, we had a great time. The last night there, I avoided getting arrested despite my ridiculous involvement in a rather serious altercation on the school's campus. Upon my lucky release from the police station, I waited for the rest of the guys who were still in jail, with a half-full keg all for me and another guy. Needless to say, there was quite a homecoming party for the arrested folk upon their return. I drank myself into a solid blackout and was gone. I woke up in my own urine, which had soaked into my luggage—I guess I packed it sometime before passing out on top of it. That morning, still half intoxicated while walking to the train station, I opened my eyes and saw a truck stopped and my thumb up. I must have been hitchhiking. I made it to the station, where I passed out again.

My brothers found me and got us to Manhattan, where we were headed. We had a nice tour through the city, with my pants ripped all the way down one urine-soaked inseam. I was pretty well off, considering I didn't go to jail, where I belonged the night before. If my parents had found out what really went on, they might have seriously reconsidered allowing me to go to college in San Diego.

Were all these classy visits to other campuses rehearsals for my behavioral outbursts during my college freshman year? Hell no. I was just getting my green feet wet and still learning the ropes. There was no problem. I was still in high school. Relax. (And don't think, *Gee, man, it sure is*

*surprising that no one ever pulled you aside and said, "You know, I think*
*some of these things are pretty scary. Maybe you have a problem and should*
*think about getting help.")*

No, it's not surprising *that* never happened, because most of these
things went under the radar of any counselor, authority, and more important, the parents. You think I went home, and when asked, "Hey, Toren,
how was your night last night?," responded, "Oh, it was great. I drank a
forty in under five minutes, we made a double-funnel beer bong, we out-
ran the cops, and later, I blacked out and woke up in a strange bathroom
with my pants on inside out. How was yours?" Never. There was always
a normal activity or at least a smoothed-over version of what we were up
to, the imaginary side of the coin of my perfect teenage life. There was no
friend of mine who would suggest to another that anyone had a problem,
because it was all too early and too fun. What could possibly go wrong in
our worlds?

Well, there was always the law. On top of my various MIPs in high
school, there were many close calls with the police, whether they were
from broken-up parties or chases through gullies, tree farms, or other underage drinking havens. For every time I was caught, there seemed to be
dozens of either narrow escapes or flawless evenings where I made it
home unscathed or without concerning my parents. But even when
busted, the only lesson I learned was that getting caught sucked. Drinking was still just as enticing, fun, and liberating . . . it just required a bit
more strategizing at times (and sometimes it was poorly thought out or
completely absent).

Throughout college I continued to have numerous near arrests and
encounters with police. Although it was socially implicit and acceptable to
drink much earlier, ironically, as it became legal to drink, we thought all
our troubles would go away. Damn it. There were still rules of conduct
and order to be broken during college, and it was increasingly possible for
me to find myself in these situations.

The focus was driving while intoxicated, or public drunkenness. I
basically didn't drink and drive most of the time in college, because I al-

ways planned on drinking, and the odds of getting caught were just too high. As if I'd actually do something that endangered people. Not that I never drove drunk, but I usually just compromised by getting drunk in one spot, rather than trying to get to other places or trying to be everywhere all the time. My complacency was a good decision. Yaaay.

So I avoided that, but man could I get drunk in public. After my final charge for underage possession of alcohol my sophomore year in college at age twenty, I upgraded and quickly found myself in trouble with public intoxication charges. To spare the details, in 1999 I found myself in the same Santa Barbara County drunk tank with my jailwich (typical courtesy sandwich served to inmates), apple, and milk, two different times—both for stupid reasons, but always intoxicated. My final visit to a drunk tank was in San Francisco, a mere five months before entering the Peace Corps. (That time, the cops were almost as out of line as I was.) My parents knew nothing about it. Luckily the charges were dropped. I was pretty good and skunked, though, you have to give me that much.

# FOURTEEN

# A FEW MISSED PARTIES

*If there is a part of the night that you don't remember
then you blacked out.*[1]

**[CHRIS]** **Examining Toren through the underside of a**
drained beer glass distorts his adolescence; there's more
to him than a trash can full of empties. I consider his
artwork, his athletics, his acts of largesse and compassion, his ability to communicate and put people at
ease—all the things kids amass to show their aptitude and uniqueness.
But standing in the way is a viscosity that alters and devastates the outcome. It erects a barrier between what we parents learn about our son and
ultimately what we do about it. What drains through, after all, is our son's
continual pursuit of pleasure in bottled form.

During Toren's high school years, Don and I found beer hidden in
the bushes and stowed in the car trunk. A few times we smelled alcohol
on his breath. His accomplishments became diluted over time by these
discoveries, even though we tried to emphasize athletics, academics, and
Toren's positive role within our family. It's true that Toren was a pleasure
to have at home. He was willing to talk about his goals and remained positive in listening to our suggestions. We talked about his flirtation with alcohol and ensuing bad decisions, and although he agreed they weren't
particularly helping him, he always pointed out how he was improving
his life, how he was mostly achieving what he wanted. We gave ourselves
hope by stressing Toren's successful activities and his loving persona.

Toren snuck around to a certain degree, but, by his junior year of high school, he grew bolder about what he wanted. An example of Toren's classic "Eyes-Open Rebellion" occurred when we insisted that he come in by midnight on prom night. First, he argued to stay out all night with his girlfriend (who was a senior, a cheerleader, and an honors student). When we said absolutely not, Toren came home as we requested. He proved to us he had not been drinking and told us about the dinner and dance. But then he went right back out. Later the next day, he finally returned home in the afternoon. Toren had calmly warned us that he was going to stay out all night no matter what, and said that he would pay the penalty for doing so. He assured us that we could ground him for a year, he didn't care; it would be worth it. We guessed that he spent the night at a hotel in town partying with friends (while we spent a sleepless night worrying). And we had every right to worry, because the next day it appeared he had driven home after consuming a huge quantity of vodka. In broad daylight, Toren sauntered into the house wearing tuxedo pants, his shirt open, and promptly fell asleep in an alcoholic stupor. It was difficult to rouse him from his sweaty sleep. I remember it vividly, and I recall thinking how powerless I felt.

Don and I discussed the situation at length. Then we tried to talk with Toren about being responsible for his own decisions, closing doors to opportunity by unthinking behaviors, the costs of legal fees for underage drinking, and maintaining control of his life. Toren said he knew what he was doing, that he appreciated our concern, and understood that we were trying to do our jobs as parents. He said whatever penalty we imposed, he would do. But his attitude was not as cooperative as usual. In fact, this time he was hostile. I can no longer remember exactly the consequences we levied. Usually we took away driving privileges, phone time, or assigned books to read or jobs to do, and restructured his social time with friends. It always calmed things down. Toren had to walk to school the remainder of that spring, but he assured us it was good exercise and that he deserved it for staying out all night. We weren't sure how often he was drinking, but the few times we had previously managed to catch him, he had seemed extremely intoxicated. We worried about this. Should we have shipped him off to rehab then? He was starting on the varsity soccer team and pulling good grades. Don and I continued our discussion with Toren, thinking somehow we would get through to him. It kept us on edge.

---

### Is Your Kid Headed for Drinking Danger?
### 10 Warning Signs of a Drinking Problem[2]

*Studies show that alcohol is the number-one drug of choice for youth. Experts believe that a drinking problem is more likely if you notice several of these signs at the same time, if they occur suddenly, and if some of them are extreme.*

Some of the top drinking danger signs are:

1. Abuse of alcohol; drinking to get drunk; heavy drinking
2. Binge drinking (five or more drinks in a row for men, four for women)
3. Hangovers and blackouts
4. Trouble with relationships/trouble at school
5. Switching friends at school
6. Finding alcohol in a kid's backpack or smelling alcohol on his or her breath
7. Poor concentration, memory lapses, slurred speech, bloodshot eyes
8. Legal problems
9. Mood changes, irritability, defensiveness, rebelling against family rules
10. Family history of alcoholism

---

One night during Toren's junior year of high school, I had a chamber music gig away from the house. Don was working at the hospital. I returned home after the job sooner than Toren—and about thirty of his friends—expected. They had taken over the house and were listening to music, sitting around our kitchen and great room, talking and drinking.

I was able to stand for some time in our unlit entryway undetected and listen to their banter. Hearing several of Toren's friends, I knew exactly who was in attendance. Eventually, I was spotted there holding on to my viola, still in my coat. The guilty drinking kids began pouring out the back door, some through the garage, some sailing right past me. I heard them trying to start their cars; a bottle broke in the street, some guys yelled to each other. It was pandemonium for a few minutes. When the confusion cleared, a corps of kids remained at the kitchen table. They greeted me somewhat sheepishly, and I sat down with them. I noticed all of them were drinking only soft drinks. Toren joined us uneasily. In fact, he looked as though a guillotine might at any moment fall across his neck.

We talked about high school, their classes, plans for college, what they were doing at our house. ("Partying. Thank you, Mrs. Volkmann.") The remaining kids were in no rush to leave because they'd been drinking nonalcoholic beverages. I knew and liked them (in fact, I even liked the kids who'd fled without saying good-bye). Finally, after everyone had left, Toren began pacing around the house, knowing we needed to work things out. He and I talked about the growing breach of trust, the responsibility of holding such events unchaperoned at our home, the deep disappointment I felt. We agreed to some terms and penalties, much the same as writing up a no-fault divorce with two like-minded parties. It seemed this phase of the war was already over. We held on to a détente where we elected not to talk anymore about what had happened. Each time we were repeating the same phrases to one another. It was too depressing for me, and Toren sensed that I was at the end of my ability to deal with it. I don't think we even told Toren's dad. Neither of us could bear to hurt him again.

Toren shaped up, after that, for some time. At least, we weren't aware of anything going on. He talked to us often about his determination not to party, how he was standing up to social pressure. We made it through summer to the fall of his senior year of high school without alcohol incidents, then we made it on through football season. But, during the winter swim season, it ended. Toren appeared intoxicated at a basketball game (as a spectator), verbally harassed opposing fans, and practically ran over a vice principal in the parking lot. For this, Toren and several other of his friends were suspended from high school for ten days. At that time, Toren had been enrolled in a serious Shakespeare class. He wanted to see a performance of *Twelfth Night* in Tacoma with his class, but this was denied because of his suspension, as was his attendance at the swim team banquet (he was cocaptain of the swim team). Toren had worked hard in swimming and adored Shakespeare, so he was extremely disappointed. This punishment truly was a low point for Toren, we thought. We were sure he must have hit bottom and that a real turnaround would take place.

Toren missed a few parties as a result of his latest misstep. He spent a lot of time with his parents and family during his suspension, and, again, lost driving and phone privileges. It gave us all time to think. We encouraged him to make it through soccer season, his final high school sport, without an incident. He was about to graduate. It was time for him to apply for a summer job and to focus on college. Toren assured us his wild ways were diminishing, since he'd already "done it all" in high school. He talked with us about drinking and partying, and said he was planning on making it through graduation without any alcohol. I don't know if he did or not. But he stayed out of trouble, at least. I looked forward to sleeping better at night.

Each time he was kicked off a team, not only did Toren miss the end-of-the-season celebration, but so did we, his parents. Throughout our kids' youth, Don and I attempted to support them in their interests. With the public schools, this usually meant coordinating booster club activities or participating on fund-raising committees. We both contributed during soccer, football, and swim team seasons, which took hours of our time. It was a way of showing our boys that we valued their activities, that we cared. Don acted as president of the soccer parent boosters for six seasons straight and volunteered as the football on-field doc for eight years. I worked as president of the high school Parent Connection, a group committed to bettering communications between high school and home. It was not only disappointing but embarrassing to attend these events without our son (as we were obligated to do sometimes), or not go and know that people would be second guessing about why we were suddenly absent.

Recently, I heard experts talking on the radio about drugs and alcohol and high school kids, about how families with addicts are usually families where no one cares what the kids are doing. They said that, in high school, parents all but disappear; that parents stop attending conferences or events for their kids. And I've heard the opposite as well, that parents don't let their kids work things out on their own. In this case, they say that many parents are overinvolved, too pushy, too in-your-face with their kids, always trying to rescue their darlings or cover up for them. I wish I could find them, those "they" people, to see what they say about the parties we missed on behalf of our son and the parties he missed when we could catch him. What really goes through my mind is that sometimes experts have no idea what's really going on in a home, and no matter what is done, sometimes it's not enough, nor does it solve the problem.

Let's get back to the question: Was high school a time for intervention? In retrospect, I'd say yes, it had been time for an intervention or rehab program for Toren. But remember that he was still lying to us about the extent of his drinking. We still thought that the occasions we caught him were the majority of his alcohol experiences. Our attempts to change Toren's early alcohol abuse in high school seemed hit-and-miss. Much of the time we worried about how to better guide him without knowing for sure if we were doing enough about his drinking. Ultimately, I don't know whether a rehab program during high school would have been successful without Toren's willing participation. He did not seem ready to admit that alcohol was holding him back. His life was a success from his point of view, and he didn't hesitate to tell us so.

Many people forget that for most high school adolescents and their parents, drinking confrontations have just begun. Families at this stage are not ready to think of themselves or their kids as addicted. Dialogue

and questions at this time might include a broad discussion so that everyone understands the progression of alcohol abuse and its insidious way of
creeping into what some would consider normal behavior.

One treatment specialist tells me that the average length of time parents wait to seek help after the first fearful suspicions of their child's possible substance abuse is three to four years. This professional suggests that
even a resistant adolescent can benefit from professional counseling or intervention. He feels it is worth a try at this early point.

Even though much of our approach seemed unsuccessful, I now realize that the total of our efforts to stop Toren's excessive alcohol consumption *was* a *type* of intervention (although not ideal). The real
question is, could we have been more systematic in our efforts? Yes. And
could we have been more informed about what we were attempting to
do? Yes, of course.

Maybe part of the paralysis (not seeking help) Don and I experienced
stemmed from the fear and stigma of Toren or our family being labeled
alcoholic or addicted. (To us, even the label of problem high school
drinker was horrible-sounding. I doubt we even remotely considered the
idea that our son could already be on the road to alcoholism.) During his
high school years, we worried that Toren's chances of being admitted to a
quality college would be jeopardized if his alcohol abuse were officially
acknowledged. In addition, we sought to protect the image of our family
in the community. This is part of the black hole of bingeing, the shadowy
abyss awaiting friends, family, and the teen abuser. Because we parents
hate to come out and admit there might be problems with a child for fear
of being labeled, we don't know whether we've fallen into this black hole
or not. And if we do discover it's real, then we don't know how to climb
out. We want to rescue our family and loved one, but it is a whirling unknown. And it's scary. We feel alone and confused.

The stigma of the problem-drinker label can be extremely harmful
because it causes well-meaning parents to hide out and refuse to seek professional help or advice. In our case, Don and I did not wish to visit a
counselor and hear that our kid was alcoholic or addicted when, in our

eyes, he may have only been experimenting with alcohol. What would have happened had a counselor called us to discuss our son and suggested we seek professional help? Since this did not happen, we do not know whether we would have denied help or would have acknowledged the problem.

Unfortunately, the assumption is that if parents seek help, they are already labeled. What a shame that we need be fearful of this. I encourage any questioning parents to run as fast as they can to a professional and pour out the questions and use the opportunity as a chance to learn. We can leave the black hole to its own devices and not worry what anyone else says about us or our family. There are actions parents can take. The first place to start is with a series of positive steps.

---

### What To Do . . . If worried about a teen who may be drinking . . . [3]

**What to Do First**
Consider getting advice from a health care professional specializing in alcohol problems *before* talking with your teen.

To find a professional, contact your school counselor, family doctor, or a community source. *Other resources may be found in your local yellow pages under "Alcoholism," "AA," or "Al-Anon."*

**Action Checklist**
Establish a loving, trusting relationship with your teen. Make it easy for your teen to talk honestly with you. *It may help to humanize you as a parent by telling about yourself as a teen: your fears, your anxieties, your mistakes.*

Hold family meetings to discuss values, expectations, and consequences of behaviors.

Talk with your teen about alcohol facts, reasons not to drink, and ways to avoid drinking in difficult situations.

*(continued)*

---

Keep tabs on your teens' activities, check their whereabouts, and join with other parents in making common policies about teen alcohol use. *Get to know the parents of your teen's friends.*

Develop family rules about teen drinking and establish consequences.

Set a good example regarding your own alcohol use and your response to teen drinking.

Encourage your teen to develop healthy friendships and fun alternatives to drinking. *Activities in the arts, sports, and interest groups keep kids involved and busy at approved locations, and allow you to meet other involved parents. Such activities promote self-esteem, discipline, and human connection.*

Know whether your child is at high risk for a drinking problem; if so, take steps to lessen that risk.

Know the warning signs of a teen drinking problem and act promptly to get help for your child. *Do not hesitate to consult an expert.*

Consider attending Al-Anon.

Believe in your own power to help your teen avoid alcohol use. *You, as a parent, are the most powerful influence on your child. Be active as educator, confidant, and supporter.*

In addition to the alcohol education and intervention we can initiate at home, there are many free services available where no fingers are pointed. Part of stopping the cycle of alcohol abuse and binge drinking is working together with experts, who can come through the back door of our family home to help us see where we are. We may not know whether we really have a problem drinker in the family or not, but seeking professional advice will give us better perspective. Under a professional's guidance, teens and families may talk together without fear of judgment. School counselors have told me that they wish more parents would drop by to see them. Though they appear busy, they welcome the chance to guide teens and families. This is what they are trained for and the reason they work in our schools. Their doors are open to us. In addition, communities have many resources on a sliding financial scale and can network to provide adolescents and their parents the guidance needed for alcohol decisions. It only takes a phone call at the local level, a browse online, or a visit to the yellow pages to see the list of social services available.

The NIAAA and SAMHSA (Substance Abuse and Mental Health Services Association) have phone lines people may call toll-free to receive help from a *real* person at the other end. The trained operators on staff speak numerous languages, are informed about current trends in alcohol and other drug abuse, are available on twenty-four-hour call, and genuinely care about the people calling in. Our tax dollars support these lines, so we have every right to take advantage of these resources. Toren and I were invited to visit the SAMHSA office near Washington, D.C., where we talked with the project director. Had I known about this resource, I could have called after Toren's first problem at age fifteen. I could have spoken anonymously to someone who would offer me advice and reassure me.

What I have learned about getting help is that people working in addiction treatment are kind, nonjudgmental, and extremely generous with their resources and spirit. Many addiction treatment professionals are in recovery themselves. Even at the governmental level, Toren and I have experienced acceptance and professional demeanors from everyone we met. The time to call is *before* addiction happens.

Not all parents are fortunate to find help early on with a teen drinker. A portion of Toren's first letter from rehab talks about his early drinking:

> *I subscribe to the idea that there is cognitive distortion, a genetic disposition, and other things that may be influencing how rapidly I've experienced certain aspects (more physical than anything) of this scary progression. Not to mention, I've been a BINGE drinker from the start, more or less. If I had been a churchgoing, social drinker or a moderate drinker with my same genetic makeup, I may*

*not have been affected for years. But for me, I think it's been a highly reactive combo. It may have happened eventually, no matter, what. I have nothing to be bitching about and everything to live for and that is WHY I am here NOW. I'm trying to keep an open mind and listen—and ignore thoughts about Paraguay. But sometimes I wonder, what did I do? And why or how it all happened so fast.*

I see that Toren's pondering some of the same things as I. Like why did it happen in the first place? I look back and remember time after time when I attempted to tell myself this would be the last time. The *last* time. No—*This* will be the last time . . . this time. . . . I leaf through slips of paper in the "Toren" file, flitting from episode to episode. Why did I save those scraps of evidence if I was trying to forget? I find several letters he wrote to the high school administration about his suspension, where he apologizes sincerely and requests the chance to attend the Shakespeare production, where he talks about all the thinking he has done, the prioritizing. Is this not the doctrine of an alcoholic: sincere remorse then on to another foray? I wonder how I could have been so gullible. Again. And again.

Now, as a result of my preoccupation with this debacle, I miss a party. I say no to the trumpet section (really fun guys) when they invite me out for a beer. I *could* go along and drink Perrier; I know that. But somehow, my heart's not in it. I don't feel like talking to anyone, especially people who will ask about my family members. I also say no to friends calling to invite us to dinner, no to lunch on someone's boat, no to a glass of wine after work on Friday. The bubble has burst. I stay home to figure out why I didn't see my son clearly in those early days. Didn't stop him. Couldn't have helped him. (Miss a few more good parties.)

**Someone to TALK to . . .**
*for parents or teens*[4]

**NCADI Live Help**
National Clearinghouse for Alcohol and Drug Information
SAMHSA's NCADI has a staff of trained information specialists who can answer your questions twenty-four hours a day.

Call toll-free at: 1-800-729-6686
Se habla español: 1-877-767-8432
Washington, D.C. (301) 468-2600
TDD: 1-800-487-4889
Fax: (301) 468-6433

Use this feature for a confidential online text chat with an NCADI information specialist: www.health.org/help/default.aspx.

SAMHSA stands for Substance Abuse and Mental Health Services Association.
NCADI stands for National Clearinghouse for Alcohol and Drug Information.

You can also . . .

Call the National Drug and Alcohol Treatment Referral Routing Service (Center for Substance Abuse Treatment) at 1-800-662-HELP for information about treatment programs in your local community and to speak to someone about an alcohol problem.

Look at this link for frequently asked questions:
www.niaaa.nih.gov/faq/faq.htm.

**These resources are supported by tax dollars.**

**I continue to look at alcohol and its effects on our** family throughout our three boys' high school and college experiences. A creeping paranoia sets in. By now, we are unknowingly raising one alcoholic and two undiagnosed sons who admit they've done more than their share of bingeing. Slowly, I become worn down. It's hard to know what the boys are *really* doing in their social worlds, and sometimes I wonder if I even *want* to know.

Toren pressured us to allow him to study in the Semester at Sea Program his junior year of college. This paralleled his interests in global studies, psychology, and world service. Considering his history of high school and college alcohol problems (and that's counting only the ones we knew about at the time), people would wonder why we would agree to pay for this. It turns out the cost was almost comparable to his regular college tuition. Toren's grades were still good. We had several discussions with him about the program and why he wished to participate. After he researched the program, applied, and convinced us that he would not behave in the way that had some students calling the program Party at Sea or Mattress at Sea, and after he worked all summer to earn a portion of his expenses and diligently filled out the paperwork and visa applications on his own, we said okay. It seemed safer to have Toren anchored in the middle of an ocean than frequenting the 7-Eleven on the corner of campus. Another part of our deal was *no* alcohol-related trouble during the summer prior to his study abroad.

From our standpoint, Semester at Sea drifted by without a hitch. Toren was not shipped home early, nor did he get thrown into a foreign prison. Don and I guessed that his drinking may have been less, away from his usual collegiate haunts and buddies. We had been told that aboard ship the staff monitored each student's bar tab, closed the bars at set hours, and stressed a no-tolerance policy for drugs and alcohol in the cabins. Students were not allowed to bring alcohol aboard and were educated about proper conduct as international guests. Toren had previously traveled with our family to third-world destinations and embraced our philosophy not to represent the stereotypical ugly American strangled by camera, Nikes, and fanny pack. This doctrine, along with astute guidance by shipboard professors and staff, seemed to outweigh Toren's penchant for alcohol mischief. At one point on the voyage, he called from India and told me, "We love you." I was alarmed and asked, *"We?"* "Yes, Mom, it's true. We. The world. We love you."

Obviously, at this point we had no idea about Toren's heavy experimentation with drugs and extreme drinking behaviors aboard ship. Of course, I later learned that most of Toren's experiences on Semester at Sea had been glossed over. The version Toren revealed to Don and me was void of alcohol or drugs. To read his description of the voyage and compare it to my version is like boarding two different sea vessels. Once again, our two versions of Toren's adolescence, written side by side, hardly resemble one another.

Upon his return from Semester at Sea, I encouraged Toren to live in the dorms for the remaining junior semester, not knowing at the time that he had been banned from living on campus. To me, this seemed a logical way for Toren to realign himself with American culture and return to his studies with minimum fuss. He had undergone a wisdom teeth extraction as well as an extensive shoulder surgery during the Christmas vacation, and needed to get resituated without trauma to his healing incision. I called the university and requested that they give him a dorm room, and to Toren's surprise, they granted him one. I still remember the look of shock on his face when I told him about reserving the room. It was as if he thought I were a magician. To me, it seemed a perfectly normal request, and I wondered why Toren would be so squirrelly about it. I had no idea how much trouble Toren had previously created by his alcohol consumption, and apparently the university had forgotten as well. Imagine how nervous Toren must have been, knowing that I was calling the housing office, probably thinking the university would tell me why they had kicked him off campus. But that did not happen, because Toren seemed to have done a better job of keeping a low profile after his freshman year.

It seems impossible for parents or universities to realistically monitor students' alcohol consumption. Some say that students should be left on their own to weather drinking decisions. In reality, lots of students are able to survive college partying and move on without chronic damage. A campus is, after all, a setting of higher education. It is not the institution's responsibility to care for the youth we send them, to hold their hands, to predict which of them will graduate as addicts and which will graduate cum laude. There has been a movement away from cocooning college students within protective arms. Whereas colleges used to practice *parens patriae*, a type of surrogate parenthood where the administration attempted to guide and nurture students, current policy has shifted away from that practice and now diminishes the role of the hovering campus guardian. It allows students to face the consequences of their behavior on their own. Therefore, many colleges do not notify parents of students' wrongdoings.

With the chance that faculty and administration are looking the other way, students will do what they will, functioning in the limbo of their pseudo-adult adolescent existence. After all, they're over eighteen. They can legally vote. They can fight in a war. It's time to grow up. Universities are not probation officers or babysitters. The 80 percent of students who can drink successfully will thrive. But the 20 percent who cannot will cause problems. Unfortunately, these problems become not only a campus problem but a family problem, and thereafter society's problem. Yet, the university system is not "obligated" to take care of these people.

The Buckley Amendment protects a student's right to privacy. This restricts a college or university's ability to inform parents about such things as academic performance. However, federal legislation now permits colleges and universities to establish their own policies on parental notification regarding disciplinary proceedings. Every campus will have different procedures. Even though Toren's university maintained a policy of not notifying parents of student alcohol abuse, many U.S. schools are now moving in the direction of intervening with heavy drinkers and contacting families about problems. Parental notification signals a new awareness by higher education, acknowledging that drinking behaviors affect not only the drinker but all those around the drinker, including students, teachers, and community members. The consequences of heavy drinking include undermined school work, diminished student security, acts of violence, and increased dropout rates, thereby affecting not only the social climate on campus but the costs of controlling these situations. It's good economics for universities to take care of these problems.

Effective prevention of excessive alcohol consumption on campus involves clear alcohol policies, including consistent enforcement and coordination with the larger community near the campus. Active intervention services are also needed for students who manifest signs of alcohol dependence, as are methods for moving them into treatment options. (Even when such programs or interventions are offered, however, it is difficult to ensure that chronic abusers will seek out or utilize the services.)

College binge drinking is receiving proactive attention because *alcohol-related problems are a leading cause of death among college students.* Student health services provide screening and assessment for alcohol use, and the goal of such programs is to reduce alcohol-related harm. This can directly benefit students' health by reducing the estimated 1,400 deaths and 500,000 serious alcohol-related injuries each year.[1]

One university-based urgent care worker I interviewed reported that he treated an average of twenty students per day for alcohol-related injuries. College STD, rape, and pregnancy statistics inflate as students consume alcohol.[2] According to the College Alcohol Study, roughly one in twenty (4.7 percent) women reported being raped; nearly three-quarters (72 percent) of the victims experienced rape while intoxicated.[3] Women who attend notorious party colleges or join sororities face the highest risk.

In 2002, when asked, "Have you ever awoken after a night of drinking not able to remember things that you did or places that you went?," approximately 51 percent of those students who had ever consumed alcohol reported experiencing at least one blackout at some point in their lives, and 40 percent experienced one in the year before the survey.[4] National research reveals that 72 percent of college students who reported being raped in the past year (2004) were so intoxicated that they were unable to consent or refuse.[5] Some college women refer to the trek back home on the morning after a regretted sexual encounter or a hookup as "the Walk of Shame." Under mounting evidence of such damage by alcohol use, universities are now offering remedies for chronic heavy drinking and binge drinking.

Our U.S. culture commonly tells us that college days are a time for partying and drinking. Many college students come to campus with expectations that the majority of students drink heavily. Selected campuses have mounted specific campaigns to curb such perceptions of student drinking. It's hypothesized that if students perceive their peers drinking less, they may feel less pressure to drink heavily themselves. Many of these campaigns use posters, Frisbees, or T-shirts to display statistics derived from campus alcohol surveys, stating, for example, "*93 percent of students would disapprove of their friends if they drank 4 to 5 drinks every day,*" or "*Most students choose to drink moderately or not at all; in fact, 70%.*" These efforts, called social-norms marketing, were initially thought to show mixed success, according to research published in September 2003.[6] Some students appeared skeptical about these alcohol education programs. However, a study released in 2005 of more than 76,000 students attending 130 colleges and universities confirmed that most college students do, in fact, overestimate peer drinking, and that such college prevention programs can decrease high-risk drinking.[7]

When Toren and I look at such data, he always points out that social-norms campaigns are excellent for the majority of students, but that he was a student who did not respond to these campaigns, an extreme drinker on the periphery who would require more intense roadwork before changing behaviors. Evidently, some students will drink no matter what.

Substance-free dorms are now available on many campuses. Even though there is a disconnect between the idea that students under twenty-one are not legally eligible to drink anyway, campuses are providing such housing. This option for housing is popular because students in drug-free dorms are less likely to suffer drinking-related problems, like poor grades or the secondhand effects of other drinking students. Even students who choose to drink often prefer to live in a climate free of drinking problems. Recent studies indicate that students who live in these residences are less likely to indulge in smoking and drinking.[8] Substance-free housing often appeals to freshmen. For example, at Dartmouth, about 400 of the 1,075 incoming freshmen requested it. Substance-free housing also provides the benefit to colleges of less property damage and vandalism.

Taking the concept even further, some universities are offering support for recovering students or former substance abusers who want to finish their education surrounded by the support of like-minded students, because it is highly difficult to socialize on a typical college campus if one is trying to recover from substance abuse or addiction. Among others, programs at Case Western Reserve University in Ohio, at Rutgers in New Jersey, at Texas Tech University, and one at Grand Valley State, Michigan, have set up housing and support for on-campus recovery programs that enable recovering students to succeed in school.[9] On-campus recovery programs such as these allow students to stay enrolled while working on positive lifestyle choices, lessening the emotional alienation experienced by recovering drinkers and addicts. At Texas Tech University, the average

GPA for students participating in the recovery program is 3.34, compared to an overall undergraduate average GPA of 2.68.[10]

Today, campus housing options and college drinking awareness differ from what existed at the time our boys went to college. We have seen diverse college settings over the years as our three sons collectively attended seven different universities and grad schools. Moving through these various college scenarios has provided experiences I could not have anticipated. The upshot is that *I* finally graduated from Beer Bong U, right along with them. One of our sons ultimately gave me a private tasting of college life I will never forget.

It happened when Don and I visited one of Toren's brothers at a university where he was a senior. We met his friends at a party they threw to welcome us at his rental house. I discovered, though, that the true guest of honor was Triceptatrough—the beer bong dinosaur. I had told my son to get it out of our house and he had; he took it back to college with him. There it was, hanging on the back patio in all its glory and splendor, fully operational. Let me describe this demon: the Triceptatrough was constructed of a series of seven mad-scientist-looking plastic tubes hooked to funnels, with valves that looked like they could open pipelines to an Olympic-sized swimming pool. The gadget was activated by a main valve that flooded the apparatus with a beverage (often beer) free of air or obstruction. Drinkers took their places in a line underneath individual faucets.

By now, I'd become somewhat glazed. Perhaps you could even say I'd lost my perspective. I knew our son had done well in school; I'd already had commensurate experience locating and discarding any number of contraband funnels; and I realized that most of the kids attending this party were age-appropriate. We had talked with every person attending the bash, and finally met all the friends described by our son for the past several years. They were delightful kids with varied talents and interests. As the party mellowed, my husband and I watched five or six students line up under the multifunneled contraption, then open their mouths for a round of beer to pour forth. No one appeared intoxicated (except for one kid who had arrived already in that state).

The kids asked if we wouldn't like to try it. Suddenly, as half-witted as it seems, Don and I said okay. After all my lectures . . . after the infamous green binge-drinking chart . . . after expelling the dinosaur from our home . . . here I was queuing up like a hardened beer bonger! I viewed it as an experiment, I told myself. For several years I'd been hearing about this Triceptatrough, now I would try it. The dosed quantity looked to be about the amount of one can of beer. I thought I could do it and hoped I wouldn't gag. I was nervous. I planted my feet and took a place in line along with three other coeds and Don. The whole party cheered, cameras flashed and captured the moment, and we leaned back, ready for the explosion. When the beer burst through, I found it fast and unobtrusive. It just went down. I stepped back and it was over. I didn't feel bad. I felt like the same person.

No wonder. No wonder they do it.

The party dwindled down and my husband and I walked back to our hotel. We talked about how easy it had been to beer bong. How frightening. And we felt guilty that we had tried it, as though we were endorsing beer bonging in front of our son's friends. I guess we were. But my feelings still haven't changed. I look at bingeing as a dangerously seductive activity with no point. I still resent the beer bong dinosaur.

As I read in the Sunday paper that I should drink a glass of red wine each day for better health, I wonder how that news will influence my sons. I joke to my husband that beer bonging could be similar to that glass of wine at night, maybe something good for me and I don't know it. Is it possible to put red wine in a funnel? He points out that there has been much research showing that the alcohol industry is deceptive, that innumerable reports are unchallenged by media and science. The data is often misleading, unsubstantiated.

Extensive research on the media and alcohol suggests that original studies should be read to check out their accuracy. *Many articles about the benefits of alcohol are funded by the alcohol industry.* Press releases often omit dangers, especially when dealing with doses of alcohol, which are frequently harmful when increased by a single drink. There are more than four hundred substances in alcoholic beverages besides ethanol, some linked to cancer, and the alcohol industry is not required to disclose them, nor to alert the public of risks.[11]

Our experience beer bonging with college students only further reinforces my uneasy feelings about the seductive glamour of peer influence. My husband and I, perfect examples, succumbed to the beer bong. Now we become more wary with each swallow.

---

### To Beer Bong or Not

**3 Things Every Drinker Should Consider *Before* Breaking Out the Beer Bong**

Bingeing may seem glamorous. Few drinkers think about the problematic effects of continuous heavy drinking. Here's what to consider before breaking out that beer bong:

1. What's really happening to your brain every time you drink heavily? It is essential to understand how damaging alcohol is to your body and brain.
2. What's your family history with alcohol? Heredity plays into the demise of a heavy drinker.
3. The process of alcoholism is stealthy. It creeps up little by little. It's progressive and the damage it causes to relationships and behavior becomes chronic.

---

When our boys get together, they often jest about riotous drinking games they've played with their friends. Even adults play drinking games. But drinking games these days, like beer bonging, have evolved to a whole new level. A trend in college and teen drinking surrounds the commercialization of drinking games. These contests feed into risky drinking and increase the chances for alcohol poisoning. Not only do kids play drinking games at private parties, but games are actually marketed at bars near campuses. One such game, called beer pong, has players toss Ping-Pong balls into a triangle of cups. When a player sinks a ball, the other team must chug the beer and remove the cup from the table. When a side runs out of cups, it loses (and must finish the remaining opponents' cups as well). Many bars now hold beer pong tournaments, complete with leagues and statistics. There are variations of the game and its name, Bud Pong or Beirut, and there are plenty of other drinking games using quarters, dice, and cards. Some drinkers tape forty-ounce malt liquor bottles to their hands. Urban Outfitters stocks a popular beer pong kit boxed with sets of rules. Beer pong hoodie sweatshirts can be purchased on the Internet.

"When you play drinking games, you're not really in charge of how much you drink," says Brian Borsari, a psychologist at the Center for Alcohol and Addiction Studies at Brown University. "Your drinking is at the whim of other players, which can be very dangerous, especially if you're trying to fit in." It is said that beer companies stress responsible drinking at the same time as they promote beer pong accessories. The idea from Anheuser-Busch was to make the beer pong game as an icebreaker for young adults to get acquainted. The "official rules" call for water to be used, not beer. Students report that they have never seen anyone use water during an event.[12]

Not only do we worry about the drinking games our kids are playing for fun during academic sessions, but we wonder what they are doing with their time during the numerous academic breaks. Vacations during college years can present periods of angst for parents who are unable to determine what their kids are up to. Thanksgiving break (which is now being lengthened by many schools) always posed a problem for us. When our sons were in college, we chose not to bring them home for Thanksgiving holidays, because the vacation period was short and the distance great. Because of this, they united with new and former friends, congregating in such cities as Boston, New York, Santa Barbara, and San Diego to prepare their own feast. If you removed the alcohol, the gatherings could have entertained Grandma in style. The boys usually called me while struggling through their preparation of gravy or turkey and stuffing. Something always needed adjusting. But as the years passed, I grew to dread this holiday, because I knew the boys were drinking too much alcohol. They had shown me photos and told stories, and it concerned me. After one such "turkey holiday," I found out that Toren had been arrested for public drunkenness at ten a.m. He called home the following week to ask us what to do about legal procedures. We told him to find a lawyer and pay for it himself. So he did. Being two thousand miles away, I felt that I had to let go.

Was this a good decision? As I look back, I think we should also have arranged for counseling for Toren. This could have been an opportunity for my husband and me to *insist* that Toren participate in counseling or treatment. We could have told him that we required him to do so if he wanted us to continue paying his university tuition. Of course, it would have been difficult to know what resources to use from such a distance, but we could have called his university counseling center for recommendations. This would have been a better decision for us. It seems so logical now (one rehab, one halfway house, and six years of scrutiny later).

After Toren's post-Thanksgiving call informing us of his public intoxication charge, I slept less well and became a worrying mother, even though I gave the appearance of leaving my son's destiny in his own hands. We always felt that Toren should be responsible for his own actions, just as binge drinkers should be responsible for the problems they create. Is there anyone else to blame?

One could blame alcohol promoters for providing cheap drinks that cause kids to come back for more.

Or blame the campuses and communities for not enforcing minimum-drinking-age laws.

Or blame parents for not monitoring their students' behavior or not finding out how tuition funds are being utilized.

Or even blame college presidents and administrators for turning a blind eye to sports initiations, sorority and fraternity functions, hazings, and campus alcohol-inspired infractions.

The blame can be spread in many directions. Blaming someone does not get to the bottom of what is causing the problem. It is just a way to pass off ownership of a situation to which we have all contributed.

To me, it seems there must be more definitive methods for helping students. I research this area and discover several curricula written for counselors and health care professionals to reduce high-risk drinking among college students. One published by the National Institute on Alcohol Abuse and Alcoholism lists guidelines for using brief intervention.[13] Intervention programs where a student is contacted three to five times have been initiated by some colleges to head off alcohol problems. Brief interventions are primarily used to reduce alcohol use in nonaddicted drinkers and focus on convincing kids in one or two brief visits to reduce their drinking. Students can actually be screened for alcohol use disorders, with staff available to help them in a nonpunitive environment. This can cause heavy drinkers to change drinking behaviors and to not reoffend.

I spoke with a counselor who does brief interventions on campuses. When working with college freshmen who exhibit risky drinking behaviors, it is her goal to get the drinkers from the point of precontemplation to contemplation. The objective by the end of her session(s) is to make the particular student abuser "consider" that he or she actually could have a drinking problem or be an alcoholic. This is a critical step and just a small part of the eventual understanding of the progression of alcohol abuse.

Even experts who do interventions acknowledge that changing drinking behavior is a lengthy process. When they say it, it sounds reassuring. But when we experience it in our families with our teens, the lengthy wait for a different behavior seems endless.

A vacation period even more worrisome than Thanksgiving for our family was the annual college spring break. Toren disappeared during spring vacations, and I wrung my hands wondering what he was doing. While finishing up his junior and senior years, he racked up several dangerous physical feats, such as falling into poison oak (requiring steroids for treatment) and cutting his foot on a camping trip in Mexico and thereby contracting cellulitis. During college, there were times when we

## Getting Assistance for a College Student Facing an Alcohol-Related Crisis[14]

Be aware of the signs of possible alcohol abuse by your son or daughter (for example, lower grades, never available or reluctant to talk with you, unwilling to talk about activities with friends, trouble with campus authorities, serious mood changes).

- If you believe your son or daughter is having a problem with alcohol, do not blame, but find appropriate treatment.
- If your teen is involved in an alcohol violation, avoid the temptation to react to the violation. Instead explore ways to act on the opportunity the violation presents to communicate.
  What has the student learned?
  What is being done as a result of the experience?
  What will be different in the future?
- Call and/or visit campus health services and ask to speak with a counselor.
- Indicate to the dean of students, either in person, by phone, or by e-mail, your interest in the welfare of your son or daughter and that you want to be actively involved in his or her alcohol decisions (intervention, recovery, or treatment) despite the geographic separation.
- If your son or daughter is concerned about his or her alcohol consumption, or that of a friend, have them check out www.alcoholscreening.org for information about ongoing screening for problems with alcohol.
- Pay your son or daughter an unexpected visit. Ask to meet their friends. Attend Parents' Weekend and other campus events open to parents.
- Continue to stay actively involved in the life of your son or daughter. Even though they may be away at college, they continue to be an extension of your family and its values.

A majority of college and university presidents identified alcohol abuse as one of the greatest problems facing campus life and students. *A Call to Action: Changing the Culture of Drinking at U.S. Colleges* presents a

*(continued)*

series of recommendations to college presidents, researchers, parents, and students to deal with this continuing public health problem in a scientific and sensible way. Parents are encouraged to continue to educate themselves by referring to and using the following materials prepared by the Task Force. The documents are available in full text at www.collegedrinkingprevention.gov.

wouldn't hear from Toren for days. I thought it was normal, because back when I went to college, I would go weeks without calling home; it was too expensive to make long-distance calls. Now I realize that a lot of parents stay in touch at least weekly, if not daily. Internet and cell phones allow for frequent communication.

Parents hear from their children about opportunities for a cheap trip to some sunny locale, often Mexico, over spring break. Playing on the beach can seem like a well-earned reward for students who have studied hard all year long. What parents don't realize is that these trips sometimes boast an all-inclusive rate, including airfare, hotel, meals, *and* alcohol. *Lots* of alcohol, with a wristband to let bartenders know your kid has a prepaid license to constantly refill. Drinking to become intoxicated can create a serious situation in a foreign culture where there is strict enforcement of public drunkenness laws. And not only is it a legal risk, sometimes involving pricey foreign attorneys, but packs of vacationing out-of-control American youth leave an ugly impression abroad. One of my Mexican friends has told me that each year her teenage daughter dreads encountering vacationing American *borrachos* (drunks) during spring break, because they are often disrespectful.

Even within our own country's borders there are numerous designated party spots for college kids. *USA Today* covered spring break partying at Lake Havasu, Arizona. Adventures from this weeklong party are often filmed and end up on the Internet or in video documentaries, turning "a few seconds of immaturity into a lifetime of Web-based infamy."[15] And then there are the spring break "camping trips" with friends, as described by Toren. Why had I envisioned rosy-cheeked college kids hiking along the trail in a breathtaking national park? It's really tough for a parent to get the straight story. No matter how hard we try.

---

**Top 10 Things to Discuss with Your College Student Before Spring Break[16]**

1. Talk to your college student about the health and personal physical safety dangers of excessive alcohol consumption—both by themselves and others (e.g., fighting, drunk driving, alcohol poisoning, and rape).
2. Give your college student tips on how to protect themselves, such as traveling in pairs, having money for taxis or public transportation, carrying medical insurance cards and condoms.
3. If your son or daughter is using a tour company to plan their trip, ask to see any promotional materials that helped your college student decide. Make sure that the company is reputable, and that it isn't using excessive alcohol promotion to target and influence students.
4. Ask your son or daughter to provide the names and numbers of any hotels they will be staying in, as well as cell phone numbers for themselves and their friends.
5. Talk to your son or daughter about your expectations and limits with regard to alcohol use.
6. Give them a prepaid calling card and establish a regular check-in time.
7. Offer to cover the cost of participating in an alternative spring break program.
8. Teach your son or daughter the dangers and warning signs of alcohol poisoning, so that they can better protect their peers and themselves.
9. If your son or daughter is under twenty-one, make sure that their spring break destination has the same drinking age limitations as do U.S. locations. International locations may allow students as young as eighteen to legally purchase alcohol (e.g., Cancun, Mexico).
10. Warn your college student about the danger of drinking and dehydration.

As parents, we did our best to keep tabs on Toren. Sometimes his behavior was more suspicious than others. An example of this occurred after his shoulder and wisdom teeth surgeries his junior year of college. I doled out painkillers to him whenever I thought he needed one. Toren acted insulted, but by this time, I had become wary. Even while taking these medications, he seemed in a lot of pain. Then, one day I found the stash; he hadn't taken them and was stockpiling them. I asked him why, and he said, "To sell." I became nervous once again. When I further questioned Toren, he told me he could get five dollars for each capsule. Secretly, I speculated that he wasn't selling them, but that maybe he planned to use them recreationally after he returned to campus. Toren had been willing to endure a fair amount of agony to hoard away those meds. I wondered what kind of son we had raised. I fretted.

He would be graduating from college soon. I felt relieved that Toren would be living in the dorms. He took a full class load as well as a preparation course for the GREs, where he memorized hundreds of vocabulary words. Toren claimed he wanted to get the GREs out of the way, that he could eventually use the results for grad school applications. He called me frequently to chat about a psychology internship he had at a local children's hospital, his prep course, and his final work in school. I thought the frequent and friendly calls were a good sign. Toren talked about applying to the Peace Corps. He could go away and be successful, escape his drinking buddies. I began counting the minutes to graduation.

# SIXTEEN
## IN DESCENT

 **Before I entered the Peace Corps, I suspected** that I had a problem. I just didn't understand it.

Over my last year of college, I began to notice many new physical symptoms. It made me wonder if other people were feeling the same way I did after a long weekend. Those postdrinking withdrawal symptoms (once as simple as mere sleeplessness) had slowly escalated, leaving me devastated and in pretty bad shape for the better part of my senior year. I was, in actuality, a full-blown alcoholic by college graduation, but my mind-set told me that I could just party through until I made it to the Peace Corps, not really wanting to investigate the depth or reality of the problem. Much of me denied the possibility of alcoholism. The rest of me just wanted to keep drinking.

Being drunk for five months straight after graduating (throughout the summer of 2002 in Seattle and on into the fall, when I lived in Las Vegas) was a *choice* I made and was my way of getting the problem out of my system so that I wouldn't drink like that later. But all my choices were under the influence in one way or another, and I was really just quieting voices inside that I didn't want to listen to, the ones starting to slowly recognize that things were not right.

Throughout the months I spent studying Spanish in Mexico, I

slowed down the drinking and let my head clear up by stringing together a few pairs of weeks without any alcohol. I remembered what it felt like to be sober. But on certain occasions when I did drink, I noticed that my drinking behaviors seemed a little screwy and my withdrawal symptoms were just as bad as (or worse than) they had been after most of my weekends in college, or weeks of drinking in Seattle or Las Vegas.

One weekend during my studies in Mexico, my host family invited me and other students to a wedding, followed by a huge reception with great food, several musical acts, traditional dancing, fireworks, and plenty of alcohol. I started out the night like a gentleman and drank modestly, sampling some brandy, wine, and beer. I wanted to keep things mellow. For the most part, I enjoyed myself. By the end of the night, however, I was no longer pacing myself and the effect of an endless supply of drinks (even on a full stomach) surprised me. I was extremely intoxicated and wound up getting a ride home through the streets of Oaxaca with some students and a few locals. My last memories were of me smashed and feeling very fluid with several weeks of Spanish class spilling out while I sipped from a sizable tequila bottle. Way more drunk than I thought, I must have seemed obnoxious wearing my new cowboy hat, a party favor from the wedding.

The next morning was the tricky part. I had plans with a friend to rent mountain bikes and ride through the city and out into the surrounding mountains. Due to the effects of the alcohol, I awoke a little bit earlier than normal and assessed the events of the night before. While lying there, I pieced things together for the most part all the way up to the point of getting home, and concluded that it wasn't a complete blackout—so I must have done all right.

I had been sober for a good two weeks before that, but my nerves felt a little uneasy. I couldn't ignore the fact that I felt sort of anxious and a little bit shaky. I drank some water, and as I was writing in my journal, I glanced across the room toward my dresser and saw the old tequila bottle next to my cowboy hat, staring back at me. No. I didn't want to believe it actually occurred to me that I should drink some. More than that, it even seemed appealing. It made sense. Since I felt kind of sick, why not?

I went over and picked up the bottle and took a whiff. Mmm . . . last night . . . there I held the cause of and remedy for my current hangover. I took a couple of big, painful gulps, and felt the fire spread from my throat to my belly. I didn't vomit, but it disgusted me when I realized what I was doing. Then I took one more big pull, dumped the rest out, and threw it in the garbage. Almost immediately, I felt much better. I managed to go riding all day and have a great time, ignoring the taste of alcohol in my mouth or any thoughts about drinking again later. It was an isolated incident, so I let it slide.

During my last two weeks of travel through Mexico, I experienced a few other evenings when I drank heavily and things felt a little off. The morning after each episode my nerves crawled and I battled a desire to drink those sensations away. Drinking began wearing a hole in my previously impenetrable defense system.

While exploring the coast, I met an adventurous girl from New Zealand named Danielle. She had been traveling through Mexico and planned to continue to Central and South America throughout the next year. We spent several days together going to beaches, eating out, and talking about our travels and plans. I had been having enough difficulties with my drinking that when Danielle asked why I was going into the Peace Corps, I said to her half jokingly and half seriously, "If I weren't going into the Peace Corps, I would be headed to either rehab or jail." As extreme as it may have sounded, I knew there was some truth to it. Danielle told me that Paraguay had always fascinated her and that she would come to see me there. (Really?)

A few days later, I suffered another, more punishing blackout where almost a whole night went missing. To make a long story short, it started with some other backpackers and beer, and ended with hard alcohol and a mystery. In the morning I woke up in the youth hostel with a pounding headache, and I had no clue what had happened. The guy in the bed next to me saw me stirring and immediately asked me if I was okay. *Yes*, I thought, *should I be?* It was then that I suspected something had gone wrong. One single recollection of being in some type of dark club with black lights came over me. That was all I got. I had no clue where I had gone or whom I was with. I didn't have it in me to ask the dude next to me, who obviously had seen some of my drunkenness. When I found my smashed glasses on the floor, there was no question that some bad stuff had happened.

"Luckily," I had reserved a ticket to go horseback riding early that morning and all day through the mountains to a traditional Chiapan village. Having already paid, and stubbornly refusing to acknowledge how fucked up I really felt, I rode off at sunrise with an excited group of travelers to my own personal day of living hell.

My hangover got much worse. I couldn't help but wonder what the hell I must have done the night before. I was too wasted to even get my spare glasses for the day trip. Completely unable to appreciate the view without my glasses, I merely bounced painfully up and down on my horse all the way up to the village, and in my best moments found myself dreaming of sleep and water as I completely ignored my blurry surroundings. I didn't talk to any of the other people and just wanted to die. To make matters worse, when we stopped for lunch, I somehow managed to rub some juice from a violently spicy pepper into my eyes. My eyelids felt like they were nearly swollen shut and my mouth completely dried out. Even more blind and worthless from that point on, I would rather not talk about the ride down.

The whole trip lasted six or seven hours, and I didn't enjoy a minute of it. I couldn't see that it was, in actuality, sort of funny (in a sick way) how I paid the price for that mysterious night out. I guess I got what I deserved. Still, it didn't scare me enough and I wasn't ready to call my drinking a real problem. I determined, in general, that it was a self-exacerbating process and that it *could* be avoided. *Watch the drinking*, I thought. Or maybe it was that I just needed to plan my trips better, not leave my glasses out in vulnerable places, and be sure to wash my hands after eating dangerously spicy tacos. Yeah, I could handle the booze, but the others were things I would master in Paraguay.

I had no alcohol in my system a month later when I first met all my fellow Peace Corps volunteers, and I intended to keep it that way. We spent a few nights together in Miami before leaving for South America, and I kept to myself, trying to lie low and avoid the inevitable socializing (which to me meant drinking). I went out with some girls our last night in Miami and had a few drinks at a club. I didn't drink much and woke up feeling pretty normal, but my body knew what had happened. I couldn't lie to myself about the physiological shit going on in my brain, stuff that *I* didn't even understand. I could only kid myself by thinking it wouldn't matter.

The next day, after some internal resistance, I had a case of the "fuk-its" and downed about four beers with some other new faces. I knew I shouldn't drink, but I just wanted to drink normally. Damn it, dude. Why did I do that? I was not surprised when I couldn't sleep and had a fever on the plane ride down. *Jackass*, I thought, *same result*.

Upon arrival in South America, I was given the opportunity to wipe the slate clean. Thus began a little trial-and-error period for me. I thought I could learn to drink socially and get control of my life, as if nothing were wrong. With new faces and a new environment, surely I wouldn't feel the same pressures to drink. Although I refused to accept defeat and was afraid to look at the truth, I was becoming more cognizant that my problems were steadily present, if not worsening, when I drank.

In rehab, I learned that this type of drinking for the alcoholic is fondly referred to as "research." Many problem drinkers find themselves in court-ordered meetings or in rehab due to family pressures, but still feel the need to conduct their own research. (No, they are surely not alcoholics like the rest of them.) The duration of time for these intense investigations vary for each alcoholic, but unfortunately the outcome is usually the same. The problem doesn't go away. It gets worse.

The cyclical drinking that consumed me in Paraguay served as sufficient research for me. During my time in rehab, I was able to look back at how it had slowly unraveled, and my therapist called me out when I started bullshitting or minimizing the problems that had occurred. The months stretching from Mexico to the start of Paraguay were crucial in the realization of my alcoholism. In retrospect, it was pretty easy to see what had happened.

Although deep down I knew I was struggling when around alcohol, I was not yet ready to be open about it when first starting my Peace Corps work. I was far from acceptance and not quite desperate enough to be honest. During the early stages of our Peace Corps training, we engaged in many types of icebreakers, little games or drills that allowed us to get to know each other and start to learn names. There were thirty-four of us in all. The Peace Corps made it clear that these thirty-three other people were going to be like my second family for the next two years.

During the first week, there was one particular icebreaker called the safety circle or something like that. The idea was that all of us trainees got in a circle, and if the statement that was read aloud applied to us, we were to take a step forward into the circle. Examples of statements could be: "I was born in a country other than the United States," "I'm a vegetarian," or "My favorite kind of music to listen to is jazz." Of course it was a way of getting a feel for what everyone had in common, as well as for what made us unique. It was also important that whatever information came out in the game was to stay in that room—the whole "safe place" concept.

One question really jumped out at me and shows how sensitive I was at the time. The statement read something like this: "I have experienced difficulties in my life due to drugs or alcohol." Right as I heard it, I completely froze. I couldn't think of a sentence that could apply to me more. But, as I said, I froze. I saw a bunch of people step into the circle, but I couldn't. The moment seemed to last forever, as if to let the shame and guilt crawl throughout my whole body. I imagined myself sliding on my knees across the hard floor into the middle of the circle with my fists clenched in the air, screaming for some sort of relief . . . but of course I stayed at the edge of the circle, adamant that no one would know about the war being waged inside me. I remember looking at a couple of the people as they stood in the circle and desperately thinking, *Maybe they are having problems, too, like me*. But then I thought, *These people have no clue what it is like to experience the difficulties that I have*.

Throughout training, I tried to keep a low profile and act like I was just a normal drinker. I was still delusional enough to believe that I could control the outcome when I drank. But it was starting to scare me. It was such a big deal to me *inside* anytime alcohol was around that I became careful, cautious, and edgy. (I would have no problems socializing if I could just get away from that bottled demon.) I hated alcohol already. But it didn't take long for me to get to know the other folks and realize that they were a really fun group. It also didn't take long for me to reason that it wouldn't matter if I just got past the uneasiness of the first drinks, the silencing of my internal resistance, and I could just have fun like I always did. On alcohol.

Once I started drinking, it followed that I would almost always drink until the last people were at the bar. (And I *was* moderating my drinking. I was drinking considerably less than I used to back in the States.) Although I struggled every time I drank, I usually managed to stay under control, and only got to the point of blacking out one or two times. For a whole three months, that was a new course record. I was on my best behavior, and maybe, just maybe, I was in control and almost "cured."

On April 25, 2003, our last day of training, when we were to be sworn in as volunteers and foreign ambassadors of the U.S. government, I was hit with food poisoning, and it was a relief to me because it gave me an excuse not to drink. I was happier to be nauseous and sober than to go into another temporary battle at that point.

What was going on in my head was a complete reversal of thoughts. My time between graduation from college and admission into the Peace Corps (nine months) had taught me one thing: alcohol's effects on me weren't all that great anymore and I was definitely not like the rest of 'em. I was now starting to realize that once I put that shit in my body, a little switch flipped, like a fuel gauge in my head telling me that I was one or two drinks shy of feeling okay. When sober and completely straightened out, I hated taking the first drink or two, because I knew I was crossing over that line. It was as if I had gone through some type of aversion therapy, because inside I was saying, "No, no, no," but socially and behaviorally I wanted it to be okay. Besides, I had found it more difficult to explain, to lie, or to just say, "I can't drink" or "I'm not drinking tonight."

What kept me going back was that after a drink or four, everything was cool and I was in the clear for the next, oh, two or three hours or so. From there, along with sometimes futile strategizing, it was a roll of the dice. Circumstantially, I could usually avoid a loss of control or a blackout, but not always. The bigger issue to me was that I could never avoid the eventual withdrawal. It was easier for me either to ignore the problem when I was sober or to drown away my concerns when I was drinking. This shut up the voices in my head and fed my delusions: "I . . . am . . . okay."

# SEVENTEEN
## PROGRESSION WITHOUT PROGRESS

**Bam. Before I knew it, I was a volunteer and out** alone in my little community. But this was a good thing for me. I lived with two families, each for a month, and then on my own in a small house across the street from the school in the center of the village. I found great peace and serenity being out in the country with some of the warmest people I have ever encountered. Struggling with the indigenous language, I adapted and came into my own. I helped the villagers in the fields, where we picked and ate fresh fruit. They helped me with my language and taught me their traditional ways of cooking and living. In my off time, I spent hours playing guitar and writing in my journal.

One evening I scribbled, "A long night of drinking used to make me tired . . . now it makes me stay up and shake." What followed was what I wrote in "My Drink." I was amazed at how much I had to say about my drinking and how easily I could recall details about the way alcohol affected me. It flowed right out. My insides were full of all kinds of feelings and thoughts, yet I had been very good at bottling and storing them. That manifesto, "My Drink," poured out in one night during the first month in my village community. It was the first time I had honestly explored my alcohol problems.

What I noticed from that point on was how completely obsessed I was with alcohol. When not drinking during my service in South America, I was extremely happy to be sober and free from its bondage. But when there was alcohol around, I did everything I could think of to avoid having it offered to me. At times, I drank a bit with a family because it was normal to them (like a lot of people), and it was almost disrespectful not to take a nip of their cheap but potent beverage. It was terrible how much premeditation went into my every move around the stuff. Of course, after two or three drinks, I could feel the buzz and would suffer later in bed, either at night or in the morning, depending on how much I ended up drinking. (The only cure I knew then was drinking more.) It really was not worth it to me, and I was always looking for a way out.

For the most part, if it had stayed that simple, maybe I would have continued on at that level. I could possibly have developed an understanding that I just shouldn't drink at all. *Possibly.* And then, eventually, my language ability would have exceeded the level required to explain in my simplified version that "Toren no like alcohol. Make him feel bad man." But that's not how it worked. I still saw other volunteers about once a month. We often met in the capital city, Asunción. I am in no way blaming them. No matter where I drank, or with whom, I had trouble with alcohol. The problem was simply that when I was out drinking, I was still trying to be something I couldn't be: a social drinker. It wasn't working.

The second month in my site, to my surprise, Danielle (my friend from New Zealand) made her way through South America as she promised and visited me in Paraguay. I met up with her in Asunción, and from there we floated north by boat up the Rio Paraguay to Concepción. We set up camp on the top deck of a small tugboat hauling various cargo, goods, and a few passengers, for a relaxing thirty-six-hour ride up to the remote city. The sleepy river crawled along a flat green vista where scattered smokestacks stained the endless blue of sky. By night we watched the stars, sipped from bottles of *caña*, and caught up on each other's travels.

Awareness of my drinking had progressed and I mentioned to Danielle that my habits had been troubling me. Before I had even joined her this time, I knew that my first drink would be my biggest mistake, but I still didn't hesitate to drink and chose to believe that it would work out. On our last day together, I began drinking in the morning, but only enough to keep me going, just so I felt okay. We later shared plenty more drinks on a long bus ride back to the main terminal, where we would say good-bye. From Asunción, she planned to catch an overnight bus to Santa Cruz, Bolivia, and I would return to my community that same night.

With my own bottle of *caña* nearly finished, I watched her bus pull away. I was fairly loaded at this point and barely recall saying 'bye, nor do I remember buying my return ticket back to my village. I apparently spent the remainder of my money on the ticket. With time to spare before my bus departed Asunción, I sipped away on my bottle. The last thing I remember.

When I came to again I was shivering and lying facedown on the hard bus terminal floor near a wall. I was still in Asunción and it was early the next morning. A security guard was inspecting me as if I were crazy. He must have noticed me passed out. Hungover, dirty, and ragged, I'm sure I looked like a total street bum. The plastic bottle, now empty, had fallen out of my pocket. I didn't know how long I had been there. I still had my ticket but had missed my bus.

It was lucky I hadn't been robbed or arrested, because I had picked a bad place to pass out. Somehow I still had my backpack and my wallet. With no more money, I had to talk my way onto the next bus heading in the right direction. Finally home six hours and one unknown day later, I arrived dehydrated, miserable, empty, and expecting things to only worsen. My detox was just beginning.

Incidents such as this began to affect my attitude and I started feeling hopeless. I surrendered to the idea that I'd have to tough it out and drink when I was in certain situations. Inevitably, I enjoyed the greater part of my experiences when I drank with others. It was always later that I'd find myself bearing the consequences of the withdrawal symptoms on my own, often hoping that *this* time the indicators wouldn't happen. But they were always there.

What some people have trouble understanding is that the majority of the time I spent in my community I was actually sober. I didn't drink every day. But when I did drink, it was hopeless. The last four times I gave in to alcohol, I experienced the same progression and telltale characteristics of my binges. Always anxious and full of anticipation even before leaving my village for Asunción, I would begin to hope that I would find a way not to drink.

It's not that I was trying to quit drinking, but I was trying to avoid the truth—that I was an alcoholic. By not drinking I could feel okay, sober, and cling to the fantasy that I could still drink. Alcohol meant so much to me that I couldn't imagine a life without it. I would rather not have drunk and believed that I was okay than fight it (thereby letting reality set in). Every time I left my village, I got a little closer to reality, the truth about my drinking.

On the bus rides I would go over strategies or idealize ways to not drink so much. I knew I would drink. But every time I hoped it would be just a little. Like clockwork, though, I always lost sight of my intentions. Each time, there was a failed resolution to control my consumption. I didn't ever just say No. (That didn't make sense to me . . . yet.) Instead, I tried to moderate my intake. I would tell myself, "Just a few drinks like the rest of them, and then you can turn in early so you don't suffer all night or in the morning."

My alcoholic thinking was very stubborn. The disease of alcoholism seems to have a way of keeping drinkers feeling pinned down, thinking they have to drink, that there's no other way. It had not occurred to me that the solution to my problem was to stop drinking entirely. After the first drink, the switch would turn on, and I'd be swept away with a consistent need to maintain a level of "just a little bit of alcohol to keep me above the line," to keep me feeling normal. Invariably, it would result in a several-day binge and I would begin replacing my food intake with alcohol.

At the end of my binges, I would usually take the bus back from the city with a fever and unsettled dread about the long night and day or two ahead, in fear of seizures or hoping that this time I'd magically sleep through the hell. I often arrived home after dark, so I could walk into my village unnoticed. From there I could safely sweat it out until I had normalized and my anxiety had subsided enough to show myself. This caused a lot of inner struggle and a self-inflicted suffering that made me uneasy. Each time felt like the Sunday to end all Sundays: I was alone, depressed, and scared. I thought masking it was a good idea, but it only seemed to increase the intensity and frighten me more.

On one occasion, when I returned home from a trip to Asunción, my Paraguayan mom, Señora Francisca, took one look at me and asked if I was sick. She pointed out that I looked a lot skinnier around my neck and throughout my body. She was very observant in a motherly way, but had no idea how much drinking I was doing when I was away from my site.

When on these binges, it wasn't that I was out of control, drunk, or even drinking that heavily the whole time. I practiced basic maintenance drinking during the days for the most part. As long as I had a few drinks every once in a while, I felt pretty normal and could hang with everyone else. But it wasn't sitting well on the inside and it was becoming more absurd to me. I was now drinking like I had through the weekends in college, but *then* it had been for *fun* and with other people. Then, it felt more like a choice. Suddenly, I was doing it just to get by. For the most part, I didn't bother hiding it, even though no one else was doing it with me. I continued this behavior out of necessity until I got home to my village and could go through my "payment period" of withdrawals and could resume sober life at my site.

I had always been a hard drinker, partied hard, and accepted that if I had to die young, then so be it. At one point, I used to think aloud, "I might as well smoke, nothing else can stop me," or "Smoke a lot or not at all so you don't live to regret it." I began to think certain lifestyle choices were simply inevitable. If I were suffering, it would just be part of being a hard drinker. As my brother pointed out once, it would be a self-fulfilling prophecy if I accepted this and went along with it.

As my disease worsened, I began believing this type of rationalization. My thinking had become so distorted and twisted that I'd completely lost sight of objectivity or what was normal behavior. But I knew something was wrong.

By July, the third month in my community and my sixth month in Paraguay, I was extremely worn down by the seemingly inevitable cycle of my binges. Around that time my brother came to visit, and I became borderline panicked about how to handle my drinking. My insides filled with anxiety and confusion and I felt like I was ready to implode. I had considered telling him how I felt about alcohol, saying what was happening to me every time I drank, or just letting him in on my mounting fears and concerns. I was near distraught, looking for answers—but I didn't make it appear that way.

We met up in Asunción. I found him and his friend peering at me from a cheap hotel balcony over a busy downtown street. We caught up over some big bottles of beer and made plans for the next few days that we'd be spending together. They had traveled extensively and had seen a lot of amazing places and had just arrived in Paraguay. I was very excited to show them where I lived, and introduce them to some of the families in my community. We even talked about visiting the giant waterfalls of Foz do Iguaçu across the border.

Even with my best intentions, I never found the proper way to address my problem with alcohol. Instead I just gave in and started to drink like I normally did and tried to ignore what was going on underneath. With those first drinks, my alco-switch flipped, and for the remainder of the trip I drank constantly to keep everything either in or out of control, depending on how you looked at it. One night we drank quite heavily, and after a lot of hard alcohol, I apparently began gushing about how destroyed I felt when I drank and how difficult the boozing lifestyle had become for me. I had finally blurted out some of my problems in late-night fashion. It wasn't that I cried out for help, but just vented. I didn't give them reason to think much of it. Nor did I make too big of a deal about it. I was far from ready to call it a problem or think I should get help. But I was closer than I knew.

I didn't stop drinking and still managed to have a super good time.

Bringing up my struggles didn't change a thing. In fact, I was so drunk that I hadn't remembered it. Later the next day, I mentioned everything again to my brother, as if it were the first time. He looked at me like, "Are you serious? You already said all this last night."

I wasn't trying to repeat myself. I just didn't remember. Not only had I repeated things concerning my wavering stance on alcohol, I had repeated all kinds of other things without knowing it. Apparently, when drunk and on autopilot, I became unable to filter what concerned me or remember what I was saying or thinking. It immediately occurred to me that I had been complaining about something I could be preventing, and it made me feel ridiculous and even more stupid.

We spent a few days in my community that were highlighted by a housewarming party at my place and a festival in our village. My brother, his friend, and I, along with the help of my friend Lucio, prepared a special dinner for the families who had hosted me the two previous months. We drank and ate like kings, and later played a sing-along jam of George Michael's "Faith" on the guitar that community members still talk about to this day.

A festival of horse racing and a fiesta with plenty of loud music, drinking, and late-night dancing capped off the final day and night. The kids in my community were amazed by my brother and his friend's blond novelty, "rap dancing," and otherwise foreign ways at the party. Having that many young, lively foreigners visiting at one time was highly unusual. All three of us ended up in pretty amazing shape by the end of that night, having drunk all day with the locals. That next day we three blond, dirty, smelly gringos left the village and headed for Brazil. In general this visit with my brother and his friend—who we said was my cousin—was all my Paraguayan friends would talk about for my remaining time there.

I drank throughout the next two days until I had to return from Brazil back to my site and we parted ways. I'd had a great time with my bro and his friend. Like usual, I compartmentalized the anguish of my drinking away from all of the fun. But with these kinds of ups come the downs. My journey back was tough. I think that particular trip home to my village stood out as the loneliest set of bus rides I have ever endured. With about ten hours total travel, I felt like the world was slowly ending the whole way home. That last morning in Brazil I tried to put off my withdrawals with a few final beers, but finally gave up and succumbed to the evil process. I didn't even drink the final beer, a brand called Quilmes. No matter the pronunciation, I remember thinking *kill me* the whole trip back.

After arriving home, I left that beer sitting around my house for a week or two. Drinking it wouldn't have stopped the withdrawals I had coming, so at that point it was over and I knew it wouldn't help me. I pretty much felt like nothing could.

My last bouts with drinking were all the same. They consisted of social situations where I became less and less able to pull myself together. The events always started out fine, with me having a lot of fun, but when I began to get intoxicated, my agony leaked out. I turned into a disaster. Things inside me constantly stirred, waiting to boil over.

I repeated a very similar scenario sometime in August while reunited with volunteers in Asunción. It had been a solid weekend and I had made it to my phase of obligatory maintenance drinking. A bunch of us went out to eat at a Mexican restaurant. I had already been drinking all day, here and there, and I am pretty sure I didn't have any food in me. It was all fun and games until I decided to start talking to one of the bartenders and downing cheap shots of vodka. I should have seen it coming. But I don't remember thinking (this time at least), *Here we go. I'm going to get wasted*.

It is really hard to tell what I was trying to prove, what I was thinking, or why I would drink this way. By this point, one would think I had learned my lesson . . . but there was no reason or logic inside me to be found. Already buzzed, I walked right into my own alcoholic trap, trampling any caution or common sense that remained. Only trying to have a good time (and I suppose I was having fun), not one part of me made a decision about my intake or thought about it twice. There is no mechanism in the alcoholic drinker that says, "Slow down." The only thing I remember doing was taking shots as if it were my job, as though I were programmed. Or perhaps, more fittingly, rewired. I believe I remember up to shot number five, and after that, things go dark. My black box completely shut down—over and out.

Sometime later we all ended up hanging out in a few different hotel rooms. Depending on whom I talked to, there were good or bad things that happened. A few of the volunteers told me that I was hilarious that night. They said that I was pretty crazy and out of control, and eventually, by some sort of unanimous decision, they all decided that I should be put to bed. They told me that even when it was my bedtime I seemed to think the whole scene was comical. Apparently, as they literally carried me to my room in the hotel, I was singing Eddie Money's classic '80s song "Take Me Home Tonight." Although I was disturbed that I had blacked out yet again, I thought it was funny that at least whatever personality had taken over my body showed a sense of humor. But that wasn't all I learned about this special evening.

From a different source, I found out that during this same night I'd dredged up a pretty serious breakdown when talking to a small group of volunteers. I don't recall any of it, but apparently whatever I said really concerned a couple of them and made a pretty big impact on them. I'm sure I went on about how shitty I felt after drinking, about my anxiety and withdrawals. I wonder if I informed them that I was blacked out at that time as well? Obviously not. I had no clue. This really made me sick to hear about. For me to talk privately to a friend is one thing, and that was coming, but for me to be drunk, out of control, and spitting out my problems all over without even being aware of it was not cool. I wished I would either shut up or just not drink. It wasn't my nature to bring everyone into my head, which was swimming with alcohol and confusion. It became apparent to me that I was quite ill and that the results were beginning to spill over into all areas of my life.

In general the frequency of my blackouts seemed to be increasing. I started to notice a lot more unpredictability. It seemed like every time I began drinking again, month by month, the blackouts worsened. I was either losing my grip, or alcohol was tightening its hold on me. It was insanity. The infrequent weekends when I did go out, after a few days of seminormal drinking, the last hurrah seemed like a suicide mission.

In my village I spent much time sober, thinking about how crazy things had become. Inside I just wanted to rid myself of the problem and resume my community life, where, for the most part, I was at ease and content. Somehow I couldn't seem to let go of drinking.

One of my close volunteer friends, Tomás, stopped over sometime thereafter and stayed with me for a couple of days. We always had a good time together and were becoming pretty close. It was cool to show him where I lived and all the different fruit trees I had in my yard. My garden featured everything from coconuts, oranges, mandarins, lemons, limes, mangos, papaya, guavas, and grapefruits to bananas. Tomás and I started the process of making a homemade wine from grapefruits. We gathered a bunch of grapefruits and added a lot of sugar to their juice, but fortunately it didn't ferment in time, so I never allowed that brew to damage me, as I'm sure it would have.

For the better part of a day, Tomás and I cleared a field behind my house, where we planted rows of mandioca and corn. Mandioca is a variation of the yucca plant and is everywhere. It is basically the bread of Paraguay. I couldn't wait to have my own supply. During the time we worked, I talked openly with him about where I was with my drinking, among the many other things that we covered.

Talking to Tomás about my issues was a big step, a benchmark moment for me. It allowed the wheels to keep spinning and enabled me to address my problem in a constructive way. I was completely sober and took the chance to think out loud and bounce some of my thoughts off him. Of course I described my withdrawal, how my blackouts were troubling me, and generally how it all seemed to be on my mind constantly. He asked me if I had ever thought about quitting, or drinking less. I remember telling him that I enjoyed partying and drinking in general and that I didn't feel that my time was quite up yet, but that I realized someday I may have to think about cutting back, or even stopping. What I failed to mention to Tomás was how often I actually *had* tried to cut back or not drink so much during certain occasions. I don't think I told him because I hadn't yet realized that I truly couldn't stop drinking once I started. Besides, that would have meant I was an alcoholic.

During training, we volunteers spent plenty of nights at one particular bar. I had observed how much other people were drinking, and how fast or how slowly. I think it was partly an attempt to see if there was something wrong with me. I knew that Tomás usually only drank a few drinks at a time and that was it. I never saw him drunk, but he always seemed to have a good time, and sometimes he even cut out early. He told me that he had seen alcoholism in his family and that his own heavy drinking had run its course. He didn't like how it affected him near the end of his partying days. So he didn't drink as much and that was it. I really respected Tomás, how he managed to limit his drinks and stuck to it. It seems there must have been a very fundamental difference between the ways our bodies processed alcohol.

Tomás and I shared the same upcoming birthday in September, where we would be meeting up for an All-Volunteer Conference, followed by another two-day workshop for all the newest volunteers in my group, including a chosen member of each volunteer's community. I thought about the conversation with Tomás and felt like this would be a good opportunity to prove myself and make some sort of change in my drinking tactics. I didn't want to repeat my mistakes and planned to be "present" during the workshops and conferences. Thankfully, I couldn't see the future. It was then that I would finally give up the fight and blow my brains out, metaphorically.

# EIGHTEEN
## HOME SWEET UNSAFE HOME

### DRINKING WHILE DRIVING

> . . . . . . *I am happy*
> *riding in a car with my brother*
> *and drinking from a pint of Old Crow.*
> *We do not have any place in mind to go*
> *we are just driving.*
> *If I closed my eyes for a minute*
> *I would be lost, yet*
> *I could gladly lie down and sleep forever*
> *beside this road.*
> *My brother nudges me.*
> *Any minute now, something will happen.*
>
> —Raymond Carver[1]

**The Volkmann brothers' unwavering loyalty to one** another creates a bond that can be divided by only one thing: rock, paper, scissors. This game decides who gets the last scoop of ice cream, who goes first off the diving board, who takes out the garbage, or who cleans up the broken vase. With only twenty months between their births, Toren and his two older brothers are close not only in years but in steadfast devotion. They shared the same bedroom until we relocated to a larger house. When they reached mid–grade school, Don and I thought they should have their own rooms. The boys cried and argued with us when they were "required" to be separated. What resulted was that they still spent all their free time together inventing games and adventures, playing rock, paper, scissors, and parted only when it was time for lights out.

In high school and college, the three brothers negotiated a well-stocked and never-ending supply of communal friends on athletic teams, in classes, within our close-knit neighborhood, and throughout our community. Opportunities for camaraderie multiplied times three. Their best friends became universal, in the sense that they spent time with any of the Volkmann brothers. When kids dropped by our home, it didn't matter who was there to greet them; they shared friends unconditionally. Friendships that began in kindergarten are still going strong.

"O-town," as the brothers fondly refer to it, is Olympia, the place where these three kids grew up. We moved there when our oldest son began second grade. "It's the Water" was the motto of Olympia Brewery, which reigned with beer legacies of Olympia, Pabst, Schmidt's, and Miller—corporations that offered free tours. You could not only drink the beer there but see how it was made. The boys often met friends at the brewery when returning to town from college, and they would again take the tour (they probably could have guided it themselves) and down a free brewski afterward.

Lots of different boys rotated through our family, often joining us for weekend trips to a rustic family cabin on the rugged Pacific Coast. There we spent hours walking the beach, running ourselves ragged climbing hogbacks, building forts and rafts, cooking outdoors, chopping firewood, playing board games under the light of a lantern, and talking together about everything possible. Don and I had the unique opportunity to be thrown in the midst of these kids over a span of twenty years as they spent this expansive time with us. Because the cabin is one room and completely isolated from development, the boys and their friends were forced to interact with us. The hours spent driving there in our jam-packed Suburban, pitching in for chores and beach excursions, and talking together in front of a crackling fire with no other agenda provided many fond memories. If we had not had this chance to know the boys' friends so thoroughly, perhaps I would feel more jaded upon learning the extent of Toren's infatuation with alcohol and parties. But I have seen both sides. I have seen both the safe and the unsafe, the tentative morphing of boys into men.

It may be difficult for Toren when he emerges from rehab, since he and his brothers share the same dangerous DNA, along with a composite of party memories and a posse of mutual buddies. I wonder how these friends will socialize with Toren when he is unable to consume alcohol, and whether he will choose to see them—or they him.

After Toren's startling revelation to our family, his brothers check out the rehab Web site for themselves. They call to ask what we've heard from him. I inform them about Toren's recent letter from rehab, his battle with the Higher Power. I don't tell them what the therapist said, that Toren's own brothers could be hazardous for him. That maybe Toren shouldn't be around them for a while because they used together. "They drink a lot?" she'd asked me for verification. But it was really more of a declaration.

That reminds me of the wallet I've kept hidden away on the top shelf of my closet. Inside is a bunch of fake IDs used by the boys, some bearing each other's names, friends' names, even one with the name of one of Don's friends. They're from diverse states, but they all have pictures of one son or another. Fake IDs are easy to get nowadays. It's just a click away on the Internet. As I took them away from the boys over the years, I stockpiled them. I'd thought that someday we could pull them out and laugh. But not now; it's not so funny.

When the boys came home from college in summertime, they stayed close, packing lunches for one another and sharing rides to work. At one point they stretched a long cord from bedroom to bedroom, tied to each of their wrists, which they pulled in the mornings to be sure they would awaken on time. On weekends, they divided up friends and social invitations. Within a range of five to six years, if one brother had something to celebrate, any number of friends would show up to join in. Our family did a lot of burgers, boating, and sports tournaments with the boys and their friends. We incorporated these kids into our family and treated them as our own.

One Monday morning in the summer after Toren's freshman year of college, Toren did not get up to go to work. When I returned to the house around noon, he was still in bed. I could tell he was hungover, and we had a long talk about it. "Toren," I warned him, "if you're too hungover to go to work, it's a red flag. You need to pay attention to your partying, because this is a sign of alcohol problems." Toren had great difficulty responding, but he knew I was serious. He scrambled out of bed and didn't let it happen again. Now I wonder how he managed it. Little did I know.

What made our home unsafe? Probably the fact that because we were so happy to have the boys back, we didn't challenge their social habits enough. Our house is ten miles out of town, and we preferred the boys not drive home after drinking alcohol. For this reason they often stayed in town with friends on weekends. We also figured that since they were now in college, they could set their own hours, as long as they had steady jobs, respected our home, and helped out when needed. We wanted them to manage their own time and build some independence.

Toren and his brothers attended extended family events, worked at their grandparents' house, and visited Don's father across the mountains. They helped us with projects. We enjoyed having them around. When some of the boys' college friends dropped by to visit, they called me "VolkMom" and recalled times we'd seen them on campus. Some of these students were Triceptatrough seniors. No wonder they liked us. "You Volkmann bros have the coolest parents," they said. Right.

That incident aside, probably the most palpable danger at home was the ability for the brothers to get into mischief together, to set one another off. Who can jump off the highest cliff? Who can eat the most greasy hamburgers? Outdrinking one another could be a contest as well. Rock, paper, scissors determines designated drivers. And when a brother nudges a brother, it means something is important, whether it's happening now or is about to happen; or even if it's never happened. That's why our family lives in a Home Sweet unSafe Home. The coalition of brothers holds up the wall of loyalty and protection. Nothing can penetrate it.

And normal things? Normal is a myth. Our family is ready to discuss a new definition of us. Now that we've unearthed the Volkmann genetic blueprint, our sons are looking at home somewhat differently. When they return here after Toren has finished rehab someday, we know it won't be the same. Already, when we phone one another, it's changed. We're all talking about alcohol, how much we're drinking, how much we used to drink, if we should, can we never?

"What could I have done to prevent this?" I ask the older two.

"You did great, Mom," they assure me.

"Maybe I could have instructed him better. . . ."

"Program Toren?" They laugh at me. "Mom, he's grown up. He makes his own decisions. You're free after graduation. On your own, like Toren was in the Peace Corps." He was beginning his life.

What has our "You're on Your Own after College Graduation" plan done for our kids? Where did it get them—those brewery-head boys we raised? All those dinners together, mountain hikes, family times with grandparents, reading *City of Joy* as a family, symphony concerts together. I wonder if it helped. Sure thing, we shouldn't have bought those kegs for the first two boys' college graduations. By the time Toren graduated, we said, *No more big parties*. Because maybe we knew. Maybe we saw the unsafety of our home: a finality of success and graduation with three tuitions paid off, the relaxed thinking. We thought it was finished. Now, we pay the real price.

In our home, presently empty of boys, my husband and I look at our own alcohol usage and our lifestyle. We've been known to go out dancing with our sons, to accompany them to sports bars or to receptions where alcohol is served. Alcohol has not been central to our family activities. Yet, it was there. As we face an addicted family member, we scrutinize our home differently. What used to be reassuring appears threatening; there's a shadow hanging over our front door.

I gather the clues in order, things that we missed seeing. Every family varies, and problems with alcohol manifest differently. No one addiction is the same as another. No teen acts exactly like other teens. No alcoholic has identical symptoms. For this reason, it is difficult to say specifically what parents should look for. But in our case, I can recall instances when, if I were a parent telling another parent how to make home safer, I'd say, "Look out!" Because here's what we neglected:

---

### Things I Would Change

✓ Seeing or learning about our son intoxicated and not signing up for professional counseling. *(This could have been addressed in high school.)*

✓ Allowing our high school–aged son to visit college campuses without being accompanied by a parent. *(Some kids may be mature enough to do this, but we should have known better with Toren.)*

✓ Not knowing exactly where our son was during some of his college vacations; leaving too much unstructured time on his spring breaks. *(It would seem a responsible college kid could handle this on his own. Too much hand-holding wasn't our style, but in this case we were remiss.)*

✓ Seeing our son in legal difficulty at *any* time as a result of alcohol use and not pursuing counseling. *(We told him to handle his own problems, but did not aid him in professionally dealing with the cause of his difficulties.)*

✓ Seeing our son trembling or sitting around breaking a sweat for no reason. *(These late-stage symptoms may not be visible with every teen. We did ask him about it, but he said he wasn't feeling well; we believed him. And, well, he wasn't feeling well!)*

✓ Not working out a secure, structured plan for immediate postcollege time. *(We thought we had this covered with Toren's imminent plans for language school in Mexico and ensuing Peace Corps employment. Toren's plan was to party and drink, while we thought it was to find a job and take care of himself. He did land a summer job in Seattle before leaving for Mexico, and somehow he func-*

*(continued)*

*tioned well enough to get by, at least on the surface. His time spent in Las Vegas was obviously frivolous. Our downfall was that we ignored his extensive partying. Since he didn't live with us, we were unaware of its pervasiveness.)*

✓ Repeating over again any of the above mistakes and trying to rationalize it.

After writing these observations, I show them to Toren. He comments that no matter what we'd have done, he probably wouldn't have cooperated until he was good and ready. He says that our efforts may have been wasted had we pursued any of those avenues. Jokingly, Toren suggests he needed intervention even *before* he drank one drop.

"But what about the D.A.R.E. program you had in middle school?" I ask him.

"That was too soon," he explains. "The information was good to have, like all the facts I was presented, but I didn't think it applied to me. And I didn't care about it."

"And what about intervention after college?"

"By then, it was almost too late."

*Never too late*, I think. "What about counseling in high school?"

"It might've worked, but I probably would've thought my problem wasn't that serious." He goes on to say, "I had to have enough time to make a pile of bad decisions in order to realize I had a problem with alcohol. The only way to find out I had a problem was to let it manifest itself. You can't intervene too soon."

Toren led us to believe that he was an average college kid doing the average kind of college partying. The same, for that matter, in high school. Very talented at hiding and minimizing the problems caused by his alcohol abuse, he was even able to hide it from his brothers, his friends, and himself. As much as parents want to believe what their kids swear to be true, Toren's portrayal of his average kid's life was much different from his reality. When I go over this in my mind, knowing now about the extreme risks he took both with alcohol and other drugs, I wish that we could have done more as parents to prevent what happened.

When to interrupt the suspected abuse is the key question. But I keep thinking, *What if . . . ?* Maybe, by me saying this, some other parents will have the courage or foresight to make an attempt.

# NINETEEN
## NOTHING SOCIAL ABOUT IT

**[TOREN]** **On the evening of September 11, 2003, all** Peace Corps Paraguay Volunteers met in Asunción for a conference focused on goal setting and coordinating volunteers with varied skills to work together in cross-sector projects. Many of the newer volunteers from our group, including myself, had invited Paraguayan representatives from their individual communities to join in for two more days of a project design and management workshop. This meant a five-day stretch of extremely helpful idea sharing and a great opportunity to get to know the entire group of volunteers. I was aware that alcohol would be around and wanted to limit my drinking and participate without any craziness. For once, I wanted the results to reflect what I could accomplish when I was sober and that I was able to do things right. I had very good intentions, but, unfortunately, I still hadn't realized that control and drinks didn't belong in the same arena for me.

The first night was fine. I would have chosen not to even drink or had just a few (right . . . ), but because it was my birthday, I thought I'd ease up a bit and enjoy myself. For the most part, I drank somewhat normally, by my standards. I went through the whole next day with minimal side effects. But the switch *had* been flipped, and by early that afternoon the deal was pretty much sealed. I'd be drinking again soon. Every time my sobriety was broken, it seemed easier to keep sliding downhill in social situations. Although it didn't feel exactly like a craving, I knew I wanted to drink. My body wanted it. I chose the easy way. I'd rather drink than walk uphill the hard way to get out of the situation. Avoiding more alcohol, enduring withdrawals, and eventually feeling better no longer worked for me. It was easier to continue drinking than to stop and detox.

I knew that I would drink that next night. And I did. Like the usual progression, I began earlier, I drank a lot more, and I went a lot later. I made two late-night runs to the store for boxes of wine, but it was only because we were having such a great time and I didn't want it to end. I knew that more drinks would keep it going. At least it would for me. Once I was drinking, that's all I wanted. I could have gone on drinking the entire night. At least it felt that way, and my body said I could. Not once did I actually stop and think, *Maybe this is the type of drinking I shouldn't do. This is what always fucks me up. This is what I always dread and am trying to avoid.* No. Instead, all my plans to moderate my drinking or not drink at all were washed away by some tipsy, whimsical desire to keep drinking until the night just faded away and slipped into darkness.

The next morning I woke up in a bed on the other side of the facility in a different sleeping quarter. I had completely blacked out, and a few of us had slept through the morning lectures. Normally I wouldn't care, but I was already fed up with this routine, and that pissed me off. Unpredictable. The night had been a blast all the way to the moment I pulled a disappearing act from my own memory. To remedy the effects, I drank a lot of water. Along with some minor shakes and tremors, I noticed that food was starting to seem pointless and foreign to me. That afternoon, I was able to appear normal and enjoy myself, but still, my thoughts were completely preoccupied with when I could get to the next drink. I may have been present physically, but my mind was already anticipating the ensuing relief of the drinking that seemed inevitable.

At this point, I realized I was at a crossroads. I had two options. I could either fight it and suffer a pretty nauseating withdrawal and eventually recuperate after tremendous anxiety, discomfort, and another long night or two, or I could continue to drink and put off the problem and act as if everything were normal. My tainted alcoholic mind gave me no choice.

"Yeah, right, you're not putting yourself through that now or tonight." Besides, all the volunteers would be at a bar that night. I was already wet in my mind. My community representative and friend, Lucio, loved to drink. This meant that while he was with us I wouldn't have to withdraw. Nor would I have to conceal my drinking. I could just keep up the momentum and make it through. It was an ugly situation, but I was running out of options. My sense of humor and reason were both by the wayside at this point. I could fight any uneasiness with a few more drinks. In my brilliance, I was avoiding pain and solving the problem. Temporarily.

This third night at the bar I drank slow and steady because I didn't want to black out and lose it all—neither the control nor my memory—like I'd apparently done the night before. What I didn't realize was that my control was already gone when I picked up my first drink. Completely clueless. By the end of the night, I'd maintained a pretty constant buzz and managed to avoid a blackout.

I noticed that as my disease progressed, walking the fine line of maintaining myself between withdrawal, overintoxication, or blacking out for an extended period of time was increasingly difficult and dangerous. I needed X amount of alcoholic drinks in my system to feel normal or a bit better, like most normal people or moderate drinkers feel. But if I got to another plateau a bit further along, I began to let all my guards down, which is common with heavy drinkers. Unfortunately, there is another part to the alcoholic system that told me, "Yes, yes!! This is it. Keep doing this, it's working!" And, somewhere in there, I'd go from a normal buzz to a heavy buzz (and keep drinking while thinking everything was cool) to gone. This is the essence of the brain disorder.

During all of this, I wouldn't remember a thing, but I could be around for hours more, and often my drinking accelerated. According to some, a real blackout artist can lose days or more at a time. It was a terrible feeling to wake up and have no clue about what I'd missed. Or what I'd done. Attempting to appear like I knew what had happened the night before, I'd have to play detective to figure it out.

When I met my community representative, Lucio, at the bus terminal on the fourth day at noon, I'd already had two beers to take the edge off. After all, I felt good. But inside I realized how ridiculous it was. Basically, for the next two and a half days I struggled to keep my urges to drink at bay. I was at a loss for how to do this. I had completely lost sight of:

Why I was at the conference;
What I was supposed to be doing for my community;
How I had planned *not* to drink;
What really mattered;
What I wanted.

All I could think about was drinking when my system got low. I didn't consider it a craving. *It was a physical necessity.* Before my eyes, I had watched my will completely deteriorate over the duration of six days. I had compromised everything for alcohol. It was my new priority. Not only was there *nothing* social about it, but this was the first time that my drinking was completely and directly interfering with my work and what I was trying to do in the real world. Not one other volunteer was drinking with me. I started leaving in the middle of lectures or activities to gather myself, get fresh air, or strategize. It was moment to moment until my avoidance could no longer postpone what I saw as inevitable. My next drink.

About ten blocks away was the same store I'd gone to a few nights before. I understood that two or three drinks would stop the suffering and shut it all off, returning me to feeling normal and functional, the only things I really wanted. At that point, I didn't care. I had to do what was necessary for me, so I could get past my craving and back to participating in the conference.

I went to the liquor store, disgusted with myself, but at the same time relieved that I could at least end the discomfort. The very anticipation of the first drink was always incredible. Once I had a bottle or can in my hand, had simply given in or decided to drink, I could already feel relief. Before I even tasted it in my mouth or the alcohol reached my system, I felt better. Just knowing that I would get the next drink was reassuring. The discomfort would end. I would feel okay again. And that is what took me to the liquor store.

On the way back from the store, walking through a ritzy neighborhood, I encountered a horse and buggy. I did something I never thought I would: I took a ride in it. I felt bad about this, because all the other volunteers were doing what they were supposed to be doing. Not me. But the ride sure was novel. *¡Viva Paraguay!*

When I returned to the conference I downed my few drinks, even though they tasted like varnish. I attempted to rejoin the normal folks. Very few knew that I had left to get alcohol, much less about my horse-and-buggy adventure. I was pretty good at faking things at this point.

I was completely aware that I had lost the battle and was now one step closer to the stereotypical closet drinker. I had reached a new low. My will was broken. I was hiding drinks and actually ashamed for the first time. I believe I was more scared about what was going on than I'd ever been before, but there was no way in hell I was ready to bring another volunteer into my poisoned world. I chose this sordid path and it was my deal. A drink was always the cure to ignore the problem.

Toward the end of the conference, things got pretty blurry to me. The only thing I know with any reliability is that any time my fuel level was low, I would drink a bit to keep it under control. What finally urged me to go to the medical office at headquarters still baffles me. I don't remember a definitive moment where I said to myself, "This is it. I'm turning you in," or anything like that.

But I do remember one foot in front of the other, up those steps, through the door and sitting down in a chair facing the nurse behind her desk and staring blankly. This same nurse had driven me to the terminal to pick up Lucio three days before, and she had smelled alcohol on me then. Everyone must have known I smelled like alcohol except me. The nurse sensed that I wanted to talk about something, and it took very little for me to open right up.

I was ready. I immediately began to feel relief and comfort, because I could finally talk about what was up and get it out of my swelling head. After my score tallied more points than were possible on a question-and-answer test for alcoholism, it was now just as clear to her as it was to me that I had a problem.

From this point on, all possible procedural steps were taken to get me back to Washington, D.C., ASAP, where I could be properly helped by the best of professionals.

Uh-oh. What had I done? I'm not sure if I knew what was going on, except that I wanted help.

I was given Valium and put in a hotel room to detox in the care of some of my good Peace Corps friends. This detox for me was not my usual. Normally, I bore it all alone, and if people were around, I never told them what I was feeling inside: an almost inexplicable discomfort, which was always there. But this time with Valium, the withdrawal effects were subtle and nearly undetectable.

From the medical office, the nurse called my friends at the hotel and asked them, "Have you ever been around anyone coming off alcohol?" She then explained the seriousness of it, and that they'd have to get rid of all the alcohol in the hotel room, that they should monitor my Valium intake, and that I'd be sweating a lot. Although my friends didn't realize it, they'd been hanging around with me long enough that they definitely had witnessed someone coming off alcohol various times. Only now had it been formally acknowledged. We managed to have a good time in spite of the underlying darkness of what the situation really meant. Beneath the smiles and conversation, there was sadness about what I was going through. Many said conciliatory things and that they were proud of me, but nobody knew it was really time to say good-bye.

The next afternoon I was driven to my site to pack some items for Washington, D.C., a trip that I figured would last a week or two, tops. Still on my Valium detox plan, with my friends in Asunción three hours away, I absentmindedly threw some CDs together, got my guitar, and pulled out some clothing, which would not be sufficient for the unforeseen fall temperatures at rehab.

As for the trip to Washington, D.C., well, I'm still on it.

Thankfully, before leaving my village in Paraguay, I got to briefly see my two families and my buddy Lucio, who had witnessed some of my struggles and desperation in my final days. I had no idea that I was leaving the place permanently and that those were my final good-byes to the community and all the volunteers. And maybe those were also my good-byes to drinking. Believe it or not, that last one is the hardest to comprehend for a drunk like me.

# TWENTY

## CALLS FROM REHAB

ALCOHOL

*Let her*
*fall in love with you and you*
*with her and then . . . something: alcohol,*
*a problem with alcohol, always alcohol—*
*what you've really done*
*and to someone else, the one*
*you meant to love from the start.*

*—Raymond Carver[1]*

**October 2003. Finally, after more than eight** days, we receive our first phone call from Toren. He has survived the initial week of rehab, supposedly the toughest. I listen to his voice for the tone, his inflections, for any indication of his mood. He sounds thoughtful, focused. There is noise in the background because he must use a phone located where visitors are received, which extends for two hours on Sundays. A baby cries in the background. I picture people chatting and laughing amidst friends and relatives, while Toren is all alone. He speaks clearly. "I'm working on acceptance of the cost of my alcoholism. This week was intense." He mentions quickly the haunting trio of anger, guilt, and shame. "I know now that I'm worse off than I thought. I'm trying to do whatever they say," Toren confesses.

It must have been grueling. The person speaking doesn't sound like the guy I talked to days ago. His voice is level, and he doesn't seem discouraged when he admits, "I might have to leave South America for good."

"That's not what you wanted," I suggest.

"The worst part is, I didn't have closure with my village. I left without explaining things. That is so hard for me to deal with."

"What will you do next," I ask, "after rehab?"

"I can hardly think more than one day at a time. I just do today. But they're saying I might consider living in a halfway house, that it's what might be best." He stops here.

"Well, what do you think about that?" I ask, recalling how a halfway house once reared its prefabricated siding in our former neighborhood. That'd been almost twenty years ago. And I'd joined with other neighbors to lobby against it ("I just don't want my children associating with that type of person," I'd justified). Then I'd signed a not-in-my-backyard! (NIMBY) letter. Now *my* kid is talking about going to some town to live in one. I immediately feel guilty but grateful to those citizens if they'll give him this chance. I know Toren will be nice to his neighbors.

"I'm not enthused. It's not appealing," he says, "but I'm here to listen to what they tell me." His voice has lost the early fervor of the call. It takes on a slightly forced tone, one of resignation, somewhat hopeless.

It took courage for Toren to turn himself in and admit he had a problem when he was so enamored with his life in South America. He'd had to give it up. I remember he'd said he wouldn't have come forward if he'd known they would yank him out of his service. What if he'd died in Paraguay? Detoxing from alcohol is extremely dangerous and can even be fatal. Repeated untreated withdrawals (such as the self-detoxing Toren endured) have a cumulative effect and create more serious future withdrawals. Some alcoholics develop a seizure disorder that causes brain damage. Professionals believe that chronic alcoholics should receive drugs to control withdrawal symptoms, thereby reducing the potential for further seizures and brain damage.[2] I shudder. Maybe a halfway house isn't such a bad alternative. It would give Toren organization for his life, a positive spin. Hopefully he wouldn't run into any disapproving NIMBYs like me.

"If you live in a halfway house, you'll have structure," I say reassuringly. "You'll be able to relax because temptation will be out of sight." I look at Toren's free time after college graduation, where it had put him. I had disliked his choices then, and suddenly this halfway house sounds even better.

The phone call changes pace when Toren asks if we know about the Family Education Program. I hear someone hacking away at a cough in the background as I tell him we're planning to come; in fact, just that day I'd been working on flight arrangements.

"You and Dad?" he asks.

"Yes, and your brothers, too."

*"Oh, Lord."*

"What?" I'm not sure what Toren is trying to tell me.

"You said the whole family's coming? Oh, Lord," he repeats. Then he spills out, "It's going to be hard on our family. You'll have to write letters to me telling me how I've hurt you. I don't want anyone to feel betrayed, to feel like they have to 'sign up'—to change their lives because of me." Toren sounds panicked. "I thought you and Dad might come, but my brothers? Are you sure they can come?"

"Yes, I've called them, and they're clearing their schedules. They both had conflicts on Thursday, but they'll fly out on Friday in time to be there Saturday morning. We've checked out flights already."

"Our family's going to have to be honest," Toren warns. He's worrying about us, about his brothers being coerced into attending. I wonder if there might be some other reason he's so concerned. Toren comments that one of his brothers wrote him a letter trying to be sensitive. "I think coming here will really affect them, because you have to be honest about yourself in regards to what you want in your life and how actively you're going after it. I don't want my brothers to feel threatened about their drinking, but this could be difficult for them."

I tell Toren that this weekend symposium will be good for all of us. "We have to live together [hopefully] a long time, Toren, and if we can't be honest, then we won't have a good relationship."

"Our family's probably the healthiest family they'll ever see here in rehab," Toren comments. "Really, it'll be embarrassing. It seems like everyone's families are either torn apart or damaged. But the education program will cause our family to be more open with each other."

He goes on to tell me that he has been worrying not only about how his brothers will react to him but what his longtime friends will do when they hear the news. He thinks that only a few buddies would be able to understand him never drinking again. "I might have to give up a lot of my former friends. I don't know how and when to tell people."

I suggest that Toren talk with his therapist about his brothers and his friends, and he agrees it's a good idea. It seems strange for me to be slinging around the term "your therapist" so casually with my son, like something out of an old Woody Allen movie.

Then I ask Toren if he has been receiving my cards and letters. He tells about opening his mail in front of the guard, a hardened man who has seen everything and is notoriously stoic on the job. But Toren got a smile out of him when he showed him an old photo I'd sent of the brothers as kids.

Toren comments on the family alcohol history sent to him by Don, how it surprised him. "I can't believe all the alcoholics in the family. Did you know about it?" he asks. I tell him it was startling to me as well.

Toren continues, saying, "I'm constantly busy here. There's hardly time to make a phone call." He explains that there're a lot of lectures and group discussions, but downtime, particularly Sunday, is slow because he can't be alone. He is required to be interacting with someone and to remain in public. The only reading material is the *Big Book* (AA material). "It's hard to sit here blindly not knowing what to do or what I will be doing in the immediate future. I don't know what to prepare for."

I ask Toren what he wants from us, for us to do.

He says, "Feel good for me. Don't feel bad or sad."

So I try to do that. I will myself to cheer up. After all, I *am* proud of him, of his brutal honesty. The rest of the week I'm busy renting a car, finding a hotel, and facilitating arrivals at the airport near Toren's rehab facility. Gretchen, Toren's therapist, calls to ask if I have any questions about the weekend program and Toren's progress. She casually brings up the halfway house, and I do not tell her about my former negative attitude. She tells me that the aftercare team is looking into good placement options for Toren.

Aftercare. I think about the stigma of telling friends that my son's living in a halfway house. That sounds humiliating enough, but the feedback from Toren's brothers is even more quizzical.

"I think they're overreacting with this rehab program," one of his brothers tells me. "Yeah, I've had the shakes. Are they going to enroll me now? And this halfway house stuff, isn't that for addicts?" (Yes, son, it is.)

Now I realize why we need the Family Education Program. Like much of the population, Toren's brother hardly considers alcoholism an addiction. It's sort of "an unfortunate situation." But an addiction? Isn't that label a bit serious? Lots of people drink too much, after all. It's an accepted norm of society. We don't have to saddle them with the label of addict, do we? It's so much easier to say alcohol problem than alcohol addiction. It sounds better.

The Family Education Program seems like a seminar custom-built for us. After all, we're the near-perfect nuclear family. Two still-married parents: an endangered species. And two sons willing to support an addicted brother: unflappable. Other addicts may not be so lucky as to have such resources. In reality, our family problem may not be so groundbreaking; the history of traditional American values has always included alcoholism and addiction. Millions of families have been in crisis and flux over the last two centuries, and our family is another example of the exploding myth. According to family scholar Stephanie Coontz, no single type of household has ever protected Americans from social disruption.[3]

With Toren being far away and rehabbing in secret, I miss being able to talk with close friends about what is happening to our family. There is a tremendous lack of support for me and my husband. At the same time, I know this disease is not all about me, it's about Toren. At least that's what I think at this point. I will later be told that alcoholism takes down not only the alcoholic but the entire family. That's the logical reason I'm in such turmoil. But at this point, without resources and help, I am frankly slipping into a whirlpool of panic. I lack emotional control when talking to people because I don't yet know enough about this disease. After Toren's phone call, I hit the Al-Anon Web site in near hysteria; I look for information on the Internet about drinking. But what I really need is someone who will talk with me about our son, someone who knows him and is working with him.

Two days later, Toren again phones. He finally announces to Don and me that he has given up on returning to Paraguay. His voice is resolute and victorious. "I've accepted it," he proclaims. "I've been through denial, anger, and all the way to acceptance." Toren says he stood in front of the group just that day and announced that he wouldn't be going back. He says it felt good to share it.

Don and I discuss with Toren the advantages of living in a halfway house, of being with people who are clean and sober. Toren's still trying to decide where to do his halfway stint. Much of the country is off limits to him since he used in practically every western state. Toren is considering several eastern locations. He will find work; there are options. Toren likes his therapist and says she's cool. It's a relief to us that there is someone out there who's able to discuss things with Toren, subjects that were impossible for us to bring up. Toren says that immediately after rehab he will go to Washington, D.C., for closure with the Peace Corps. After that, he will go to the halfway house selected by him and his therapist. He doesn't know about finances, but stresses that he wants to do this on his own. He had saved summer employment funds in his bank account and feels this will get him by until he can find a job.

After Toren hangs up, I want to ask him if he can manage, if he needs us to help him move. But inside, I know that he has previously relocated to a foreign country and unfamiliar village culture on his own. Finding his spot in an American town should be relatively simple in comparison. Before we have time to comprehend all that Toren has told us, his therapist telephones. She checks on our visiting arrangements, our arrival times, and talks about setting an appointment for our family to work with the education team. She reports that Toren is doing very well and is beginning to understand his problem. Gretchen says the letter Don sent about our family alcohol history is excellent and shows outstanding support for Toren. She is working with Toren to narrow down his halfway selection to three choices. Again, she stresses that Toren should not be near his brothers. He needs to do this move on his own to prove himself, because he was floundering after college. He was not making good decisions about drinking; he was all over the place.

We talk about support for Toren and whether Don and I should help him in the transition. Gretchen suggests, "Tell Toren you want to be there for him and ask him what you can do. Ask Toren to tell you if it gets to be too much." She says that Toren processes things internally and doesn't tell people what he needs. "He solves everyone else's problems but doesn't take care of himself. It's something I talked with Toren about today."

I explain to her, "I'm concerned Toren won't tell us if he's unable to function, because look at how he's hidden things from us before!"

Gretchen reminds me that Toren is learning to go to people when he needs help. I now remember that during Toren's phone call he mentioned appreciation for sharing some of his burden with the group. Maybe he can do that with us.

Before Toren left for the Peace Corps, I asked him if he had any regrets for his misconduct (only the things I knew about at that point). I needed to verify the real Toren: my son, the kid who had treated me so well, the boy who talked to me about injustice, world causes, and sonnets. Many times, it seemed his acting out hadn't matched the person I knew at home. I remember the day before he departed, we crossed a rainy parking lot on our way to pick up his eyeglass prescription. The glasses had to be ordered and barely arrived in time; the following day Toren would launch himself into his South American mission. I believed he had joined the Peace Corps to contribute to the betterment of the world. Now I wanted him to convince me that he had finally realized the negative impact of certain past actions. (In my mind, I was validating the intelligent, thoughtful young man I thought I knew. Who was he, really? Although he had often pushed limits, I needed reassurance that he was not as self-effacing as he'd sometimes seemed.) Obviously, he was now ready to turn over a new chapter in his life, one of commitment and leadership.

Trying to keep it casual, I asked him, "Do you regret any of your behavior in high school and college?" We continued toward the store entrance, plodding through random puddles, cigarette butts, and dented latte lids. He looked at me as though he couldn't understand why I would ask such an obvious thing. I rephrased it, "Do you think your life has been more difficult because of your decisions?"

Toren answered me, "No, my life's been good. I wouldn't give up my experiences."

"Even when you got into trouble?"

"Yes. Even then." He remained resolute.

Does Toren believe that now? How good has it really been?

# TWENTY-ONE
## VISITING HOURS

**[CHRIS]** *October 12, 2003. His voice is clear and strong,* even cheerful. "I know that I need help," Toren tells us. "I've been working with my therapist and I think we've figured out the best option. I'll probably go to a halfway house in Florida for three months, maybe even six." He speaks with conviction. Toren sounds like he wants to settle in; become accountable. And sober. He says he was tempted by New York City, but no programs there were recommended by his treatment center. He doesn't know yet where in Florida he'll be, and asks us to bring some clothes for temperate weather when we come to the Family Education Program. Toren reads me a list of things he will need, since most of his belongings are still in South America. We're allowed to deliver them to the rehab facility, where they will be stored until he has finished his treatment; the program does not want anyone smuggling in unauthorized "stuff."

Toren's take is upbeat. We decide that I'll bring him a duffel bag. He requests long-sleeved shirts, a hooded sweatshirt, swim shorts, blue jeans, his flannel pants, some favorite T-shirts, his old Windbreaker, and a beanie hat from the bottom of his sock drawer that says "Alcoholics" on it. . . . I wonder what he will do with it? He also wants his drum pad.

Toren's full of news. He says he performed a song at the rehab chapel

205

for some two hundred people, a song he wrote himself. He sang and played the guitar. Toren is enthused about the priests there and their message to addicts. He goes on to say he likes his mail, especially letters he's received in Spanish and letters from volunteers and staff in South America. Toren seems lucid and cogent. It makes me realize that it hasn't been that way for a while. I think we're seeing him truly sober for the first time in years.

I spend the next evening packing things for Toren. I include an article on how to make a budget, an envelope with Tibetan mandala sand and blessing music, some mints, and, along with his requested favorite clothes, some new shirts, socks, and shorts. It's reassuring to get out his clothing, to see it and think that he will be wearing it sober. Sober. What a wonderful word!

I wonder if he needs more luggage. Toren left us nine months ago carrying one suitcase and a backpack. We have no idea what things he's brought back to the United States on unexpected notice. Those "things" aren't incredibly important. It's so much more essential for him to possess his health, his sanity, his wits, his courage to carry on: his fire to be the best person he can. Toren is fortunate at this moment to have people guiding him who care about him and know what is best for people with an alcohol addiction.

I'm thankful I can finally follow someone's direction to take care of this progressive disease, the malaise that overtook our family the past nine years. Just placing things in a suitcase seems a positive step and fills me with hope. We leave tomorrow for the Family Education Program. I don't even care how hokey the name sounds. I want to get smart, to learn about this thing that has happened to Toren and our family. I'm weary of feeling overwhelmed.

Before leaving, I phone Toren's brothers to remind them they cannot wear torn jeans or logo shirts to the rehab facility. This is one rule among other policies that ensures the safety of the patients. It's the first time I realize that ordinary symbols of drugs and alcohol, product brands or rock band names, even certain clothing styles, can be triggers for relapse. The

staff at the rehab center tries to prevent clients from experiencing unnecessary anxiety when visitors unthinkingly wear something that might remind them of their addiction.

The brothers go over meeting arrangements with me. Both of them
are adjusting study and work schedules to make this trip. They've agreed
to attend because I asked them to. They adore their brother; if he reaches
out for help, they want to be there for him. Still, I sense they cannot understand why it's necessary to have the whole family with Toren. We have
not been together as a family for over nine months, so even though this
venture is laced with dubious speculation, we can't help but look forward
to seeing one another.

I am somewhat nervous, knowing we must meet with people who
could easily see through us, who will be evaluating our family, and who
probably know quite a bit about us prior to our arrival, since they've been
working with Toren for almost three weeks now. My emotions thin, I
wonder how I will hold up even with my family at my side; all my fears
and joys mesh into one slobbery knot. It isn't the most reassuring image.

En route to the rehab facility, I'm on my own because Don and
Toren's brothers are unable to break away until Friday evening. An airport van arrives for me on Thursday morning at five a.m. amidst a down-
pour. The Pacific Northwest autumn mood wears a dour gray patina as I
board the van, joining two women inside, one going to Arizona to meet
her high school girlfriends for a spa reunion, the other dressed for an
ecology business conference in Jasper, Canada. They chatter on in lively
banter about their plans, as though it were three in the afternoon. When
they ask where I'm going, I tell them the name of the state.

"Do you have business there?" the ecology girl asks.

"No, my son's there."

Then the other, the one who just loved high school, wants to know,
"Is he a student?"

"Yes." A student of alcohol. My emotions rush to my face and I'm
grateful for the darkness of predawn. It's too early for conversation. They
recognize that I must not be a morning person. I'm not talking.

There's plenty of time to adjust to what I'm about to do. Six hours on the plane and the ensuing drive in a rental car allow me to prepare for meeting our son, while I ponder the relentless scripted captions that run through the skulls of all mothers, like: whether Toren's had a recent haircut, whether he will be lean from readjusting his diet, whether he will still have his sparkle and bounce, whether he will be happy to see me or embarrassed, whether he has a warm enough jacket.

With my directional dyslexia, I can barely find my way around my own neighborhood, let alone driving through a foreign state to a rambling rehab center with hazily labeled buildings and other lost-looking people. But I do it. There's a sense that I'm not really here, not really carrying out this mission. It's nothing I'd imagined doing; no dream come true. Upon arriving at the facility, I find my way to the location of the coffee hour, where we are scheduled to meet other family support members who will be spending the weekend with us. When I enter the meeting room, I immediately sense that it is not a fantasy visit for the other twenty or so people in attendance either. We all look miserable, like we have been sent there for detention. Eye contact is nil.

But the staff at rehab centers are expert at what they do. And their purpose this weekend is not to humiliate us. All of us are here because we care deeply for someone in treatment. As the morning passes, we begin to recognize that. We all want to experience some form of success and understanding with our family members. It occurs to me that other people are not so pleased to be seeing their loved ones as I am to be seeing Toren. In fact, some appear to dread it; others look reasonably angry. I try to hide how excited I am to get my arms around my son.

The first day of the program is devoted largely to education about addiction, about the disease of alcoholism, and about the role of the family in relation to the alcoholic. The presentations are dynamic and informative. I take notes. It's fascinating to me. I realize that this disease has tracked down my son and ravaged his brain in the same relentless manner that threatens 20 percent of our population. My son is not alone in his addiction. But he is one of the lucky ones: he has sought help.

Apparently, I'm one of 80 percent of the population who is able to drink alcohol. Our facilitator explains that such social drinkers regulate their drinking, perhaps after a few bad experiences with alcohol, and can continue to do so throughout their lives. But the other 20 percent face alcohol abuse or addiction. And as I learn from other participating family members, this disease is nondiscriminating. It selects people from all walks of life. It seduces even those of strong and good character into its clutches. And the despair it creates surrounds me in the meeting room that morning.

The disease of alcoholism, like other diseases such as heart disease or diabetes, is treatable. The goal of the rehab staff is to allow people to die *with* their addiction instead of *from* their addiction. The cost to U.S. society for the consequences of alcohol use alone is staggering, approximately a thousand dollars per individual who consumes it. In terms of morbidity and mortality, a drinker loses ten years to alcoholic liver disease, compared to two years from cancer and four years from heart disease.[1]

The most interesting part of the presentation is the discussion of addiction. An accepted definition of addiction is *The repetitive, compulsive use of a substance despite negative consequences to the user*.[2]

---

## The Characteristics of Addiction[2]

Addiction features three or more of these seven characteristics:

1. Increased tolerance
2. Withdrawal
3. Attempts to cut down or control use
4. Use despite adverse social or personal consequences
5. Use despite physical or psychological harm
6. Large quantities of time and effort and money spent on obtaining substance
7. Substance taken in larger quantities or for longer amounts of time than intended

*Why does an addict keep using?* The reward circuit of the addict's brain craves a substance called dopamine, and such things as food, sex, or addictive drugs (alcohol included) produce the release of dopamine. Scientists are just now realizing the strong role of dopamine in addiction and how the brain and body adapt to levels of dopamine production.[3] Drinking alcohol increases the release of dopamine in the reward centers of the brain. Studies show that the increase in dopamine activity occurs only while the concentration of alcohol in the blood is rising, not while it is falling.

So during the first moments after drinking, the pleasure circuits in the brain are activated. But the dopamine rush disappears after the alcohol level stops rising. This is what separates a normal drinker from an alcoholic. An alcoholic consumes more alcohol in order to raise the alcohol level and start the pleasure sequence again, called "chasing the high." The problem is that although the rush is over, there is still plenty of alcohol in the body, and continued drinking in pursuit of pleasure could push the blood alcohol concentration up to dangerous levels.[4] The addict's or alcoholic's abnormality tells him to keep drinking.

When alcohol levels are lower and dopamine quantities in the brain level off, the addict is no longer able to sustain enough of the chemical to relieve withdrawal symptoms. Then the body and brain demand the chemical (alcohol) to stop withdrawal symptoms, and the addict (alcoholic) is no longer using the drug for pleasure, but to relieve pain and the unpleasant effects of withdrawal. It makes the alcoholic feel anxious and restless, to crave the drug, and therefore to feel the need for maintenance drinking.

So what's the difference between a "normal" drinker and an alcoholic? The alcoholic drinks more and more to raise the alcohol concentration, keeps chasing the high, and ups the amount of alcohol consumed. For this reason the alcoholic's tolerance increases as well. This malfunction keeps alcoholics feeling like they need more of the substance, and causes them to overindulge and lose control. Such drinking or drug use leads to addiction. A regular drinker will stop drinking at a certain point and will not increase doses, and therefore may not become addicted. During the addiction process, physiological brain patterns change. Once this happens, the reaction to the drug (alcohol) is altered, and subsequent ingestion of the drug will continue to affect the way the drug is processed. Thus, addiction is a progressive brain disorder.

Actual experiments using an MRI of the brain have measured levels of dopamine produced when an addict receives a drug of choice. On these films, it's possible to observe how brain patterns change physiologically and how neural circuits are modified by chronic use of alcohol or drugs. Since the frontal cortex of the human brain is not fully formed until age twenty for women and between ages twenty-two and twenty-four for men, it's possible that heavy drug or alcohol use can alter that development. Studies are still being run in this area. From what I learn in this class, I realize what has happened in Toren's brain, and I better understand his increased use of alcohol.

Now I see how addiction and control are two opposite concepts. By the time Toren cultivated his taste for alcohol and experienced the enhanced levels of dopamine, his brain never looked back. When modification of his neural circuits took over, good sense was blotted out with the overriding desire for dopamine.

With my head full of lingo and my notebook crammed with facts, I'm finally allowed to meet with Toren. We rendezvous in the foyer outside his therapist's office. I'd wondered what he'd look like and how he'd be dressed. But when I see him, there is only the essence of my big strapping son. We hug one another as if we haven't seen each other for a year—which is about true. Suddenly, just embracing Toren is the most joy I can imagine. It doesn't seem possible that I'm kissing an addict, someone who would go through extreme pain and deception to get his drug of choice. I realize how much I love him and how much I desire for him to live a productive and healthy life. The hugs are meant to enfold and protect him. But he's too full-grown. I know that Toren must do this for himself.

Another couple waits in the foyer as well, chatting with their loved one. They must be astounded by how happy I am. No one should be so joyful when greeting an addict. But I am. Toren's hair is damp and he explains that he'd just jumped out of the shower after playing touch football with a bunch of guys. Outdoors, a dusky autumn mist rises across the sweeping lawns. The peace I feel, the knowledge I've gained today, and finally seeing my son in his new soberness thrills me. Toren hangs on me and lets me know that he's happy, he's alive and fighting, alert, and looking for something better in his life. It's the exact moment I've been yearning for.

Toren and I spend over an hour with his therapist. Then we go to dinner at the cafeteria, where we sit as long as possible and try to catch up on a year's worth of changes. The last time I saw him, he was walking away from us at the security gates of the airport, heading to his assignment in the Peace Corps, neither of us dreaming our next meeting would be in a therapist's office at a rehab center for alcoholism. We separate that evening, knowing we will meet tomorrow with the entire family. Toren tells me how nervous he is to finally see his brothers.

When I return to the hotel that evening, I prepare the arriving family members for our seminar over the next two days. We watch an excellent documentary called *The Hijacked Brain* about alcohol addiction, and discuss a packet of handouts I had collected that day. Together we compare our feelings about what has happened and mentally ready ourselves to meet Toren. We eat pizza and vegetables in our hotel room as we go over the materials. No one asks for a beer.

Our family's now due for a big vaccination. We know we need it and that it's good for us, but we don't know if we want to go there. I realize how anxious I am when I turn into the parking lot the next morning. It's the same general location where I'd parked the day before. I should recognize where I am. But it's a different stall. I feel disoriented. "Where's the meeting being held?" my husband asks me.

"Over there," I tell him. Then I look at the agenda. "No, I mean, I think it's over *there*, in that bigger building." I point to the other side of the road and everyone looks the opposite direction.

"What do you mean? Don't you know?" Don questions me. "Weren't you here yesterday?" Our sons sit quietly in the backseat, like they did in grade school when their parents argued . . . waiting to see who would give in, what would happen. Uncomfortable.

Meetings the prior day had been in various locations throughout the campus. We'd climbed up and down the hill and been transported hither and thither in the official van. By now I don't know for sure where I should be at the moment. "Give me a break!" I look out the car windows hoping I will see something—a facade, a bush, a revealing sign—something to indicate where the hell we should be getting educated. I suddenly begin crying, holding my head in my hands above the steering wheel.

"Get ahold of yourself, Chris," my husband orders.

And I realize what a basket case I am. The saving moment occurs when I glimpse a participant from the prior day entering a building. "Over there!" I holler, thrilled to again be in control. But my sons are looking at me in dismay from the backseat. They hadn't realized how bad off I was. Now they know. I'm barely hanging together. (Weeks later I e-mail the brothers to tell them that I'm now able to enter a parking lot and find my destination without having a nervous breakdown.)

When I'd first heard about Toren's alcoholism I was both horrified and relieved. Now we're here to "fix" it, and I know realistically that this weekend won't be enough. The reason I know this is because Toren himself said, "There's not a single answer to this problem. That's what you're in rehab for, to find your own solution, one that works for you. You figure it out for yourself and get to work on it. No distractions allowed."

That's what our family has arranged for and what we're going to get. No distractions allowed. As the weekend unfolds, we spend hours with Toren and a few selected families, learning about how we will go through this together, about addiction and its impact on the family. Our boys express their love, looking at Toren as someone who is trapped but kicking. And I see them dig in their heels to join up. Tears flow like a sprinkling fountain as we individually meet the disease and agree to do battle.

We hate the disease and detest what it has done to our family. But in its face, we unite so that it will not rob us of our joie de vivre. We stand up to it to declare that this disease will not destroy us. Our once "perfect" family is now a somewhat humbler family learning about alcoholism. We admit we've been jerked around by our own shortsightedness. And at the same time, we may thank this destructive disease for allowing us to come together, to wake up to a progression of behaviors that could destroy any one of us. Together we talk with Toren to create a plan for all of us, one that allows his success and encourages our involvement. Each of us states how we will support Toren, how we will communicate with him, and how we plan to contact one another if any of us has a concern about Toren's well-being. This agreement forces us to confront our own part of the equation, perhaps our enabling or codependency issues. We writhe as we think of what we need to do for our own lives.

On Saturday evening, Toren has a required activity at the rehab center, so we part and the four of us head out to a steakhouse for dinner. Another dagger hits home when I realize we are dining on red meat (in the type of place that serves those exploding batter-fried onions) and we're *not* drinking alcohol. Our sons are in their mid-twenties, and if it had been a normal dinner out on a Saturday night, we would've probably ordered a beer or a glass of wine.

As we sip our lemonades and Cokes during the meal, we can't help but go over all that has transformed us. We laugh; we talk about the boys' lives. They're in transitional phases and we seldom have the luxury of meeting together without other people or intrusions. The evening takes on a philosophical bent with a dash of science when we discuss the rehab program from the health care perspective. Critiques are made in good spirit. We realize that there are those who question the spiritual nature of the twelve-step program, its definition of addiction as an incurable disease, and the long-term dependence on the program.[5]

Certainly, other approaches to the treatment of alcoholism exist. There is more than one choice for an active, diligent recovery, and some programs may be well suited to one person but not to another. Presently more than 93 percent of U.S. treatment centers utilize the AA approach.[6] Toren has selected a regime oriented to the Twelve Steps, and we are here to encourage him and to stand with him. We're on a learning curve, and even with our own questions, we honor all that we've experienced and heard because we wish for Toren's healing and growth. And we love him.

By the end of the weekend on Sunday afternoon, we've met some of Toren's new friends, his favorite priest, his therapist, and countless others who help us map our journey as a recovering family. This baptism into alcoholism has transformed our family dynamics, as Toren had predicted. Now we are armed with better knowledge about alcohol addiction; we have taken the opportunity to ask Toren about his disease; we have told Toren how the disease has affected us; we have worked out specific strategies to help Toren within our family; we have promised to support one another and Toren in his recovery.

At our final lunch with Toren, we find out even more about his deterioration over the past two years. He talks to us earnestly about events in Paraguay, the realization of his alcoholism. He answers our questions, saying, "I didn't want anyone to know what I was going through." He had managed to hide his addiction from all of us. There are so many more questions we want to ask Toren. The whole sudden immersion of our family into this world of alcoholism seems both preposterous and calming at once. But our time is running short. We will have to hold our questions until our next meeting, whenever that will be.

For spontaneous recreation, the brothers have a few moments to elbow one another and chase around the parking lot (as they have always done in every existing parking lot for no particular reason). It convinces me that things could get back to "normal."

Then we say good-bye. Toren has nine more days of rehab to complete, and we must return to our lives in other parts of the country. Our farewell hugs are strong and fortifying. We know that all of us have changed. Visiting hours have ended.

# TWENTY-TWO
## SHATTERING MY WILL

**[TOREN]** *All in all, I was in rehab for thirty-three days. Be-*fore checking out of my D.C. hotel and checking into rehab, my assessment counselor, Carl, had told me that I probably wouldn't get to return to service. I said okay, I guess, but had asked that they please keep an open mind to the idea and not fully close the door on it, because I knew that I'd be able to handle going back. Carl had said that after my time was up in rehab, I might not feel ready to return to South America. Sure, whatever.

The staff in rehab stressed that they were trying to squeeze a year's worth of education and information into one month's time through lectures, seminars, one-on-one and group therapy, and other activities. With a big cheesy smile, a counselor always repeated the same thing to us, "Oh, no, don't worry, people, there's only one thing we plan to change about you here, and that one thing is everything." Ha, ha. Good luck.

Eventually, toward the end of my stay in rehab, I was able to say, "Hi, my name is Toren, and I'm an alcoholic." I began to realize what it all meant. I had to take apart and undo much of my thinking, reexamine my attitudes, and confront things that had always seemed normal to me in my social settings. Some attitudes conducive to my drinking no longer worked for me. I had to learn that alcoholism was not only a disease, but that I had it. I wrote this passage in my journal early on, but didn't really believe it until weeks later:

> *These (older) patients here are not acting. They are fighting every day and they were **YOU** once. You need to listen to them. You are here for a reason and **HAVE** time to choose your path. **THIS** will destroy you if you don't believe that you could be them and that you have this. This **DISEASE** will ruin you and take everything you love and that loves you. Listen and be glad.*

My circumstances seemed so much better than many other people's. I was still young, had less physical and emotional damage, and I had no pending legal issues by comparison. More importantly, I had escaped without devastating a family or any person I loved and had not killed anyone or myself. It is hard when you are good at looking past and minimizing your own issues, especially when you are living in rehab, where almost everyone seems more screwed up than you.

In that case, the forever-kicking disease in me says that I'm not so bad. I am okay and this is all an overreaction. *That* hasn't happened to me (yet). It is easy to see all the fun I had and listen to other people's stories and start to tell myself that I'm really all right and I certainly haven't hit bottom. Somewhere in the *Big Book* (the AA book), a writer says, "You hit bottom when you stop digging."

If I am anything like other alcoholics—and I am—my path is leading to the same place most untreated alcoholics end up: jails, institutions, or the grave. I had the opportunity to be what they call here in the world of recovery a high-bottom drunk (which means that rock bottom was higher for me than for some). What I was quickly made aware of by my counselor is that, in my mind, I tended to glorify drinking and completely minimize how serious it had become for me. It has always been part of my nature to shrug off the bad, find the good, and move on. I was told that in this case I needed to focus on what was going wrong for me in the last few years, and to examine the trail of legal and behavioral problems I had left behind. Ooohh, yeeeahh, that.

To me, the good times easily outnumbered the bad tenfold. But scattered problems consistently checkered my past. Unlike an athlete or performer who may easily see and remember past mistakes, my alcoholism enabled me to recognize only the pleasure. I completely erased all the unpleasant consequences as soon as possible, whereas someone normal may have quit or been scared straight.

Part of alcohol addiction is the insanity surrounding the disease, shared by the alcoholic and the family or loved ones around them. There is an irrational conviction that things are going to get better, change, or that the problem will go away. And after doing the same thing over and over again—drinking—I was consistently getting a similar result... things were simply worsening. What had been tolerable in the beginning started to add up and eat away at me. Lying in bed at night sweating or twitching and fearing seizures eventually broke down my stubborn alcoholic defenses. I knew I was screwed up, but it took a lot for me to believe it, to want to confront it, and to go to anyone about it. (Asking for help is for sissies, right?) But I had lost control.

One of the biggest parts of the process, and a foundation of the Twelve Steps, is admitting powerlessness. If I can't accept that I am powerless, there is a good chance that I will have to go another round or two with whatever was kicking my ass all the way to rehab.

Powerlessness was a tough one for me, like most alcoholics, who think they are in control and delude themselves into believing it through distorted perceptions and sick thinking. I had to come to terms with the fact that once I started drinking, I was exercising less and less control every time I drank and was beginning to behave just like any normal addict in pursuit of his substance. It was terrible. *Not me*.

During one of our evening meetings in rehab, we were asked to share our thoughts and feelings on powerlessness and how it relates to our use and recovery. Suddenly it occurred to me that I had the perfect little anecdote to share about my powerlessness.

I told the group how my will had been completely shattered through my last days of drinking at the All-Volunteer Conference in Paraguay, and how I had become aware of it as it was happening. I went from thinking I would just drink a little the first night, to blacking out the second night, and then later on in the week having to scurry to the store midway through lectures to get liquor in order to prevent detox. I had become totally powerless and was beginning to realize it for the first time.

My aforementioned encounter with the horse and buggy seems to perfectly capture the progression of my addiction and loss of control. But there's more to it than I previously described. Here's what really went on:

On my way to the liquor store, walking through the upscale residential area (when I should have been attending the project workshop), the horse and buggy I came across was actually unattended. I thought, *What would I do if I were me?* I decided I would not impulsively jump in, that I'd wait to see if the buggy remained there when I returned. How rational and responsible. Then I purchased my liquor so I could fix my problem.

As I approached the still-unattended rig for the second time, yet to open my high-octane beverage, I concluded that this *was* the kind of thing I would do. And besides, I was down in South America to experience new things, and this opportunity presented a crazy chance to live in the moment and go for it. *¡Viva Paraguay!*

I gave an innocent look around and saw no one. Trying to act as normal as possible, I climbed into the square wooden cartlike vehicle. There were two black horses attached to the reins I now held. I lit up, trying to hide my smile, and the adrenaline rushed in.

What the hell was I doing? I gave them a whip and a feeble, "Heeyaah." Nothing happened.

This time with some excitement, "HeeeyaaaAAAAHHH!!!" Again, there was no response.

I stood up, laughing at myself, wondering what I had to do to get these bastards to get a move on. I gave 'em a good tug, followed by a whip and an assertive, *"Jaha!!"* (Let's go!) and we jerked forward.

We were finally moving and I was elated. I passed a pedestrian on the fairly wide neighborhood road, smiling, trying to cover up any signs of mischief that may have been showing on my face. Cracking the whip two more times, I moved our trot up to a more satisfying pace. We proceeded along pretty well, when suddenly we veered left at a forty-five-degree angle onto another street. This hadn't been my command. We were now headed in a new direction, one that wouldn't get me any closer to where I wanted to go—our volunteer workshop.

Since there was no one around, I gave another crack of the whip and a shout like I knew what I was doing. I was good! After the initial excitement wore off, I thought about slowing down. On the left an oncoming car passed me, and I began thinking that I should end my joyride. I tried to get the horses to decelerate with a few inventive pulls and jerks, like I'd learned riding horseback, but they ignored my commands and only seemed to speed up. We continued to race pretty fast. I pondered a Hollywood bailout over the side, then reconsidered.

Up a block, I noticed a parked car that seemed to be zipping toward us. I tried again to slow the horses, to steer, but we were hauling ass and they had their own agenda. If the horses were trying to dash away from me, it wasn't going to work, because they were pulling me right along behind them. I started getting freaked out. *Oh shit, oh shit*, I thought, *these guys have to know what they're doing*. I sure didn't. The parked car sped directly at us, and we were aligned to clip its whole left side. It now occurred to me that these horses weren't worried about me, the cart, or anything. They seemed to be sprinting out of fright. Whoops. *No way, no way, no way in hell! This isn't happening!* ran through my mind.

I wanted to jump out, freeze the situation, or start the ride over. But it was way too late and certainly out of my hands. Suddenly, we nailed the car. We hit the left front part of the bumper, scraping along its side. My weather-beaten cart slowed down just enough for me to leap out. Then the crazed horses madly thundered on down the street with the cart rumbling behind, leaving me with my disaster in complete disbelief. Incredibly, there was still no one around. Petrified and shocked, I felt damn stupid. Guilty.

What the hell was that? The problem I'd caused was overwhelming, and I was at a loss how to fix it. So, like any good foreign ambassador of the U.S. government, I took off to avoid blame. Thank goodness, in the end, everything was okay. For me.

This potentially exhilarating escapade quickly turned horrifying. But experiencing this humiliation still wasn't enough to stop me from drinking. In fact, it was even more reason to drink: to calm the old nerves and reflect on what a crazy mishap I had just created.

With further reflection, this significant moment embodied a lot of my experience with alcohol. It had started with curiosity, experimentation, and a bad decision or two, then moved to excitement and adventure, which progressed into an episode of problems, consequences, and eventual loss of direction and control.

Overall, I tried as hard as I could to regain control of my drinking and my life while I was living out in the Paraguayan countryside. As my little wagon ride shows, some of my screws were good and loose by the end. I was not all the way there. But even before that, I was a walking, living example of powerlessness when it came to alcohol—I just didn't realize it. I really tried to not drink, but as I got immersed in my community, my guard slowly came down. In hindsight this was the very same guard that dropped when I was with new faces on Semester at Sea, new volunteers during training, and finally among strangers in my new community. It was always easy at the start to conceal my drinking tendencies. But what I consistently failed to realize was that they were always there waiting for me to get comfortable, or to convince myself that there was no problem, or to simply give in to that basic desire to go out and have a good time. My drinking slowly emerged when my comfort zone and my new environment began to mesh into one, and from there it could begin to progress again.

But this time, in Paraguay, I was trying to fight it. Rather than being on a mission to party, I realized that I was in a position of responsibility. I had made up my mind to be a good influence on the young people in my community. And I had finally even given up cigarettes before entering the Peace Corps, and felt very good about not smoking around the village families or kids, although I wanted to sometimes. There was a part of me that wished to finally grow up and be an exemplary member of my community.

I got to know the families, and also a lot of the youth and young adults in my community. And for the same reasons that I drank with my volunteer friends, sometimes I ended up drinking at my site. I wanted to be social, but I felt like I was being torn in two directions. As much as I tried, I could not constantly chain up the alcoholic inside me. Although I stayed sober most of the time, there were a few questionable times that I can think of where things didn't quite turn out the way I wanted.

One of those nights, in particular, I was "coaxed" into going to a fiesta in a neighboring community. In other words, the part of me that wanted to not drink and be responsible lost out to the part of me that wanted to have some fun. That latter part also liked me to think that I could handle my drinking. The party turned out to have a Paraguayan polka band that played before the usual activities started. The typical rural Paraguayan party has music, drinking, dancing, bingo, a raffle, and more drinking. The rules for dancing are simple and very old-fashioned: girls dance in one line and opposite them in a parallel line are the guys who have asked them to dance. Foreshadowing: Intense eye contact is not made unless there are other intentions or some romantic interest—or you're a drunken Peace Corps volunteer.

My friend Lucio and I got to the party and shared a cheap bottle of *caña* with two girls he had introduced me to. We watched the band play, continued drinking, and I began to feel more and more comfortable. Toward the end of the party (as I remember it anyway), I was dancing with one of the girls and all cultural discretion had gone out the window.

By the end of the night I found myself lip-locked with this girl and completely oblivious to the fact that maybe it wasn't the smartest way to be carrying myself. Somehow, my judgment seemed to be a little off. The next morning, with a pulsing headache, I sought out Lucio, who, with admiration and excitement, gave me every last detail of the drunken romance. It ended up not being such a big deal. The girl's name was Anita and she lived in the next village over. In some ways I knew that I should not pursue the relationship, but part of me was a bit lonely and just plain interested in the chase. Unfortunately, along with my drinking, the saga progressed.

A month later, a weeklong fair came to San Juan Bautista, a larger town some three kilometers away. Of course I accompanied Lucio and some other friends out for a few of the nights. I saw Anita on the second night. We talked and seemed to hit it off again. On the last night of the fair, my partying grew wilder. Lucio and I shared drinks on the bicycle ride to town. The one thing I do know is that a bunch of us ended up at the plaza, drinking and hanging out.

This was the third time I had been out drinking that week. My comfort level was a lot higher. My alco-switch had been flipped and my consumption became more out of control. I think a part of me had felt caged up being in training and living with families, and that I was ready to let loose. I remember sitting at a table with Lucio, Anita, and a couple of other familiar faces, while we passed around a bucket filled with wine. I had a great time and recall having a mean buzz on. It was one of those euphoric buzzes that told me I was in the company of great friends and all was good. I felt ecstatic. You would think by then I would have recognized this as a warning sign. It only goes downhill or fades out from there . . . but to me it only meant "keep drinking." One of the last things I remember is seeing my reflection in the surface of the wine as I tipped my head back and chugged from the bucket. I'm not sure who I was trying to impress, but it didn't pay off in the morning.

A sharper, pulsing headache awoke me this time, and there was a lot more confusion. I could sense that I had a serious blackout on my hands. When I sat up, I noticed my whole body was sore. I had cuts on my hands, bruises all over, and felt like I had been in a car wreck. If it weren't for Lucio, I wouldn't have had any clue what had happened. He told me that we'd had to leave the table sometime later that night because I had argued and actually started shit with one of the guys whom Anita used to date. I almost didn't believe him, but why would he lie? Anita confirmed for me later that I had acted completely *loco*. Apparently all the scrapes and bruises came from futile attempts to ride my bike home. Laughing, Lucio told me I couldn't do it for the life of me and that I was *super borracho* (drunk). He had walked me all the way back home that night.

Like so many times before, my drinking had spun way out of control and I had not seen it coming. Not once had I planned on getting that drunk. I did not decide to lose control. I couldn't drink normally. Consequently my alcoholism converted me into a drunkard who would rather chase girls, start fights, and act with general disregard for the exact life I was trying to create for myself and others. It was like two battling personalities. I was pretty shocked to see how fast I was on my way to being more of a town drunk than a volunteer. The harder I resisted drinking, the easier it was to lose control once I started. Powerless.

In rehab, I was able to learn and eventually start to accept the ugliness of the disease of alcoholism and how it began to take shape for me. It seems like the progression of my drinking had some sort of yo-yo effect. For a few months here and there, due to certain environmental factors, forces, or changes, I could control my drinking. But it never lasted long . . . soon enough I would get comfortable and the tight leash would let out more and more slack. I suppose this cycle could continue on throughout my life. All I have to do is continue trying to drink socially.

# TWENTY-THREE
## WHAT TO TELL GRANDMA

**[CHRIS]** *October 2003. They come around in the most* innocent way and ask a question that knocks you flat. "How's Toren doing in Paraguay?" or "What've you heard from Toren lately?" You can't escape friends and family.

It's hard not to be honest. We remind Toren during his rehab program that people are constantly inquiring about him and we don't know what to say when they ask. It's been three weeks now that we've been avoiding their questions.

And then, at the Family Education weekend, Toren says to us, "Go ahead, tell 'em. Tell anyone. I want everyone to know." It's a relief to hear that. Now I can inform the people who care. Now we can get the support we need. Now I can be honest.

Toren wants to phone his closest friends upon his release from rehab. All the family agrees to wait until he's had a chance to do this before we contact any of them. Alcoholism is not a secret. All those around must know, especially if they are to support the alcoholic's recovery.

I am able to tell my best friends about Toren as soon as I return home from the Family Education Program. These confidantes are women who have stood by my side throughout the years, who harbor my hopes and fears, who have cried and laughed with me. I practice the story in my mind. Then I invite two of them to my home, pour tea and coffee, and make a fire. We sit down and they know I am about to explode with some sort of terrible news. They've watched me avoid my life for the past three weeks, lose weight, not return their phone calls, and they know I recently disappeared for an entire weekend for no reason. Once again I mentally rehearse how I will begin. Then I burst into tears when I tell them—finally.

It has been too long keeping this angst to myself. They listen, then, surprisingly, express their happiness that Toren has come forward on his own, that he has decided to take care of this for himself. The judgment I'd feared is absent. In its place is empathy and understanding. As I begin to learn, almost everyone has an alcoholic in their family, and countless people have endured the dysfunction of this disease. My friends line up beside me to fortify our family; they write letters to Toren expressing confidence in his recovery. I feel a burden has been lifted. During the following week, I spend time contacting several of our closest friends, especially those who have supported Toren through the years.

Each time I see someone in the community, I wonder if I should explain what we have faced recently. When they ask about Toren, I have to decide if they are ready to hear about him and whether they really care. Some of them are mothers of his classmates. Knowing what I do now, I think, *Whose kid is next?*

Don works each day with numerous nurses and surgeons in the operating room. Conversations about their children and what they're doing are common, especially when a case drags on for hours. There are some medical personnel whom Don feels comfortable telling about Toren. But on the periphery, there are those who are asking about his family in the same way one would say, "How're you today?" Don decides to tell only his closest associates. With each disclosure, he is comforted by those who have faced similar obstacles, and by those who fear potential problems with their own adolescents.

Family Education at the rehab center gives us realistic hope for Toren's future and a spot for friends and family in his recovery. But it also

offers a terse warning about relapse.[1] We are told that relapse rates for addictive diseases range from 50 percent (for resumption of heavy use) to 90
percent (for a brief relapse). "Relapse should not be viewed as a failure; it
is part of a learning process that eventually leads to recovery," writes Susan Gordon of the Caron Foundation.[2] I realize that it's important to let
our extended family know about Toren as soon as possible so that they
can aid him in being honest about himself and his goals. There remain
grandparents and aunts and uncles to be informed. These visits and phone
calls seem even more ominous to me than meeting with our friends. I
steel myself to make the plunge.

At the same time as I prepare to contact our family members, newly
humbled Rush Limbaugh has just returned to his radio show after five
weeks of rehab for addiction to painkillers. "This is not something someone can do alone," he admits in *USA Today*.[3] Limbaugh has twenty million fans (and perhaps a grandma) to support him, even though he has
previously blasted drug abuse, saying users should be jailed.

Even though approximately 53 percent of men and women in the
United States report that one or more of their close relatives has a drinking problem, Toren could face strict judgment from those individuals
who march the moral high road.[4] These are often people who see only
one path for spiritual belief and maintain that Toren (and all of our family) could better solve problems by joining their particular faith. When
measured by their standards, of course we fall short. Don and I and our
boys have talked together about how we will deal with this. We feel our
hearts flutter and our stomach acids boil as we anticipate approaching
these relatives. But they are family. We know they love us and we want to
respect their versions of spirituality.

I begin with Grandma. Here I am, approaching a family of virgin
drinkers; there has never been a known alcoholic in this family tree.
We're testing the first branch. To ease into it, I play a game of racquetball
with my father, and then take him and my mother to lunch. At this time,
I tell them what has happened: how Toren is now back in the country;
how he committed himself to a rehab program; how our family attended

## Attitudes & Alcoholism[5]

Seventy-four percent of the general public acknowledge that alcoholism impacts the daily lives of Americans.

More than two out of five Americans say they have encouraged a loved one to seek help for an alcohol problem.

Yet, stigma persists, with 63 percent of Americans believing alcoholism is a moral weakness versus a disease (34 percent).

"Alcoholism is a chronic disease that is influenced both by a person's genes and by his or her behavior. Despite years of scientific evidence, misperceptions persist about alcoholism that can impede people from seeking treatment."
—General Arthur T. Dean, CADCA
Community Anti-Drug Coalitions of America

### Did you know that . . .

- Nearly 19 million Americans, or 8 percent of the U.S. population, need treatment for an "alcohol problem," but only 2.4 million have been diagnosed with the disease.
- One in four children lives with a parent who is dependent on, or abuses, alcohol.
- Harmful and hazardous drinking is involved in about one-third of suicides, one-half of homicides, and one-third of child abuse cases.
- Consuming at least four alcoholic beverages a day significantly increases the risk of developing any type of cancer.
- Alcohol abuse and dependence costs the United States $185 billion in direct and indirect social costs per year, with more than 70 percent of the cost attributed to lost productivity.

the Family Education Program; and how proud we are of Toren's courage and fortitude. I talk about the disease of alcoholism, give them the Jellinek Curve and some articles about the brain and the effects of dopamine and addiction. I explain to them ways they can support our family. Both grandparents seem understanding, though crushed. They are so shocked that they don't react much. But I fear there will be *those* comments.

The next day I receive a call from one son saying he just talked with Grandma, who asked him why he and his brothers drink while his girl cousins don't. She also remarked that had Toren been reading his Bible, he could have saved himself. Our son is upset and doesn't want to tell Grandma she has insulted our family. He wants our family to be unified, but I hear the discouragement in his voice.

The next day, I print out a large index card for my parents and leave it on their kitchen counter beside the phone. I hope that seeing the written words will reinforce some of the ideas we had talked about the previous day.

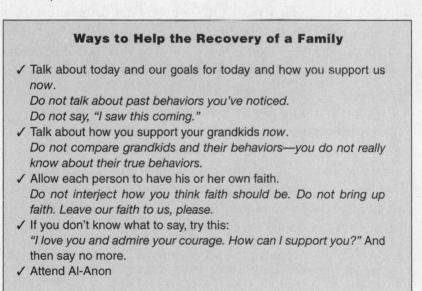

### Ways to Help the Recovery of a Family

✓ Talk about today and our goals for today and how you support us *now*.
Do not talk about past behaviors you've noticed.
Do not say, "I saw this coming."
✓ Talk about how you support your grandkids *now*.
Do not compare grandkids and their behaviors—you do not really know about their true behaviors.
✓ Allow each person to have his or her own faith.
Do not interject how you think faith should be. Do not bring up faith. Leave our faith to us, please.
✓ If you don't know what to say, try this:
"I love you and admire your courage. How can I support you?" And then say no more.
✓ Attend Al-Anon

After leaving the prompts for Grandma, things go better. My father confides to me several weeks later how proud he is of the way Don and I are handling it all. Both of my parents attend Al-Anon with me. We begin our recovery as a stumbling bunch of neophytes.

And then the aunts and uncles in our family step up. One uncle, a minister and college professor, volunteers to meet Toren at his rehab graduation and drive him back to Washington, D.C., for his exit interview. Other family members clamor to visit him, but it is impossible because they live too far away and his rehab is almost completed. I spend hours talking with each relative about the things we've learned and our family's commitment to face our disease. It's a relief to confess what we've discovered, to realize that people will accept us. Toren calls me after we arrive back home from our weekend education and comments, "I've received a lot of mail and cards. I must be really popular or really sick."

The truth is, religion or no religion, our family came through in a big way. The relatives were helpful and loving and supported us beyond our wildest hopes. Our fears of judgment were, for the most part, unfounded. Perhaps this, too, is a lesson that Toren instigated in our family. It forced us to let down some of our spiritual barriers, to realize that no matter what a person believes we are all in this together, and that the family rallies around when a member is in need.

The first step of the Twelve Steps is admitting our powerlessness over alcohol—that our lives had become unmanageable. I realize that this Step not only applies to Toren, but to our family. By letting go of the control, I am learning the language of recovery. I see how it covers various aspects of my life, not just the specific disease of alcoholism. When I am able to give up controlling the image of my family and be truthful about our challenge, I become empowered by the support of my friends and family who move toward us.

We talk with Toren's brothers about a new way of socializing in our family. Without alcohol. One brother says, "Our brother's not different to us. We will still throw the football around and goof off. We've gone most of our lives without alcohol and it won't change for us. If someone else can't do that, then they don't have to be with us." I smile and realize that, after all, we weren't constantly guzzling alcohol in the household. It

---

### Let Go[6]

This is a helpful set of ideas to review whenever we feel pressure to change someone or manipulate something outside our power. In place of fixing, blaming, or forcing, we may offer compassion, wisdom, and understanding to our loved one by letting go.

✓ To let go does not mean to stop caring, it means I can't do it for someone else.
✓ To let go is not to cut myself off, it's the realization I can't control another.
✓ To let go is not to enable, but to allow learning from natural consequences.
✓ To let go is to admit powerlessness, which means the outcome is not in my hands.
✓ To let go is not to try to change or blame another, it's to make the most of myself.
✓ To let go is not to care for, but to care about.
✓ To let go is not to fix, but to be supportive.
✓ To let go is not to judge, but to allow another to be a human being.
✓ To let go is not to be in the middle arranging all the outcomes, but to allow others to affect their own destinies.
✓ To let go is not to be protective, it's to permit another to face reality.
✓ To let go is not to deny, but to accept.
✓ To let go is not to nag, scold, or argue, but instead to search out my own shortcomings and to correct them.
✓ To let go is not to adjust everything to my desires, but to take each day as it comes, and to cherish myself in it.
✓ To let go is not to criticize and regulate anybody, but to try to become what I dream I can be.
✓ To let go is not to regret the past, but to grow and live for the future.
✓ To let go is to fear less and to love more.

---

seems that the last few weeks it was all I could think about. As if it were served at every meal. It wasn't.

While our own family seems comfortable with the concessions of alcoholism, the brothers' level of socializing with buddies will be a greater adjustment. They admit that they've relied on alcohol to fuel their fun when they're among friends. One brother says, "I have no problem with not drinking. But it'll be weird with our friends because we've done it for so many years. And we have the same friends." The boys are now thinking about this. When the time comes, when one day Toren returns home, then they can discuss it and deal with it. For now, I see the value of a halfway situation. It will allow Toren time to develop social tools so he can navigate outside his safety zone.

Don and I laugh as we realize we've now gone forty days and forty nights without drinking! If Grandma knew, she would fall to her artificial knees in gratitude. It seems like our family's getting smarter about alcoholism. Toren has offered us this chance, even when we wanted to push it away. With this, I understand that wisdom is what you know when it's already too late.

# TWENTY-FOUR
## PICKING MY POISON

 ***October 30, 2003. I completed my rehab. Every-***thing's cool, right? Now send me back to South America. I still have unfinished business and a lot of work to do. But unfortunately, I may have more work to do here than in South America.

Whether I could return to service and complete it successfully with what I now know is unimportant. It is obvious that I should not go back right now. I learned that I need to stop making all of the decisions and be open to suggestion, be willing to ask for help and stay close to the program.

Still living in a halfway house doesn't exactly sound great. I've gone from living on my own in South America to living under strict supervision. Hey, after a month, my curfew gets extended an hour later! I can already taste the freedom.

But I know the biggest thing I need to do is come to terms with my disease. This means consistently accepting it and understanding what it means to say that I am powerless over alcohol. I was a pretty firm believer that I wasn't addicted to alcohol and that I had control over it. But that was just what I wanted to believe. Anything else was too painful. My delusions protected me from the truth.

Now I am learning about alcoholism. I have learned that I am an alcoholic. This means that when I start drinking, it becomes increasingly difficult to stop or control the amount of drinks I put into myself. To anyone, this should sound just like a heroin addict, right? Always at risk of overdosing. It is. Once clean, no one tells a heroin addict or a cokehead to just shoot up with moderation, on weekends, or after work. Or to just do one or two lines. No one tells a former chain-smoker, after having quit for a year, to have a social smoke on occasion. Alcohol isn't any different for the alcoholic.

The concept of alcohol being as dangerously addictive to an alcoholic as heroin is to a heroin addict isn't often voiced, partially because business booms around alcohol. Society condones its legal use. Alcohol is still a drug, and some people don't process it normally. Just like with heroin, the tolerance level rises. Addicts do more and more heroin because they physically need it and they will do anything to get it. In the end, they lose control. With alcohol it tends to be a slower progression. Because this process happened pretty fast for me, I discovered I was an alcoholic fairly early. It isn't always noticed by age twenty-three.

If one isn't an alcoholic, there is no reason to say, "Okay, self, I'm only going to have three drinks this time." Normal people don't sit around and think up plans for how much they are not going to drink every night. They do whatever feels right and it doesn't progressively go downhill. If you think you have a problem with drinking, you probably do. According to most alcoholics, drinking problems don't get better or go away.

There are lots of misunderstandings about twelve-step programs, and that is fine, because if you don't understand them or haven't found yourself in a position to be exposed to them, congratulations, you may never need them. The thing that struck me most about the twelve-step program was that it's really just a simple plan for living. You may hear about people who are constantly working the Steps or following a tight program, or you may not. Again, congratulations.

## The Twelve Steps of Alcoholics Anonymous[1]

1. We admitted we were powerless over alcohol—that our lives had become unmanageable.
2. Came to believe that a Power greater than ourselves could restore us to sanity.
3. Made a decision to turn our will and our lives over to the care of God as we understood Him.
4. Made a searching and fearless moral inventory of ourselves.
5. Admitted to God, to ourselves and to another human being the exact nature of our wrongs.
6. Were entirely ready to have God remove all these defects of character.
7. Humbly asked Him to remove our shortcomings.
8. Made a list of all persons we had harmed, and became willing to make amends to them all.
9. Made direct amends to such people wherever possible, except when to do so would injure them or others.
10. Continued to take personal inventory, and when we were wrong promptly admitted it.
11. Sought through prayer and meditation to improve our conscious contact with God as we understood Him, praying only for knowledge of His will for us and the power to carry that out.
12. Having had a spiritual awakening as the result of these steps, we tried to carry this message to alcoholics, and to practice these principles in all our affairs.

Surely there are other ways of getting and staying sober, and the Twelve Steps may not work for everyone. For most alcoholics and addicts, though, continuous sobriety and full recovery does not come easily. The principles and lifestyle that the Twelve Steps suggest seem to be the most effective and most universal. I have spoken with a lot of people who are skeptical about the program's effectiveness. The bottom line is, alcoholics in general do not stay sober very well. The program cannot have guarantees. It is in the hands of the individual. Sobriety works for people who want it. The Twelve Steps is just a plan to achieve it.

Many have heard people say (between drunken sips of beer), "I went to rehab and it didn't work at all." Well, some of these people may have also had several car crashes and DUIs, and those don't seem to be working, either. Most treatment centers will work if people are willing to put forth effort. Everyone reaches their own bottom differently, and a lot of people don't view their own consequences as a big enough reason to change, or they simply don't want to give up their vices and sober up. We must all pick our poison. People only recover when they honestly believe they can't control their drug or alcohol use and they are an alcoholic or addict. Only then are they ready to recover.

The Twelve Steps are not a system where one graduates from one Step to the next and then moves on, never working the previous one again. The Steps require constant acknowledgment of powerlessness, acceptance, reliance on sources of help outside one's self, admittance of one's faults and correction of wrongs, as well as help of others. These aspects, constantly being worked, allow one to concentrate on oneself from the inside out, to eventually heal spiritually, and to repair damaged relationships in one's life. It is actually surprisingly in line with a lot of the fundamentals of mainstream organized religion, while focusing on staying open to individual interpretation. The Twelve Steps are relevant to any faith, and all persons are able to pray to a God of their understanding or a Higher Power to help them do what they couldn't do for themselves. It could be considered more of an all-denominational rather than a nondenominational fellowship.

I freaked out during my first days in rehab because of how many times I heard God mentioned in the Steps, in prayers, and in the program's reliance on "His" powers to take away our character defects, as well as to abolish our obsessions and compulsions to drink. Healing an addict is considered to be impossible through human power alone. I still have a hard time with this.

I have always had strong reservations about certain aspects of organized religion, to say the least, and hated feeling pressured to be something, whether it be Buddhist, Christian, Muslim, Hindu, Jewish, or, I

guess, Alcoholic. Besides, our own extended family has been divided by our religious differences. How did this Supreme Being divide our family rather than unite it? What would this same "God" do for me in recovery?

As mentioned earlier, for my Higher Power I decided to rely on my family, friends, music, and nature in all its perfection and imperfection. I figured that would cover it. Some theologians would probably say that God manifests Himself in all of those things. Well, great, then we're all happy. I learned that rather than jump right to God, I can turn to the program for help and use the people in the fellowship as a source of guidance and strength. They are a Higher Power in and of themselves. This made it a little bit easier on me. I didn't have to fake it.

One of the more influential chaplains at rehab once said that if you are searching for God, then you have already found Him. When I was speaking to one of my uncles, a minister and Bible teacher, about some of my issues and questions concerning recovery and the search for God, he asked, "Well, can you imagine what it would be like if your search *did* end, and you *did* find what you were looking for?" Whoa . . . good point. New subject.

There. I'm fixed.

I know I'm an alcoholic. I have my twelve-step program, ten thousand versions of God to choose from, and I know that as long as I don't drink I won't suffer anymore, right? Maybe. But what about all the fun everyone else is still having? Why did that same bastard Higher Power make me a drunk?

This Higher Power that is so merciful and is going to bail me out of all these crazy problems had to make me different in the first place, huh? Maybe it isn't so great after all. Saving me? Hardly. Now I'm not going to be able to do what most people do throughout their twenties and thirties, or even their whole lives: drink and socialize without problems.

I may be sobering up, but that doesn't entirely fix the problem. I know that asking for help and being honest with myself probably made things a lot easier on me. Instead of trying to be an apple among oranges, while totally suffering and trying to control my drinking, I can start to deal with this and move on.

I know that leaving South America and being in rehab was what I needed, not what I wanted. Now I'm a graduate from rehab and I get to live in a halfway house. Now I'm officially an Alcoholic. Damn. Now I'm another statistic, newly categorized, and all those wonderful stigmas can follow me and be attached to my family, as well.

Now everyone can worry about my sobriety, not my drinking. Now everyone can be self-conscious about drinking around me, joking about drinking around me, or just thinking about drinking. Now the seed has been firmly planted in my head and I can never go back and think of drinking normally again. Do I sound happy? Who cares? I'll get over it. There has to be a brighter side somewhere to suffocating my social life and not having fun anymore. Right.

I guess what is more important is that I need to comprehend that it's not the world's responsibility to understand my problem. There certainly won't be a holiday on Fridays, extending the weekend for the rest of the partiers because Toren quit drinking. I guess I have to get over myself, and maybe I should stop whining like anyone else cares.

What's that? Did someone ask what might have been done to prevent this from happening? Ban alcohol. Whoops. We already tried that. Prohibition didn't work. Ban all alcoholics from reproducing, maybe? Now that's an idea. I bet my Higher Power is smiling now. If we eliminated addicts and alcoholics, then we wouldn't even need any Higher Powers, right?

I guess what I wasn't trying to say, but mean to say, is that alcoholism is not easy to prevent. Young kids or teenagers are not apt to cooperate. They'll meet restrictions with resistance. An adult may say it's not cool to drink, but most kids know that all the cool kids are drinking. Besides, teens want to make their own choices. I sure as hell didn't want to comply, and I still have trouble taking back all my questionable decisions and defiance. They were good times that I shall no longer glorify.

It is said that the older the habit, the harder it is to break. It looks like it's tough to prevent underage drinking or treat alcoholism from any angle. I think the key to this is having the desire to stop drinking (or using drugs)—something I hope I actually have and can stay in touch with. As far as preventing it from even starting, good luck with that. People need to learn from their own experiences, and this often needs to run its course. For example, when climbing a mountain, how many would stop before reaching their intended destination if a couple of people on their way down said, "It's not worth it." People need to see it to believe it, whatever it is. Even if the view isn't so pretty. Well, I did anyway.

Looking back, it may seem obvious that I had a problem from the beginning. One of the biggest questions may be whether intervention would have been a good idea, and, if so, when? I think it should be emphasized again that most people in the early stages of addiction are in denial (at best), and usually extremely stubborn about any idea of change. Before great losses or consequences surface, the path to powerlessness is well under way. Authorities, concerned family members, or friends may recognize warning signs before the abuser admits to having a problem. If an intervention is used, the type of intervention and how it would be implemented should be carefully strategized. Some chronic drinkers may be more receptive than I would have been. Normally, the impetus for change begins further along, when the abuser is desperate for help.

It is easy to keep second-guessing the seriousness of an alcohol crisis. No one wants a real problem to exist. Each alcoholic's symptoms manifest in different ways, and some may present themselves more slowly than others. Certain alcoholics may get into trouble with the law, while others find themselves acting out and treating people completely differently while intoxicated. Others may have control issues or black out from time to time. Many alcoholics may not experience much difficulty in the beginning, which makes comparisons among addicts misleading. There is plenty of room to rationalize and redefine the idea of an alcohol problem when being forced to look closely at oneself or asked to actually change behaviors. It often becomes difficult to say who really has a problem until it is too late.

Alcoholics love to drink. No alcoholics will stop drinking just because they may have a problem someday. It doesn't make sense to a real alcoholic to drink less, and a life without alcohol is usually unimaginable. A telling sign of an alcoholic in the early to middle stages is the outward denial of a problem that persists. Alcoholics drink however they want to drink, until greater problems begin to complicate their lives even further.

The power of denial is stronger than one would think. In May of 2002, I drove up the coast of California with a good friend of mine named Ryan. We had grown up together and were both seniors in college at the time. He opened up a direct line of communication by speaking about his own drinking problems to me. But I still wasn't ready for it. I wasn't able to understand or see its relevance to me.

Ryan explained to me that he *knew* he was an alcoholic and had been bouncing in and out of Twelve Step meetings. I was kind of surprised. He told me that he *knew* he was powerless over alcohol. He could not stop drinking when he started, and he almost invariably lost control of his intoxication and, consequently, a lot of his actions. I tried to console him, without daring to mention that I felt I had my own problems with alcohol.

There I was, staring my own disease in the face. I was so unwilling to admit my own problems that I didn't even want to accept that he had a problem. *Us have a problem?* I told him he should simply limit how much he drinks. "Just don't drink so much, dude. You're all right." I didn't believe Ryan when he said he couldn't stop drinking or that he was losing control. And I sure as hell didn't want to apply any of what he said to myself. My indifference and lack of understanding came as much out of fear as it did out of self-defense. (We drank away the whole next weekend together, both electing to ignore our issues and keep the party going.)

It took me another year (and then some) to begin to understand my own problems . . . the hard way. After further research in the field of binge drinking, Ryan and I entered different rehabs the same month without contacting each other or knowing that the other had finally given up.

How many other people could be reading this and not be willing to look at their own problems with alcohol? My guess is a lot. I know I could have. Alcoholism may hide behind its numerous faces and its variety of symptoms, but these symptoms worsen and don't go away. For this same reason, both Ryan and I threw in the towel. Many others may find that the fight is not worth it anymore and that there is hope. It seems to require a different path for each person to discover an understanding of this twisted disease.

My perception of reality had slowly been altered for so long, I could endure almost anything as long as I knew I could do what I wanted. It never occurred to me until way too late that I didn't have to go through all the abuse. It is no different than any unhealthy or exploitative relationship, and perhaps is similar to someone with a serious eating disorder. We grow accustomed to it. Abnormal is normal, and unsafe becomes safe. Someone in an abusive relationship gets used to that type of treatment, stops questioning it, and even begins to think that she deserves it or that it is her own fault. Much of this was true in my case. All of my negative consequences were the result of my "choosing" to drink, and when things got even worse, I began to accept things as normal that were actually self-destructive.

I was willing to do whatever it took to continue drinking the way I wanted, both in high school and college. I knew it was extreme, but I never thought I was sick or that my behavior was inappropriate. I blended in with others who drank heavily, and that made it difficult for me to be identified as alcoholic. Punishments and threats just created more secretive behaviors and, at best, short-term compliance. Grounding me, kicking me off sports teams, taking away social privileges or my car, putting me in jail, making me pay fines—all did little or nothing to change my drinking patterns.

Intervention early in my drinking may not have ever worked because the majority of my drinking was social, in a party atmosphere, and without regret. It may have been hard to convince me that my drinking was a problem when I felt like I was in control of my life. My grades backed that up. Only when I was flung to the other side of the spectrum, where I was met with seriously adverse physical symptoms, did I even come close to considering an alternative. By that time, however, it was far too late. I had already become an alcoholic. All the red-flag behavioral issues and consequences that could ideally have been prevented were said and done.

I could have been shipped off to rehab in high school or maybe college, but it may have been too soon. In my eyes, I just wasn't ready. I most likely would not have changed my mentality. The classic "at least we tried" may have comforted some, but in the end, I had to come to terms with drinking decisions on my own. In short, I should have been intervened on the first time I even saw a can of beer. With my genetic makeup and poor aptitude for decision making, maybe I should have been enrolled in some sort of "prehab" program.

---

### Offering Support for Young Drinkers in Danger

**To assist a young person in drinking danger, parents can use subtle approaches for offering support.**

- Start education about alcoholism and addiction early.
- Maintain a consistent position on underage drinking—set firm, clear expectations.
- Be honest about your own personal history and genetics/family history.
- Keep an open dialogue about outcomes of alcoholism—use real-life examples.
- Discuss differences between binge drinking, daily drinking, and responsible drinking.
- Instead of enabling, continue to point out warning signs or red flags.
- Offer persistent emotional support—you cannot control someone else.
- Consider attending Al-Anon.
- Never give up—recovery is a process and starts before the last drink.

There are some factors that influenced my awareness of my drinking in a positive way. Many were subtle, but they finally added up. Some weighed more heavily than others as I wove my way in and out of trouble. Recovery is definitely a long process that starts well before one's last drink. The exact nature of the disease is that the alcoholic is often the last person to see the problem. As an alcoholic's drinking progresses, he or she may become more receptive, honest, or ready to listen, but it takes time. It can be difficult to know how to assist a person in drinking danger. I think one of the least effective ways to communicate an idea to an abuser is by making threats of car crashes or eventual outcomes that seem very unlikely. In my case, hearing about everyday life examples that had relevant application gave me more to think about.

For example, learning in those initial AA meetings (the ones required by my college RD) that frequent blackouts don't happen to normal drinkers and that I was at risk for alcoholism helped me first become aware of the danger signs. The people in those meetings shared their experiences with me, and whether or not I was receptive, I absorbed some of the information. Having another alcoholic tell me, "Welcome, you may very well belong here," was not what I wanted to hear, but it did register. Granted, I still drank for another four years or so, but the seeds were planted.

Some of the most useful information came to me from dialogue with my parents. My mom scolded me one time during college summer vacation when I had been out drinking, slept late, and missed work. It got one clear point across to me: "Toren, this is serious. It is not a good sign. If you are missing work and not meeting your responsibilities, then there is a problem. That is a major red flag." I shrugged it off and tried to ignore it, but those words echoed around in my swollen brain for a long time and I didn't take it lightly.

That was probably the same summer when she told me about another kid who had gone to my high school, Dustin, who had left college after experiencing alcoholic seizures. On my own I had noticed that I was starting to experience unusual hangovers, anxiety, fevers, and sleeplessness after drinking heavily. Without wanting it to apply to me, I continued to drink heavily, hoping I was not headed in that direction. But those symptoms slowly grew more frightening.

It was a combination of all these little things that overturned some of my resistance to the idea that I may be alcoholic, while acceptance and the act of getting help was a whole different category and still far off. Obviously I didn't relate to the alcoholics in AA. But I began to think about my experiences, my withdrawals, and how they only seemed to be getting worse. It definitely dawned on me why I missed work or why I wasn't performing in class after big weekends. I recalled the video of me when I was totally out of control—how I was ten times drunker than I had realized. I also remembered the scenario about the class drunk at the high school reunions. It may have been painful, but it was not difficult to connect the dots and think, *Wow, that could be me*. But denial is thick, and we will stop fighting only when we're truly ready to recover.

Knowing that alcoholism is a disease, that it is passed on through heredity, and that it is prevalent in my family helps me to understand my situation better today. More than that, knowing that alcoholism is a chronic disease that I can learn to live with makes me feel fortunate. The important aspect of this disease is that there is plenty of hope for the hopeless. All they have to do is want assistance.

It helps to know that we are powerless over other people, powerless over certain substances, and powerless over many events going on around us. We can't control everything. We don't have to. What a relief. This actually creates a freedom. Keeping this in mind, the twelve-step programs can literally save anybody from that sense of futility.

Recognizing my problem and becoming aware of its consequences has allowed me to get better. I was educated about alcohol and all the warning signs were pointed out to me. I am thankful that when the time came for me to look for other options and start to make changes in my life, I had a supportive family. They showed me love rather than pointing fingers. I owe a lot of credit to my parents, to various counselors and nurses during college, the Peace Corps in Paraguay, Washington, D.C., and to my treatment program. These people helped me whether I wanted it or not. On top of everything, the desire for change was crucial for me. As long as I am honest with myself, I am halfway there.

---

### A Personal Strategy for Surviving Rehab and Early Recovery

- Shut up.
- Stop fighting.
- Listen to people with experience (other addicts or therapists).
- Realize that "my way" wasn't working.
- Read some twelve-step literature.
- Do not be afraid to ask for help.
- Stay honest with myself.
- Remain teachable.
- Get over spiritual barriers.
- Be open and willing to do whatever is necessary to recover.
- Get with "the program."
- Find healthier cravings (V8, fruit, vegetables, peanut butter).

# TWENTY-FIVE
## WHAT PARENTS CAN DO

*Parents are the most potent—and underused—tool in
preventing substance abuse.*

—Joseph A. Califano, Jr.[1]

 **December 2003. With sobriety on the platter, I**
wonder what our next family holiday will be like. I
question how we'll set up our household to withstand
the odds of relapse and how we will survive it. Our extended family generally does not indulge in much alcohol at family gatherings. It has never been an emphasis. And besides,
keeping my son sober is not my problem. It's his. I have to let go.

"I don't think that anyone can understand powerlessness until it's way
too late," Toren comments. He says this while Don and I are visiting him
at his halfway house in Florida. He's been there about one month and
we're talking about his fall into alcoholism and how he climbed back out.
He equates it to struggling in a riptide . . . being pulled out to sea, giving
up to powerlessness, and going with the currents down the shore until
you've regained enough strength to swim back in. Then, you swim with
the rip. You quit fighting and go with it, knowing its strength. But you
don't give up. You maintain your sense of self.

Within our family, we now have the courage to talk about high-risk
drinking. It's easily discussed because the disease is with us. We acknowledge it, watch it closely. Drinking is now considered as dangerous as a
bad sunburn—a weekend souvenir that becomes a haunting cancer and
can progress to death.

Toren's brothers tell me they plan to visit Toren at his halfway house. I recall what his therapist in rehab warned about "the brothers," so I write each of them an e-mail:

Before you take your well-deserved trip with your brother to visit Toren, I wanted to send you some thoughts. I know I've mentioned this before, but I HAVE to emphasize one more time the importance of not drinking around Toren. My personal feeling is that even though he may tell you it's okay, it isn't. Here is why: He lives in a restricted, sheltered situation. Even though it has allowed him to be successful, he is tired of it. Toren has been frustrated by the kind of people he is living with, and he welcomes you cool bros so he can at last have fun and talk to someone who knows and understands him. This could cause him to let down, to think it would be okay to try a drink. He could get off course.

The reasons for not drinking in front of Toren are: IF he should decide to return to the Peace Corps (which I don't hear him talking about, but at this point, he needs all doors open), he must have been sober for three years. He must finish his halfway program successfully. He will have a drug screening after being with you guys prior to returning to the halfway house. Toren must not flunk this test. After the huge effort and disappointment he has faced in the past months, he must be successful in this halfway program. In fact, I believe he must be successful for at least one year. It is so important for his self-esteem to make it one year without messing up, and you bros can help him at this point.

It is said that a newly recovering person is extremely vulnerable. I have been talking with Toren several times a week, and he is still working through a lot of issues and just now beginning to face his future. I believe he is concerned about how he will find friendships without alcohol and wondering if he can possibly do so happily. By not drinking around Toren, you will help him see that this is possible. If you bros stay clean and demonstrate to Toren that it can easily be done, it will give him courage. You don't have to be-labor it. Just act nonchalant.

I think our whole family needs to do this at least for the first year of Toren's recovery (even though Toren will say otherwise). I know Toren will not want us obsessing over him, but truly I believe sometimes he is putting the best foot forward and giving the impression that he is strong, whereas inside he is still mourning the loss of alcohol and wishing his life were different. When a person is vulnerable this way, it is important to have those around him in a position of contented strength.

Once Toren successfully navigates outside the halfway house on his own and passes drinking decoys successfully, he will be in a better place to hang with his "drinking family." I don't know if my gut feelings are correct, and you bros may think I am overprotective, but I love you both and need to tell you how I perceive this whole thing. Blow me off if you need to, but at least I said it!

Love and hugs—
Your Mom

Even if Toren says we can drink around him, abstaining is a symbol of our awareness and support. Toren's brothers agree with this idea and call me to say that it is not the slightest problem for them. Don and I wonder if they are drinking less alcohol now that they have had the chance to become more educated about the chronic progressive symptoms of alcoholism and our family's genetic background. We don't know; they live too far away and we only see them once or twice a year. But because of what we have been through, it is easy to bring it up, easy to question not only the routine of their younger brother but all our lifestyles. Each of us is fair game now. But Toren reminds me, "What my friends and family do about their drinking is up to them. I'm busy taking care of me."

Talking about one of his friends, Toren comments, "She doesn't understand how I can't just go have one beer. She wasn't trying to talk me into anything. But I can see that she doesn't get it, that I can no longer control my drinking. I said to her, 'I *never* drank a beer just to drink a beer. You might as well give me all of it. One beer never benefited me.'" Toren goes on to say this is a great deterrent for him. He never needs to drink again, since one single beer isn't his style. "If I can remember that," he says and grins, "I'm set."

I ask him about years down the road, how he can face never having a drink. He's suddenly quiet. I see that it's overwhelming for him to contemplate.

"I can't think about the future," Toren answers. "I just think about today, that I don't need to drink today. The rest of my life is almost too much to fathom."

Toren is fragile. I see he has undergone a transition that has left him translucent. In the past, he always seemed to know everything and would announce his destination with determination (even if, in reality, he wasn't headed there). Now he's telling me that he lives for "now only." In the present. He's pliable, recovering. I remind myself to let up, to not push him. It surprises me that he seems incapable of looking ahead. He senses this and reassures me that the program emphasizes making it through each day. Otherwise, for someone that age, a whole lifetime might be too much to promise, a setup for failure.

"What do you think about the rules at your halfway house?" I ask him.

Toren smiles. "They're a safety net. I don't have to worry about messing up. There's no temptation around here."

Toren is referring to the simple regulations required by his halfway program: house rules. Staffed with an advisory/consulting board of psychotherapists and a physician, the sober living program where Toren resides requires a daily curfew, attendance at meetings and commitment to a recovery program, full-time work or school, and agreement to behavioral, language, and grooming standards. Possession or use of alcohol, drugs, mood-altering substances, or paraphernalia is prohibited. Residents must attend a weekly meeting of all occupants. The apartments support over eighty recovering addicts, all graduates of various inpatient rehab programs. Smoking is permitted only outdoors. No persons other than the residents and staff are allowed on the premises (this means no visitors or girlfriends). Two-bedroom/two-bath facilities with TV, dishwasher, swimming pool, exercise room, tennis courts, and Jacuzzi, as well as towels, kitchenware and linens, utilities and phone, are provided by the facility. Each resident shares a room with a roommate so that four persons occupy an apartment. Toren was able to move in with minimal possessions, search for a job, open a bank account, and begin his sober regime.

"I'm so happy to be functioning in a normal life," Toren says. He goes on to explain, "My first night at the halfway house, some of my roommates and I went to a meeting. Then afterward, we went into a sports bar. I never thought we'd go to a place like that. We ordered bottled waters and soft drinks, food and snacks, and watched football games while we laughed and talked." Toren smiles. "It was just like things could be, without drinking."

Toren is looking for a job, eager to be busy. He explains to me that many recovering alcoholics face discrimination and hardship when looking for work. Some people in recovery have never before held down a job successfully. Toren adds, "The attitude of the counselors at the halfway house is, if you can work without getting high or drinking, it's a miracle. I know I can." Toren faces a unique situation. He is transitioning from having lived in a foreign culture for almost a year, to then landing in a highly structured rehab environment, and finally to experiencing the relative freedom of an apartment with basic ground rules. Thankfully, holding down a job is nothing new to Toren. He figures it's a matter of time before he finds one.

Toren has lived on his own, but never without his former closest companion, alcohol. Settling on the opposite side of the country will be a fresh experience for Toren. He says he is content to find a new life; he is ready to move on from his days in South America. As an indication of this transition, Toren calls his former Paraguayan mom, Señora Francisca, in the tiny village to talk with her about his remaining possessions. They decide to raffle off his furniture, with proceeds going to the village school. He discusses with her who should get some of his most valuable items and describes what articles he wants shipped home. Toren tells her honestly about his disease and his difficulties with alcohol. Señora Francisca certainly understands, because alcoholism is a problem for people in her community as well. Toren tells me that he feels great satisfaction finally communicating with her after having departed from his village so abruptly.

"I called some of my old friends. They took it better than I thought." Toren talks about informing past high school and college buddies. "They didn't give me a hard time. I don't know if they really understand it, but at least they still want to be my friends. I don't know if I can see them for a long time, though. It's never going to be the same." He looks disappointed. When phoning Ryan, his former high school friend, Toren discovers that Ryan completed alcohol rehab as well. He suggests I talk with Ryan's mother. Toren jokes, "When we're back in town for our high school reunion, my friends and I can attend meetings together while you moms go to yours."

It takes all kinds of people to combat alcoholism. I get ahold of Ryan's mother, and, to my surprise, she divulges that Ryan's father had his own issues with alcohol. For years I'd dropped Toren off at their house, never knowing.

There is another thing on my mind as we visit Toren at his halfway program. I have read what Toren wrote, I know him in my heart, but I do not hear him talking much about remorse or regret, except that he was not able to finish his work in South America. Perhaps expressing apology isn't necessary if Toren sees that his former life didn't work and is motivated to move on. His actions will now do the talking. But if Toren insists he has no regrets, what does this say about his attitude toward other people in his life? For example, does he not regret his treatment of his high school administrators, coaches, and fellow teammates when he was expelled? Does he not regret his disrespect of the RD in college (the RD was only doing his job and he does have feelings); the horse cart driver in South America who faced a damaged cart; the campus police, who were obligated to shadow him and shine lights onto his balcony (surely they had other things to do); the hapless custodian who had to clean up the burned-out trash can; any miscellaneous persons he might have offended and can't even remember? How can he not regret the inconvenience and nuisance he inflicted upon these people?

The sober Toren I've known is not a person who would harm someone thoughtlessly. At one time, when I saw his reluctance to express remorse, I would have said, "How can Toren do this to me?" But now I say, "How can Toren do this to himself?" Since this issue has not resolved itself, I can only await more understanding, for both of us.

I look at what has been made available for Toren's well-being. Counselors, programs, and people in the recovery community have been very helpful. While there are many sources for guiding youth through decisions about substance abuse, what parents say and do may be *the* most potent weapon.

Evidence indicates that we parents who drink influence the behavior of our children at a surprisingly young age. At Dartmouth Medical School, researchers studied children age two to six, who were instructed to choose from 133 items to get a Barbie doll ready for an evening going out on the town. Those children whose parents drank were more likely to choose wine or beer, and those whose parents smoked were more likely to select cigarettes. Interestingly, children who watched PG-13 or R-rated movies at home were five times more likely to choose alcohol. This study, published in September 2005, provides a mechanism for parents to watch children mimicking their own behaviors.[2]

The running dialogue parents have with their kids from the time they are toddlers is the beginning of how teens mimic such practices as tolerance for people with differences, sexual mores, violence and fighting, and decisions about substance use. There are countless things we parents do to influence our kids' drinking behaviors. Moderate drinking, or even the decision not to drink, can be modeled by parents at home as well as in the community.

Some parents may shy away from talking about alcohol choices because they feel kids should be able to work it out for themselves. But look at other facets of behavior shaped by parents, such as stealing, for example. Here parents take a stand. We instruct our children about honesty; we talk to them about not stealing things from stores, about not shoplifting, and about the reasons why it is important to behave honestly. We are direct about our instruction. We do not say, "Well, someday when you're in the store and see a candy bar you want, just deal with it. Make your own decision." *No.* We say, "Do not *ever* steal from a store. It's wrong."

The same education should go into instruction about underage drinking. This is our chance to direct our children's behavior and let them know our expectations, along with the consequences of their decisions. Here we can say, "Underage drinking is harmful. It will damage you and I don't approve of it." Parents have twelve years to instruct and model appropriate drinking behavior to children prior to adolescence. Not only are kids listening to what we say, but they are watching what we do. These are behaviors that we can practice from the time our kids are young. The decisions we adults have made about the way we choose to drink (or not to drink) can be discussed aloud and modeled often from the earliest age until forever.

Some people are hesitant to talk about moderate drinking in front of underage drinkers. The reality is, we parents cannot be sure if our kids will choose to drink or not. We will probably not be there for the first unauthorized sip. Even before kids begin facing decisions about drinking, explicit instruction about how to drink responsibly is in order. These days many colleges are educating students (even underage students) about moderate drinking on their school Web sites and in freshman orientations; perhaps we parents should use the same principles with our children at home.

## How to Be a Moderate Drinker
## (Guidelines for Responsible Drinking)

If you choose to drink alcohol, here are some tips to stay safe and maintain moderation:

- Plan ahead.
  —Set a responsible limit (number of drinks) for event/evening and stick to it.
  —If you're at an event where servers are circulating and refilling glasses, keep track of your intake.

- Check your mood: alcohol intensifies it.
  —Best to pass on the alcohol if you are upset, angry, sad, depressed, or anxious.

- Keep track of the amount of alcohol in your drink.

- Slow down your drinking.
  —Sip your drinks.
  —Remember, it takes about twenty minutes to feel the effects of a single drink.
  —Drink water between alcohol drinks to keep yourself well-hydrated to dilute the effect of the alcohol.
  —Add ice to your drink—if sipped slowly, the ice will dilute the drink, decreasing potency.

- Eat food before drinking alcohol.
  —Alcohol has less effect on a full stomach.

- Use a designated driver if drinking away from home.

- It is always an option not to drink alcohol; many people choose to abstain.

Points I would include in a conversation with an adolescent about moderate drinking include safe partying. This is basically the same kind of plan responsible adults follow with friends, mates, and partners when attending social events, *even when not drinking*. A party plan emphasizes safety and takes into account that those participating agree about behaviors and care for one another. All participants can be mindful of safety while partying.

Recently, campus programs began instructing women drinkers to watch their drinks and their friends' drinks when they leave them unattended. Many women do not allow men to bring a drink from the bar, but prefer to accompany the buyer to the bar, or buy their own drinks.[3] No matter what the plan, it is well understood that the most dangerous date-rape drug is alcohol itself.

---

### What You and Your Friends *Can* Do to Stay Safe at a Party[4]

- Don't drink alcohol.
- Know your limits—men should never have more than four drinks per occasion and women should never have more than three drinks per occasion.
- Have a designated driver to get you home.
- Go with friends and have a party plan, and stick to it!! (For example, we will all leave together, we will not get drunk.)
- Don't allow anyone other than a designated bartender to make drinks for you, do drink only out of the can or bottle *that you open for yourself* rather than a glass or cup.
- Beware of what's in a punch bowl.

---

As parents, *the way* we say something to our kids is very important. How to say it requires both practice and timing. Sometimes when we are overcome with worry, it is difficult to choose our words. Since new information about adolescent brain development and family genetics has become available, we parents have all the more reason to learn how these factors influence our children. One parent wrote me and said that her top priority was to get her girls through high school without their succumbing to the pressures of underage drinking. She and her husband believed it was their obligation and right as parents to be informed about when and where their girls were going. "What we [parents] should be concerned with is the long-term effects of the messages we send our children during their very impressionable years," she wrote. While raising Toren, it was important that Don and I didn't try to be his best friend. We took a stand about underage drinking, and even though he didn't always obey, we stated our message consistently.

It takes courage for parents to draw a line and constantly enforce expectations. One addiction counselor informed me that problems often develop when parents fail to clearly define household rules about drinking. Toren sometimes reacted adversely to our ground rules, but it was important that we not give in. He needed to know that his parents cared about him, while at the same time receiving a strong message about expected drinking behaviors.

"But what can be done before it's too late?" I ask Toren. I want to encourage others, suggest something that would really make a difference in their drinking choices.

"Talk to kids about their drinking habits. Threats won't work, but education about alcohol, what can happen with alcoholism as a disease, about family genetics and family patterns of drinking . . . all this helps." Toren stresses, "Kids need to know what the red flags are. They should be warned and educated rather than threatened or punished. The punishments make it into an 'us versus them' situation."

"Do you mean in high school?"

Toren tells me, "Maybe. The earlier the better, I guess. High school is when it started, but in my case, college was when I was doing my heaviest drinking. That's when some people start to develop real drinking problems. That's when I needed more help, probably. Punishment doesn't do jack shit."

Educate kids about their choices, about the potential for disaster. That's what Toren says we should do. At least, that's what he tells us now, in hindsight. I think of the warnings he received from his RD in the dorm; the requirement to attend AA meetings in the summer. This was a way to educate Toren and it did impact him, even though he did not fulfill the entire regimen. Some information filtered through. I also think of chances we missed to force him into counseling, like after his Thanksgiving arrest. Perhaps Toren would have been secretly grateful for a chance to talk about his drinking by this time. Having the courage to insist on professional help is very difficult, because what is really happening with an adolescent and what parents are told can be totally different.

While Toren is still in the first months of his halfway program, I mail him the first portion of the manuscript for our book from Washington State. He has been sending his chapters to me on the Internet from the public library in Florida. For the first time, Toren sees what I have written, and, for the first time, he reads our combined work. He does not call me back for several days. When he finally phones, he confesses, "Reading what we wrote sucked a lot of energy out of me. I never knew what a dark moment it was in my life. I can't believe what I was doing—and over and over again . . . dumb-ass. I never realized how my actions were affecting so many people besides myself. I was just doing things for me, out of control. I was sinking."

As I listen to Toren say this, tears well in my eyes. Toren has always possessed an optimistic personality that overlooked bad things and moved on. Maybe this hurt him because he diminished the harm of his actions. I've always joked about an image I'd had of Toren submerged in the bay with bricks strapped onto his feet, gurgling all the way down, "Oh look, there's a species of crab I've never seen! And look at the fabulous colors, the way the light filters through the water! Even though I'm surely suffocating and will soon die, this is a marvelous experience. I never could've had this insight if I weren't drowning!" Or sinking. As he just admitted.

But this same optimism probably pulled Toren out of the clutches of the disease when he insisted, "Yes, I deserve happiness. Now I'm seeing my life turning dark. I want my life back. I will get it back. I will have it. It's mine."

Since discussing drinking choices is not a once-in-a-lifetime duty for parents, we can continue the dialogue throughout all phases of our lives and our children's lives. Our kids will relate to conversations differently depending on their age and experience. Guidelines for raising kids are like a rope bridge; directives will adjust and sway as a child grows through the years. And as happened with our family, agreements may get trampled or ignored. I remind myself that it took nine long years before our family woke up, too late by some accounts. But no, Toren is alive, functioning in his new situation, and could possibly be figuring out his new life as I write this sentence. What happened to us is now a part of our family acreage.

So what is the plan to fix this world's problem with alcohol? Like rehab, each person, each family, has to deal with it individually. And our nation must face it as well—educating people about the costs and consequences of alcohol consumption. It's not a disease we can Band-Aid. Battling alcohol abuse and addiction takes a personal strategy. It requires awareness of the progressive effects and the courage to bring it up even through pain. If we work together as parents, we might be surprised what we *can* do.

---

### Parents *Can* Influence Drinking Decisions By:[5]

- Informing other parents about the marked impact of parental modeling of heavy drinking on their adolescents.
- Encouraging parents and policy makers not to perceive adolescent drinking as inevitable and unavoidable.
- Sharing these facts with other parents and adolescents:
  —Alcohol is not a benign substance.
  —Alcohol consumption in high school is often associated with serious adverse consequences.
  —Alcohol consumption in high school can also lead to alcohol abuse later on that can permanently affect the abuser's achievement of life goals.
  —Easy access to alcohol is a principal factor in heavy drinking.

# TWENTY-SIX
## HALFWAY HOME

 **Late February 2004. I'll never be given enough** time to figure this all out. As it stands right now, since trudging up the stairs to the Peace Corps nurse, I'm going into my fifth month of sobriety (hold applause). After this small amount of time to reflect, I can only say that I always plan to be reevaluating my life. What started as innocent journal writing (where I first sprang a leak and began investigating the reality of my drinking progression) has turned my life backward and inside out.

Many volunteers go into the Peace Corps for two years hoping to gain life experience, to give back, and to come out with a better understanding of themselves and another culture. As it turns out, I have achieved these things in far less time and in a very skewed manner. In Paraguay, amidst a foreign environment, my alcohol problems were completely unmasked, and shortly thereafter, in rehab, I found myself facing an entirely different culture: one where people want to, try to, and often struggle to be sober.

I'm beginning to better understand my situation. The first time I spoke with my parents on the phone from Washington, D.C., and told them about my drinking difficulties and what I was suddenly doing back in the United States, I felt about a thousand pounds of pressure lift off my back. Finally, I was no longer burdened with my secrets. (I considered mentioning my struggles to them earlier, while I was studying in Mexico, or perhaps when they would have come to visit me in my Paraguayan village the following May.) Having put myself out there and confronted my problem, I no longer had anything else inside eating me up. All the feelings and internal struggles no longer had to be suppressed, stuffed away, or silently borne.

By now, I don't have much left to hide. My drinking has been dragged to the surface and I'm better able to deal with my problems. The odd part about all of this is, if I had known the clinical severity of my addiction, there is absolutely no way I would have so clumsily turned myself in and asked for help. None of this was what I was intending or hoping for in life. All I knew was that things were getting worse fast and I was desperate. Luckily I was semi-buzzed and didn't think about all of the procedural repercussions that would follow.

Over the last few months in South America, I had really begun to integrate myself into my Paraguayan community. It had taken a long time for me to achieve a sense of acceptance there and I had finally forged close relationships with some of the families. To be torn so quickly from all that, and suddenly find myself sitting in an office chair in a semicircle sharing about feelings, acceptance, and powerlessness with other men didn't seem possible. To me, life had become surreal. Within a period of six days I had confessed in a nurse's office and then detoxed in a hotel room; I had traveled across Paraguayan dirt roads to pull my belongings from my village; I had squatted three nights in a hotel in Washington, D.C., while being questioned and assessed by all kinds of counselors; and, finally, I had surrendered to a northeastern U.S. rehab program.

There was nobody more sure than I that I'd found my village home for the next two years and that I would be happily working in Paraguay during that time. Experiencing some sort of inverse culture shock by being transported from South America to a treatment center, it seemed like my soul still remained back in my village. Through all this confusion, my alcohol problem was the one thing that stayed with me.

All of this happened with few decisions being made by me, which is probably what allowed it to take place. There was no point when I was allowed to step backward and withdraw my previous statements or reconsider the direction I was going. It was too late. The term "rock bottom" is relative, but being so desperate that I traded in my whole world without resistance reflects the bankruptcy I was experiencing inside. These feelings of despair are the same ones that have allowed me to continue listening to outside help and intervening suggestions. As opposed to all the times before when I was in trouble with my parents or authorities, this time I was ready to consider other options. Losing my would-be life in South America forced me to confront the seriousness of my situation and also made it difficult to hide from anyone.

Surely, when my friends see me, they'll wonder, *Wasn't he supposed to be in South America for another year and a half?* This significant turning point allowed me to be honest with myself and everyone else. I have finally identified what now seems like the beginning of a nightmare, one that I have somehow awakened from.

Near the end of rehab, I was given choices for what they call aftercare—where to go and what to do after completing treatment. This was packaged with a strong recommendation for me to live in a halfway house.

"What? Are you crazy?"

My therapist kindly pointed out that I didn't have any clue how to live like a normal adult in society. College didn't count. She then reminded me of my five continuous months of drinking, from my May 2002 college graduation to my studies in Mexico, prior to my trip of self-discovery with the Peace Corps in 2003.

"Ooooh, right, thaaat." It was a painful realization, just how correct she was and that she knew what she was talking about, partially because of my self-incriminating honesty. I was prime halfway house material.

Now, in late February of 2004, a little more than four months into my approximately six-month stay in the halfway house, I'm a sort of blank slate. It's similar to how I felt when I arrived at my village in Paraguay.

The difference is that this time my supporting community is a bunch of sick addicts instead of the rural farming community that had me as their struggling volunteer. In this halfway environment, I am no longer searching for a functional way to socially drink. Opting to be in a corner of the United States where I know next to nobody, I have had plenty of time with myself to think it all through, lick my wounds, and react to a new emerging lifestyle, one that I'm not sure anyone like me can completely embrace from the get-go. Boring . . . bored . . . bored . . . bored-boredboredbored.

Reluctant to fully accept that I will always be sober and never again drink alcohol, I have learned to focus more on each day as it comes. I try to worry less about all the times I will be the shoo-in designated driver and all the times I may be counted on to clarify blurry details of someone else's drunken nights. People will still drink, I guess—just not me.

I have noticed several differences in a sober me today. Some make me question myself and wonder if I have completely sold out and turned into this sissy recovering alcoholic who is overly revealing about his problems. But there are changes in my life I have appreciated. I have noticed that I'm no longer living to drink, and more important, as it was quickly becoming, drinking to live. Increasingly, my life revolved around the time I was drunk. The time I was sober counted less and less. It had gotten to the point that I only tolerated the times I wasn't drinking. Instead, I looked for the next chance to get liquored up and disappear into oblivion—just waiting to drink all the time. Now I'm no longer just going through the motions with a bottle or tall can lingering in the back of my mind. I have no strings attached to my next good time and I can be more in the moment and give myself to the situation.

Sure, I'm healing, but I'm not cured. I am still a sick bastard when it comes to my thoughts about drinking. I have insidious, crazy relapse dreams where I am suddenly drinking or drunk. Sometimes I dream that I am doing obscene amounts of cocaine, ingesting bottles of cough syrup, or smoking pot like I never even used to smoke. The dreams seem very real, and in them I always feel shitty, guilty, and have to deal with people seeing me drunk and out of control, or finding out that I relapsed. The sickest part is that in the morning, although I am relieved that the dreams weren't real, I often regret that I didn't take advantage in some lucid way and enjoy a nice warm Schmidt's Ice. There are no consequences in dreamland, so why don't I just get down or go a little crazy? I guess deep inside I really am scared of these potential situations, so in my dreams I am unable to block out the feelings of regret, shame, or disappointment that would follow an authentic relapse.

Even more revealing is that I still think about the last times I drank with a sick and twisted fondness. I still remember the last beer I slammed in Paraguay before getting help. I look at my last moments before I entered rehab sometimes and wonder, *Why didn't I drink in that hotel room in Washington, D.C., before I went into rehab to learn how fucked I was? It may have been my last chance.* I suppose the Valium was working. Besides, a last-minute drink would have undermined my asking for help and negated all of the professional detoxing I'd done in South America by putting me back in the exact hell that had beat me down in the first place. By then, I guess I knew what the problem was, and apparently I was looking for a solution, because it's not like it didn't occur to me that I had the freedom to go out and buy beer. As stupid as it may sound, as an alcoholic I still see that final day as a missed chance to have one last romantic dance with that sickly love of mine.

So in some ways it is obvious that I miss a lot of the fun that came with drinking. But now I'm able to appreciate life much more without weighing it against exaggerated extremes or having to wait out reality so I can go crazy for a few days. My existence used to operate on a basis of rewards. I was always fulfilling a requirement in order to earn the next chance to drink and have fun. Most people operate on a basis of personal rewards, but, by the end, my system became reliant only on alcohol. I was most concerned about drinking and, therefore, unable to direct myself toward anything else. I had a complete mental obsession with alcohol. It ran

my life. Even when I wasn't drunk or physically exposed, my body anticipated it and my brain looked for the next opportunity to blissfully self-
destruct.

Sobriety has definitely shown me a more stable version of reality.
Gone are the times that I lived for during the better part of the last nine
years. Since I appreciate a taste of chaos, spontaneity, and excitement, this
new tranquil consistency is almost traumatic. If it weren't for the days of
guitar playing and simple living down in Paraguay to cushion this unforeseen transition, I may have had more difficulty. I no longer look to the
weekends as a source of endless drinks, wild late nights, loss of inhibition
and control, and the subsequent memory lapses into oblivion that were so
normal to me. And as a result, I no longer face waking up to shakes and
sweats, dehydration, or any of the total confusion, insanity, or regret that
used to follow a typical benchmark evening. Also gone is the absurdity,
hilarity, lunacy, and knee-slapping silliness that I always counted on.
Where can I still find some of that?

Dear Toren,

   You speak of your halfway experience as dull. Monotonous. Mind-numbing. This ennui can be a form of simplicity, a rehearsal for the next step. It's the repetition of doing undemanding things right, having them turn out in simple form, then being prepared to face added frustration and complications without falling back into old habits.

   In the halfway situation, layers and seasonings have been stripped from your life. You are geared down to essentials. Gone are your gadgets, posters on the wall, e-mail contacts, friends and social schedules. Your Peace Corps work, which was meaningful and inspiring to you, has vanished. In its place is tedious, unrewarding work. Therefore, your life has the appearance of being dreary and lackluster. But you are not a boring or uninspired person in reality. You must remember this as you repeat again and again waking up, going to work, then repeating again. You are building muscle memory to walk you through the next steps. This gives you rhythm before you add chords or elaborate riffs.

   At the halfway house, you are preparing, just as you do in any school, for the chance to continue on. What appears to lack depth and flavor is like practicing musical scales, going over them until you *can perform them in your sleep perfectly, three octaves. Then one day when you have a meaningful choice, you are ready. You will flourish. In any key.*

*You, the real Toren behind the halfway shell, are still there practicing without distraction, looking at yourself over and over and over in the mirror after returning home at curfew, deciding how you will set off onto the next phase. You need this time to heal, to forgive, and to nurture your spirit without the interruption of all those people who would unduly influence, mistakenly guide, or destroy your concentration. You must do this on your own. You still possess the same substantial capabilities. But in the privacy of the halfway house, you don't feel the pseudo-pressure to act (as you have so aptly put it) "all happy, skippy or preachy, as though I have finally conquered the world."*

*It's not a production for someone else. What you are doing is just for you.*

*You know your disease is still with you. But you are stabilizing yourself so that you will someday be able to carry it on your shoulder without it concerning or distracting you. You are reinventing who you are, repositioning the load, and looking forward to the time when you move on, lugging this thing which, in reality, no one will notice. To you it will be like an old scar, of no current consequence or power, but there as a reminder of what you refuse to become.*

*Love,*
*Mom*

# TWENTY-EIGHT
## BREAKING THE SOBER ICE

 **March 2004. At Christmastime, I had the chance** to fly home for a few days and test uncharted territory: the old stomping ground, without alcohol, without the crutchlike supervision of my halfway house rules and regulations. I was extremely anxious about reentry into my former life with everything turned upside down, not being able to converse normally with anyone because of everything that was going on in my life.

"Hey, great to see you, too. Happy Holidays! Cheers!"

I found that a lot of this struggle was really more in *my* mind than anyone else's. As it turns out, not everyone is dwelling on my misfortunes and thinking about my circumstances 90 percent of the time.

Whether I should return home so early in my halfway experience was a decision I wondered about. I wanted to go, but at the same time I dreaded it. Some things are inevitable, and the pain of anticipation proved to be far greater than the actual events. I knew I was going to see all my old friends and would have the option of putting myself into potentially dangerous situations. There were many possibilities to consider. People in the rooms of recovery say, "If you want to be miserable, go hang out with a bunch of people who are drinking." Others take it to the next level and say, "If you hang around in a barbershop long enough, eventually you'll get a haircut."

I finally got to face my family and friends. Basically, I feared that I'd have to constantly explain myself, tell people where I was at and reestablish whatever I had going before I chose to disappear South. I worried that I would have to justify not drinking, or make excuses to people who had always partied with me as to why I couldn't drink. I was afraid they'd think I was betraying them, that my situation would threaten them in some way, or that they'd say I'd changed.

The last part can't be denied. I'd had to change. What I found out was that people were not expecting explanations, nor were they waiting for me to break down and cry myself a drink. I guess my actions and living arrangements spoke for me more than anything. I felt acceptance and understanding, that people were still happy to see me, same as always— drink or no drink.

Upon my arrival home I noticed that there was *no* alcohol in our usually diversely stocked fridge. The liquor cabinet was practically deadbolted and the once all-too-vulnerable wine cellar was now mysteriously locked. *Oooh, yeah*, I was reminded, *their drunken son has come home for the first time*. What a special feeling. The dry Christmas, something I guess I should get used to . . . boooooooring. Really, it was no big deal for me and our family in terms of our time together. Socializing with our relatives has never been about drinking, anyway. I was concerned about feeling a sense of moral inferiority, but once again there was no reason for this, because I was embraced warmly by the entire family.

My parents, brothers, and I spent some time at home and then took off for a few days of skiing. We were all just the same together, joking and sarcastic as always. We discovered what could now pass as either funny or offensive on our newly installed alco-sensitivity meter. Is anything still funny? What can be said and what can't? Who cares? I'm the only one with weak willpower and a drinking problem. *Ha!!* That was funny, wasn't it? Halfway.

Against the recommendations of numerous voices of wisdom in recovery, I went out several nights and saw my old friends and put myself in old places—all situations where my disease would most likely want me to be. One could say that being in early recovery means that I have a very tenuous hold on sobriety. But I don't sit around wishing I could drink all the time. For almost a full year before the time I began working in South America, my body and mind were completely at odds with alcohol, and I was slowly torturing myself to the point of complete surrender and defeat: to the point of asking for help. This long process didn't just disappear from my consciousness. Many thoughts still come to mind when I think about alcohol and drinking in general, but when it comes to those ideas and *me,* it is very easy to remind myself about the pain and aftermath of drinking and its recent effects on me. These reminders make being the designated driver seem almost attractive in comparison to drinking the way I used to.

My first night out was a shock. I went to a house party with a friend and one brother. In preparation, we had agreed that we would leave the party at my first inkling of discomfort. All of us wanted my experience to be successful. I found myself at a larger-than-anticipated gathering, with seemingly everybody I could think of that my therapist in rehab had said I would need to avoid. After getting past the initial distress of really being back and no longer under the illusion that living in Florida was an extension of my excursion to South America, I began to talk with people, searching for common ground and dealing with my new empty-handed antics. As I conversed with people, my eyes were overwhelmed by the beer cans in everybody's hands. Not having been around alcohol for three months was strange enough, but this abrupt reversal of overstimulation was more than my sheltered brain could absorb.

Taking a panoramic scan of the room, all I saw were blurry images of people with cans and bottles popping out of their grasp. With every person I talked to, I had to make an enormous effort not to let my eyes wander down to stare at their beers. I felt like a little puppy that couldn't stop begging for food. My eyes just couldn't get past the beer. I was uneasy and flustered. The sensation felt similar to when you're wearing an itchy wool cap and you're searching for your lost keys: you're hot, frustrated, preoccupied. It literally took an hour or two until I began to feel comfortable, until I could quit sweating.

From that point on, I began to enjoy myself and adapted to this new form of so-called socializing. By the end of the night, I was ecstatic to see everyone, to have a good time, and to know I was not going to suffer like I had in recent years from my progressing alcoholic disaster.

After that evening, I was not at all hesitant to go out seeing old friends the remaining nights I spent in town. I even found myself in a few bars here and there without much temptation or discomfort. "If you hang around in a barbershop long enough, you're gonna get a haircut." Maybe so, but I doubt that an already balding patient fighting a life-threatening form of cancer would.

I noticed a lot of things about my social excursions with friends. The first and most important was this: it didn't make much difference that I wasn't drinking. For the most part, people couldn't have cared less. What was also striking to me was that most people weren't getting extremely intoxicated. So many of my party years had been about either getting wasted or trying not to get too wasted. The big difference was that I no longer needed to have any of this on my mind. There was no voice telling me I needed another drink before I did this or that, or that I needed a drink just to feel better. Nor was there a voice telling me, "You better slow down!," nor the voice that should have warned, "Dude, you're gonna black out soon!"

For the first time in years, I really didn't rely on alcohol to make me say or do things that I normally wouldn't. From the moment I went out until I got home, everything stayed the same. I experienced longer-than-usual nights where my buzz never came and nothing ever changed. I was consistently either unprovoked or stimulated based solely on my natural response to a given conversation. Neither did I go through those all-too-comforting, euphoric feelings that used to keep me coming back. In return, I got the sanity of knowing I was no longer screwing myself over on the inside. There was no internal conflict. No anticipation. No anxiety of withdrawals. I was fine with that. I'd never known that the solution to my drinking problem was to *not* drink. Damn it.

Going out and seeing everybody and breaking the sober ice was definitely necessary for me. I got that out of the way and now I can continue on, knowing that the world didn't end because I can't drink. I realize that most of my friends don't feel betrayed, aren't giving me the ol' "You've changed, man," or whatever I thought would cave in everything I used to care about. There's no doubt that I feel a disconnection from my past and from my friends. But that probably would have happened to anyone who was out of the country for virtually a year, not to mention returning from a plan gone awry and living in a halfway house.

Back in Florida, I'm once again strapping on the training wheels for another few months to live out my commitment of a six-month stay. More than anything, I've been given this time as yet another opportunity to test my growing patience. Living under a constant curfew, having people check to see if I make my bed daily and confirming that I'm in bed every night are just some of the little things that put me to the test. The real joys of the halfway house come from living in an apartment with three other strangers, guys who don't necessarily get along with each other and whose only commonality is that their pasts crumbled and brought them together in the wake of their own personal destruction. Learning what is best for me may not always be what I want. It's a character-building experience, right?

I now have to face the whole idea of, "Okay, so I keep waking up and it's not a dream. I'm still not in South America as planned, and I am still not drinking." Both still seem so unreal. The last time I checked, those were my two short-term reasons for living: working in Paraguay and drinking. I'm not about to pretend that I have suddenly stumbled onto the meaning of life just because I've forced myself to sober up. Actually, I feel like I'm still wiping my eyes and trying to figure things out. What do I do with myself? I have removed the one constant that fueled my social life and everything I chose to do. Suddenly I'm dealing with a whole new reality. What do I do with all this time and energy?

I'm still not sure. Similar to "out of control," the term "normal" is relative and subjective. I don't know what normal necessarily is, because what seems normal to me is abnormal, and what normal people do seems boring to me. I have a hard time knowing how to go about replacing my behaviors with others when much of what I used to do seems like an all-or-nothing package deal.

Who knows what will come through the loss of my Peace Corps experience and the realization of my alcoholism? It appears this process and reevaluation of my life won't ever end. Some wise man may say that "Every time a door closes, a window opens." But that window might not appear as sparkling to the person who has to climb through it.

I'm tackling my problems just as others have dealt with their predicaments: by facing them. The severity of my physical reaction to alcohol forced me to confront my disease at a relatively early age, and I feel fortunate that this did not drag on for another decade. Some people never find the Twelve Steps or recover at all.

Where this will take me is not my big concern, as long as my journey isn't a loop. Along the way, the more I seem to learn, the less I feel I know. My existing halfway situation has given me a whole new model of living, a new focus. Words like "powerlessness," "acceptance," and "willingness" are etched into my latest vocabulary. By remaining honest with myself, by leaning on the twelve-step program, and by using my friends and family for support, I am given a second chance to move into unmarked territory. Today, I live more for the present.

# TWENTY-NINE
## WARNING LABEL

**[CHRIS]** *May 2004. When I first began writing, I thought* the subject was my son and his drinking. By now, I realize my scribbling is also largely about the alcohol culture and how families fit into it. What should be so simple, sipping a glass of spirits, has turned into an exploding cocktail. Our family is only a fraction of the way through this dousing. As Toren's halfway program draws to a close, I'm living in Washington State and he resides in Florida. Now Toren tells me that he plans to move to New York City this summer. When I hear this, I want to say, "*No, no. That is not a good spot for you.*" But where is a good spot? Where should a bandaged and raw survivor go to live? The truth is, no one can protect my son from himself.

I feel as though we aren't finished yet, like we're in the middle of a shipwreck without the necessary safety gear. The chapters are spilling out, and each time Toren sends me his writing, I hold my breath. I wait for him to assure me that he's on the right course and that I shouldn't worry. His hesitant words disappoint me. He's not fixed yet. Then I realize I am expecting too much. I can't predict or manipulate how he is feeling about himself. He must launch on his own, and I will find out only afterward which currents he has followed. So I slap his written portion into our emerging book and also paste in mine, hoping the overlap will one day align and we will again be a family rowing along *with* the current instead of against it. The life jacket is stowed. I can grab it and snap it on at a moment's notice.

Toren plans to play music in New York. It's the type of setting his rehab professionals cautioned against. Yet they also said he has to make it on his own. I recall what he has told me on the phone: "Mom, I've practiced for this. I'm ready to go, now."

So far, so good. After his brothers visited him in Florida this past winter, I heard it went well. No one sent word of a relapse or problems. Even though I don't ask for many details, the brothers tell me they had a good time in the never-ceasing rain, that they felt comfortable together. When sons report to moms, particulars can be scant. It's not like they are calling me every day on the phone or writing me huge e-mail messages, darn it. But I'm used to it. Many parents operate by this form of insight. You have to guess whether something is going wrong or right, smile a lot, and hope for the best. (Remember the life jacket: out of sight but right at hand.)

Toren and his two brothers are at the age experts now refer to as Emerging Adulthood. When I took education classes for my teaching degree, we learned about stages of child development. In those days, after adolescence came adulthood. No longer. Now kids get an extended phase to blossom. Dr. Jeffrey J. Arnett proposes that the time of life roughly between ages eighteen and twenty-five be considered a "distinct period" called Emerging Adulthood.[1] It's a time when individuals consider themselves too old to be adolescents but not yet full-fledged adults, a period offset by our technological society with high levels of education and well-paying jobs, when people postpone marriage and having children. Apparently during this phase of life there is a high correlation to risky behaviors, especially heavy drinking.[2] (That's quite an understatement, from my perspective.) It's predicted that after this stretch of time kids will exit the emerging adulthood stage and morph into adulthood, where they can assume responsibility (and not be addicted to a substance).

The problem is that after an adolescent has practiced the social habit of heavy drinking for nine years, from age fifteen to twenty-four, it may be difficult both emotionally and physiologically to change behaviors. As with Toren, symptoms of addiction can overtake, beyond the control of the emerging adult. Toren and I often discuss his concept of socializing, when he felt it necessary to have alcohol in hand. He could control it to a point. Then, before our family's open but unseeing eyes, he transformed. For a teen addict, emerging into adulthood is problematic. Some research indicates that addicted teens face lagging emotional development. If so, Toren could bloom later than predicted.

No one likes to think that using alcohol will delay the emergence of adulthood, but the fact that alcohol can kill someone is something our society *really* hates to acknowledge. Part of the eyes-closed infatuation with alcohol and other drugs is that people feel there is no harm in using them. The press often focuses on meth and steroids, even though alcohol is still the number-one drug of choice among teens.[3] Experts and athletes came from across the country to testify to Congress about sports and steroids, some of them lying during their testimony. Worry about steroids is legitimate, but if Congress were also to hear from the fourteen hundred families that lost students to alcohol last year, perhaps our nation would better recognize that underage drinking carries great risk. It is a startling fact that *"the federal government spends twenty-five times more on illegal drug abuse prevention than on underage drinking prevention, despite the fact that alcohol kills six times more youths than all other drugs combined."*[4] The battle against steroids and other drugs on school campuses and baseball fields is important, but with 10.1 million youths between the ages of twelve and twenty using alcohol, 2.1 million of them heavy-drinking youths, underage drinking is a gripping area of concern.[5]

Some alcohol prevention professionals prefer that binge drinking be labeled "heavy episodic drinking" or "dangerous drinking" or "high-risk drinking." It is said that if students believe binge drinking is the norm on their campus, then common use of the term might encourage them. This controversy about terminology means that people who work on campuses in such areas as public safety, district court, the dean's office, the counseling office, housing, and university support are paying attention. Colleges want not only to define the drinking problem better but to deal with it. Even Toren's university alumni magazine has published articles about campus drinking, and recently interviewed Toren and me about alcohol awareness.

In reality, binge drinking can be any amount of alcohol that impairs a person's judgment and causes him or her to make unsafe choices. Another important part of binge drinking to consider is the consequences, which can include personal, economic, academic, social, legal, and medical problems, not to mention symptoms of dependency, such as withdrawal, tolerance, and loss of control. No matter how it's labeled or who is doing the labeling, the culture of binge drinking and alcohol abuse is a huge problem, especially if campuses, students, and parents deny that it is happening.

Not only is binge drinking a concern at the college level, but we need to be reminded that in 2004, one in five eighth-graders were current drinkers. By twelfth grade, one out of every two was a current drinker. "We have a huge public health crisis in this country with our kids drinking, and as a nation we are in denial," said David Jernigan, the research director at the Center for Alcohol Marketing and Youth.[6] The number of adolescents ages twelve to seventeen admitted to substance-abuse treatment increased 65 percent between 1992 and 2002.[7] In 2004, 1.6 million youths aged twelve to seventeen (6.2 percent of this population) needed treatment for an alcohol use problem. Of this group, only 126,000 youths received treatment at a specialty facility, leaving 1.4 million youths who needed but did not receive treatment.[8]

People wonder where young kids are getting all the booze. A 2005 study by the American Medical Association revealed the eye-opening fact that kids don't have to look too far for a steady stream of alcohol. It's right at home, sitting in the fridge next to the milk. Two out of three teens, age thirteen to eighteen, said it is easy to get alcohol from their homes without parents knowing about it. I remember one time intercepting one of our boys clanking bottles in our liquor cabinet. When I entered the living room, he hurriedly tried to close the doors to the cupboard. A high school freshman, he explained that he needed alcohol for a science experiment. I challenged him, but he vehemently insisted on it. Since both of us knew he was lying, the subject was dropped. He left the living room. I decided that we ought to lock the liquor cabinet from then on.

For some kids, access to alcohol only requires asking an adult. One-third of kids age thirteen to eighteen responded that it is easy to obtain alcohol from their own parents *knowingly*; 40 percent said it was easy to obtain from a friend's parent. In all age groups, girls nearly always ranked higher than boys in obtaining alcohol. Surprisingly, girls aged 12–14 are actually more likely than boys to have used alcohol in the past thirty days.[9] *And one in four teens has attended a party where minors were drinking in front of parents.* That's because one out of four U.S. parents (26 percent) with children age twelve to twenty agrees that teens should be able to drink at home with their parents present.[10]

We often question where Toren got his supply of alcohol. One troubling incident occurred during high school, before a spring formal. These special dances always put Don and me on alert, because curfew would be later and after-dance parties at other kids' homes presented opportunities for unsupervised alcohol consumption. Prior to that dance, Toren's after-hours plans seemed dubious, so I ducked out to look in the trunk of his car while he was showering. My suspicion was correct; he had stowed a collection of beer and other alcoholic beverages. I confiscated the drinks and asked him where he had gotten them. Toren refused to tell me. We feared that one of his brothers had provided the alcohol for him. Toren's story at that moment was that he and his friends had asked a stranger to purchase it at a local supermarket. These kinds of behaviors, unfortunately, are typical for teens who want to hide drinking from their parents. Years later, Toren admits that he not only used various fake IDs for purchasing alcohol, but that he often raided alcohol from *our* garage or liquor cabinet. I don't think I had ever gotten around to locking the doors. Somehow I couldn't imagine our boys stealing our liquor. How naïve I was. Sometimes, as the research indicates, we were providers for our teens, unknowingly.

Most teens believe they are justified in asking why, if alcohol is okay for adults, it is not okay for them. This is an attitude Toren expressed during his adolescence. Where do kids get their ideas about drinking? Dr. Dwayne Proctor asks, "Imagine if four out of ten adults engaged in behavior like going out four or five nights during the workweek to gulp down six or seven beers, knock back several shots of liquor, and then head home for a nightcap? Yet such a daily scenario is played out weekly across the country involving thousands of college students, many under the legal age to purchase alcohol."[11] Is this the way we have influenced our kids to drink?

It has been said that "Alcohol is so potent that, if discovered today, it would be classified as a Class II drug, available only by prescription."[12] Adults who willingly provide minors with alcohol often think they are doing them a favor, especially when it occurs within the confines of a private home. But in fact, providing young people with alcohol can contribute to violence, driving under the influence, sexual assault, and binge drinking. By allowing underage drinking, parents are sending the message that it's okay to drink. Parents may not be able to control the actions of intoxicated youth once they have left a party, or even within the confines of the home. Car crashes and injuries following parent-hosted parties are a huge risk, and parents can be held liable for these incidents. Recent information about the susceptibility of adolescents to severe damage from heavy drinking causes me to stop and reconsider attitudes about serving alcohol to underage kids. Collecting car keys and allowing minors to party in the basement may be more detrimental than most parents realize, even without considering the destruction caused to the adolescent brain. Which of us parents wishes to be responsible not only for destroying cells in our children's still-forming intellects but for the crashes, sexual incidents, and violence brought on by underage abuse of alcohol?

A report concluded that the cost of alcohol use by *youth* was $53 billion in 1996, including $19 billion from traffic crashes and $29 billion from violent crime.[13] Since 1996, rates of underage drinking have risen.

Families such as ours, who are looking the other way while teens drink, pay closer attention when the consequences spill over into our own lives. All people are affected by teens who abuse or are addicted to alcohol, and it will take the efforts of our whole nation to bring about changes in drinking attitudes.

One way to change the perception of the youth alcohol culture would be for us parents to present facts about alcohol in an organized way.

### 21 Reasons *for* Teens to *Avoid* Alcohol[14]

1. Underage drinkers consume more alcohol per occasion, and drink more frequently, than adults, thus doing much more harm to their health and increasing their risks of deadly consequences.
2. Underage drinking results in *permanent* damage to the memory and the part of the brain where critical thinking and learning take place.
3. Teens who drink have more difficulty making judgments, and heavy use of alcohol arrests development of emotional and social maturity, causing difficulties in communication and coping with everyday life.
4. Adolescents need only drink *half as much* as adults to suffer negative effects on their memory, learning ability, and critical thinking faculties. *Drinking a six-pack of beer affects a teenager about the same way a twelve-pack affects an adult.*
5. Underage drinking usually leads to lower grade point averages.
6. Teens who drink frequently usually *do not outgrow alcohol use*, and they do become problem drinkers or addicts as adults.
7. Underage frequent drinkers *cannot catch up with nondrinkers in brain development* in adulthood, and therefore suffer academically and socially.
8. The younger a person is when starting to drink, the higher the chances of alcohol addiction; in fact, the risk is even higher for them than it is for people who have a family history of addiction.
9. Increasing numbers of young people are becoming addicted to alcohol and other drugs before the age of eighteen.

*(continued)*

280 FROM BINGE TO BLACKOUT

10. Young people with ADHD are at great risk of developing alcohol addiction as an adult.
11. Teens are more susceptible to advertising than adults, and more advertising targets them. Television, radio, magazine, and in-store advertising contributes to increases in underage drinking. Even commercials for alcohol during sports programs reach more teens than adults.
12. Alcohol causes increases in the hormone that causes *stress*.
13. Teens who frequently use alcohol, marijuana, and other illegal drugs are likely to experience "episodes of *major depressive disorders*" as young adults.
14. Experimenting with alcohol and other drugs at a young age usually leads to *multiple addictions*.
15. Most teenagers do not use alcohol and disapprove of their peers who frequently use alcohol.
16. Underage drinkers are six times more likely than nondrinkers to have *unplanned and unprotected sex*.
17. Alcohol stimulates violence and crime. Most rapes among teenagers are "acquaintance rape," and 90 percent of them involve the use of alcohol by one or both individuals involved.
18. Underage drinkers who start to use before age fifteen are ten times more likely to be injured or killed in accidents.
19. Nationally, 4 percent of young drinkers, age twelve to seventeen, and 27 percent of those age eighteen to twenty-five, drove under the influence of alcohol in the past year, increasing the probability of fatal car crashes.
20. There are no benefits to teenagers in drinking alcohol. And there is no safe level of drinking for teenagers. The only "safe" level of drinking—for those who are taking no medications and have no other risk factors—is one per day for adult women and two per day for adult men.
21. The benefits of delaying alcohol use until after age twenty-one outweigh the negative consequences of underage use of alcohol.

Many surveys are conducted on college campuses to ascertain levels of student drinking. I learn from an alcohol counselor that college kids who fill out data surveys asking the number of drinks they consume per occasion will typically fill in the number of drinks they consume at a given event, but will not include the drinks they consumed at the preparty or postparty. Moreover, the size of these individual servings can vary greatly.

Doses of alcohol are typically standardized in the United States at 5 ounces for wine, 12 ounces for beer, and 1.5 ounces for distilled spirits. Because it is the amount of alcohol one drinks rather than the type of drink that matters, it's always good to know the alcohol content of whatever one is drinking. Alcohol affects some people more or less strongly than others, and can affect the same person differently. This depends on body weight, metabolism, tolerance from prior use, food in the stomach, and other factors. In reality, there really isn't a standard dose of alcohol.

Even wines vary in alcohol content per bottle. Standards within the wine industry differ according to individual labels, and alcohol content is creeping up. Going back thirty years, the average level of alcohol per bottle was about 12.5 percent. Today we see an average of about 14.5 percent to 15 percent.[15] A person must know her own limits and pace herself. A standard alcoholic drink is metabolized out of a person's system in approximately two to three hours.

One study from the University of Maryland reports that college students overestimate the number of ounces of standard servings of wine and liquor.[16] The average student definition of the amount of liquor in a mixed drink was more than twice the standard definition, and when free-pouring drinks, students consistently poured drinks larger than standard definitions. This suggests that when a college student reports five drinks consumed at an event, the actual quantity could well surpass that amount.

At many college parties, it is common to see kids carrying around large bottles of malt liquor, or forties, as kids call them. Why do kids drink malt liquor? When I ask Toren, he says, "It's a no-brainer. We drink them for the same reason as the homeless: they have higher alcohol content; they're readily available; they come in larger quantities; and they're cheaper." Researchers at Drew University found that malt liquor drinkers were drinking three times more alcohol on a daily basis than their beer-drinking counterparts.[17] Toren could have saved researchers time and money.

I never realized that malt liquor can have as much as 8 to 9.5 percent alcohol, compared to beer at 5 percent. It's obvious that young people drink malt liquor for the high alcohol content; it's not a taste issue. Furthermore, there is evidence that the alcohol industry has recognized the popularity of malt liquor and is marketing it to African-American men, Latino men, and college-aged white males, knowing that the way to reach young suburban drinkers is through the masculine culture associated with the hip-hop community. The catchy logos and clever branding on forties and tall cans glamorize these beverages and obviously target contemporary youth culture: Olde English; Colt 45; Schlitz's Blue Bull; Steel Reserve 211; Camo; King Cobra; Mickey's; Country Club; Big Bear; and Crazy Horse—to name a few. When Toren and I go over these brands, he refers to them fondly as if they are old friends, easily recalling and describing their distinct features. Some researchers are suggesting that malt liquor should not be marketed under a regular beer category, and that the public needs to be educated about the difference. We need a warning label.

I can remember seeing Toren and his friends sipping from big bottles of malt liquor on summer evenings or while watching holiday bowl games. I had no idea they considered this forty-ounce serving of 8 percent liquor a single serving. Or did I? Maybe I was trying not to pay attention, hoping the scene would just go away.

Since Toren and I have begun talking about alcohol openly, more people approach us to ask why, why, *why* do we drink in our society? What is it people are looking for when they open a bottle of beer or sit down at a bar? It starts so simply. Yet when an addictive genetic makeup is coupled with a society that encourages excessive indulgence, the disease of addiction seems inevitable. Toren's downfall was the classic substance of alcohol. But look at all of our options today. "Feeling good" through enhancement by a substance or behavior extends far beyond alcohol: we can choose from weed, coke, heroin, meth, OxyContin, and ecstasy—and let's not forget food, pornography, gambling, and sex. It's incredible that all of us aren't addicted to something.

At first glance other drugs or habits may seem more risky than drinking alcohol. Parents panic when thinking about their kids smoking weed after school; they don't want their kids to blimp out by overeating fatty snacks and candy bars; they abhor a child's potential involvement with porn and sexual promiscuity. As far as vices go, alcohol has a much safer, reputable image. It's more accepted by society. But really, alcohol is just another "feel-good chemical."

A student writes, "We're always taught to pay attention in school; to go to college and get that great job; to find a soul mate, house, car, kids, and all that stuff we 'need.' Maybe this is what drives us to drink. Maybe we're just a bunch of wimps who have nothing better to do than wait around until our 'problem genes' catch a whiff of the wrong substance and send us spiraling downhill." I've met the writer of these words. He's a deep-thinking, creative young man who loves the outdoors, investigates diverse cultures and languages, and isn't afraid to ask why he's here and what he's doing with his life. He's pondering why we're drinking and drugging ourselves to such extremes. Maybe it's as simple as people drinking to relax, to have fun, to forget troubles, to feel more comfortable in their skin, to gain acceptance by a person or group, to prove they're tough; or perhaps they indulge themselves because they can, or because they think it's cool. Maybe that's how we get addicted.

A family friend chimes in about the question of why we drink, remarking that throughout the history of humankind, people have tried to alter their consciousness in order to cope. "Life is hard. Maybe it's necessary to use *something* in order to get through things: alcohol, religion, caffeine, sex, nicotine, support groups, drugs, exercise. Is it all the same? Which is 'healthiest,' with the least risk of being abused?"

Let me vote on that. When I line up the aforementioned options (alcohol, religion, caffeine, sex, nicotine, support groups, drugs, exercise), it's difficult to determine which activity *is* most healthy, or moreover, which has the least risk of being abused. Looking at the list, I ask: Which substance or belief group won't break up my family if I'm abusing it? All the categories make me wary, because I've personally seen damage from their excess or misuse. Nothing seems really safe. I've even read of people dying from drinking too much water. A person can be fanatical about any ideal or practice. But at the same time, I might need *something* in my life, as our friend suggests. No matter what I choose to endorse, it seems that I must temper it with common sense. This could be the part of the discussion parents fear, because in order to do this, we must be honest to our kids about what is important to us. We must really talk about things such as exercise, sex, food, gambling, drugs, prayer or meditation, nicotine or alcohol. And then we must back up our values with our lifestyle. Our kids deserve that honesty.

So I return to the issue. What's best to help me get through tough times? Every indulgence or passion seems to carry a warning label. Perhaps I need to look for a lifestyle that does not rely on escape but encourages a direct embrace. Grabbing on to something I cherish and value, something constructive, will allow me to direct my energy forward instead of pulling a mask over my feelings. In doing this, I must model it for my children first, before I ask them to do it for themselves.

# THIRTY
## *SOBER: SO BE IT*

**Fall 2004. I continue to examine the different** phases of my recovery, and I realize that the process of "undoing" an addiction happens at a different rate for everyone. It takes time—just like it does for someone to become addicted. During my six months in the halfway house, it wasn't all growing pains, sadness, and strife. I worked my ass off at a few restaurants, saved some money, and along the way continued to put my experiences down on paper, wrote songs, and made plans for my next step.

Overall, the time I spent in Florida in my halfway situation ended up being very productive, and it did several things for me. First, it gave me a good foundation for sobriety. I learned that I could live a relatively normal life and maintain a routine without countering it all by drinking. More important, it sent a message to family and friends that I hadn't just come home from the Peace Corps because of a problem with drinking, but demonstrated that I was actually serious about getting better and changing my life. After all that, what friend would want to be held responsible for messing up my life again?

One of my old buddies, Fitz, had been living in New York City for about two years and had visited me while I was in rehab the previous fall. There we had talked about the possibility of me relocating to New York.

This was a very attractive idea to me, and it became even more enticing when I found out that another longtime friend named Charlie had arranged a music-related internship in Manhattan for the summer. Since I had returned to the States, Charlie and I had exchanged tapes of some of our new songs and talked about the idea of playing them together. All of this came about at the right time. I couldn't have dreamed up anything better than moving to Brooklyn and playing in a band.

I left the halfway house in good ol' Delray Beach, Florida, took a train straight up the coast, and eventually arrived at Penn Station. Fitz met me at the platform and helped me with my bags and guitar, still basically the majority of what I had with me from Paraguay (the rest of it was eventually sent back to Olympia in a huge box).

Before I settled in, I got on my horse and found a Twelve-Step meeting. This established some continuity from my halfway house. My sponsor had told me that if I didn't make a meeting right away I would be drunk in no time. I didn't totally believe that, but I wasn't ready to prove him right, either. It was reassuring to attend meetings and receive the same type of support as in Delray Beach.

I stayed on Fitz's couch for about three nights before I walked into a really good deal on a loft space that turned into our place. Throughout the summer, things seemed to work out that way. I found a well-paying freelance job, and during periods when I didn't work, I made my way to different meetings throughout Brooklyn and Manhattan while maintaining a fairly consistent routine of exercise at the park. Summer was under way and life was pretty good.

Shortly after Charlie moved in, we went to an open mic at a Brooklyn bar in trendy Williamsburg. We were each to play two songs, and by the time I was up, all the bar patrons had departed. For my second song, Charlie joined me and sang the harmonies. It was just us (and the sound guy as an audience) at this point, so we acted kind of wild. After we finished, he asked us if we had a band, and as I was preparing my explanation (getting ready to say no, pretty much), Charlie interrupted with, "Yeah. We have another guy. . . . We're a three-piece." Turns out the sound guy also did bookings and had a date to fill a couple of weeks later. And before we knew it, we were riding the subway home, laughing and scratching our heads because we knew that there was no turning back. Fitz played enough music to make this all possible. But we still needed a bass, amps, a drum set, a set list . . . and time to get our music together. This, of course, was the only way that things could have actually happened.

We pulled off the first show, performing some of Charlie's and my songs and switching instruments throughout. We had a lot of fun. I tried not to make a big deal about it. I once would have thought that there was no way I could go out and try something like that without getting super boozed up before. The truth is, nothing like this could have ever happened for me if I *were* drinking. I had always been on the verge of playing music with friends, or jamming here and there, but what it came down to is that in the past, I had always put drinking and getting fucked up with my friends before music . . . before everything. I felt envious of people who played music or wrote songs, but I had never thought it possible for me.

My prior choices in life had always yielded to alcohol. Most of my desires or remaining aspirations had been sucked up or blotted out by drinking. Before, I never really did anything beyond sitting around and talking in jest, satisfied with a life of debauchery and actively listening to a lot of *cool* music. I had basically been a bystander in my own life, because alcohol had always kept this imaginary party going and told me that I had everything I wanted. The differences in Florida and then Brooklyn were that I no longer spent Sundays, Mondays, and even Tuesdays braindead in front of the TV after drinking away all my nights. I was able to put my energy toward doing things I had always said I wanted to do. I could write songs when I felt like it, and I found that I could be just as creative without using drugs or alcohol.

They say New York is the city that never sleeps. I guess that is true, but I never found it necessary to stay out too late, with my little condition and all. And it doesn't seem to matter where you live or where you go out, people are drinking. I was consistently around alcohol all summer long. Sometimes I got fed up and wanted to get away from it, and other times I felt empowered. I liked that I could be around booze without drinking and have just as much fun as everyone else. Life seemed exhilarating compared to the rule-laden existence at the halfway house. We enjoyed many great outings to see good bands play, had plenty of awesome rooftop and backyard barbecues, and I found myself basking in a newfound free will that included a desire to stay sober. What a paradox for a guy like me.

In midsummer, I began spending more and more time with Julia, a girl I'd known three years prior to getting sober. She had just finished college and was living in Boston, and suddenly our old friendship/romance started up again. I had not gone to New York City in hopes of getting involved with someone. In fact, I had been curious to find what the life of a sober bachelor could offer me. Yeeeooowwww!!! Look out, ladies. I also knew that it wasn't recommended to get involved during the first year of sobriety. Surely, compared to the relationship she and I had when I was drinking, whatever was starting now could only be an improvement. For sure, this summer was the start of something new for me . . . and for us. Although I felt more than a little resistant to the idea of having a real girlfriend (commitment? honesty? intimacy? what?), I slowly opened up and began to let some of my guard down.

In a lot of ways, this time with Julia seemed like my first real intimate experience with a girl. All my previous pursuits had come second to drinking. Alcohol had stood as my first love and my most important relationship for many years. Consequently, whatever part of me that remained had been channeled into fleeting romantic interests. I had always cared a lot more about Julia than my actions may have shown, and I realized that my alcoholic ways had complicated our past. I had never really told her how I felt before. I was good at hiding my feelings . . . mainly because I couldn't convey them or didn't care. Also, in my own drunken, me-first world, by not fully getting involved, I couldn't hurt her—or any girl—whom I may have inconvenienced while drinking.

By taking alcohol out of my life, I have gained the chance to look at how I acted. Now I feel like I have much more choice in how I conduct myself. It comes down to this: How do I really want to live and what kind of person do I want to be? I don't want to live like a dirtbag anymore, and I don't want to be a shitty person. Period. No more malt liquor, no more shitty behavior.

All in all, the summer was a huge success. I felt like I had proven to myself that I was serious about being sober and that I could still have a good time. Also, I had found a way to mix my old life with my new sober life. Musically, our band ended up playing three shows and separated with vague plans to keep the dream alive the following summer, after Charlie had finished school and I had finished whatever I was planning on doing. I was working on being sober, that was it. That *is* my job.

It seemed to be in the cards that both Julia and I would move back to the Pacific Northwest after the summer. I planned to work on the book and speaking engagements, and she anticipated saving money before moving on to her next step. Translation: we'd both be living with our parents.

There were good and bad things about moving home and residing again in the town where I had grown up. I received another chance with my folks to make up for those lost years and wacky summers spent sneaking around, hiding my drinking, or just avoiding home in general. How many times had my parents woken me up drunk after passing out, had I shown up drunk and out of control with random friends, or had I gone drinking and stayed out the entire weekend because I was too trashed to come home? Plenty.

Instead, my parents and I were now able to enjoy meals together and actually interact meaningfully, with no distractions. I didn't have to manipulate stories, or battle anxiety, sleeplessness, mood swings, or the all-too-familiar onset of shakes and fevers. I could just be. I even remember the first time they went out of town for two weeks and left the house in my hands. And they didn't lock the wine cellar. Hmmm . . . either they know I'm a total loser or they really trust me. I guess it turns out to be a combination of both. I mentioned to my mom in passing that they left the wine cellar unlocked, and she replied, "At this point, Toren, you've been sober over a year. If you're gonna drink, there is nothing I can do about it. You obviously know where to find alcohol . . . anywhere." Don't give me any ideas.

I still had it in me that I wanted to return to Paraguay, but that would be on the back burner until the winter. Throughout the fall, my mom and I saw ourselves working together and speaking at high schools and universities around the country. Coming out with my drinking problem was pretty bizarre, really. I hugged more strangers than I could have possibly imagined. Their emotion and connection to my experiences made it clear how unoriginal my struggles with addiction really are. Everyone has a brother, aunt, daughter, or friend with an alcohol problem.

It was strange for me to casually sit with my otherwise conservative grandparents and literally tell them how it had been to drink like an alcoholic, act like an alcoholic, and then slowly turn into one. It was also satisfying for me to be able to tell them what it is like to be sober, to still go out and be with people who drink, and to talk about how I relate to my friends after such lifestyle changes. Through all that, they listened and still supported me.

Finally back on the West Coast, I found a pretty good balance in my life . . . er, as good as can be expected for a twenty-five-year-old still living with his parents, that is. I spent a lot of my free time with Julia. Both at home again, we sometimes felt like we had warped back to our teen years—cooking dinner, watching movies, going to shows, stealing kisses, and so on—but it felt good to reestablish a social life that had less to do with alcohol. Even if our activities didn't seem overly adventurous, we had a lot of fun together. I continued to redefine what fun was without alcohol.

I went out with quite a few of my old friends who either had moved back to Olympia or still lived in town. For these occasions, having a car was crucial, because I could always leave when I got tired, things got old, or I simply just couldn't hang. I found that it helped when I put some distance between such social outings (the ones involving drugs or alcohol). Everything was fun in small doses. Otherwise it got to be too much. There were quite a few instances when a random friend would pull me aside for a one-on-one (after a fair share of beers) and say, "Dude, I really respect what you're doing . . . if you want, man, call me sometime and we can hang out sober . . . you know, seriously, and just watch a movie or something. . . ." Their efforts were really considerate.

Another great way of keeping my life balanced was going out with my mom and giving workshops at conferences or speaking with educators or students at high schools and colleges. Sharing my story definitely has proved to be a good way for me to keep my experiences fresh (especially the worst ones toward the end of my drinking). No, I have not forgotten the humiliation of some of my blackouts, nor how it feels at the onset of withdrawal. *Death*. No more mental anguish, please. (Although the subject of my presentations addressed addiction, I learned that this activity was no substitute for going to a meeting with other people in recovery.)

To my surprise, I found it rewarding to share my experiences with people. I don't mind the fact that some young person (or older, in some cases) may relate to the things I said and decide they don't want that for themselves, or that their self-destruction may be leading them down a similar path to mine and maybe causing them to think about it. I guess you could say that it feels pretty good to carry a positive message, to say that life doesn't have to be that way. And if it turns out that way, to say that there is still hope.

Even more refreshing is letting high schoolers talk or ask questions. After a good-sized assembly at my high school alma mater, one girl dryly asked, "Don't you think you're overdramatizing this whole thing just a little? I mean, why didn't you just chill out and enjoy partying but not drink so much?" I understood her point, but like most people, she misunderstood the true nature of addiction. Afterward, she proceeded to tell me (and I swear it was like talking to my own know-it-all self at age seventeen), how she and her friends drank all the time, and that none of these things (shakes, loss of control, arrests, blackouts) ever happened to them.

I congratulated her, and did my best to explain as concisely as possible that those weren't big issues for me at her age either, but that for certain people it is a progression that doesn't stop if the heavy drinking continues. Choice and control slowly disappear from the equation. I told her that this fact would be hard for her to believe at her age, but to think about and remember our conversation. One day, almost invariably, some of her hard-drinking friends or classmates would experience symptoms and problems that they didn't want. They might have to deal with the consequences of their heavy drinking. Not everyone, just the *special* ones: the alcoholics.

At a college presentation, a kid raised his hand and remarked, "That's great and all, but what's the point of drinking if you're not drinking to get drunk?" Almost the whole class seemed to nod their heads in agreement. *Great*, I thought, *I get to argue with myself on this one*. It was hard for me to answer this question (without feeling like a hypocrite), since I obviously never got to the bottom of that question either. I tried to explain that, believe it or not, there comes a time when people stop wanting to get so out of control and crazy. Suddenly it's awkward and it isn't so amusing to be around people who are drinking until they're sick, are overly drunk, or are more obnoxious than they realize. Some of these people are on their way to alcoholism.

The point is that many people (clearly not myself, by the way) prefer to grow up, enjoy the taste and variety of an alcoholic beverage as a social agent, and choose to drink it moderately and responsibly. Most kids are clever, and not many would buy into my response. Perhaps that is why we're sent off to college, to figure these things out for ourselves. It worked for me. Well, sort of . . .

Although the average student won't want to take my word for it, especially ones of the heavy-drinking persuasion (I know how I stood on taking advice), it has been gratifying to be able to tell kids that life doesn't have to revolve around drugs and alcohol. At least I tell myself that. But it is very promising when I can authentically say that my life has been just as badass, fulfilling, and interesting since I have been sober. I don't advise people how to drink or tell people not to drink. Nor do I need to tell people how to stay sober (the solution is out there in any community . . . twelve steps away). But I can honestly describe what happened to me because of my drinking. Others get to decide for themselves.

My life may have dried out in a way, but it is far from over. No, I haven't shriveled up dead or gone into hiding since I checked out of rehab. In fact, life has gotten juicier. I think the only part of me that may have died was the part that had a death wish and wanted me pickled and wrapped around a telephone pole.

I've learned that just because I choose not to drink or use drugs today doesn't mean I can't kick back or have a good time. At the risk of sounding brainwashed, I will reiterate that life can still be fun. Maybe I *am* brainwashed. But wasn't I basically brainwashed before by my own denial? Yes, brainwashed all those previous years, listening to voices in my head telling me that I didn't have a problem. Now, I actively choose the form of brainwashing that will open doors for me rather than close them—that is something new to me, I might add. It's so new it almost hurts.

Maybe life doesn't have to be fueled by drugs and alcohol, after all. It sounds so simple, but seriously, it's something I forgot about along the way. I used to associate all the pleasurable and cool things I did with alcohol, because almost every leisure activity I participated in from age fifteen on involved drinking. I have found that I can keep my identity. (Alcohol was not my identity. I just drank so much, so often, that they always seemed to coincide.) I feared that my unique ways of thinking, my personal philosophy, my interest in music, and my attitudes about life would be compromised when I got sober. For the most part they haven't changed. I still see and do things the same way but with a less-destructive, healthier spin. Go team!!! I can be who I want to be, say whatever, and do what I want with my life—and just not drink.

I thought my lifestyle was going to be restricted by not being able to drink, but I find that I now have more choices. It is pretty amazing how it works. The biggest difference now is selecting constructive things to do and healthy outlets for my energy. The crazy part is, if things would have gone how my alcoholic mind wanted, I'd still be drinking with no consequences or addiction. All of this would have continued under the illusion that I was doing what I wished with my life.

I guess everything happens for a reason. I know I was not meant to be drugged into a numb existence with fewer and fewer brain cells, and less and less meaning every weekend. There are a lot of options out there that I didn't see before. I'm happy to say I'd rather be a part of something bigger than my own perpetual blackout.

# THIRTY-ONE
## *POWER ME UP*

**[CHRIS]** ***When the first of our three boys turned twenty-***one, he celebrated his birthday with us. He happened to be attending college nearby, so we had dinner, then Don and I took him out for his first legal alcoholic beverage. We ordered special drinks and casually discussed bar conduct, drinking etiquette, and the types of drinks he hadn't yet sampled. Later on, when he joined his friends, we returned home. Our second son celebrated his twenty-first while away at college. We called him on the phone to wish him well. By the time Toren turned twenty-one, we were thrilled that he was of legal age. He was still in town before fall semester, so we went out and played a few games of pool, bought a round of beer for him and his friends, then returned home. In all cases, our kids partied on without us into the early hours of the morning.

When kids go out to celebrate a twenty-first birthday, no one intends that they will drink themselves to death. Parents think that by the time kids are twenty-one, they already know about drinking. And kids, of course, think they know what they're doing as well. To many parents, it's a huge relief. Time to celebrate! Worries about underage drinking violations evaporate. But celebrating a twenty-first birthday can prove lethal, because drinkers that age are relatively inexperienced and susceptible to friends' social prodding. They feel they can survive anything. While

295

pleased that at last our kids can drink legally at age twenty-one, we parents ought to be fervently praying that they will live through the celebration.

Some parts of the country initiate twenty-one-year-olds with a celebration called power hour. Apparently this "21 for 21" is a popular tradition, a custom where the twenty-one-year-olds go to a bar at midnight on their birthdays and try to chug twenty-one shots in the hour or two before closing time. Over the past five years, six states have reported deaths from this deadly rite of passage.[1] Even so, many bars near colleges promote twenty-first birthday celebrations. Some businesses even provide a souvenir bucket for retching at the table. The number of shots ingested by the celebrant is often written on his or her forearm or forehead, while friends chant slogans or taunts at the drinker. Kids commonly assume that their friends will watch out for them and not allow anything bad to happen. But what sometimes occurs is that birthday drinkers die afterward in their sleep of acute alcohol poisoning while their friends have no idea it is happening.

There is criticism of bars that serve power hour patrons. These celebrations have become so popular and lethal that several states have passed laws prohibiting bars from serving alcohol to twenty-one-year-olds until eight a.m. on their birthdays. Minnesota and North Dakota have experienced problems with kids killing themselves in honor of their birth. These states hope that enacting the power hour law will lower the rush to drink twenty-one shots of alcohol in less than two hours.[2] Some bars limit the celebration to a mug of beer, with no shots served. The power hour trend serves as a reminder that attitudes about drinking can prove fatal. Some wonder how a law could stop a twenty-first birthday celebration. Will the parties then move to private locations? Others say that such laws save lives by allowing kids to have a whole day to drink their twenty-one shots. (Hmm. Now *that's* a smart idea.) Some predict it will relieve peer pressure and end the practice.

On the other hand, celebrating a noteworthy occasion with kids can be a festive way to acknowledge a special day, while at the same time modeling moderate drinking for teens. Parents are not always able to be with their sons and daughters on their twenty-first birthdays. If not, going over celebration plans could be helpful. Some kids may not completely understand the difference between moderate drinking and bingeing. Parents can review information about alcohol poisoning and discuss the consequences. This is a good way to talk about celebratory drinking with teens.

## What Happens to Your Body When You Get Alcohol Poisoning?[3]

Alcohol depresses nerves that control involuntary actions such as breathing and the gag reflex (which prevents choking). A fatal dose of alcohol will eventually stop these functions.

It is common for someone who drank excessive alcohol to vomit since alcohol is an irritant to the stomach. There is then the danger of choking on vomit, which could cause death by asphyxiation in a person who is not conscious.

A person's blood alcohol concentration (BAC) can continue to rise even while he or she is passed out. Even after a person stops drinking, alcohol in the stomach and intestine continues to enter the bloodstream and circulate throughout the body. It is dangerous to assume the person will be fine by "sleeping it off."

### Critical Signs for Alcohol Poisoning

- mental confusion, stupor, coma, or person cannot be roused
- vomiting
- seizures
- slow breathing (fewer than eight breaths per minute)
- irregular breathing (ten seconds or more between breaths)
- hypothermia (low body temperature), bluish skin color, paleness

Each year we hear of numerous college-aged youths who have died due to alcohol toxicity. In 2004, there were nineteen such deaths, not including other accidents, violence, and crashes due to intoxication.[4] These tragedies suggest that there is more work to be done. Every parent with whom I have spoken who has lost a child to alcohol toxicity has told me that the family was unaware their teen had been a heavy drinker, and explained that there had been other circumstances involved (such as being passed out overnight in cold weather or simply "drinking more than he realized"). Parents of some of these youths have started memorial foundations to educate the public about alcohol poisoning and to develop counseling services to reduce future risks of alcohol abuse. The B.R.A.D. 21 foundation focuses especially on twenty-first birthday celebrations and responsible use of alcohol;[5] the Gordie Foundation focuses on the dangers of alcohol and promotion of self-worth to prevent alcohol poisoning, binge drinking, and hazing;[6] and the SAM Spady Foundation educates youth on high-risk alcohol consumption and alcohol poisoning.[7]

Nineteen-year-old Samantha Spady died on September 5, 2004, at Colorado State University after drinking approximately forty shots of liquor and beer. The sophomore business major had a blood-alcohol level of .436, and with her five-feet-six-inch, 126-pound frame, "her blood-alcohol content was indicative of thirty to forty 12-ounce beers or 1.5-ounce shots over an eight-to-ten-hour period," said the deputy coroner.[8] (A BAC of .400 is considered a lethal level.) I talked with Patty Spady, her mother, about the SAM Spady Foundation and efforts on Samantha's behalf—on behalf of all youth, for that matter. She spoke softly, yet with conviction. "If we can save just one life, it's worth it," she stated. "Too many parents don't know the quantities their kids are drinking. We're doing whatever we can so that what happened to us will not happen to other families."

The most serious consequence of alcohol poisoning is death. When there is a heartbreaking story about an adolescent death in the newspaper, it often involves a parent talking about the child, saying how surprising it is that the calamity happened. It occurs to me that Toren's drinking inci-

## What Should I Do If I Suspect Someone Has Alcohol Poisoning?[9]

- Know the danger signals.
- Do not wait for all symptoms to be present.
- Be aware that a person who has passed out may die.
- If there is any suspicion of an alcohol overdose, call 911 for help. Don't try to guess the level of drunkenness.

## When Alcohol Poisoning Goes Untreated

- Victim chokes on his or her own vomit.
- Breathing slows, becomes irregular, or stops.
- Heart beats irregularly or stops.
- Hypothermia (low body temperature).
- Hypoglycemia (too little blood sugar) leads to seizures.
- Untreated severe dehydration from vomiting can cause seizures, permanent brain damage, or death.

Even if the victim lives, an alcohol overdose can lead to irreversible brain damage. Rapid binge drinking (which often happens on a bet or a dare) is especially dangerous, because the victim can ingest a fatal dose before becoming unconscious.

Don't be afraid to seek medical help for a friend who has had too much to drink. Don't worry that your friend may become angry or embarrassed. Remember, you cared enough to help. Always be safe, not sorry.

dents could be interchanged with those of any youth lost to alcohol toxicity, and my experience from the parent's perspective could be that of any other mother. Fatalities among young binge drinkers seem random. I am grateful that our family can continue on and am mindful of other parents' losses. Throughout our travels, speaking with parents who have lost their children to alcohol abuse is the most tragic conversation imaginable. It hits home how senseless these types of young deaths can be.

The process of writing a book has given Toren and me many chances to go over details of his upbringing. When we began working on the first edition, we spent three days together in Florida poring over material we had compiled for the beginning chapters and formulating our goals. By the second time we met, Toren and I had completed part of the manuscript.

Six months later, it is different. Toren has finished his halfway program and moved on. Don and I find him happily installed in a Brooklyn warehouse loft, playing music, working a job, and negotiating his new territory. This is the third time we have met to sort through our scattered notes in order to glue our family back together. For this rewrite, we meet in Manhattan, street noise muffled in the background, to discuss final changes to our work.

In order to better understand what we have put on paper, we decide to say aloud every word. As we sit in a hotel room overlooking the city, Toren reads my chapters to me, then I read his chapters to him. Hearing my own words in Toren's voice changes the perspective of our lives so completely that it forces me to listen with new ears. I can't believe what I hear myself saying when it comes from his mouth. On the other side, when I read Toren's words, it causes him to stop me at several points so that we can talk about troubling issues. This reading transforms our struggle into an audible storm that seems insurmountable at certain moments. The tangle of our conflicting stories about Toren's growing up and how our family dealt with him sounds like something from some other family's experience. In addition, speaking someone else's worries aloud makes them more real. Suddenly our very personal situations cannot be ignored, because now another voice has acknowledged it. Uttering and hearing such sad and depressing descriptions of ourselves overwhelms us. After an hour or so, one of us begs to stop. Then, a solitary walk follows, in two different directions.

Much of our visit is spent going over the manuscript. Toren and I huddle over dingy laptops, rearranging parts of our lives throughout the past nine years. To my surprise, fresh stories still spring from Toren's past. New details of his former drug and alcohol escapades continue to shock and concern me. I wonder when the bombshells will stop dropping. And he then admits to me that yes, after all, he really *had* been drinking at the river party when first arrested at age fifteen. All this time, even during rehab, I had continued believing Toren's original claim that he had only *attended* the party of drinking upperclassmen. We look at each other in disbelief over the ridiculous idea that either of us could have been so pathetic: him to lie about the event, and me to swallow his story. There seemed to have been no middle ground for discussion when Toren was fifteen.

"We need something to help people talk about alcohol," I suggest to Toren, "some sort of tool where families can find out if they've at least covered the basics." Toren nods.

After talking more, we create what our family might have found useful. Or better yet, something that could have been utilized years before the event occurred. Having this tool might not cause every family member to be honest about what is being said, but it could allow for discussion and thinking. That's what parents and kids need first. The truthful part might not come until ten years later.

---

### Is Your Family Talking About Alcohol?[10]

### Three Questions for Parents:

- Has our family talked about the developing adolescent brain, blackouts, and the damage caused by heavy drinking between age eleven and twenty-four?
- Has our family talked about the genetic history of alcoholism in our nuclear and extended family?
- Has our family talked about binge drinking, alcohol poisoning, and the fact that even one binge experience could cause irreparable brain damage to a teen?

Even one "no" answer indicates the need for more talking!

*(continued)*

---

### Three Questions for Young People:

- Are you aware of the severe risks of heavy drinking and its effects on the still-developing adolescent brain (between ages eleven and twenty-four) and that one binge experience could cause irreparable brain damage?
- Do you know about the disease of alcoholism and the role of heredity in your family?
- Have you thought about your drinking choices and talked about them with your parents or a caring adult?

Even one "no" answer indicates the need for more talking!

The above are questions we wish we had asked sooner.
Alcoholism is a family disease.

---

Months later, after the first edition of the book has been released, Toren and I travel together to Washington, D.C. Toren suggests we visit the Peace Corps nurse who assisted him more than a year ago during his assessment upon his return from Paraguay and prior to rehab. Since we are in town on business, Toren and I go together to her office, where we are ushered into a conference room. Toren has told me about this remarkable woman, her compassion and expertise, and the efficient but sensitive way she dealt with him. I am pleased to be able to meet her, to thank her for the care of my son.

She greets us both warmly. When she asks how Toren is doing, he summarizes his rehab and halfway experiences. Before she can pose more questions, he opens his backpack and places *Our Drink*, the first edition, on the table. Her mouth falls open. "I can't believe it!" she repeats over and over. Recovering from shock, she admits that it is highly unusual for someone who has undergone treatment to return to see her, and even more to have written and published a book about it. This occasion, suddenly momentous, marks an exact moment of realization. Here is the instant when both Toren and I can step back and see progress through her eyes. She graciously allows us this moment of basking, which heals and blesses our efforts even as faltering and naïve as they had been. All of us swallow back our tears and laugh at how absurd it is to be sitting together, celebrating our pain and our joy at the same moment.

This flow of healing begins to build. Now as Toren and I speak to more people about what happened to our family, we do not feel like experts, only learners. We are invited to offer presentations for educators, students, and counselors in high schools and colleges across the country. Waiting in airports allows us even more time to go over the past and reflect on what we could have done differently. I sense Toren's confidence growing. Every moment we spend together fastens our lives back together and offers another chance for our family to rediscover itself.

Midway through the fall, Toren announces, "I've decided. I'm going back to Paraguay."

Not surprised, thinking he might go in the spring, I ask, "Do you know when?"

"I'll have enough money saved by December. So that's when I'll leave. I'm going to stay there for a while. Maybe six weeks, so I can adjust to the pace of the country. And maybe I'll do a little traveling in South America."

This December. As Toren explains his plans, I brace myself for whatever catastrophe this could present. It does not seem possible, even as well as things are going, that he could be successful. What if he can't find his family? What if there are hard feelings? What if no one else is as supportive as the nurse in Washington, D.C.? And how could he think of missing Christmas with the rest of our family?

Gazing at him and his determined manner, I can see how important this goal is. I reassure myself that when he is able to make arrangements on his own and save the money to go, it will be a sign that he is capable of facing his past. I realize that Toren's recovery does not necessarily include me and what I think *I* need. I reason that he is stronger than I'd realized. His power to succeed enables him to move forward. It isn't for me to worry about. So I don't.

# THIRTY-TWO
## A SIP OF CLARITY

**[TOREN]** **Before this goes any further, it may be necessary** to point out that I am talking less about alcohol and more about what is going on in my life. There is a simple explanation for this: although the objective of this writing is to portray my life in relationship to alcohol and my recovery from alcoholism, I now have more sobriety under my belt, and I find that I am able to start doing what I want with my time. An existence that was once completely dominated by alcohol has now been freed up, and I am experiencing life in a much different way.

It may also seem that my tone has changed from being desperate, bitter, confused, or hopeless to optimistic, content, and upbeat. The difference is that I no longer feel defeated or ruined. Some time has passed now, and slowly but surely I am re-co-ver-ing. My life has opened up and my outlook has changed in many ways. I am only ready to move on to each new phase when the time comes, not one moment before. By the time I bought my return ticket to South America sometime in the fall of 2004, I had just reached a year sober, had survived a summer in New York City on my own, and no longer felt like I needed protection from the real world.

It is hard to pinpoint exactly why I thought I needed to go back to

Paraguay. I knew I could no longer be a volunteer, but I wanted some form of closure. I still didn't know if I could face the community I had, in essence, abandoned. My return had a sense of urgency, though. I had not been in communication with most of the volunteers, and few of them really understood what had become of me. My visit would only make sense if the rest of the volunteers in my group were still there, so I had to return before their two-year service commitment was fulfilled. I wanted to know what had gone on since I had been extracted from the equation. Part of my healing process would not be complete until I went back and saw things for myself. I itched with curiosity and wanted just one more taste of the life I had lost to my drinking.

I traveled light, with just a backpack, but thought it worth the inconvenience to bring my guitar along. One thing I didn't take with me was a plan. I had given myself six weeks for travel, more than enough time. In roughly two-week increments, I thought I'd travel a bit, visit Paraguay, and then travel again. There were many things I wanted to see, but I realized that no matter what, I would always feel like I was missing something.

On my layover in Florida I reached my friend Tomás by phone. He was the volunteer to whom I had confided some of my worst drinking struggles and the one I felt closest to. I mentioned to him that I was on my way down, so he gave me some general directions (go to so-and-so town, take this bus to random village in the middle of nowhere, and ask for the American is basically how it went). This was the invitation to find him. After dreaming up various itineraries on the plane ride, I arrived in Buenos Aires, Argentina. Still no plan. I decided the best thing to do was to start with Paraguay right away and save the superfluous travel till later.

From the Buenos Aires airport that morning, I started the next leg of my trip: overland travel to Poncho in the district of Itapua, Paraguay. The bus ride from the airport into downtown took almost two hours. Then I walked forever to get to the bus terminal, only to find that I had to wait until later that afternoon for my next thirty-some-hour bus ride to Encarnación, a town on the Paraguayan border. From there I would find the bus that Tomás described and begin my search for the American. The bus ride was long, but I felt energized.

The next morning, a bit before sunrise, I was awakened and ushered off the bus at the border so that the police could check papers and my passport. It was still dark, and I was close to my destination. After I got back on, in my groggy morning haze, I noticed that we had already passed through the main part of a town and seemed to be continuing out into darkness again. Finally I asked and found out a little too late that the bus was continuing on another five hours to Asunción, the capital of Paraguay, and we had just passed through the town where I needed to catch my connecting bus. Of course they told me I couldn't get off. Finally I convinced them that I *had* to get off. They stopped, and I was spit out onto the dark highway.

It smelled like heaven. Strange familiarity flooded my senses. A rush of aromas and sounds elicited all kinds of good memories. It was drastically warmer than I was prepared for, and the sun was just starting to rise. My heart finally stopped pounding from the misunderstanding on the bus, and I began to trace the red clay highway back to town. I walked for what seemed to be a good hour until I finally found the bus station. There I learned that the bus I needed didn't leave for a few more hours, so I killed some more time. Welcome to Paraguay.

I stayed at Tomás's village for just over two weeks. It was great to be part of that world again, a chance to experience a simple way of daily living. Not that tourism really exists in Paraguay, but I didn't feel like a tourist. I got a chance to see the relationships that Tomás had forged with the kids in the community, and by the time I left I had become acquainted with a handful of families and felt comfortable with some of his closer friends there. Once again I felt at home with the people and culture of rural Paraguay. There I received an extraordinary, if brief, second chance at the opportunity I had missed.

After being away from Paraguay for more than a year, I no longer found the responsibilities and hardships of their daily life as desirable. It was reassuring to experience their lifestyle in my detached way, but I knew I didn't have the drive to be a volunteer, as I once had when starting out. My intervention and subsequent recovery somehow had made the two mutually exclusive, and forced me to move on. I had grown apart from the culture just enough to be appreciative of it, as well as to observe how much things had changed for myself and for all the other volunteers.

Tomás and I hiked a trail that passed through various fields of soy, peanuts, corn, and sunflowers, and down into a steep, wooded valley, where Bernardo, another volunteer, lived. We planned to stay only one night, and fittingly, it began to rain. In Paraguay this means that the world stops turning. Most of the rock-hard red roads turn into long clay Slip 'N Slides, and nothing gets accomplished. That following afternoon we bought and killed a chicken. We enjoyed a good meal, and I recalled how filling the time during such downpours had become an art form for most of my volunteer friends. In the United States, people are accustomed to having something stimulate their senses at all times, or they depend on constant entertainment. Being in rural Paraguay is like turning back the clock seventy-five years. It was pleasant to just mellow out and see what it's like to pass time without a specific objective.

During my visit with Tomás in Poncho, we usually ate lunch with one of the nearby families. Because Poncho is located close to Brazil, several families of German descent had come there in recent generations. They retained excellent traditions of agriculture and cooking, which had rubbed off on Tomás. He pickled cucumbers from his garden and could raise yeast and bake up a hearty loaf of bread on a self-constructed brick oven by the time I came to visit. A creek ran through the property where bathing and laundering took place. Living in a house he had built himself upon arrival, with the permission of his neighbor family, it was obvious that he had invented his own version of the Peace Corps dream.

Since getting sober, this venture in Paraguay would be the first time I had been away from my routine world of Twelve Step meetings. I had talked about it (to myself mostly), and thought about what temptations might lay ahead for me. Early in recovery, I halfway joked that when I reached a year sober, I could drink again . . . or that if I went on vacation, say, to South America, that maybe I could drink there. Why not? No one would have to find out. I could detox myself on Valium like the last time. That was so easy. Besides, on Semester at Sea I learned that Valium, among other things, could be easily obtained without a prescription. For sure these are the kinds of thoughts that a recovering alcoholic or drug addict faces.

As much as I preach how wonderful it is to be sober, it is a safe bet to say that most alcoholics and addicts still miss aspects of drinking or using and would love it if there were no such thing as consequences. Luckily, as the months pass and more sobriety soaks in, I realize that I would be risking a lot and throwing away growth, all for some short-lived-moment-turned-long-run-disappointment. So of course, I drank.

But it isn't like it seems, so let me explain. First of all, it *was* the day after Christmas. Tomás and I visited one of the German-Brazilian families, where we were treated to a wonderful barbecue with exquisite food and a good time. I had refused drinks at meals with them before, so this time it wasn't as uncomfortable. (Without proper explanation, it is always a little strange and awkward.) I declined with no problem.

It wasn't till afterward, when walking home, that the trouble started. We stopped by a neighbor family's house for a visit, the same home where we had celebrated Christmas along with the entire family the previous night, eating dinner, then counting down till midnight while singing Christmas songs. There was enough family for several choirs, so it wasn't too obvious that I had stayed out of the rotation when drinks were passed around.

On this afternoon, we joined some of the family, who sat on rickety wooden chairs in their habitual place, shaded under a big mango tree. Meanwhile, the oldest brother (of many) asked if Tomás wouldn't mind accompanying him and his wife to a town that was quite a distance away. It seemed to be an overall pointless task, but somehow Tomás was suckered into the role of chaperone. Realizing how long and time-consuming the trip would be, his parting words were, "I'll be okay, Toren. Stay here, save yourself." In light of his sacrifice, I planned on visiting with the family a little more and then heading over to Tomás's for a bit of guitar, reading, some good old peace and quiet, or even a nap. Life was good.

With Tomás gone, I sat around with two of the other brothers and their soft-spoken, proud father. Something about this family struck me. They seemed to have an overwhelming sense of calm and peacefulness that spread to me when I was with them. Still, these stare-down-type situations can often be tricky for volunteers when they first spend time with a new family. Sometimes there just isn't a whole lot to say. After talking about the weather, the neighbors, and the Olimpia and Cerro Porteño soccer teams (the only two teams that seem to matter to Paraguayans), or how the weather affects the animals and the crops, things can get tough. Customarily, then, someone breaks out the yerba maté and a pitcher of ice-cold water. This refreshing and energizing (nonalcoholic) tea is then passed around, becoming the focus of the occasion. Usually, at this point it is again best to address the weather from a different angle. But not on this fine day.

After a long silence, I saw the father get up and run back to the house with an almost boyish excitement. He returned with a pitcher of the traditional holiday drink they had shared the previous evening. The beverage, called *clerico*, is like a Paraguayan Christmastime version of jungle juice (a fruity alcoholic drink).

In this type of situation, usually one glass is poured and passed around, or if it is a liter bottle of beer, they will just pass the bottle around. Normally each person takes a turn and leisurely passes it on. (If someone is holding it for too long, distracted by their own talking, sometimes you'll hear someone say, *"No es un micrófono."* It's not a microphone. In other words, pass it on!)

As in any culture, in Paraguay there is a long list of dos and don'ts. Many of them are forgivable, especially when these cultural norms are broken by confused foreigners. I had already turned down offerings of alcohol in various settings, but I knew this was going to be a bit more difficult. After the father took a few sips, he passed the cup of *clerico* to me and gave me this look that seemed to say, "I offer you this most holy and precious Christmas drink. It is only available here and now. By drinking it, you will dignify me as a host. Your refusal will bring shame to my family and all generations to follow."

"*No, gracias,*" I said.

Without even a flinch, he offered it to me again, and assured me that I would really like it. "Go ahead, try it."

It felt like a situation right out of some D.A.R.E. skit we used to do. I told him no, thanks, that I had just eaten a really big meal. (Even though it was true in this case, using this phrase is an accepted way of refusing unsanitary water or otherwise dangerous offerings without insulting the host.)

Still, the father insisted that the drink would sit well with the meal and that I would really like it. "Here, try it."

I told him, "*No sé como tomar alcohol,*" which literally means "I don't know how to drink alcohol." That was the truth for sure, but in Paraguay they will ask if you "know how to eat a certain thing" in order to allow you to express whether you like it. The phrase is a way of indicating whether you want any.

My response didn't faze him. All that mattered was that I try his drink. I looked around helplessly. Where was Tomás? He was naturally a brilliant communicator and a master at defusing awkward situations such as this. I hesitated. I didn't know what else to do. Having exhausted all my excuses, I couldn't just walk away. My confusion only seemed to make matters worse.

Then I reached for the cup. I brought it toward my lips for a while but hardly sipped much in. I tried not to make a scene or think too hard. A mix of cola, wine, and chopped-up fruit came into my mouth. It lingered there, and then I swallowed it down. I detected a trace of the wine among a surge of overly sweet flavors. I tried to ignore the alcohol but feared another part of me wanted to see if I could actually taste it and soak it all in. When I passed the still nearly-full cup back to the father, I confirmed, "*¡Que rico!*" Delicious! He gave me a satisfied look. There, I had fulfilled my requirement.

At this point the illicit drink could mean whatever I wanted to make of it. I could dwell on it and make a big deal of it, or remember that I chose to respect the family's culture and take the path of least resistance (get over it). I am proud to say that I didn't accept the next drink that came around, and I excused myself from the situation as soon as I could do so without being offensive.

Did I just relapse? Not really. I felt no desire to actually drink. I experienced the alcohol a bit, but it tasted more like a bad idea. It tasted like fear. It wasn't enough to trigger any physical reaction or to awaken my disease per se, but I did *not* care to see how much alcohol I could drink without losing control. That would basically mean that I was looking to get drunk. On this day I didn't want to get drunk. And I didn't. I may have walked a fine line, and taken a cultural pass, but I was not trying to get away with something. I still believe there is absolutely no good reason for me to pick up that first drink.

My two weeks in Poncho proved to be a perfect crash-course review of Paraguayan culture, where I slowly reabsorbed a lot of the language that my poor brain had tried to learn a year and a half earlier. I partially owe my longer than planned stay to an illness that resembled giardia-like encounters I had experienced before. It was an excellent reason to continue on and spend Christmas with Tomás and the friendly people in his village.

Overall, this visit was the perfect way to get reintroduced to the Paraguayan lifestyle and to capture a satisfying taste of what I knew I had missed out on. I now felt prepared for my impending interactions with families from my former community. I'd had a great time seeing Tomás again. It seemed like it had been forever since I had thought aloud about my drinking problems while he and I had planted mandioca and corn behind my house my first time in Paraguay. Only three months more of service remained for Tomás and the other volunteers in my former group. A lot had changed.

# THIRTY-THREE
## DEADHEADING

**[CHRIS]** *Winter 2004. Raising a child is like deadheading* a plant. We pull off spent blooms and remark how wretched they look. What was once vibrant and beautiful has become faded and worn. The flower tarnished, we wonder whatever will become of this withered plant that once flourished from careful tending. It seems like all those special composts, fertilizer, and grow potions may not have been worth it, let alone the hours spent weeding and watering. This is the point when we'd like to give up. But our master gardener friend whispers to us that we should snip off the bad stuff; then work all the harder with the soil; utilize exposure to sunlight and resources, and watch patiently. "Keep nurturing it," she stresses. "If the still-living plant thinks you've given up, it will go to seed. Yet, if the plant is encouraged to bloom again, it will put out a whole new set of blossoms." She advises waiting for the next flowering and assures us that we won't be disappointed.

Well, some of us have to wait season after season with discouraging results. What we are raising seems like a forever-dormant garden. But lately ours has been showing signs of life. We have welcomed Toren back home. At this point Toren has not only returned to our home for fall and winter, but meanwhile has departed on his return trip to Paraguay. At age twenty-five he landed briefly back in the family plot and we have read-justed to a third resident.

Don and I are pleased to have him home. Toren and I adopt an office-hours professionalism as we work on speaking commitments. I am reminded how pleasant he is to have around. Don and I steal this unex-pected time with him against the deficit we experienced while he was a rebellious teenager. Recapturing these moments is another unexpected gift. Our garden again blooms, though out of season.

Toren takes the opportunity to visit my parents and returns with bags of homemade snickerdoodles and gingersnaps. "It's really great how I can talk to them now," he says and grins.

I nod. "Is it so different than before?"

"Oh, yeah," Toren explains, "*everything* changed when I was in the halfway house. It happened the first time when I called Grandma and Grandpa from there."

"When had you last spoken to them?"

"Not since before I left for the Peace Corps, for over nine months. I was dreading talking to them from Florida, because I knew they would tell me how I could have prevented my drinking problems. But I called them anyway." Toren bites into a cookie and continues, "They asked me how I was doing, and I told them a little bit about rehab and my situation, how I was living. It was just me talking for quite a while."

"How did they finally react to you?"

"Well, after I described what I was doing in the halfway house, it was just plain quiet. Nothing. They didn't say anything. Then after that long pause, Grandma said, 'Well, Toren, we love you. And we admire your courage.'"

"That's all?"

He smiles as he recalls the story. "Then Grandpa slowly said, 'Just let us know how we can support you.' That's it. That's all they said. I've *never* had such a short conversation with them. And I was like, well, that's cool. That's really cool. They love me."

Toren goes on to say that he had been expecting advice, their version of how he should have been behaving, but they surprised him. "What happened because of this was that I felt supported, not blasted or criticized. Their acceptance caused me to be more open with them." Toren laughs. "At the time, I had no idea they were reading text off an index card you had placed by their phone. And it still doesn't matter, because it got us off to a fantastic start." He crunches down on a second cookie. It's obvious he is basking in their love and is willing to accept it, offered either by phone or via Grandma's batch of mouthwatering cookies.

The new version of our family is now known within the community as well. One acquaintance at my health club remarks to me, "Some people will do anything to get famous," and grins broadly. A musician friend tells me that she has added our autographed book to her prized collection, along with Kurt Vonnegut and Captain Kangaroo. Toren's grade school piano teacher meets him at a signing and asks, "Do you still know where middle C is?" All of these remarkable friends come forth to humor and support us. Toren and I feel their encouragement guiding us along our road.

Several book groups invite Toren and me to their discussions. After one meeting, Toren marvels, "It's just like talking to you and a bunch of your friends. They are so outspoken and rowdy. But they really care." That's because many of them are already familiar with this battle of drinking decisions and feel that they already know us after having read our book. Many of them have kids who are teens right now, or else they have struggled on their own or with their friends' kids. The women talk openly about their conflicts, and the discussion is sprinkled with personal stories and comparisons to our family. We laugh about the spontaneity of the group, how during the discussion a mother endearingly called Toren "You little shit!" Toren had never before met this woman from a distant town, but the way she playfully addressed him seemed to sum up every parent's exasperation at a disobedient or wayward teen. Toren and I spent hours talking with these people, attempting to get to the bottom of

Toren's behaviors, our family's reactions, and what these parents could take back to their own families from our experiences.

Mentors beyond the family, many who live outside our community, lend support to Toren and his brothers. These close associates provide a protective blanket. Throughout the years, our boys have stayed close to a number of people who impact and assist them. The development of such a friendship between a teen and another trusted adult (such as a teacher or family friend) can create a partnership that will fill the role of observer, as well as provide a vital confidant who is able to counsel or support the teen in ways a parent can't. Having the backing of a mentor prior to adolescence and throughout the ensuing journey to young adulthood can be a huge stabilizer for a teen. Toren and his brothers have several adults who have stood by them through the years, no matter what, and their support continues to bolster Toren through his recovery. Many of the friendships have evolved into relationships independent of Don and me. Toren is free to contact these inspirational friends on his own and has developed a personal rapport with them.

Outside mentors provide quiet assurance not only for Toren but for our entire family. When such respected friends magically appear or telephone to ask how things are going, or when they express interest in what the boys are doing, it calms us as parents, and also lets our boys know that others are interested in our family's well-being.

Relatives from Don's family call, sometimes laughingly identifying themselves by their pseudonyms in our book. Tim and Grant, two of Don's cousins, arrange to attend our speaking presentations, and Grant brings his grown daughter to a signing, where he spends two hours talking with us, going over past drinking habits and the relief he has found in sobriety. "You're going to feel better and better as the years pass by," he predicts to Toren. "It takes a long time for the body and mind to readjust. But you'll be thrilled by how fantastic your life will be." His daughter listens quietly as he talks about the dissolution of his first marriage and the loss he experienced before changing his ways. Certainly she could recall some of his tales firsthand, since she had been a young girl during this turmoil. This is honest family talk without barriers, so open that I can hardly believe we are sitting in the middle of a bookstore discussing such aching memories. Few people have the chance to sit down like this with family and touch one another's hearts. Or maybe families *do* have the chance, but don't take it. I admire Grant for arranging time from his work schedule to reach out to us. Our written words have allowed this part of the extended family to know us, and now they wish us to know them. It's a generous offering and we enjoy our time with them.

Our family visits Granddad out of town. He is eighty-nine years old and professes, "I'm getting easier to get along with all the time." A disciplined two-war army vet, retired orchardist, truck driver, and a man who has overcome more than enough hardships in his lifetime, Granddad places spiritual and ethical beliefs first. Anyone who has met him knows where he stands, even though he struggles as he repeats, "I can't see; I can't hear; I can't walk; I can't breathe; but I feel great!" Toren's granddad has not seen Toren for two years and wants to find out what has gone on, even though we have attempted to explain it to him. He now brings up Toren's decision to go into rehab as we are traveling in the car on the way to dinner. He hollers toward the backseat, "Hey, Toren, can you tell me how long you were in the clinker before you gave up and went on the wagon?" A huge, dead pause sinks inside the car. Toren's brothers, who are passengers, look over at Toren and practically fall into hysterics. Everyone restrains themselves as I calmly ask Granddad to explain his question. Apparently he thought Toren was sent to prison for drinking and then had decided to reform. (Well, I guess Toren's drinking was sort of like his own self-imposed prison.) Toren again explains his decision to enter rehab to Granddad, and we marvel at the example of Granddad's unconditional love, how he had thought that Toren had been in jail for who knows what, but still accepted and loved him.

We celebrate Granddad's ninetieth birthday a season later and the extended family pours in. Groups of relatives who had not been seen together in years show up. Even though no one talks about it overtly, the outing of Toren's drinking has allowed us to embrace one another with unspoken but solid loyalty. Granddad sits on a special throne built for the occasion so that family and friends may approach him at hearing-aid level for well wishes and congratulations. When Granddad's minister appears, Granddad pulls Toren over and introduces him to the clergyman in a tumultuous voice, "This is my grandson, *Toren the alcoholic*." Reported so matter-of-factly with amplified pride and dignity, it almost seems like Granddad is announcing an award. The minister blushes and we see that he is uncomfortable. Toren later tells me that he almost burst out laughing when he heard his new title. What a family we are becoming.

Surrounded by the warmth and acceptance of family members who know what we have faced, I suddenly realize that what to us seems practically normal (living alongside an alcoholic) can be quite unsettling for someone on the outside. Whereas our family considers Toren's disease a part of our life, as one would consider the everyday diagnosis of someone who has diabetes, this disease of alcoholism may be considered embarrassing or even shameful to someone else looking in. Because no one is making a big deal of Toren's "label," our family continues to function and enjoy one another while doing everything we can to sustain success. The minister's discomfort is an insight into how the rest of the world might perceive us, and I am learning how important it is to proudly accept my son and stand up for the person he is and for the family he represents.

While at a book signing on a university campus, Toren and I experience yet another powerful reunion with the other side of our family. We sit behind our signing table on a cold autumn day, meeting random students and parents who are attending a rousing football game on Dads' Weekend. Since it is my college alma mater, we had previously driven around the campus, while I tried not to bore Toren with rambling stories about my college days, where I'd lived, how things had changed, and different escapades I'd experienced with his father (who at that time had been my college boyfriend). Also living in that same town are two of my sisters, whom I had not seen in many years, the result of a lengthy and painful family estrangement. From our upbringing in a family of five girls, two of my sisters have chosen to remove themselves due to religious differences. As a result, these sisters are able to avoid our mom's (Toren's grandma) sometimes acerbic comments, but they also miss out on her fabulous cookies, her passionate zest for life, and her enfolding love. I guess they've also missed the chance to support *my* family. And we have certainly missed knowing them.

I try to call one of them while picking up breakfast, but I no longer have a working phone number, and we run out of time before the signing. I figure it is futile anyway; my sisters would probably not be interested in a book about addiction. (My other fear is that they might be too interested, and perhaps stop by to harass me about my alcoholic son.)

While greeting our readers, one woman catches my eye as she enters the bookstore with a teen in tow. I can't place her—until, suddenly, like looking in a wavery mirror, I see my own sister. And then her daughter. It has been about thirteen years since we'd been together, but I know it is her. We practically fall over the table trying to reach one another.

"I heard you were in town," she tells me. "It was on the radio this morning."

But my eyes can't leave her daughter, for there before me is almost a replica of myself. We all realize it, Toren included, and he blurts, "You look like my mom!" His eyes dance, because this is the first time he has ever met his first cousin, a sparkling teen ingénue.

Despite years of unspoken sentiments, none of us can keep still. We talk for close to two hours, though our conversation is slightly stilted for fear of offending any absent family member or saying something that would bring up old roadblocks. After sharing coffees, hugs, and parting wishes, Toren exclaims to me, "They seem so normal! Why don't we see them?"

And I can't logically tell him why or what has destroyed the relationships between my two sisters and me. He and I discuss it for six more hours as we drive back home. I can only think that this whole experience is a miracle, this alcoholism, this bringing to the forefront our imperfect family, so that we can be approached by sisters, cousins, and strangers all in one. I don't know if I will ever see my sister again. She said she would read our book. But maybe Toren will one day learn to know his cousin, because they obviously relished every second of their introduction.

By now it has been over a year since Toren entered rehab; lived in Florida; worked in New York; and then returned home to our doorstep. During the six weeks Toren travels to Paraguay, the house returns to a quieter state. Toren's brothers come home over the holidays and we celebrate Christmas without him. We hear that Toren has spent the holiday with friends in a small Paraguayan village. He calls once or twice during his travels to say that all is going well, but gives few details. His voice sounds secure and I speculate that he is finding satisfaction in his travels.

It is reassuring to have Toren's brothers with us. Our family has worked hard to stay healthy and connected, to hold on to our roots. We have clung to survival every way we could. I often reflect where our children have come from. When the boys were small, they helped me with the yard work. One job was weeding. In the Northwest, cedar and fir trees volunteer all over the place between tulips and under rhododendrons. The boys hated pulling them out, knowing the tiny trees were destined for certain death, so I allowed them to transplant the seedlings to a backdoor section of earth alongside our house. They dubbed it their tree farm and spent hours stabbing tiny sprigs of cedar and Douglas fir into the soil. Years later, after the boys had graduated from high school, I found several of the transplanted seedlings in a juvenile stage, still growing furiously. Despite all odds they'd survived. Sometimes you just can't explain it, that persistence. I think of this tree farm now and how our boys have grown up. The odds they've faced.

With an empty spot in our garden, I think back over the winter, looking forward to spring, when new color and life will emerge. I have faith in the vigilance and care we have put into our family. On an especially cold day when I turn over a dead log, I find tiny green sprouts poking through. I now know that it just takes time.

# THIRTY-FOUR
## LA VUELTA DEL GRINGO

**[TOREN]** **Since departing Paraguay to return to the United** States for treatment in September 2003, I had only made direct contact with my favorite Paraguayan family one time. I had used a calling card and talked by telephone to Señora Francisca, my Paraguayan mom, about what to do with some of my belongings. I made it clear on the phone that I wouldn't be returning as a volunteer, but that I was hoping to come back and visit sooner rather than later. I don't think she really believed me, though. I tried to call her again a few months later and finally gave up. A message said the number was no longer in service.

While previously in Paraguay, I had spent my entire second month with Señora Francisca and her amazing family. They had become very special to me. Even when I lived on my own for the remaining few months, I passed a lot of my days there and ate about half my meals with them. The family inhabited a spacious ranch that opened up over an extensive, verdant plain, which filled out the backdrop beyond their livestock and garden. Señora Francisca's husband bought and resold cattle. In talking with Señora Francisca, I eventually found out her family wasn't really from San Juan Bautista (the location of my village), but from Pilar. She told me they had come from Barrio Takuara, outside of Pilar. Sometimes, almost as if she were joking or warning me, she threw out the idea that they would leave there before I did. That thought had seemed unbearable to me at the time. I relied on them and enjoyed our time together. The family was well respected and quite active in the community and would surely be missed if they moved on. And in fact, they ultimately did leave the village and return to Pilar.

Upon my arrival in Paraguay for the second time, I didn't know if I was ready to revisit my original community. For the most part I was scared shitless of the idea. Señora Francisca's family had been my biggest incentive to go back to the village, and I now realized they were no longer there. I knew I had to see the family no matter what, so I figured that visiting them wherever they were should be my next venture.

In order to locate the family, I found my way to the bus terminal in Pilar, and with a returning confidence in my language capabilities, I asked around until I was led to the bus driver, who navigated the bus to Takuara on a daily basis. I remembered *takuara* was their home because it meant bamboo in Guarani, and that had stuck in my mind. Besides their names, that was the only lead I took with me on my quest. I was told that the bus driver would know every family that lived out there, and that if I could tell him their names, he could find them. It was true. Without any address or other clues, he confirmed that he knew who they were and where they lived. The bus would leave the next morning around ten a.m.

The next day, after some watermelon and *chipa* (a special ubiquitous bread of Paraguay), I returned to the bus terminal and found my new driver/guide. The bus filled up with people and random cargo and we set out to God knows where—it became a mission of faith very quickly. This part of Paraguay is amazing because it is even flatter than the countryside I had previously seen. It is also known for its mythically beautiful women, white sands, and fresh fish from the bordering river. Several times along the way, I got up and initiated eye contact to make sure the bus driver hadn't forgotten about me. Then I sat back down and started running through my head what it was going to be like to see my family again. With no warning, I was going to practically fall from the sky and greet them in this strange new place they called home, fifteen months after last seeing them. What was I going to say to them? I wasn't even sure I'd be able to express what I wanted to say.

After many leisurely stops, drop-offs, pickups, and detours, the bus driver discreetly got out to urinate. Upon completion of his business, he motioned for me to get off the bus. There was no reason not to believe him. What would be in it for him to leave me stranded in this random little village? I got off with no choice other than to completely trust his knowledge of the people on his route and the names I had given him. He pointed to a house on the corner of two sandy, intersecting roads (like the ones we'd been driving on all day), and said simply, "They live there." I tried to hide any skepticism I had about the situation and graciously thanked him. As the bus pulled away, I knew no matter what I would probably be staying awhile—whether I found my family or not.

It must have been about two p.m.—the hottest time of day, when most families stay inside, hiding from the sun or rain, or work, or lack of work. I suddenly felt guilty about showing up at this time, or at any time without any notice. What was I doing? Arriving at their house without warning was something I used to do on a daily basis, and they never once made me feel unwelcome or appeared inconvenienced. Not once did they act too busy or seem unwilling to let me join in on whatever was going on around the home. It always made me think about how we view our time in the States, and how generally we are unwilling to drop what we are doing to make time for foreigners, acquaintances, or even family and friends. Don't mess with *my* schedule. Still, this was no routine visit.

I approached their house and gave a few loud, pronounced claps with my hands, and waited. (This is the universal Paraguayan doorbell.) I'll be honest, I was nervous as hell. All kinds of thoughts raced through my head as a neighbor looked on with curiosity from the sandy road. From around the corner of a covered entryway a little head popped out. Then, just as fast as the head had appeared, it disappeared. It was Natalia, the youngest of the three daughters. She darted back inside, and in the distance I heard a faint yelling.

A long minute passed, then out came Señora Francisca with Natalia clinging to her leg, looking at me suspiciously. Francisca smiled and play-fully greeted me, "Hola, Toren," as if I had come back from yesterday's visit to pick up something I had forgotten. She always took everything in stride, anyway. "Take a seat," she said, pointing to some wooden chairs in the front yard. It wasn't long before Francisca's husband and another daughter, Leti, came out to see what the commotion was. Their oldest daughter was not around, and the oldest son was still serving in the mili-tary, so the rest of us sat around a shaded table as we tried to make sense of my visit.

Francisca brought out a watermelon and we all picked away as we worked through the surprise of the situation. It seemed like there was so much to say that sometimes nothing was said. Every once in a while one of my comments would be followed by a "... *dios mio!*" from Francisca, a laugh, and then there would be another long pause. Then the father would follow up with a confused and rough accented, "Toren ... Toren ... Toren ..."

I wasn't really sure what they understood about my alcoholism or the treatment I had received and what it all meant. As much as I wanted to set it all straight, I surely wasn't going to rush it—explaining my sobriety is complicated enough for me in English. Nor did I want to tell them about all the outwardly luxurious details of my life since leaving (rehab, halfway house in Florida, playing music in Brooklyn, moving home to Washington State to work on a book). I simplified things and told them that after getting better, I had lived in New York City for a while to make some money, and then I moved home with my parents to continue to save money in order to fund my return trip to Paraguay.

It was interesting to catch up on all the gossip from the old commu-nity. They were still in touch with a few of the families and asked if I had been back there yet. I told them that I was going to go there next, thus pretty much sealing the deal.

I passed the afternoon at a swimming hole with the daughters and some of the neighbor kids, and then in the late afternoon tended to some of their cattle with Natalia, before helping to prepare the meal. Immediately I was in my old role of asking questions, shadowing Señora Francisca as she worked inside the house, and joking around with their daughters.

I had some good opportunities to talk one-on-one with Francisca. I told her more about my condition with alcohol, how I had been basically sick the whole time I was in Paraguay, and that I had no choice but to go home in order to learn how to live with it. I explained to her that I was fine now, but that I could not drink again, at least not normally. That was part of the sickness. Señora Francisca had a very worldly intelligence and seemed to understand, despite coming from a rural, primitive setting in a country that allowed very little opportunity for such people.

Drinking is a problem in Paraguay as well, she acknowledged, and we discussed various people we knew from our old community who were afflicted with this same disease. One gentleman of whom we spoke was a father of five children and a hard worker. I remember he would often wander the streets at night, mumbling and saying nonsensical things to himself. A few times he invited me to drink, almost pressuring me, along with some of the other men. It always felt awkward. His wife was sweet, and it was apparent that the kids were ashamed of how drunk their dad sometimes was. Still, the response to this man's drinking was very matter-of-fact in the community: "Just ignore him. He has had too much to drink." The man wasn't intoxicated all the time, and when I saw him sober, he was outgoing, energetic, and social. How could this be?

I could tell that Señora Francisca longed for the old life they had left. She said she missed some of the people, their house, and the lifestyle there. The house where they now lived was nice as well; it was the one she had grown up in. I found that part of their current source of income was derived from making and selling *chorizo*, a sometimes spicy variety of sausage. In the evenings, their yard turned into the neighborhood hot spot for volleyball. There, they sold beverages to people in the community. I am pretty sure they saw more money come in from selling the drinks than from the *chorizo*. You better believe alcohol is as large a revenue generator down there as it is in the United States.

I didn't know what the protocol was for such a random visit as this one, but I was hesitant when I told them that I was on a tight schedule. I felt really bad about it. Overstaying my welcome was probably not going to be the issue. Rather, it could be an insult to the family to pick up and leave too abruptly. But I couldn't stay long. Deep down I realized that there was nothing I could do about it. A brief visit was as good as it could get without moving in and reintegrating myself into their lives and the neighboring community, as I had done before. There was only so much catching up to do before I came to realize that we now represented two entirely different worlds fused together more by our past than by this one visit. In the end, my stopover served mostly as acknowledgment of their importance to me.

Just before dinner, the father obliviously asked me, "So what will we be drinking tonight?," implying that I would buy the drinks, usually wine, *caña*, or beer. I realized that the parts didn't necessarily add up to the whole, given that I had only told him a fraction of the complexity regarding my relationship to alcohol. He just didn't understand that I couldn't drink. I told him I wasn't going to drink but that I'd be happy to pay for whatever everyone wanted. He seemed more confused than offended, but part of him was still trying to coax me into joining the drinking. He began to realize I wasn't budging right as Francisca chimed in with something along the lines of, "We'll obey the crazy boy's wishes and it will be just fine." So we all drank soda along with our dinner.

It wasn't like not drinking really made sense to me the last time I was there, so why should I expect them to get it so suddenly? In order to change my own viewpoint it had taken a month of intense education in rehab and six months in a halfway house, and even after some time sober, I still think drinking sounds like a good idea sometimes.

I was fed very well and didn't know how to thank the family. I took some pictures that I promised to develop and send to them before I left the country, imagining that the bus driver would deliver them. Who else would? In bed that night in the spare room, I went to sleep with an overwhelming sense of relief and satisfaction at having found my family and spent the whole day with them. There was still a sadness knowing that early tomorrow would be the real good-bye, maybe forever.

Now it became clear to me why I would need to return to my former village and site. There would be too many what-ifs and questions left unresolved if I departed from Paraguay without making the effort. I also knew that my community would eventually discover that I had returned to Paraguay, and they would be hurt if I hadn't visited. It would be difficult to rationalize avoiding them. I was also interested in meeting my replacement volunteer to see what had happened since I had disappeared.

Despite unpredictable weather, I departed. The bus passed through several daunting downpours en route, each time making me think there was no way it'd be worth walking the three kilometers into my former village. But as I reached San Juan Bautista, the rain was light enough for me to make the venture in. I walked along the red dirt road like I had so many times before, and I wondered whom I would run into and what was going to happen. Although I still felt bad for having started relationships and work that I couldn't finish, I decided I didn't owe anybody anything and that I would not stay in any situations that would make me feel uncomfortable. Of course all the uncertainty proved to be the toughest part, like always.

I marched right into town. Wire fences lined the beat-up road all the way in, where I could take in either fields of crops or cattle stretching out between each house, seated low in front of a horizon speckled with palms and random trees. Sometimes I could walk quite some time before running into the next visible structure. Many of the places seemed exactly the same as when I had been there before. It felt like a strange dream. Most of the houses had minimal electricity, no running water, and were constructed of wood or brick, depending on the family's economic means. The only two local stores operated out of oversized windows and counters inside families' homes, and the school and church constituted the sole communal property. Much of the community relied on food from local fields, gardens, and livestock. A lightly wooded, green countryside kept moist by the humid air and sporadic thunderstorms engulfed the perimeter of the village.

The first house I visited was my former residence, where the new volunteer now lived. I could tell he was eager to speak English and to share his newest revelations on life, the encounters he'd had in his community, and the frustrations he was having with locals. From the start I saw that his experience was entirely different from mine and that we had divergent views on some of the families and what the life did or did not have to offer. Most interesting, he told me many of the things he had heard about me. We got to confirm or clear up some of the rumors that had developed, or evolved, you could say. It was nice to be able to set the record straight.

I had a chance to see another family I had lived with during my first month. It was great to sit and chat with the father, who was a professor at the school, and his wife, alongside the grandpa and their two kids. I explained to the grandpa, who had been a mentor in a lot of ways, that I hadn't had a drink in almost sixteen months. His bushy eyebrows shot up and he gave me a familiar grin. Then the professor loosely alluded to the idea that Grandpa had been talking about quitting drinking, or should, or something of that notion. It had never occurred to me that he had a problem. I summed up the solution for me by saying that it was simply a daily decision not to drink. One day at a time. But even the grandpa pointed out that he knew it always started with the first drink. I didn't have it in me to explain how much treatment, effort, and support had gone into my getting and staying sober. Had I the time and the ability, I would have loved to talk about the Twelve Steps and the awareness one can gain from applying them to addiction. But I was sure that, linguistically, I couldn't do it justice.

That evening I visited with my good friend Lucio. I saw one other family I had spent a fair share of time with, and then my replacement volunteer and I ate dinner with some of his closer Paraguayan friends in San Juan Bautista. The volunteer invited me to stay with him, so I got one last night in what was once my place. We listened to music, both played some guitar, and talked more about living in Paraguay and our community more specifically.

The next morning, I left relatively early. I wished the newer volunteer luck, shook hands with the grandpa and the professor, and made my way out of the village. This was the moment that every volunteer thinks about . . . when they finally leave their site. Of course, my situation was much different, since I had not actually come close to completing my service. Still, for some strange reason, I departed feeling like it was far more complete than it ever could have been any other way. I walked out of there with a sense of pride, satisfaction, and excitement. It felt like a huge act of finality, or some sort of triumph over those lasting feelings of defeat that I had carried around with me for so long since leaving South America the first time.

Ultimately, I spent New Year's Eve 2005 in Asunción. It was a big step up from the halfway house in Florida, where I rang in 2004. Just like anywhere, I had to make sure I was wearing the right attitude to go out, and I had to arm myself with an escape plan and surround myself with people who understood my situation. Whether they had dosed themselves with mushrooms or were sticking to booze, most volunteers understood what I had been through with my drinking. After careful consideration, I saw no good reason and felt no real temptation to alter my state of being that New Year's Eve, and by midnight (horaaaayyyy . . . kiss . . . kiss) I was ready to make a break for it and call it a night. Of course the real festivities didn't start for a few more hours, in typical South American fashion. It was my second sober New Year's.

I spent a few more days and nights in Asunción hanging with the last of the volunteers from our group, who were either returning from vacation or clinging to the last of their holiday celebrations. During this time, I returned to the Peace Corps office and visited with the same doctor who had helped me detox on Valium and had actually escorted me personally out of Paraguay, all the way back to Washington, D.C. The doctor was thrilled to hear about my progress and to see that I had been practicing my Spanish. He said he would pass on a thank-you to the nurse who had originally diagnosed me. It was gratifying to be able to thank him in person. I also had the chance to meet with the Peace Corps Country Director. I told him what my experiences had been, and when there was not much else to say, he and I exchanged clichés about sustainable development and recovery respectively. It was great.

One of those evenings, a group of us volunteers went out to dinner. I got to chatting with a few of the young women, and one confided to me frankly that if she were in my place, she didn't think she would have been able to return to Paraguay after what I'd been through. Without an inkling of judgment, she plainly asked, "Don't you sort of feel . . . sheepish?"

"Well, not really." Unsure how I was going to respond to that question, I answered off the top of my head, saying, "When I lived here the first time, I was sure that I belonged with this group, and in my community. Now I still feel like I am a part of the group." I continued to say that, obviously, I had been through a lot in regard to my drinking, and it is just a part of my story. I'm far from ashamed of it. It is part of who I am. At home and everywhere I have gone since, for the most part, I've been pretty up-front about my drinking problem.

It was refreshing to be able to speak honestly and candidly about these things, to be able to look someone in the eye and say what was really going on. Before, I had held so much locked up inside me. My life is better now, and I think the volunteers could tell that I actually meant it.

During one of those nights in Asunción, a volunteer friend surprised me by recounting my final drinking episode. It was revealed that after I had initially spoken with the Peace Corps nurse, I returned to the hotel and decided to have one last hurrah with some of the volunteers. This was of course against the directions of medical staff and more in accordance with the rules of most true alcoholics. I have no idea how much I really drank that night.

Along the path of uncovering my story, I had never really remembered this (probably due to the six previous days of drinking and abuse I had put myself through). I honestly thought I had remembered my last drink being the one I swigged before talking to the nurse. Maybe some-day I will see photos of my last run when I was desperately holding on to the habit that finally kicked my ass. But it had to have been a sad night, considering my state going into it. I guess it goes to show how worthwhile drinking was for me in the end. If I can't even remember it anymore, what is the point?

In talking with the volunteers in our group, I also learned more de-tails about what had happened to some of them since my departure to re-hab. A few had switched sites due to robberies. Some had gone home, others had become involved in deep relationships with locals in their vil-lages, some were known for pulling off ambitious projects (health, urban youth, education, business, environment), while others were known for their propensity to socialize more exclusively with other volunteers. There were a lot of obvious changes in most of the volunteers.

When I had departed the first time, we were still a bunch of green, good-intentioned, hopeful volunteers who struggled to communicate. By the time I returned, many of the volunteers had become excellent com-municators in Spanish and Guarani. They also knew the routes and times of the local bus systems, and understood how to deal with cultural differ-ences and frustrations. In a strange sense, they had each become guides or experts of their own region. A lot of them had endured traumatic experi-ences, bouts of loneliness, depression, or anger, as well as many personal triumphs and successes. Some of them were looking for ways to stay in Paraguay or South America, and I was surprised to see that a few had be-come extremely jaded, fed up, and were more than ready to leave. All the romantic Third World bliss does wear off, and I guess life can be just as shitty or great no matter where you end up. But it was clear that they had developed many meaningful friendships with each other and with other Paraguayans. I learned a lot from my fellow volunteers, and I could tell they also had discovered a lot about life and themselves.

My return to Paraguay lasted just over a month. It wound up being much more fulfilling and enriching than I could have planned. The whole time I was there I couldn't help but liken my return to some life-after-death scenario. I had vanished in one instant and was injected back into the scene some fifteen months later. The only thing that remained of me was an evolving array of rumors, some more accurate or complimentary than others. You always wonder what it would be like if you died or just disappeared. I got an inside glimpse and found out that life goes on, as does the world, regardless of whether you're in it.

My last two weeks I made a mini-whirlwind tour of the Southern Cone of South America. As much as I like to travel, it became apparent to me that it takes planning, effort, and efficiency to see a lot for a small amount of money, and I didn't feel like making some impossible itinerary. I thought about how my brother had traveled the greater part of the globe for over a year and I realized I just didn't have that in me. I knew there was too much to see and too little time, so I lowered my ambitions and enjoyed whatever I could.

As strange a feeling as it was, I felt ready to just get back. I had accomplished my goals and found closure, and I missed my girlfriend. To end the journey, I hiked around the epic and wondrous waterfalls located on the Brazilian, Argentine, and Paraguayan border, and met a friend from South Africa on the crowded resort beaches of Uruguay. Together he and I traveled south to the mountainous lake district of Argentina and Chile. By then I had enough time to loop back north, stopping through Santiago and finishing up in Buenos Aires.

I left South America with pretty much the same stuff I had brought: my same old backpack and guitar. But for sure, it felt like there was one less bag to carry home.

# THIRTY-FIVE
## *MOVING ON TO GRAVY*

GRAVY

*No other word will do. For that's what it was. Gravy.*
*Gravy, these past ten years.*
*Alive, sober, working, loving and*
*being loved by a good woman. Eleven years*
*ago he was told he had six months to live*
*at the rate he was going. And he changed his ways*
*somehow. He quit drinking! And the rest?*
*After that it was* all *gravy, every minute*
*of it, up to and including when he was told about,*
*well, some things that were breaking down and*
*building up inside his head. "Don't weep for me,"*
*he said to his friends. "I'm a lucky man.*
*I've had ten years longer than I or anyone*
*expected. Pure gravy. And don't forget it."*

—*Raymond Carver*[1]

**Spring 2005. When Toren returned from Para-** guay, it was obvious he had healed to a new level. He immediately began planning his next move and arranged to live away from our home in Washington State. I could see that he felt confident enough to deal with life on his own terms. Don and I helped him tune up Granddad's 1993 Ford Tempo (conveniently available, since Granddad could no longer drive it) for a road trip to his next destination, New Orleans, where he planned to work and play music. It was obvious that all those who joined together for Toren's benefit had been influential in his recovery. And Toren's efforts toward his own recovery couldn't be overlooked, either. Even though we had enjoyed having Toren at home, it was time for him to move on. Don and I anticipated a quiet summer, just the two of us.

But the disease of alcoholism is still sneaking around. Perhaps I've long known what this book would be about. Could be that's why I had those nights of tossing and turning. The thing is, I just don't know what the last chapter will say. *There is no last chapter.*

The real word about drinking isn't out yet. It hasn't hit the cul-de-sac. The end of the road, a niche where you can turn around if you want to, is perceived to be a safe place to raise your family. But in reality, this is a semicircle where we parents tremble in fear as we collect the morning paper, dreading to find our passed-out teenager flopped in a flowerbed since two a.m. the morning prior. Or discovering our kid parked in the driveway, slumped inside the car with windows up and the motor still running. Things like that ruin the newspaper article we were about to read over a cup of coffee.

When we finally do think we have a handle on things, we're still learning about the power of this disease. Alcoholism, after all, is a lifelong battle. There is no end. I vividly recall the first day I went to the Family Education Program at Toren's rehab facility, sitting down by a matronly woman in a purple shirt. I chose to sit by her because I was scared and humiliated to be there; somehow I thought the purple color of her clothing would comfort me. The stark chairs in the meeting room felt uncomfortable even while the purple woman smiled at me. So I forced myself to look squarely at her name tag. (Her first name only, of course.) And we whispered our introductions. She beamed sweetly as she explained, "This is my second program. My son relapsed last week." Then, as if to reassure me, she added, "But the other program was on the West Coast. We decided to try this one."

I thought I would become ill. It seemed incomprehensible that someone would go through a program like this even *once*. But twice? How could it be? I looked her over more carefully. She was well-groomed and she looked calm. There must be a reason she would have a relapsed son. My son certainly wouldn't do *that*. There I sat in my inhospitable chair, emotionally frozen, and speechless as I realized that maybe *perhaps* just *somehow* not only would I be completing this program one time, but two times. Or three. What was this disease of alcoholism, anyway? Did it have no sense of when to stop?

Ultimately, the woman and I both graduated from Family Weekend. I don't know how she and her relapsed son are doing. Well, I hope. But as our son begins his new phase, sometimes I wonder if he will be able to move on to a new town and find people he enjoys, people who will be a positive influence on him and who will be supportive to him. What about his return trips home for the holidays, when all his drinking friends corral at the local taverns? Will he continually be able to fend off temptation and maintain his course? Wearing a new set of habits, it could be daunting to return to Olympia, a site where he used—*It's the water!* The brewery's motto and the name of the town are synonymous, just like the American image of alcohol as a benign legal beverage. (Coincidentally, about the same time as Toren has gotten sober, the former brewery in our town is being purchased by a water bottling company. Is that a good omen? The dark side of me is laughing hysterically. Now my sons can meet their friends at the brewery for water-making tours!)

Recently, while I was conversing with another parent, she commented to me, "I don't know what our kids are doing. They seem to plug into society later than we did. They're waiting longer to choose a career, longer to select a partner, longer to support themselves."

"Right," I agree, "not only are they slow to be plugged in, they want an extension cord."

And I mean it. Our kids don't have to face a military draft or the Depression. Their abuses or dalliances could be considered frivolous. But no matter what generation, even back to Great Gatsby parties or the Dust Bowl (or whatever era we want to consider as either glamorous or painful), there has always existed the disease of alcoholism. And we still have its lugubrious effects filtering drip by numbing drip down through the generations—perhaps a major factor for the past legislation of Prohibition. (But everyone knows that idea was a failure. How we love to break a rule if someone will just write it out for us!) These days we're living

longer and longer. We have more time to make mistakes, to become addicted.

The good news is that we also have time to correct our mistakes.
Every individual is eligible for the hope of sobriety and productivity.
Thank goodness we have tools to help us through our vulnerabilities.
They are innumerable, varied, and individual, and perhaps there is one
that will serve each of us.

Toren and I have seen how alcoholism cuts across boundaries, classes,
and cultures. Our family's struggle is no different than obstacles faced by
others fighting this disease. We have met doctors, clergy, artists, kids,
moms, athletes, and educators who grapple with alcohol abuse and the aftermath of its destruction. Throughout Paraguay, Toren was struck by
the immediacy of rural villagers wrestling with alcohol abuse and its effects. People of all nations and positions experience this struggle.

One of the most nerve-racking speaking engagements Toren and I
accepted took place with the Yakama Indian Nation. As we drove to the
location across peaceful plateaus of hops, vineyards, and alfalfa fields, we
discussed what we could say to high school kids whose ancestors have
waged a serious genetic war against alcohol for generations. We shrugged
inside our whiteness and wondered how we could be inspirational to
these students. Yet when we stood before these Native American youth,
we could visibly perceive understanding and knowledge of the disease.
They listened without judgment, perhaps hoping as vehemently as we did
that sometime, somewhere, our society will begin to recognize the sickness stemming from an abusive alcohol culture. Following our presentation, a student athlete stopped by to chat with me. He talked about his
struggles with drinking, how alcohol abuse had affected his grades and
sports, but emphasized his determination to overcome this halting start.
As the student and I grasped hands, we sought mutual encouragement.
And we felt like kin.

At another of our high school presentations, a student whose family
hardly spoke English purchased a book to read aloud and translate to her

mother because of serious drinking problems with an older brother. These issues transcend all language.

In late spring while in Mazatlán, I joined a Mexican friend for lunch. I had plotted how to tell her about our changed family. In order to prepare, I double-checked translations for words like "recovery" and "addiction." But instantly, two mothers began talking, and she already knew what I was trying to say. Her family has had the same problem, she said. Before lunch was over, it was she who presented a speech. I listened in amazement as she talked about drinking traditions in her culture and the difficulties it has caused. The problems she described are no different from what Toren talked about after visiting Paraguay, and what is experienced daily by all ethnic groups.

Across the United States, people are beginning to look at alcohol differently. Compare this to cigarettes. Over the past thirty years, the United States has seen a huge shift in the way smoking is viewed, with growing pressure on advertisers and distributors of tobacco products. Now people are beginning to demand the same of the alcohol industry. Representative Tom Osborne of Nebraska and the American Medical Association are petitioning the NCAA to curtail alcohol ads at college events. There is a strident campaign by legislators and communities to reexamine underage drinking and advertising.[2] After alcohol-related behavior problems during football games, the sale of alcohol within stadiums has been banned by the University of Southern California and several other schools in the Pacific-10 Conference.[3]

Legal ramifications are hitting the alcohol culture. Lawsuits have been filed against those who overserve young drinkers. In 2005, two Vermont bars were sued by a parent whose son was served seventeen beers and shots of liquor in four hours. (After passing out, the teen was brought to the hospital thirteen hours later. He never regained consciousness and died in a hospital after twenty days.) Also named in the suit was the teen's drinking companion.[4] Those who advocate for healthier changes in our nation's drinking awareness will cause a cultural shift in attitudes about heavy chronic drinking, just as we are seeing a cultural shift regarding smoking.

Dr. Peter E. Nathan from the University of Iowa suggests solutions to alcohol problems by changing the community drinking environment through such means as bar regulations, entertainment options, and unwillingness of citizens to tolerate public drunkenness. Harvard researchers have indicated that when substantial environmental changes are adopted, reductions in binge drinking and decreases in harmful secondhand effects of bingeing, such as date rape, assault, and vandalism, can be expected. That's good news for any community.

---

### What Communities Can Do to Modify Rates of Binge Drinking[5]

- Educate bar owners that, in the long run, binge drinking by underage students is not good for the community.
- Educate local citizens that binge drinking by underage students negatively affects their own quality of life.
- Participate in creating more attractive, alcohol-free entertainment options.
- Help create a community climate of unwillingness to tolerate public drunkenness.
- Limit alcohol access among the least experienced student drinkers by raising the age of entry to bars and taverns to twenty-one years.
- Help students understand that:
  —there are a range of alternatives to binge drinking every weekend evening;
  —alcohol is not a benign substance;
  —abusive alcohol consumption in high school and college is often associated with extremely serious adverse consequences;
  —abusive alcohol consumption is associated with alcohol-related problems after graduation or dismissal from high school or university that can permanently affect achievement of life's goals.

---

How do we ordinary parents and teens bring about attitude changes regarding alcohol use to our own towns? How can our nation address this epidemic of heavy underage drinking?

A good place to start is by persuading universities and surrounding communities to support changes that deemphasize alcohol as a part of college life, such as enforcement of minimum-drinking-age laws, limiting access to low-cost, high-volume drink specials, and changing social perceptions about the amount people are drinking. Parents can encourage university administrators to implement comprehensive campus-wide programs. This can be done in college towns and also in our hometowns.

Community coalitions can address substance-abuse issues, with parents, educators, health professionals, law enforcement, and local government working together to bring about change. The Community Anti-Drug Coalition of America (CADCA) is a membership organization of over five thousand antidrug coalitions, each working to make their community safe, healthy, and drug-free. Teaming up with such an organization brings clout to communities where parents and teens wish to see changes in attitudes about adolescent alcohol consumption.

We parents can visit middle schools and high schools to talk about bringing alcohol abuse out of the closet, out of the alley, and away from the back parking lot—straight onto the school board agenda. There needs to be more help offered to concerned parents. An alcohol awareness assembly offered for school kids, or presentations for incoming college freshmen, will be twice as effective if coupled with parent education programs designed to inform families about teen drinking and the alcohol culture. There can be alcohol awareness and recovery programs offered in public schools for *both* teens and parents, and a friendly, supportive environment for all those who have questions about teen alcohol use.

Of all the points to consider about heavy teen drinking, I am most struck by the fact that oftentimes young drinkers and their parents don't realize they are in trouble until it is too late. It can be *after* college graduation that symptoms become pronounced, just at the time when an emerging adult begins to seek out lifelong goals. Abusive alcohol consumption is associated with alcohol-related problems after graduation that can permanently affect the achievement of a young person's dreams and aspirations. As with Toren and our family, the results of this continual abuse will finally stack up until it falls with crushing force onto our heads.

The consequences of heavy drinking have changed the dynamics of our family. Toren and I have talked about what we should do when entertaining friends during the times he is visiting us at home. I still do not wish to drink in front of him. Toren tells us to relax, not to make a big deal of it anymore. He does not want to be singled out, and says, "I have to deal with people drinking around me. It's not up to them to stop what they're doing because of me. It's up to me to do what I know is right for me."

Just the same, for me, it's a personal decision not to drink in front of Toren, and a way I can easily support him. We talk about going out with his brothers. Toren volunteers that when his brothers visited him in Florida while he was still living in the halfway house, they did not drink, even when the three of them entered bars or restaurants serving alcohol. I recall the e-mail I had sent to his brothers prior to that trip where I requested they abstain in front of Toren. Until now, I had not known for sure what they did. When Toren tells me about this, I feel thrilled that they supported him so thoughtfully. Almost two years later, I know that they now sometimes drink in front of him. But I also observe that they are extremely sensitive to him.

At one of our appearances, Toren is presented with a T-shirt lettered in bright red that reads "2 out of 3 consume 5 or less." This is a sample of the type of apparel used by college campuses for social norming campaigns. My mother saw Toren wearing this eye-catching shirt and asked him, "What does it mean?" She pointed to the logo.

Toren replied, "It's how much students drink." His grandma frowned, and Toren continued, "At least it's considered by campuses to be a good thing. Schools use it to educate kids and bring out the fact that many students drink five or less drinks."

"Really? Oh my. All at one party?" she questioned. "That seems like a lot."

While it appears that educators are celebrating that students consume five or less, Toren's grandmother considers five to be excessive. Disparity in attitudes about drinking is widely divergent and personal. In reality, no one really knows the amount of alcohol someone else is consuming. Grandparents, teens, parents, and even college prevention teams may be at odds about what is considered a normal amount of alcohol.

Over the past years, our family has thrashed through parenting and adolescent decisions, tallied up the pros and cons, bemoaned the results, and, finally, accepted them. We have had to forgive others and ourselves. When Toren returned home after finishing his halfway house experience and living for the summer in New York, he brought up the subject of the first video Don filmed of him when he was intoxicated at age fifteen. Toren asked if we still had it around. After some searching, we found it, and then we all three decided to watch it. Together on the family room couch, Don, Toren, and I relived that ill-omened night some nine years prior.

This incident was not an event we had ever planned to include in our family footage. The pathetic debacle had defiantly wedged itself on a tape between miscellaneous soccer scrimmages and quick random clips of one of Toren's older brother's high school graduation. Interrupting a chain of fast-forwarded family events, the dizzy nightmare flipped onto our screen with brilliant immediacy. Suddenly a helter-skelter image peppered with intense voices pulled us into our troubled kitchen, reviving the painful drama. In the middle of that summer night, a family script unraveled before the camera, capturing a bathrobe-clad mother and her disheveled son sitting under glaring lights at a table, not communicating. The son held his head in his hands while the mother loomed toward him.

From the couch we observed ourselves back in our former kitchen, all wearing the younger bodies we had forgotten we had. Toren, Don, and I listened to ourselves on the soundtrack, and we tumbled together into that fearsome black hole, just as deep and scary as before. Even though we thought we had learned all about it, the intensity sucked us under while we watched, and none of us dared to catch our breath. Nor could we glance to the side to see how anyone else was holding up while stale images caught us by surprise and the garbled interrogation held us paralyzed.

Images of Toren slurring, retching, and evading overtook us. Don's questioning and prodding came from behind the frantic lens, capturing a teen's plummet into oblivion. In and out of focus was my sighing, pleading, frowning, and propping. Why did we have to watch this again?

Because it is a reminder to us. We could clearly see our frustration and fear as parents, alongside Toren's vacant indifference. Terse questions and a lack of coherent responses shredded everything Don and I had known to be real at the time. It laid bare how hard it is to be a parent. It showed us how quickly the personality of a young drinker could turn sideways. It revealed what a real blackout could be (even though I had no idea that the son I was trying to talk to was already gone).

We watched it spellbound, as though we had never experienced the saga before. And as suddenly as the trancelike episode had begun, it ended, like footage of one of those violent hurricanes on TV with just destruction and bad feelings left lying around afterward. Still shocked and staring at the screen, three disheartened people lingered on the couch contemplating a bunch of kids playing soccer in place of someone crawling around on the tile floor vomiting. Toren said nothing. None of us wanted to bring it up, but it seemed like we had traveled back in time too abruptly—to years before rehab. And we had torn open a partially healed wound. We couldn't stop the pain, but we might prevent further infection.

"Is that how you remember it?" I asked Toren.

"No," Toren said. "I hardly remember any of it."

"Well, there it is. Look where we've come." I attempted to put closure on the haunting images that never seemed to end.

Toren didn't respond. Immersed in renewed disappointment, he hunched under unmoving shoulders, lowered while his body relived powerlessness. Don sat beside him, amazed at what he'd filmed but not seen.

"We need to get rid of it," I offered. "Move past it. It's over."

Toren nodded. He looked over at me for the first time, his eyes flashing relief.

With that, I pulled the cassette from the player and tossed it a few feet away into an empty wire trash can sitting underneath a desk. The plastic case echoed as it crashed to the bottom of the receptacle. Just to be sure it had no real life, I eyed it from my peripheral vision. It hadn't budged. "Okay, Toren. We're done with it. No one will ever see it. So let's move on."

We sat there longer. I wondered if we could get up off the couch again. But we did.

When I remind Toren about throwing away the video one year later, he tells me that he *still* has trouble remembering it. He can't picture it, nor can he recall me throwing it away. Such a rotten experience hardly deserves a memory. We must travel on from that point.

It's important to stay in today, to look forward to what we are doing now and to not dwell on the past. Through all this overwhelming information about binge drinking, blackouts, and the alcohol culture, our family continues to thrive. Toren's bravery and courage seem almost a miracle for us, although I wouldn't have requested this addiction. Don remains a staunch supporter of Toren's recovery and the process to share our story. He quietly senses what we require and facilitates our work. One of Toren's brothers currently lives and works in Brazil, while the other scurries between schools from West to East Coast. Both of them stay in touch and frequently send us relevant information about trends in addiction and alcohol education. Aunts, uncles, and cousins chime in to lend encouragement. We treasure grandparents and longtime friends, along with diverse acquaintances met along the way. As both friends and strangers take time to ask about Toren and our family, we are overwhelmed by the generosity of their energy.

What saved our son? I think it was that, ultimately, he possessed a combination of his own determination and our love. He cherished his good fortune even as he made poor decisions, and then he used his desire to stop drinking to make his life better. Don quotes the proverb, "Luck happens when preparation meets opportunity." Perhaps Toren's years of missteps presented him with the opportunity to find himself. Toren listened to what people said even though he acted otherwise. When at last his life became unmanageable, he had the fortitude to bail out. All these qualities added up to his enlightenment. Here was a kid who continued to take risks and who continued to self-destruct while his parents and mentors persisted in pointing out bad patterns and pushed for better behavior. It was not a miracle combination. It was a mishmash of luck, effort, education, and readiness. All this paid off.

Now down the road—after worrying about the allure of beer bongs, meeting up at rehab, and getting honest with Grandma—people ask me how I look differently at our family. One thing that is very different is my attitude about Toren's judgment and his honesty. I used to worry about his decisions in high school and college, and even somewhat while he recently traveled in South America. I've learned that I can't control his life (or anyone else's). Now, the first instant I feel insecure, I can immediately go to Toren and speak outright about my concerns. He will give me an honest answer. Just that openness between us puts my qualms to rest. Each day I attempt to offer that same honesty to the rest of my family.

Our family *is* changed. Now we're more precious to one another than ever. Each of us will determine the role of alcohol in our lives. We know there are severe consequences when we abuse it. Although we cannot force another person to change a behavior, we can talk together about it. It is never too early to honor our family by discussing drinking choices, and never too late to repair a habit or to ask for help. Refusing to give up becomes a part of our life, uniting what we lost with what we have found.

# THIRTY-SIX
## COULD YOU SPARE SOME CHANGE, PLEASE?

**[TOREN]** *October 2005. I remember when the thought of* me having ninety days sober seemed impossible. When I got there, it felt like the achievement of all achievements. Don't get me wrong—it is. At the time, I couldn't imagine anything beyond that. Even twenty-four hours is an accomplishment for most addicts or alcoholics, and no matter how much time one has sober, it is only the twenty-four hours of today that are important. Having maintained continuous sobriety for well over two years, it has become clear to me that it is still my choice and my responsibility to stay sober, yet I am still only one drink away from a whole new horrific, ugly, soul-scraping adventure.

There is no question that, at the beginning, I was looking for a way out of this whole recovery thing. I tried to remain convinced that I wasn't a *real* alcoholic, or I liked to think that if I did this or that, I'd be able to drink again. The last thing I wanted to be sentenced to was a life of Twelve-Step meetings and burnt coffee. When I finally accepted that I couldn't drink normally, I went through a phase of telling myself, "I know I can't drink alcohol, but I can still do other drugs socially on occasion, maybe." Right. Let me think about the last times I was coming off a hearty cocaine bender, an ecstasy binge, or a long, distorted mushroom or

344

acid trip. Alcohol was always there to ease the comedown. More than that, I used most other drugs so that I could drink like a machine for much longer periods of time. In other words, alcohol was a necessary ingredient during and immediately after most of my drug indulgences. I don't even want to imagine how I would handle coming down off hard drugs without alcohol. I'm sure I would have that same jump-off-a-building feeling that I had when I used to suffer through my alcohol withdrawals. Do I really want to start this cycle back up? Today, I think the costs finally outweigh the benefits for me.

I'm sure a lot of people wonder, *Well, what would happen if you did drink?* For me, all I have to do is think back to my last few drinking cycles down in Paraguay, when I still was holding on to the idea that I was a normal drinker or that maybe I just had a bit of a problem to fix. Sometimes back then, when I was not drinking—physically sober, like I am now—all it took was a few drinks and invariably a physical response would follow. This adverse reaction developed and progressed over many years and is still with me. I'm told that my two years of sobriety (or any amount of time) would go completely unrecognized by my body if I were to drink again. Although my tolerance would initially be lower, the time lapse from active drinking would make very little difference in how my body processed alcohol.

The tiny sip I took in Paraguay wasn't enough to start the process, but it wouldn't take much more to get me going. My alco-switch would again be flipped and my fuel gauge would be activated. In other words, I would probably, just like all the times before, experience sleeplessness or fevers, even if I drank only a little bit. I probably would have cravings and urges to continue drinking, and if I actually drank heavily and got drunk (losing control and most likely blacking out), I would end up drinking myself back into the process of eventually having to experience shakes, sweats, and painful withdrawals again. And let's not forget that along with the accompanying guilt, regret, and embarrassment, I would have broken over two years of personal growth, progress, and momentum.

Surely, just like any good crack addict or nicotine fiend, I would probably be off to the races with a mean case of the fukits. The terror level would again be raised to HIGH.

Sobriety has a whole new meaning to me in a lot of ways. It is more than just not drinking or not using drugs. While *not drinking* is the essential element, sobriety really is a process of change or growth—both emotionally and spiritually. Sobriety aside, isn't that indeed what life is about? Great . . . I guess that is exactly the point. As an active, drinking alcoholic, my life was clearly not about change or growth. My life was about doing the same shit over and over again in a self-indulgent, self-destructive manner, while struggling to pass it off as fun. Looking back on a lot of the consequences from my more serious drinking days, I was hardly living when I was drunk or recovering from drinking, and when I was sober, all I wanted to do was start drinking again. Nothing was changing.

I'm not a drunk anymore, so I have found that I have to stop living like one. It really is a package deal, and part of being sober is taking responsibility for my actions and being aware of how they affect other people. Maybe that means if I care about people, I should treat them thoughtfully all the time, not at my convenience. Studies have indicated that alcoholics who drink heavily during their adolescent years virtually stop their emotional development and don't learn how to deal with relationships and daily problems. No wonder getting sober can be such a pain in the ass. We have to face life for the first time as emotionally underdeveloped adults.

The ideas and the principles laid out in the Twelve Steps allow the afflicted alcoholic to nurse himself into a lifestyle pattern where he can begin to deal with both relationships and problems. I have to identify the destructive or otherwise damaging behaviors in my life and begin to improve or change how I may be treating myself or others. The underlying concept is that if I can learn to be more aware of my actions and their effects, I am a lot less likely to go back to drinking.

While speaking with various friends or acquaintances over the course of my sobriety, I have sometimes mentioned that I have been attending meetings, or that I haven't even gotten all the way through the Twelve Steps yet. A lot of times the reaction is something like, "Oh, you still go to those?" or "You actually have to work the Steps?" Yes, I am afraid so. It seems that some of my friends are even in denial for me.

I realize that it must appear painful to have to put all this effort toward something so stigmatized. But wouldn't my behavior be just as or even more stigmatized if I were always the too-drunk guy going out with my friends, dining at restaurants, or at family gatherings? I'll take the stigma of going to meetings any day over being the token drunk guy for the rest of my life.

It may be a stunning revelation to my friends that every day presents a new challenge for me. They may learn this, perhaps, but not everyone can truly understand my struggles. That is why meetings are so important. I may or may not continue to attend meetings as often as I do now, but I enjoy the gatherings and find they can be very spiritual. This is where we "abnormal" people can talk about our "abnormal" frustrations and feel understood. It gives me a chance to listen to people whom I have either been like or could be like sometime in my life. Step meetings are also full of people I don't want to be, or could only hope to be like. I learn a lot from other people in recovery, and it is important to be there for others who need the same help I have received.

Being sober still isn't what comes naturally to me. Looking back, the patterns I established from very early on in my life point to the fact that I may have had this coming to me from the start: from not following rules on the playground, to acting out in class, to frequent trips to the candy store (with or without permission), to antagonizing peers, to throwing things at cars for sport, to sneaking out at night for various combinations of those things.

Continuously living a life where I ignored the consequences finally caught up to me. I guess I am ultimately learning that I can't get away with this type of living. Even when I can, it just may not be worth it, contrary to the beliefs of the fifteen-year-old who hijacked my social life some ten years ago. What kind of person would I rather be today?

I still have a lot of friends who drink. An easier way to put it is, I can show the number of sober friends I have on one finger. My friend Ryan is still sober as well, and we both celebrated two years of continuous sobriety in the fall of 2005. Since getting sober, he and I have developed an even deeper friendship and understanding of one another. Both Ryan and I are lucky to have gotten help when we did, and now we can be there to support anyone else who comes through those same doors.

A lot of our friends seem to respect the choices we have made, while others may feel threatened or skeptical. Some friends have said things along the lines of, "I think it's cool what you're doing . . . but I could never go that route . . . I could never go straightedge, completely sober." I used to think that exact way, too. It really comes down to the fact that this is the only direction I *can* go if I want to have a seminormal, productive life. And for now, that sounds like something I should want, right? I don't want to be enslaved to toxins that disconnect me further from living. That's where I was when I was last drinking. So I can mirror similar sentiments to those friends of mine respectively: "I think it's cool that you still drink and use drugs . . . but I can't go down that road . . . it would destroy me."

I am dealing with that lifestyle clash constantly. The craziness of my old ways seems to linger and haunt me at times, through my friends' drinking styles or when I am out at bars. But sanity still triumphs. I wonder if there will ever be a time when I can completely relax and say that alcohol no longer impacts me. Alcohol seems to be around in most social situations, and that probably won't change. I have found that I am getting much better at feeling comfortable in its presence, but that I have become less tolerant of the whole idea of getting wasted. I guess that is my natural reaction, because I know how much it was messing me up. Alcohol has really lost its allure.

Often when I am with my friends, I have found that staying out later than one or two in the morning can be a big mistake. As people get drunker (and often stupider), I usually start to tire and have problems relating to them. After my first year of sobriety, I stopped ingesting caffeine in order to keep up, and actually ended up abandoning it altogether once I found myself misusing it and feeling like I needed it. (Give me any substance and I'll probably abuse it. That is what alcoholics and addicts do.) In general, I have found it very helpful to leave bars or parties when the night is still on the upswing, before it gets depressing, ridiculous, and is completely spoiled (for me).

I have managed to stay out with friends till the wee hours on some occasions, and the next day I am always surprised at what they don't recall. Evidently, I have become so removed from the drinking scene that it is hard to remember what it was like to *not* remember things from the night before. When I'm talking to day-after partiers, I'm usually thinking, *Are you kidding, you really don't remember that?* Being a master of blacking out myself, it is strange that I can now see the events only from my sober standpoint.

It is bizarre to be around drunken people who aren't doing much else but drinking for the sake of drinking. I see this sometimes because I am trying to have a seminormal social life while still not drinking. These two worlds inevitably collide. When I am out and am in a good mood, I can have a fantastic time. But if I make the mistake of staying around too long, the nights generally seem pretty uneventful. From my new perspective, I notice that when people have drunk a lot, no one seems to be doing anything *that* amazing or having *that* much fun.

When all is said and done, I am curious to know, were they really having *that* much more fun than me? Often it doesn't appear that way outwardly, but then again I know how much I loved boozing away my Friday and Saturday nights (or any night). I can't measure the chemical activities or dopamine levels in the pleasure centers of my friends' brains, so I usually conclude that all the good stuff must still be going on internally. Why else was *I* drinking all the time?

Now, almost invariably, I look back on the previous night and, whether I had a great time or not, I think how glad I am that I wasn't drinking and that I don't have to endure what I used to.

---

### Practical Advice for the Recovering Alcoholic (Who Still Wants to Go Out with Drinkers):

1. Don't go out with people who drink or use* (especially if you are still tempted to drink or use).

2. If you do go out with people who drink or use:
   → Don't do it all the time. It is tiring and can be difficult.
   → Do so only when in a good mood.
   → Don't go out tired or hungry.
   → Leave when you are uncomfortable.
   → Go out with people who *know* what your situation is—that you're in recovery.
   → Don't be committed to drive people—so you can leave when you want to.
   → Don't stay out too late—people only get more drunk, and you become less tolerant.

3. Find new friends who are in recovery or whose lives aren't centered on drinking.**

*Maybe, in some ways, I'm all talk, but you can't hide from reality forever, and reality says that people still drink and use drugs.
**I like my old friends and still see most of them when I visit their various locations and frequent their watering holes—*but I only stay out when I am wearing the right attitude!!!*

---

Alcohol plays some role in almost all of my relationships because the majority of my friends still drink, and we live in an alcohol-happy society. Luckily, my more important relationships continue without relying on it. Sometimes it can get a little tricky when people I really care about are drinking. When around my best friends, girlfriend, brothers, or even other family members who drink, I have learned that I have to be in the right place mentally or I don't need to be there.

Going out sober takes getting used to. Being where people are drinking and altering their mood can be a challenge for me, since I no longer choose to do this for myself. Sometimes I just don't feel like being sober. In the past, altering my mood was fun and easy. Sometimes I want those feelings back. I just want to relax or to go out and have some fun, do something that makes me feel different, to get fucked up—to lose control. But that option has run its course, and I know where the outcome will take me. I know it's no longer worth it. I can't let it ruin me when others are drinking, even though sometimes I feel left out.

I have to realize that it isn't about me, and that I can't take other people's drinking personally. Still, I admit, sometimes it is tough and I can't help but think, *Can't we just go without alcohol every once in a while?* Around my friends, generally that answer is still no, and that's something I have to continue to accept. When people are drinking socially and not drinking heavily, it is easy for me to remember that I literally *never* drank that way. So why would I suddenly want to start now?

People are often curious to know how coming out with my alcoholism has affected my brothers and our relationships. In certain situations it has changed how we interact, but on the whole we are still very close, seasoned with the same outlook on life and shared sense of humor. They are still both heavy drinkers at times, but there have been situations when I can tell they have made efforts to drink considerably less or not at all when I'm around.

I remember one specific time when I asked them about a weekend that included a bunch of our friends in San Francisco. It was one of the first big rendezvous-type weekends after I had been back in the country and newly sober, so needless to say I stayed out of the picture. This would be the exact kind of scene (a long weekend binge with a lot of our hard-drinking friends) that I would still, to this day, not really care to be around. Of course, I was curious to know what they all did.

Over the phone I asked how it was and they told me something like, "Oh, it was cool, so and so was there, we went to such and such place, ate this and did that . . . it was really fun to see everybody." I couldn't help but notice the watered-down version both of my brothers had given me. These kinds of weekends in the past usually called for long, graphic, and entertaining e-mails among us, recapping all the details and hilarity. If not that, there would be at least some sort of summary by phone reporting all the various adventures and highlights that went down: who passed out where, who may have hooked up or not hooked up, who got kicked out of what bar, or what ridiculous drinking game was invented, among the rest of the activities that took place over the weekend.

This time, none of these details came to me from my brothers. Not right away at least. I don't think they were doing it on purpose or necessarily hiding anything from me. I think it was more that a lot of these things were still sensitive topics, and my brothers were probably unconsciously protecting me or censoring what my pure little ears could no longer handle hearing about. In general, I am sort of out of the loop from a lot of this type of talk among my friends nowadays.

"Well, it sounds to me, Toren, that you still hang out with a bunch of alcoholics."

Yep. Or not.

Are my friends really alcoholics? Are my brothers alcoholics?

Who knows?

Do I really think they're alcoholics?

That's their own business. Besides, it was obviously hard enough for me to come to the conclusion that I had a problem, so what good is it gonna do for me to walk around and try to diagnose my friends, or anyone else for that matter? That isn't my job. I can't worry about other people or try to change anyone else. The best I can do is keep remembering that I am an alcoholic, continue to stay sober, be willing to talk to others about my situation, and not judge other people who may be experiencing their own issues—just like I once did. Of all people, I know how tough it can be to honestly look at oneself and decide to either change or ask for help. It isn't an easy or fun process.

Although it may not always seem like it, my brothers *have* been there for me. Just recently I had a conversation with one of my brothers about all the changes and the events we have weathered. We had a good laugh and spoke about all the different stories that probably belonged in a book. He and I recounted when all three of us lived together in Las Vegas and I was trying to quit smoking.

A combination of continuous drinking, some serious drug use, and pending legal problems from a previous arrest in San Francisco had me stressed out of my mind. On this night, it all seemed like too much to handle. I was trying to cut back on my smoking. All I could think about was a cigarette. In my confusion and narcissism, everything felt like it was crashing down on me. And nobody could understand. One cigarette would make it better.

This overpowering need for a cigarette catapulted me into a ridiculous drunken breakdown. I completely lost it. I lay there on the floor and bitched and sobbed and argued as my brothers tried to reason with me—to tell me to get over my smoking. Pathetic? Yes. Desperate? Yes. But this was just another addiction and another facet of my powerlessness, my disease, and my life spinning out of control.

I cried and whined as they both stood there and told me how each cigarette was more and more pointless, damaging, and reinforcing to my addiction. They reminded me how I had promised to quit smoking after high school, and then vowed to quit again during college, saying that it was a stupid habit. I acknowledged how evil it was and how it had gravely affected both our granddad and nana. No, I didn't want cancer or emphysema. Nor did I want to be immobilized by a lack of breath someday. But I still wanted a few more smokes. I wanted to quit on my own terms (as I had said for years). "I'll quit after this one."

"You're gonna have to quit someday, and the longer you wait the harder it gets. What are you waiting for?"

My brothers would not give up. And they would not be outsmarted. Screw both of them. They were right. And it was hard on me. Even tougher was that they cared. I didn't want them to. I felt all the more ridiculous. (I got my nicotine that night, and shortly thereafter I finally did quit.) Their support (and stubborn pressure) kept me headed in the right direction. Recalling this story reminds me of how much I rely upon my brothers and how I value their input.

After this recent conversation with my bro, the other one e-mailed me and asked about the book, the progress I was making. He mentioned a woozy, drug-induced conversation we'd had a long time ago, when we analyzed our lives, drifted through all sorts of existential thoughts, and sorted out our friends, our futures, and our destinies. At some point, we acknowledged that I had already fucked up a lot and that I appeared headed down the wrong path at times. Half of our thoughts seemed to be transmitted without words.

I agreed that I'd done some stupid things but vowed that I was not going to take it all too far. I wasn't going to be a fuckup. I wasn't going to lose control. We paused. There was something that wasn't being said. I mentioned that I didn't want to die. "No, man, I'm not going to be the one to overdo it, you know, like, Uncle Ric." The moment I said this, something struck a nerve. It felt as if some spirit escaped my body. My brother felt something strange, too. We both realized what it meant. We knew. Neither of us wanted to have this happen to me—or anyone in our family. Although we were into some risky things at times, we wanted to prevent another tragedy in the family. (My dad's brother, Ric, died of a drug overdose when he was thirty-one.) I decided right then that I would choose life.

Today I am still holding on to this decision. I truly believed then that I would never let myself lose control, even though I continued down that wrong path for quite some time before I was ready to accept my addiction. I did lose control, but I didn't lose my life. Along the way, my brothers (and some of my good friends) have been very understanding and helpful to me.

The idea that I need to get an entirely *new* social life has been recommended to me, and I would have no problem suggesting it to most people in recovery. I'm working on it . . . sort of. With the support of my friends and brothers, I am prepared to embrace change. I admit that I have fantasized about having a group of companions that doesn't rely on alcohol for fun . . . or even drink at all. But that isn't my reality. There have been times when I've been frustrated with how alcohol runs our social scene, and I swear to myself that I will find some new friends. But they have been hard to come by. Part of it has to do with moving around a lot, part of it has to do with really enjoying my friends, and part of it has to do with not putting myself out in new sober situations often enough. I'll get right on that.

Stepping out to bars and to parties with drinking friends can present enough challenges, and even with the most understanding people, sometimes I know I just don't belong. I have to protect myself. My life is awesome, but when I am around alcohol, at any given time it can become complicated. Sometimes my thoughts just aren't right and I start feeling a little crazy, or like an outcast. Even though my friends try to be there for me, I have to know my limits and ability to be around alcohol. I choose not to drink, and sometimes I need to choose not to be around drinking at all. That will not only keep me sober, but sane.

I know that I can't run and hide from reality for the rest of my life, though. I want to be able to be in situations and not let alcohol dictate whether I can be somewhere or whether I can have a good time. I may live and die by that rule, but for the most part I have maintained contact with my old friends and probably will continue to do so.

As some of my peers become less interested in drinking just for the sake of drinking, things will slowly work out. I feel like drunkenness and loud music in bars are losing their appeal, whereas coherent conversation is gaining momentum as we settle into our postcollege state of confusion. *I* like to think that way, at least. Hopefully, as time goes on, I will attract and be drawn to people whose lives don't revolve around alcohol.

Being sober makes me a much more dependable guy, but it doesn't necessarily simplify everything. My not being able to drink, for example, makes me somewhat of an incompatible date for my girlfriend. It isn't that she is particularly a heavy drinker. It is more that we both have to make sacrifices due to our lifestyle choices when we are out together. Sometimes I may be less enthusiastic about being out at a bar or going out with people who drink, but that is what our friends often do. At the same time, for various reasons, Julia will often drink considerably less when we are out together. I remind myself that social drinking is something that should not affect me, surely not offend me. And for the most part it doesn't.

Of course I have heard the suggestion and given thought to the idea that I could be or should be trying to date someone who is sober as well. But that discounts so much of what Julia and I have. Just because some other girl may be completely sober, meaning our lifestyle choices would be aligned, doesn't guarantee we will automatically have the spark and chemistry that Julia and I have. We have an attraction, a passion, a friendship, and an understanding that make our lifestyle differences seem minuscule.

Julia has seen good and bad parts of my drinking as well as what has become of me since I have sobered up. With her, I've found myself involved in a much deeper relationship than I ever thought myself capable of. For the first time I am emotionally connected to a girl. I am not afraid of commitment and have been able to experience and express feelings that I didn't know existed. I have also found out that alcohol use does not have to precede sex, and in fact (cover your eyes), an amazing sex life is possible without the presence of alcohol at all. That was news to me. Most important, in a lot of ways Julia has taught me how to love. While it is still an abstract term to me, love is now something I can experience.

The more I turn the corner on my old, saucy lifestyle, the more I'm glad I don't have to go back to it. Recently, while road-tripping with my mom, I began laughing out loud at myself. I started thinking about all the shit I put my parents through (yes, I'm sorry). I was busting up and saying, "Seriously, how could I really have not known that I had a problem? It was so obvious!" Even in high school. Kids don't repeatedly get in trouble like I did: getting kicked off teams, picked up by the police, coming home drunk and vomiting or blacked out, or coming home—as my dad put it—"smelling like a burnt hemp field." I always felt like a victim or a magnet for trouble, but I refused to look at why I was always in trouble. I guess the most difficult patterns to identify are those too close to recognize or too scary to believe.

At times I do regret the misuse of my time, my potential, and my creative energy. There is no question that I was more interested in drinking than practicing when I began to learn how to play guitar or the drums. It doesn't help to wonder, *What if I had actually really learned to play the guitar as a teenager?* (What alcoholic is into discipline or dedication?) The best thing I can do is take back the life I was wasting.

Some people would say I'm still young. No matter what I did or did not do, much of my purpose was slowly siphoned away by drinking. It isn't too late to have music as a passionate creative outlet, with guitar and songwriting as a constructive influence. Taken one step further, this avocation has given me another purpose and added meaning to my life.

Today I get to focus on living. I'm not ready to worry about what I should be doing with the rest of my life. I'm not afraid to dedicate some time and effort toward pursuing a passion of mine, a dream, a life that I was throwing away. These are my last youthful years to investigate possibilities, and I am willing to be naïve and take a risk or two. It may seem like I have no shame, but more than that, I am no longer afraid of failure. I failed my way off plenty of sports teams, was nearly kicked out of college, and was finally coughed up and spit out of the Peace Corps and into rehab and a halfway house. I had it coming to me for a long time. From this perspective, I'm bouncing back from failure. What more have I got to lose?

Sometimes I get ahead of myself and start wondering where I am going with all of this. Where will I be a year from now? Am I spending my time wisely? Can I really be disciplined and dedicated enough to accomplish what I want with music? Am I crazy to be in love with a girl while we live on opposite sides of the country and mesh different plans for our lives?

Luckily, if I apply what I have learned in recovery, I quickly remember that I am living for today and that I cannot control everything or worry too far into the future. I also don't need to set expectations that I know I can't meet. The only time I feel pressure is when I apply it to myself, and most of the time it is unnecessary. I feel fortunate to get the chance to play music and to be able to do what I want with my life. Today I can put my sobriety first and work toward my goals in the present, a little at a time. All the rest will follow. Whatever that may be.

When I take a big whiff of my circumstances today, they seem far from tragic. They are, in fact, pretty awesome. I have lots of room for change and growth, and I have a lot to learn. I may have some mistakes to make, but I will find a way to correct them and learn from them. I still have some amends to make, but the way I choose to live on a daily basis will allow this to happen. I still have troublesome dreams about drinking relapses, but I wake up relieved that it's not real. I choose not to drink, one day at a time.

I've come to terms with my past and am starting to understand who I am and what I want in life. This is just the beginning. All of these challenges I face, the goals I am chasing, and the relationships I have today are a result of my sobriety. None of this deliciousness would be possible if I were still drinking. Now sober, it is hard to imagine life any other way.

## Toren's Timeline

1994 spring: eighth grade, age 14, drinks first beer

1994 August: begins frequent experimental use of marijuana and alcohol

1994 September: ninth grade, quits freshman football team

1995 winter: successfully completes varsity swim season

1995 May: arrested with MIP at river party; kicked off high school junior varsity soccer team with 3.79 GPA

1995 July: caught by parents drunk, blacked-out; grounded, driving privileges postponed by parents

1995 October: tenth grade, caught smoking cigarettes on campus; kicked off high school varsity football team

1996 winter: successfully completes varsity swim season

1996 March: arrested drinking with friends; MIP: kicked off high school varsity soccer team

1996 fall, eleventh grade, successfully completes varsity football season

1997 winter: successfully completes varsity swim season

1997 spring: successfully completes varsity soccer season, selected most improved player

1997 May: eleventh grade, caught by parents drunk, blacked-out on day after prom, driving privileges revoked by parents for remainder of spring

1997 fall: twelfth grade, successfully completes varsity football season, named to second team all-league defense

1998 February: twelfth grade, caught drunk on campus; kicked off high school swim team, loss of team captain position and suspended for two weeks

1998 spring: successfully completes varsity soccer season, selected most-inspirational player

1998 June: graduates high school, Olympia, Washington; 3.63 GPA

1998 fall: freshman year, starts college in San Diego, California—first, second, and third alcohol offenses issued by university staff, makes dean's list with 3.6 GPA

1999 March: kicked out of lower campus dorms; relocated to main campus

1999 spring: spring semester GPA 2.33

1999 summer: spent at home in Olympia, Washington, working, forced to attend first AA meetings

1999 November: sophomore year, arrested for public drunkenness in Santa Barbara, California

2000 May: cited with MIP returning from Santa Barbara, California

2000 summer: spent at home in Olympia, Washington, working

2000 fall: junior year, studies abroad with Semester at Sea program

2001 March: arrested for public drunkenness in Santa Barbara, California

2001 summer: spent at home in Olympia, Washington, working

2002 May: senior year, graduates from college in San Diego, California; 3.19 GPA

2002 June: moves to Seattle, Washington

2002 August: arrested for public drunkenness in San Francisco, California

2002 September: moves to Las Vegas, Nevada

2002 November: leaves for eight weeks of travel/study in Mexico

2003 January: enters the Peace Corps, Paraguay, South America

2003 September 20: last drink (to date)

2003 September 21: medically evacuated to Washington, D.C.

2003 September 25: enters thirty-day in-patient rehab program

2003 October 27: moves to Delray Beach, Florida, to live in halfway house

2003 December: visits home in Olympia, Washington, for the first time sober since middle school

2004 April 28: leaves halfway house and moves to Brooklyn, New York, to play music

2004 August: first edition *Our Drink* released

2004 fall: moves home to Olympia, Washington; travels in support of book

2005 September 20: celebrates one year of sobriety on the road in Portland, Oregon

2005 June: moves to New Orleans, Louisiana, to play music, continues speaking presentations

2005 August: begins work on *From Binge to Blackout*

2005 September 20: celebrates two years of sobriety on the road in Lubbock, Texas

2005 October: relocates to San Diego due to Hurricane Katrina

2006 August: *From Binge to Blackout* released

2006 September 20: celebrates three years of sobriety and on goes the story . . .

# APPENDIX II

## Why This Book—*From Binge to Blackout*

Our goal is to talk honestly to kids and families about alcohol choices and the consequences of heavy drinking.

We hope:

- to fill in the gap between what's really happening with young drinkers today and what society perceives about young drinkers;
- to help someone possibly recognize early symptoms of alcohol addiction/abuse;
- to help parents and kids talk more openly about alcohol use;
- to inform others about alcohol addiction and the disease of alcoholism;
- to support parents and enable them to realistically examine alcohol use in their family;
- to educate kids about their drinking choices;
- to dissolve the glamour of chronic heavy drinking;
- to heal our family.

---

### *Honest Talk* for Families and Teens

*From Binge to Blackout* **Honest Talk** is a quick aid for families and teens to determine if they are adequately informed about drinking choices. The reminders below cover essential elements of alcohol awareness.

*By talking together, you will create:*
**openness** among family and friends;
**understanding** of alcohol issues;
**reality** of alcohol's influence in our world;
**ownership** of your own drinking choices.

*Don't forget to discuss these* **Binge to Blackout** *topics:*

| | |
|---|---|
| **Blackouts** | Blackouts are an indication of alcohol abuse and a warning sign of potential alcoholism. |
| **Red Flags** | Problems at school, legal and financial difficulties, problems with relationships, and drinking to get drunk are signs of alcohol abuse. |
| **Family History** | Genetics play a huge role in risky drinking and alcoholism. |
| **Neuro-effects of Drinking** | The adolescent/young adult brain is extremely susceptible to permanent damage. |
| **Knowledge of Alcoholism** | It's a progressive disease that starts with the first sip. |

---

## The Michigan Alcohol Screening Test (MAST)[1]

The MAST Test is a simple, self-scoring test that helps assess if you have a drinking problem. Please answer YES or NO to the following questions:

1.  Do you feel you are a normal drinker? ("normal"—drink as much as or less than most other people)
    YES or NO

2.  Have you ever awakened the morning after some drinking the night before and found that you could not remember a part of the evening?
    YES or NO

3.  Does any near relative or close friend ever worry or complain about your drinking?
    YES or NO

4.  Can you stop drinking without difficulty after one or two drinks?
    YES or NO

5.  Do you ever feel guilty about your drinking?
    YES or NO

6.  Have you ever attended a meeting of Alcoholics Anonymous (AA)?
    YES or NO

7.  Have you ever gotten into physical fights when drinking?
    YES or NO

8.  Has drinking ever created problems between you and a near relative or close friend?
    YES or NO

9.  Has any family member or close friend gone to anyone for help about your drinking?
    YES or NO

10. Have you ever lost friends because of your drinking?
    YES or NO

11. Have you ever gotten into trouble at work because of drinking?
    YES or NO

12. Have you ever lost a job because of drinking?
    YES or NO

13. Have you ever neglected your obligations, your family, or your work for two or more days in a row because you were drinking?
    YES or NO

14. Do you drink before noon fairly often?
    YES or NO

15. Have you ever been told you have liver trouble, such as cirrhosis? YES or NO

16. After heavy drinking, have you ever had delirium tremens (DTs), severe shaking, visual or auditory (hearing) hallucinations? YES or NO

17. Have you ever gone to anyone for help about your drinking? YES or NO

18. Have you ever been hospitalized because of drinking? YES or NO

19. Has your drinking ever resulted in your being hospitalized in a psychiatric ward? YES or NO

20. Have you ever gone to any doctor, social worker, clergyman, or mental health clinic for help with any emotional problem in which drinking was part of the problem? YES or NO

21. Have you been arrested more than once for driving under the influence of alcohol? YES or NO

22. Have you ever been arrested, even for a few hours, because of other behavior while drinking? YES or NO (If Yes, how many times _____)

## SCORING

Please score one point if you answered the following:

1. No
2. Yes
3. Yes
4. No
5. Yes
6. Yes
7 through 22: Yes

Add up the scores and compare to the following scorecard:

0–2 No apparent problem
3–5 Early or middle problem drinker
6 or more Problem drinker

# ADDITIONAL RESOURCES AND LINKS

**A.A. (Alcoholics Anonymous)** Alcoholic Anonymous is worldwide, with A.A. meetings in almost every community. You can find times and places of local A.A. meetings or events by looking in your telephone directory or by going to their Web site at: www.alcoholics-anonymous.org.

**About Alcoholism** Includes College Binge Drinking Issues, What You Need to Know About Alcoholism/Substance Abuse, and other articles. Go to http://alcoholism.about.com/cs/college.

Alagna, Magdalena, *Everything You Need to Know About the Dangers of Binge Drinking* (New York: Rosen Publishing Group, 2001). Geared to teens with reading difficulties.

**Al-Anon/Alateen** Your inquiry is confidential and anonymous. If you are concerned about someone else's drinking, browse their Web site for information about the program. Call 888-4AL-ANON, Monday through Friday, 8:00 a.m. to 6:00 p.m. ET, for meeting information. E-mail: WSO@al-anon.org; Web site: www.al-anon.alateen.org/.

**Alcohol 101** Go to www.alcohol101plus.org/ for the Century Council's interactive CD-Rom, which explores alcohol decisions in at-risk college settings.

**Alcohol Policies Project** Advocacy for the prevention of alcohol problems. A self-test is offered online to assess drinking patterns, as well as personalized feedback and links to support resources, including a database of twelve thousand treatment centers. Go to http://cspinet.org/booze.

**AlcoPRO** Drug and alcohol testing products for home use. PO Box 10954, Knoxville, TN 37939, 1-800-227-9890, www.alcopro.com.

**A Matter of Degree (AMOD)** College environment advocacy group that furthers changes in college life to reduce alcohol abuse. Go to www.amodstrat.net and www.hsph.harvard.edu/amod.

**BACCHUS & GAMMA Peer Education Network** Promotes peer-to-peer strategies as effective tools in health and safety education and prevention programs. Go to www.bacchusgamma.org/.

**B.R.A.D. 21—Be Responsible About Drinking** Educates young adults (high school and college age) and their parents as to the responsible use of alcohol, the effects of alcohol, and how to deal with excess use by others. Go to www.brad21.org/about_us.html.

**Caron Foundation** Excellence in Addiction Treatment. Adult and adolescent residential treatment. Go to www.caron.org.

**CAS, Harvard School of Public Health College Alcohol Study** A study Web site for higher-education alcohol-abuse research. Go to www.hsph.harvard.edu/cas.

**CASA, the National Center on Addiction and Substance Abuse at Columbia University** Over the past twelve years, CASA has released fifty-five reports based on intensive research on the relationship of substance abuse and addiction to a variety of the nation's social problems and conditions. CASA reports have covered such topics as the child welfare system, the dangers of nonmedical marijuana, America's underage drinking epidemic, the diversion of prescription drugs, and the nation's adult and juvenile justice systems. Go to www.casacolumbia.org/.

**Center for Alcohol Marketing and Youth (CAMY)** Fact sheets, marketing of alcohol, research on alcohol and youth. Go to http://camy.org/.

**Community Anti-Drug Coalition of America (CADCA)** CADCA is a membership organization of over five thousand antidrug coalitions, each working to make their community safe, healthy, and drug-free. Go to http://cadca.org/.

**Core Institute** Provides stats on college students. Go to www.siu.edu/departments/coreinst/public_html/.

**Facts on Tap** Prevention initiatives for high school and college students. Go to www.factsontap.org/.

**Gordie Foundation** The Gordie Foundation is dedicated to the memory of Gordie Bailey, who was an eighteen-year-old freshman at the University of Colorado when he died of alcohol poisoning as a result of a fraternity initiation ceremony for pledges on September 17, 2004. The mission of the Gordie Foundation is to provide today's youth with the skills to navigate the dangers of alcohol, and through education and promotion of self-worth, to prevent alcohol poisoning, binge drinking, and hazing. Go to www.thegordiefoundation.org/home/default.asp.

**Higher Education Center for Alcohol and other Drug Information (HEC)** HEC develops, implements, and evaluates programs to reduce student problems related to alcohol, drugs, and violence. Go to www.edc.org/hec.

Jay, Jeff, and Debra Jay, *Love First: A New Approach to Intervention for Alcoholism and Drug Addiction* (Center City, Minn.: Hazelden, 2000).

**The Jellinek Curve** Go to www.in.gov/judiciary/ijlap/docs/jellinek.pdf.

**Join Together** Join Together helps community leaders understand and use the most current scientifically valid prevention and treatment approaches to advance effective alcohol and drug policy, prevention, and treatment. Subscriptions to Join Together's electronic newsletters and publications are free. Go to www.jointogether.org.

**June Russell** Health Facts about alcohol consumption categorized under specific topics. Go to www.jrussellshealth.com/index.html.

Ketcham, Katherine, William F. Asbury, Mel Schulstad, and Arthur P. Ciaramicoli, *Beyond the Influence: Understanding and Defeating Alcoholism* (New York: Bantam, 2000).

Kuhn, Cynthia, Scott Swartzwelder, and Wilkie Wilson, *Buzzed: The Straight Facts about the Most Used and Abused Drugs from Alcohol to Ecstasy* (New York: W. W. Norton & Company, 1998).

**Marin Institute for the Prevention of Alcohol and Other Drug Problems** Focuses on environments that glamorize alcohol, and includes a database about the alcohol beverage industry and policies. Go to www.marininstitute.org/.

**Michigan Alcohol Screening Test (MAST)** A quickly administered questionnaire to determine signs of alcoholism. Go to www.ncadd=sfv.org/symptoms/mast_test.html (*see* Appendix IV).

**Mothers Against Drunk Driving (MADD)** Provides group information and counseling for victims. Go to www.madd.org.

**National Center for Chronic Disease Prevention & Health Promotion** Trends and data for alcohol use and chronic drinking grouped by categories, from the Department of Health and Human Services. Go to www.cdc.gov/nccdphp/.

**National Clearinghouse for Alcohol and Drug Information** A national resource sponsored by the U.S. government. Searchable databases at www.health.org/dbases.htm allow the user to search papers on any topic related to alcohol use. Go to www.health.org.

**National Commission Against Drunk Driving (NCADD)** This group continues efforts of the Presidential Commission on Drunk Driving by uniting public- and private-sector organizations. Go to www.ncadd.com.

**National Institute on Alcohol Abuse and Alcoholism (NIAAA)** NIAAA provides leadership in the national effort to reduce alcohol-related problems by:

- Conducting and supporting research in a wide range of scientific areas, including genetics, neuroscience, epidemiology, health risks, and benefits for alcohol consumption, prevention, and treatment
- Coordinating and collaborating with other research institutes and federal programs on alcohol-related issues
- Collaborating with international, national, state, and local institutions, organizations, agencies, and programs engaged in alcohol-related work
- Translating and disseminating research findings to health care providers, researchers, policy makers, and the public. Go to http://www.niaaa.nih.gov/. See also www.collegedrinkingprevention.gov, which is devoted to changing the college drinking culture.

**National Substance Abuse Web Index** Information on substance abuse prevention and treatment communities. Excellent links. Go to http://nsawi.health.org.

**The Network** Addresses collegiate alcohol and other drug issues. Go to www.thenetwork.ws.

**Outside the Classroom** Colleges and universities use their product, AlcoholEdu, as a prevention effort to negate consequences of alcohol abuse on campus. Go to www.outsidetheclassroom.com.

**Partners in Prevention (PIP)** A statewide coalition focused on preventing high-risk drinking among Missouri's college students. Publications include "What

Every Parent Needs to Know." Information about alcohol and other college health issues. Funded by the Missouri Division of Alcohol and Other Drug Abuse and Missouri Department of Transportation Highway Safety Division. Go to www.missouri.edu/~mopip/.

Peterson, J. Vincent, B. Nisenholz, and G. Robinson, *A Nation Under the Influence: America's Addiction to Alcohol* (New York: Allyn & Bacon, 2003).

**SAM** [Student Alcohol Management] **Spady Foundation** The mission of the SAM Spady Foundation is to educate all parents and students on the dangers of alcohol, specifically high-risk consumption, and the signs and symptoms of alcohol poisoning. Go to www.samspadyfoundation.org/.

Schaefer, Dick, *Choices & Consequences: What to Do When a Teenager Uses Alcohol/Drugs* (Center City, Minn.: Hazelden, 1987).

**Sober Living in Delray** Early sobriety halfway facility. Go to www.soberlivingindelray.com/.

**STOP underage drinking** Information on underage drinking and ideas for combating this issue. People interested in underage drinking prevention—including parents, educators, community-based organizations, and youth—will find a wealth of valuable information here. For a helpful pamphlet, click on "Start Talking Before They Start Drinking" at http://www.stopalcoholabuse.gov/.

**Student Health 101** Promotes better health throughout college campuses. Go to www.studenthealth101.com/index.asp.

**Students Against Destructive Decisions (SADD)** Prevention programs for middle school, senior high, and college students for underage drinking, drug abuse, destructive decisions. Go to www.saddonline.com.

**Task Force on College Drinking** Sponsored by the National Institute on Alcohol Abuse and Alcoholism (NIAAA), the site offers information about the alcohol problem on college campuses, and possible solutions. Go to www.collegedrinkingprevention.gov.

**U.S. Department of Health and Human Services Substance Abuse and Mental Health Services Administration** Get help for substance abuse and mental health problems. Go to www.samhsa.gov/.

Vanderlip, Susie, *52 Ways to Protect Your Teen: Guiding Teens to Good Choices and Success* (Orange, Calif.: Intuitive Wisdom Publications, 2005).

Wechsler, Henry, and Bernice Wuethrich, *Dying to Drink: Confronting Binge Drinking on College Campuses* (New York: Rodale, 2002).

Zailckas, Koren. *Smashed: Story of a Drunken Girlhood* (New York: Viking, 2005).

# BOOK GROUP FOCUS QUESTIONS

## PREVENTION/EDUCATION

1. At what age should parents begin discussing alcohol choices/facts with kids?
2. How can parents make alcohol facts real to kids? Is this possible?
3. What fact about alcohol do you think most important to bring up in your family?
4. What ideas do you have for the earliest education about alcohol?
5. How can the glamour of alcohol and drinking be diminished?
6. What ideas do you have for the prevention of immediate and long-term alcohol risks when kids go to college? (Peak drinking is predictable. According to the Pacific Institute for Research and Evaluation, March 2004, the heaviest drinking on college campuses occurs among freshman males at the beginning of each academic year.)
7. In communities today there is an emphasis on contracts in which youth and parents agree to eliminate drunken driving. With the contracts are we saying, "It's okay to drink, just not to drink and drive"? What kind of message are we sending?
8. Try abstaining from alcohol for a month. Make observations from personal experience regarding peer pressure, belonging to a group, inappropriate behavior due to alcohol, and so on. How can this exercise help you to educate your child about alcohol/substance use and choices?

## ADDICTION

1. How is having an addiction to alcohol different from other diseases? How are a family's reactions to this disease different from their reactions to other diseases?
2. There is an ongoing debate about the genetic component of alcoholism. How much do you think is genetic and how much is learned behavior?

## MYTHS/MEDIA/SOCIETAL ISSUES

1. What is the "perfect family"? Define this for yourself. Is this realistic? How is this term a myth?
2. What is on your list of worries regarding your children? What are things that you have control over? What things do you need to let go of?
3. Why do we drink? Why has human culture always devised a way to alter our perception of reality or numb our feelings? What role do mind- or mood-altering substances or activities play in our society? Are they necessary? What are some healthier ways to elevate our moods?
4. The stereotypical view of an intoxicated woman has been worse than that of an intoxicated man. What do you believe is the current view of a drunk woman by your contemporaries?
5. The liquor industry maintains that there is no proven relationship between alcohol advertising and youth alcohol consumption. Many researchers claim there is a connection. What do you think?
6. Do beer companies, with their vast media campaigns, have a responsibility for curbing young people's attraction to alcohol?
7. Should alcohol taxes be raised to cover the health and societal costs resulting from alcohol abuse, similar to the way tobacco companies are now paying states for health expenditures?
8. Will reducing accessibility to alcohol and increasing education about addiction be enough to prevent alcoholism, or are even greater fundamental changes in our society needed?
9. What, if any, is the connection between adult family members drinking alcohol in front of underage kids and kids/society thinking that drinking alcohol is okay? Is it a mixed message we're giving kids when we adults drink alcohol in front of them?
10. What are the differences between social drinking and addictive drinking? Are there any, or is it just a matter of degrees?
11. "People seem to be more upset about kids' smoking than their drinking. Drinking is seen as a rite of passage. Many don't see the link between

drinking and trauma and injury or other negative consequences." Do you agree with this statement? Why or why not?

12. "Of each state dollar spent, ninety-six cents goes to shovel up the wreckage of substance abuse, (and only) four cents goes to prevention and treatment." (Center on Addiction and Substance Abuse, 2001.) What does this say about our priorities?

13. The federal government spends twenty-five times more on illegal drug abuse prevention than on underage drinking prevention, despite the fact that alcohol kills six times more youths than all other drugs combined (Gogek, *New York Times*, August 25, 2004). How can parents make a difference in our government's emphasis?

14. What role, if any, does the need to belong to a group play in alcohol/substance use and abuse?

15. What has the reaction been within your home community to the publication of *From Binge to Blackout*?

## RESOURCES/HELP

1. Where can a family or parent go for help the first time a child/teen comes home drunk?

2. What can parents do to encourage college institutions to develop and enforce an alcohol policy?

3. How does a parent know when an alcohol flirtation has become an alcohol problem?

4. What is the role of colleges in stemming the flood of binge drinking? Are they right to take a hands-off stand? What responsibilities do colleges have to the parents? Where do privacy rights interact with public health initiatives?

## TREATMENT

1. Chris and Toren talk about the effectiveness of various attempts to control drinking (such as D.A.R.E., the binge chart, grounding and other consequences). What works? What services in your community are needed to help parents deal with children who drink?

2. What are meaningful and realistic consequences for alcohol use during adolescence?

3. Are "Behavior Contracts" effective? How or how not? When should they be used?

4. If an adult child is abusing substances, what can you do? If they are in denial and/or not seeking help or treatment, what is your role as a parent?

5. Some therapists agree that to successfully help alcoholics, they need to work with the whole family. Most HMOs and PPOs do not cover family treatment. What are possible solutions to this problem?
6. The U.S. Surgeon General has established a goal of 50 percent reduction in binge drinking by the year 2010. What is needed nationwide to accomplish this goal? How can we get it going?
7. Do you think Toren will be successful in handling his alcoholism in the future?

## FAMILY DYNAMICS/ISSUES

1. Early in the book Chris calls herself a failure as a parent because of Toren's drinking. How much do we individually and as a society blame parents for the failures of their children?
2. How do parents know what kids and their friends are doing when they spend time together?
3. Do most parents talk with their kids when the kids return home from a social event?
4. Do parents know how their kids are spending money?
5. What social avenues promote the glamour of drinking?
6. Do most parents watch the same movies as their kids? How do kids react to the movies they see?
7. The majority of adults who drink in this country do so in moderation. How can parents model good behavior with alcohol? Is this possible with teenagers in the house?

## ASSESSMENT

1. Toren talks about early opportunities to intervene in his drinking and how he wasn't ready to face his addiction. How do friends and family cope with an alcoholic or abuser who isn't ready for rehab? What are ways to intervene before an alcoholic has admitted his or her addiction?
2. If one chooses intervention, is intervention by the family effective or is professional expertise required?

*For discussion suggestions, thank you to Cathy Williams, Kammy Minor, Peggy Ludwick, and Susan Fiksdal*

# STUDENT FOCUS QUESTIONS

1. Name three negative effects of heavy ("binge") drinking.
2. How does heavy drinking affect the adolescent brain?
3. What is the association between violence, assault, date rape, and drinking?
4. Name things you and your friends can do to stay safe at a party or in a similar situation.
5. The majority of adults who drink in this country do so in moderation. How can parents model good behavior with alcohol?
6. Do beer companies, with their vast media campaigns, have a responsibility for curbing young people's attraction to alcohol?
7. What is the role of colleges in stemming the flood of binge drinking? Should they take a hands-off stand or become involved? What responsibilities do colleges have to the parents and students? Where do privacy rights interact with public health initiatives?
8. Of each state dollar spent, ninety-six cents goes to shovel up the wreckage of substance abuse, (and only) four cents goes to prevention and treatment." (Center on Addiction and Substance Abuse, 2001.) What does this say about our priorities?
9. The federal government spends twenty-five times more on illegal drug abuse prevention than on underage drinking prevention, despite the fact that alcohol kills six times more youths than all other drugs combined (Gogek, *New York Times*, August 25, 2004). How can one make a difference in our government's emphasis?
10. What role, if any, does the need to belong to a group play in alcohol/substance use and abuse?

11. Why do we drink? Why has human culture always devised a way to alter our perceptions of reality or numb our feelings? What role do mind- or mood-altering substances or activities play in our society? Are they necessary? What are some healthier ways to elevate our moods?

12. The stereotypical view of an intoxicated female has been worse than that of an intoxicated male. What do you believe is the current view of a drunk female by your contemporaries?

13. The liquor industry maintains that there is no proven relationship between alcohol advertising and youth alcohol consumption. Many researchers claim there is a connection. What do you think?

14. Should alcohol taxes be raised to cover the health and societal costs resulting from alcohol abuse, similar to the way tobacco companies are now paying states for health expenditures?

15. Will reducing accessibility to alcohol and increasing education about addiction be enough to prevent alcoholism, or are even greater fundamental changes in our society needed?

16. What, if any, is the connection between adult family members drinking alcohol in front of underage kids and kids/society thinking that drinking alcohol is okay? Is there a mixed message given to kids when adults drink alcohol in front of them or in their homes?

17. What are the differences between social drinking and addictive drinking? Are there any, or is it just a matter of degrees?

18. "People seem to be more upset about kids' smoking than their drinking. Drinking is seen as a rite of passage. Many don't see the link between drinking and trauma and injury or other negative consequences." Do you agree with this statement? Why or why not?

19. Do you or any of your friends choose not to drink? How does this affect party behaviors?

20. Do you think Toren will be successful in handling his alcoholism in the future?

*For discussion suggestions, thank you to ALERT Labs, Nancy Harper, Ph.D., Cathy Williams, Kammy Minor, Peg Ludwick, and Susan Fiksdal*

# ABOUT THE AUTHORS

Photo by Taea Thale

Author **Chris Volkmann,** a former classroom teacher, lives in Olympia, Washington. Chris stepped away from her career to parent three sons. She attended Toren's college graduation having no clue her son was part of a not-so-hidden epidemic. She shares what every parent thinks but cannot always say.

Coauthor **Toren Volkmann** (BA in psychology, former Peace Corps Volunteer) lives one day at a time after successfully completing rehab and a six-month residence in a Florida halfway house.

For further exploration of alcohol choices and the consequences of chronic heavy drinking, and speaking engagements, go to www.BingetoBlackout.com.

## CHAPTER 1

[1] H. Weschsler, J. E. Lee, M. Kuo, M. Seibring, T. F. Nelson, and H. Lee, "Trends in College Binge Drinking During a Period of Increased Prevention Efforts: Findings from 4 Harvard School of Public Health Study Surveys, 1993–2001," *Journal of American College Health* 50 (2002), pp. 203–17. For more information on CAS, visit www.hsph.harvard.edu/cas/.

[2] Robert H. DuRant, Wake Forest Baptist Medical Center, professor of pediatrics and public health sciences, multidisciplinary study team. Research funded by the National Institute on Alcohol Abuse and Alcoholism (NIAAA), fall 2003 survey. The ten universities involved in the study are Appalachian State; Duke; High Point; Western Carolina; and the Asheville, Chapel Hill, Charlotte, Wilmington, and Pembroke campuses of the University of North Carolina; available at http://alcoholism.about.com/od/college/a/blwf050523.htm, accessed September 25, 2005.

[3] H. Wechsler, J. E. Lee, M. Kuo, and H. Lee, "College Binge Drinking in the 1990's: A Continuing Problem: Results of the Harvard School of Public Health 1999 College Alcohol Study," *Journal of American College Health* 48, no. 10 (2000), pp. 199–210.

[4] Henry Wechsler and Bernice Wuethrich, *Dying to Drink: Confronting Binge Drinking on College Campuses* (New York: Rodale, 2002).

## CHAPTER 5

[1] Thom Jones, *Cold Snap* (Boston: Little, Brown and Company, 1995).

## CHAPTER 7

[1] *AMA Alliance Today*, 1998.

[2] S. A. Brown, S. F. Tapert, E. Granholm, and D. C. Delis, "Neurocognitive Functioning of Adolescents: Effects of Protracted Alcohol Use," *Alcoholism: Clinical and Experimental Research* 24, no. 2 (February 2000).

[3] J. N. Giedd et al., "Brain Development during Childhood and Adolescence: A Longitudinal MRI Study," *Nature Neuroscience* 2, no.10 (October 1999).

[4] Cynthia Kuhn, Scott Swartzwelder, and Wilkie Wilson, *Buzzed: The Straight Facts about the Most Used and Abused Drugs from Alcohol to Ecstasy* (New York: W. W. Norton & Company, 1998).

[5] National Institute on Alcohol Abuse and Alcoholism, "Cognitive Impairment and Recovery from Alcoholism," *Alcohol Alert* 53 (July 2001).

[6] F. T. Crews, C. J. Braun, B. Hoplight, R. C. Switzer III, and D. J. Knapp, "Binge Ethanol Consumption Causes Differential Brain Damage in Young Adolescent Compared with Adult Rats," *Alcoholism: Clinical and Experimental Research* 24, no.11 (November 2000).

[7] "NIAAA Releases Estimates of Alcohol Abuse and Dependence," *Media Advisory*, March 17, 1995.

[8] U.S. Dept. of Health and Human Services, Tenth Special Report to the U.S. Congress on Alcohol and Health: Highlights from Current Research (Alexandria, Va.: EEI, September 2000).

[9] Alcohol Policies Project, "Young People and Alcohol," Summary of Findings from the American Academy of Pediatrics Survey: Teen Alcohol Consumption, American Academy of Pediatrics, September 1998; available at www.cspinet.org/booze/alcyouth.html, accessed March 11, 2006.

[10] W. Slutske, "Alcohol Use Disorders Among US College Students and Their Non-College-Attending Peers," *Archives of General Psychiatry* 62, no. 3 (March 2005), pp. 321–27.

[11] The 2004 National Survey on Drug Use and Health: National Findings, SAMHSA, Office of Applied Studies, September 2005, available at http://oas.samhsa.gov/nsduh/2k4Results/2k4/Results.htm#toc, accessed March 1, 2006.

[12] "One in Five Americans Binged on Alcohol Recently," *USA Today*, February 13, 2005, p. 4A; and Join Together, as reported in National Survey on Drug Use and Health from SAMHSA, February 13, 2005, at www.jointogether.org/sa/news/summaries/reader/0%2C1854%2C576202%2C00.html.

[13] Peter E. Nathan, "Culture of Heavy High School Drinking," University of Iowa, 2005.

[14] Kuhn, Swartzwelder, and Wilson, *Buzzed*.

[15] Michelle Healy, "Brain Damage from Heavy Social Drinking," *USA Today*, April 15, 2004, betterlife@usatoday.com, as reported in D. J. Meyerhoff; R. Blumenfeld; D. Truran; J. Lindgren; D. Flenniken; V. Cardenas; L. L. Chao; J. Rothlind; C. Studholme; M. W. Weiner. "Effects of Heavy Drinking, Binge Drinking, and Family History of Alcoholism on Regional Brain Metabolites," *Alcoholism: Clinical and Experimental Research*, 28 (April 2004).

[16] Aaron M. White, "Alcohol-induced Blackouts," Duke University Medical Center, 2004; available at www.duke.edu/~amwhite/Blackouts/blackouts11.html.

[17] A. M. White, D. Jamieson-Drake, and H. S. Swartzwelder, "Prevalence and Correlates of Alcohol-Induced Blackouts Among College Students," *Journal of American College Health* 51 (November 2002), pp. 117–31.

[18] Wechsler and Wuethrich, *Dying to Drink*.

[19] Jeff Benson, "What Does It Mean to 'Blackout'?" *Bowdoin Orient*, November 19, 2004; available at http://orient.bowdoin.edu/orient/article.php?date=2004-11-19&section=3&id=5.

[20] Kuhn, Swartzwelder, and Wilson, *Buzzed*.

[21] H. Wechsler, G. W. Dowdall, G. Maenner, J. Gledill-Hoyt, and H. Lee, "Changes in Binge Drinking and Related Problems Among American College Students Between 1993 and 1997: Results of the Harvard School of Public Health College Alcohol Study," *Journal of American College Health* 47 (September 1998).

[22]Harvard School of Public Health College Alcohol Study (CAS), *Journal of Studies on Alcohol*, 1994–2004, and www.hsph.harvard.edu/cas, a study Web site for higher-education alcohol-abuse research, H. Wechsler, Director.

[23]Vincent J. Peterson, B. Nisenholz, and G. Robinson, *A Nation Under the Influence: America's Addiction to Alcohol* (New York: Allyn & Bacon, 2003).

[24]The 2004 National Survey on Drug Use and Health: National Findings, SAMHSA, Office of Applied Studies, September 2005, available at http://oas.samhsa.gov/nsduh/2k4Results/2k4/Results.htm#toc accessed March 1, 2006, and L. D. Johnston, P. M. O'Malley, and J. G. Bachman, *Monitoring the Future National Results on Adolescent Drug Use: Overview of Key Findings, 2002* (Bethesda, MD: National Institute on Drug Abuse, 2003), available at http://camy.org/factsheets/index.php?FactsheetID=17#trends, accessed March 3, 2006.

[25]Wechsler and Wuethrich, *Dying to Drink*.

[26]June Russell, "Deception in Reporting About Alcohol"; available at www.jrussellshealth.com/alcben_paradox.html.

[27]"One-Third of College Students Have Alcohol Disorders," *Alcoholism & Drug Abuse Weekly*, June 17, 2002; available at www.jointogether.org.

[28]J. A. Ewing, "Detecting Alcoholism: The CAGE Questionnaire," JAMA 252:1905-1907, 1984, available at http://www.renascent.ca/addiction/cage.htm.

[29]Harvard School of Public Health College Alcohol Study (CAS), *Journal of Studies on Alcohol*, 1994–2004, and www.hsph.harvard.edu/cas.

[30]Healy, "Brain Damage from Heavy Social Drinking," *USA Today*, as cited in Meyerhoff, *Alcoholism*.

[31]S. T. Ennett, N. S. Tobler, C. L. Ringwalt, et al., "How Effective Is Drug Abuse Resistance Education? A Meta-analysis of Project DARE Outcome Evaluations," *American Journal of Public Health* 84, no. 9 (1994), pp. 1394–1401; C. L. Ringwalt, S. T. Ennett, and K. D. Holt, "An Outcome Evaluation of Project DARE," *Health Education Research: Theory and Practice*, 6 (1991), pp. 327–37; and D. P. Rosenbaum, R. L. Flewelling, S. L. Bailey, et al., "Cops in the Classroom: A Longitudinal Evaluation of Drug Abuse Resistance Education (DARE)," *Journal of Research in Crime and Delinquency* 31, no. 1 (1994), pp. 3–31.

[32]Wechsler and Wuethrich, *Dying to Drink*, p. 6.

## CHAPTER 9

[1]Katie Hafner, "How Thursday Became the New Friday," *New York Times*, November 6, 2005.

[2]Adapted from National Institute on Alcohol Abuse and Alcoholism (NIAAA), August 2005; available at www.collegedrinkingprevention.gov/Parents. Adapted from Wechsler and Wuethrich, *Dying to Drink*, pp. 248–49.

[3]Wechsler and Wuethrich, *Dying to Drink*, p. 158.

[4]R. Ochs, "Students Need Lesson in Alcohol Avoidance," *Los Angeles Times*, September 24, 2001, p. S5.

[5]The Doors, "Alabama Song (Whiskey Bar)," written by Bertolt Brecht and Kurt Weill.

[6]Harvard School of Public Health College Alcohol Study (CAS), *Journal of Studies on Alcohol*, 1994–2004, and www.hsph.harvard.edu/cas.

[7]Henry Wechsler, Jae Eun Lee, Toben F. Nelson, Meichun Kuo, "Underage College Students' Drinking Behavior, Access to Alcohol, and the Influence of Deterrence Policies," College Alcohol Study (CAS), *Journal of American College Health*, 50 (5): pp. 223–36, March 2002. Page 233 available at http://www.hsph.harvard.edu/cas/Documents/underminimum/, accessed March 3, 2006.

[8]Ibid.

[9]Wechsler and Wuethrich, *Dying to Drink*, p. 213.

[10]"Oklahoma University Bans Drinking in Residences," Associated Press, December 2, 2004; available at www.jointogether.org/sa/news/summaries/reader/0%2C1854%2C575330%2C00.html, accessed August 30, 2005.

[11]United Nations Population Fund: UNFPA, "Supporting Adolescents & Youth," 2003; population issues as accessed at www.unfpa.org/adolescents/.

[12]"Binge Drinking Costing Billions," BBC News UK Edition, September 19, 2003; available at http://news.bbc.co.uk/1/hi/health/3121440.stm.

[13]"Youth Drinking Worse in Europe than U.S., Study Says," *Philanthropy News Network*, November 17, 2005, from the European School Survey Project on Alcohol and Other Drugs, and the U.S. Monitoring the Future Survey, "Youth Drinking Rates and Problems: A comparison of European countries and the United States"; Join Together, www.jointogether.org/y/0,2521,578643,00.html, accessed November 29, 2005.

[14]"Worldwide Study on Fighting Alcohol Misuse," Join Together, January 21, 2005; www.jointogether.org/sa/news/summaries/reader/0%2C1854%2C575763%2C00.html, accessed September 1, 2005.

[15]Kim Bloomfield, Tim Stockwell, Gerhard Gmel, and Nina Rehn, "International Comparisons of Alcohol Consumption," Alcohol Research & Health (Winter 2003), pp. 20–27; available at www.findarticles.com/p/articles/mi_m0CXH/is_1_27/ai_112937519/pg_3, accessed November 13, 2005.

[16]"New Poll Finds Most Teens Obtain Alcohol from Homes and Adults," American Medical Association, August 11, 2005; available at http://cadca.org/coalitionsonline/article.asp?id=8477, accessed August 16, 2005.

[17]Bloomfield, Stockwell, Gmel, and Rehn, "International Comparisons of Alcohol Consumption"; accessed November 6, 2005.

[18]"Wine Labels Cause Headaches in France," BBC News, November 25, 2005; available at www.jointogether.org/sa/news/summaries/reader/0%2C1854%2C578660%2C00.html, accessed on November 29, 2005.

[19]"Teen Drinking Sets Pattern for Life," Study by the Centre for Adolescent Health at the Royal Children's Hospital, Australia, September 7, 2003; available at http://alcoholism.about.com/b/a/024359.htm.

[20]David J. Lynch, "China Finds Western Ways Bring New Woes," USA Today, May 19, 2004, p. 13A.

[21]"WHO Launches Alcohol Study," Reuters, May 25, 2005; available at www.jointogether.org.

[22]"One-Third of College Students Have Alcohol Disorders," Alcoholism & Drug Abuse Weekly, June 17, 2002; available at www.jointogether.org.

[23]Adapted from National Institute on Alcohol Abuse and Alcoholism (NIAAA), "Parents of a College Freshman—Staying Involved," August 2005; available at www.collegedrinkingprevention.gov/reports/Parents/default.aspx; and "What Every Parent Needs to Know," information about alcohol and other college health issues, Partners in Prevention, Missouri Division of Alcohol and Other Drug Abuse and Missouri Department of Transportation Highway Safety Division; available at www.missouri.edu/~mopip/.

[24]"Hispanics Now One-seventh of U.S. Population," Associated Press; available at www.msnbc.msn.com/id/8147476, accessed August 24, 2005.

[25]Center on Alcohol Marketing and Youth (CAMY), "Alcohol Industry's Marketing Overexposes Hispanic Teens," November 2, 2005; available at http://camy.org/research/hispanic1005/.

[26]National Center for Health Statistics Vital Statistics System, "10 Leading Causes of Death, United States: 2000, All Races, Hispanic Both Sexes," from *WISQARS Leading Causes of Death Reports*, 1999–2000, accessed April 8, 2003; and American Medical Association, "Facts about Youth and Alcohol," accessed April 8, 2003.

## CHAPTER 11

[1] "Gene May Be Linked to Binge-Drinking Behavior," *Alcohol and Alcoholism* (September 2003); available at www.jointogether.org.

[2] B. Grant, "The Impact of Family History of Alcoholism on the Relationship Between Age at Onset of Alcohol Use and DSM-IV Alcohol Dependence": Results from the National Longitudinal Alcohol Epidemiologic Survey, *Alcohol Health and Research World* 22, no. 2 (1998), pp. 144–47.

## CHAPTER 12

[1] Raymond Carver, "Luck," from *All of Us* (New York: Vintage Contemporaries, 2000).

[2] Adapted from NIAAA Publications, "Make a Difference: Talk to Your Child about Alcohol"; available at www.niaaa.nig.gov/publications/makediff.htm; and from Elks Drug Awareness Program, "Parenting, Identifying with Your Child About Drugs and Alcohol Problems"; available at www.elks.org/drugs.

[3] Adapted from "Taking Action: Prevention Strategies for Parents," NIAAA, 2005; available at www.niaaa.nih.gov/publications/makediff.htm#Young Teens.

## CHAPTER 13

[1] Toren Volkmann, "Alcohology," 2003.

[2] E. M. Jellinek, *The Disease Concept of Alcoholism* (New Brunswick, N.J.: Milhouse Press, 1960); available at www.in.gov/judiciary/ijlap/docs/jellinek.pdf.

## CHAPTER 14

[1] Adapted from "If there's *any* part of the night that you don't remember, then you blacked out," Washington & Lee University, 2005; for more information, visit http://life.wlu.edu.

[2] Adapted from Substance Abuse and Mental Health Services Administration, "Results from the 2003 National Survey on Drug Use and Health: National Finds," Rockville, Md.: Office of Applied Studies, 2004; and 10 Warning Signs, adapted from "Make a Difference: Talk to Your Child about Alcohol," National Institute on Alcohol Abuse and Alcoholism, 2005; available at www.niaaa.nih.gov/publications/makediff.htm.

[3] Adapted from "What to Do If Worried About a Child Who May Be Drinking," NIAAA, "Make a Difference: Talk to Your Child about Alcohol"; available at www.niaaa.nih.gov/publications/makediff.htm; and from "Suspect Your Teen Is Using Drugs or Drinking?" A Brief Guide to Action for Parents, Parents—the anti-drug, the National Youth Anti-Drug Media Campaign; available at www.theantidrug.com.

[4] "Someone to Talk to for Parents and Teens"; available at www.health.org/help/default.aspx; and National Drug and Alcohol Treatment Referral Routing Service (Center for Substance Abuse Treatment), www.niaaa.nih.gov/faq/faq.htm.

## CHAPTER 15

[1] R. Hingson, T. Heeren, R.C. Zakocs, A. Kopstein, and H. Wechsler, "Magnitude of Alcohol-Related Mortality and Morbidity Among U.S. College Students Ages 18–24," *Journal of Studies on Alcohol* 63, no. 2 (April 12, 2002), pp. 136–44.

[2] M.P. Koss, C.A. Gidycz, and N. Wisniewski, "The Scope of Rape: Incidence and Prevalence of Sexual Aggression and Victimization in a National Sample of Higher Education Students," *Journal of Consulting and Clinical Psychology* 55 (1987), pp. 162–70; and Mary P. Koss, Ph.D., "Acquaintance Rape: A Critical Update on Recent Findings with Application to Advocacy," University of Arizona, Rape Research in the Year 2000 and Beyond; available at http://www.google.com/search?hl=en&q=koss+alcohol+and+rape&btnG=Google+Search, accessed March 2, 2006.

[3] Harvard School of Public Health College Alcohol Study (CAS), *Journal of Studies on Alcohol*, 1994–2004, and www.hsph.harvard.edu/cas.

[4] Aaron M. White, "Alcohol-induced Blackouts," Duke University Medical Center, 2002; available at www.duke.edu/~amwhite/Blackouts/blackouts11.html.

[5] M. Mohler-Kuo, G. W. Dowdall, M. P. Koss, and H. Wechsler, "Correlates of Rape While Intoxicated in a National Sample of College Women," *Journal of Studies on Alcohol* 65 (January 2004), pp. 37–45.

[6] "Perception and Reality: A National Evaluation of Social Norms Marketing Interventions to Reduce College Students' Heavy Alcohol Use," *Journal of Studies on Alcohol* (2003); and Daniel Palmadesso, "Harvard Study: Students Will Drink No Matter What," *Cornell Daily Sun*, September 9, 2003.

[7] National Social Norms Resource Center, NSNRC, Michael Haines, Director, and H. Wesley Perkins, Ph.D., "Largest Nationwide Study to Date Confirms Perception as Strongest Predictor of Personal Alcohol Consumption on College Campuses"; available at www.socialnorm.org/PressRoom/release8-29-05JSA.php, accessed October 9, 2005.

[8] Tamar Lewin, "Clean Living on Campus: Does It Work? Substance-Free Dorms," *New York Times*, November 6, 2005.

[9] Wendy Cole, "Goodbye to the Binge: The Recovery House," *Time*, September 20, 2004; available at www.time.com/time/magazine/article/0,9171,1101040920695849,00.html.

[10] The Center for the Study of Addiction at Texas Tech University; available at www.edc.org/hec/casestudies/ttu.html, accessed September 20, 2005.

[11] June Russell, "Deception in Reporting About Alcohol"; available at www.jrussellshealth.com/alcben_paradox.html.

[12] Jeffrey Gettleman, "As Young Adults Drink to Win, Marketers Join In," *New York Times*, October 16, 2005.

[13] National Institute on Alcohol Abuse and Alcoholism (NIAAA), "Clinical Protocols to Reduce High Risk Drinking in College Students," September 2003; available at www.collegedrinkingprevention.gov/Reports/trainingmanual/contents.aspx.

[14] Adapted from "Parents of a College Freshman—Staying Involved," and "Parents of a College Freshman Facing an Alcohol-Related Crisis—Getting Assistance," available at http://www.collegedrinkingprevention.gov/NIAAA CollegeMaterials/parentBrochure.aspx, and "The Network—Addressing

Collegiate Alcohol and Other Drug Issues," available at http://www.the network.ws/resources.htm, accessed February 23, 2006.

[15]Marco R. della Cava, "Spring Break Gone Wild; Uninhibited Students Sometimes See the Consequences in a Flash," *USA Today*, March 30, 2005.

[16]"Discussing Spring Break," prepared by A Matter of Degree: The National Effort to Reduce High-Risk Drinking Among College Students; available at www.ama-assn.org/ama/pub/category/9914.html, March 2005, last updated March 28, 2005; content provided by Alcohol & Drug Abuse.


## CHAPTER 18

[1] Raymond Carver, "Drinking While Driving," from *All of Us* (New York: Vintage Contemporaries, 2000).


## CHAPTER 20

[1] Raymond Carver, excerpt from "Alcohol," from *All of Us*.

[2] M. Linnoila, I. Mefford, D. Nutt, and B. Adinoff, NIH Conference, "Alcohol withdrawal and noradrenergic function," *Annals of Internal Medicine* 107, no. 6 (1987), pp. 875–89.

[3] Stephanie Coontz, *The Way We Never Were* (New York: Basic Books, July 2000).


## CHAPTER 21

[1] Joseph Troncale, M.D., "Medical Aspects of the Disease of Addiction," Caron Foundation, Pennsylvania, October 17, 2003; available at www.caron.org.

[2] Kuhn, Swartzwelder, and Wilson, *Buzzed*.

[3] J. D. Berke, and S. E. Hyman, "Addiction, Dopamine and Molecular Mechanisms of Memory," *Neuron* 25 (2000), pp. 515–32.

[4] Kuhn, Swartzwelder, and Wilson, *Buzzed*, p. 40.

[5] Jane Lampman, "How Far Can 12 Steps Go?" *Christian Science Monitor*, January 21, 2004, p. 12.

[6] M. J. Lemanski, "Addiction alternatives for recovery," *Humanist* 60, no. 1 (January/February 2000), p. 14f.

## CHAPTER 23

[1] J. M. Polich, D. J. Armor, and H. B. Braiker, "Stability and Change in Drinking Patterns," in *The Course of Alcoholism: Four Years After Treatment* (New York: John Wiley & Sons, 1981).

[2] Susan Merle Gordon, "Relapse & Recovery: Behavioral Strategies for Change," Caron Foundation, 2003; available at www.caron.org.

[3] Peter Johnson, "Rush Is Back on Air After Rehab," *USA Today*, November 18, 2003.

[4] Reported at http://www.infoplease.com/ipa/A0192787.html, accessed August 30, 2005; and the 2003 National Survey on Drug Use and Health; available at https://nsduhweb.rti.org, accessed August 29, 2005.

[5] Peter D. Hart Research Associates, "CADCA Survey Finds Stigma Persists Despite Evidence That Alcoholism Is Not a Moral Weakness," September 25, 2005; available at http://cadca.org/CoalitionsOnline/article.asp?id=897, accessed October 15, 2005.

[6] "Let Go," Caron Foundation; www.caron.org.

## CHAPTER 24

[1] The Twelve Steps of Alcoholics Anonymous, Alcoholics Anonymous, 1985. Reprinted with permission of Alcoholics Anonymous Worldwide Services Inc.

## CHAPTER 25

[1] Joseph A. Califano, Jr., CASA Chairman and President, the National Center on Addiction Alcohol and Substance Abuse at Columbia University. Statement by Joseph A. Califano on CASA Web site available at http://www.casa columbia.org/absolutenm/templates/article.asp?articleid=276&zoneid=1, accessed March 3, 2006.

[2] "Young Children Emulate Parents' Smoking, Drinking Habits," *Archives of Pediatrics & Adolescent Medicine*, September 2005; available at www.jointo-gether.org/sa/news/summaries/print/0,1856,578191,00.html, accessed September 7, 2005.

[3] "More Women Drinking Defensively," Knight-Ridder, September 6, 2005; available at www.jointogether.org/sa/news/summaries/reader/0%2C1854%2C578195%2C00.html, accessed September 8, 2005.

[4] "What You CAN Do to Stay Safe at a Party," adapted from Alcohol and Other Drugs Teaching Module, ALERT Labs, Alcohol Laboratories for Education, Research, and Training, Grand Valley State University, Nancy L. Harper, Ph.D., August 2004.

[5] "Ways Parents Can Influence Drinking Decisions," adapted from Peter E. Nathan, Ph.D., "Proposed Interventions for Students Before College," University of Iowa, 2005.

## CHAPTER 29

[1] Jeffrey Jensen Arnett, *Emerging Adulthood: The Winding Road from Late Teens through the Twenties* (New York: Oxford University Press, 2004).

[2] Nora D. Volkow, "Exploring the Why's of Adolescent Drug Use," National Institutes of Health (NIH), *Director's Column* 19, no. 3 (September 2004); available at www.nida.nih.gov/NIDA_notes/NNvol19N3/DirRepVol19N3.html.

[3] Substance Abuse and Mental Health Services Administration, "Results from the 2003 National Survey on Drug Use and Health: National Finds," Rockville, Md.: Office of Applied Studies, 2004.

[4] Jim Gogek, "Putting Caps on Teenage Drinking," *New York Times*, August 25, 2004.

[5] Daniel Ari Kapner, "Infofacts Resources: Alcohol and Other Drugs on Campus—The Scope of the Problem"; available at www.edc.org/hec/pubs/factsheets/scope.html, accessed March 15, 2004.

[6] "2004: Little Progress in Reducing Underage Drinking," CAMY, Center on Alcohol Marketing and Youth at Georgetown University, February 28, 2005; available at www.jointogether.org/sa/news/alerts/pring/0,1856,576318,00.html.

[7] Report available at www.oas.samhsa.gov.

[8] Results from the 2004 National Survey on Drug Use and Health: National Findings, SAMHSA, available at http://oas.samhas.gov/nsduh/2k4Results/2k4/Results.htm#toc, accessed January 16, 2006.

[9] L. D. Johnston, P. M. O'Malley, and J. G. Bachman, *Monitoring the Future National Results on Adolescent Drug Use: Overview of Key Findings*, 2002 (Bethesda, MD: National Institute on Drug Abuse, 2003), available at http://camy.org/factsheets/index.php?FactsheetID=17#trends, accessed March 6, 2006.

[10] "New Poll Finds Most Teens Obtain Alcohol from Homes and Adults," American Medical Association, August 11, 2005; available at http://cadca.org/coalitionsonline/article.asp?id=847, accessed August 16, 2005.

[11] Dwayne Proctor, "The Time to Purge Binge Drinking Is Now," the Robert Wood Johnson Foundation, December 19, 2004; available at www.jointogether.org/sa/news/features/reader/0%2C1854%2C575352%2C00.html.

[12] Wright & Wright, 1989. J. Vincent Peterson, Bernard Nisenholz, and Gary Robinson, *A Nation Under the Influence: America's Addiction to Alcohol* (Pearson Education, 2003), p. 17.

[13] D. Levy, T. Miller, and K. Cox, "Reducing Underage Drinking: A Collective Responsibility," in *Costs of Underage Drinking* (Calverton, Md.: Pacific Institute for Research and Evaluation for the Office of Juvenile Justice and Delinquency Prevention, 1999).

[14] "21 Reasons for Teens to Avoid Alcohol," compiled by Nancy L. Harper Ph.D., Director of Alcohol Education, Research, and Training, Grand Valley State University, August 29, 2005.
(http://www.samhsa.gov/oas/2k3/AlcQF/AlcQF.htm)
(www.ama-assn.org/ama/pub/category/9416.html##)
(*Alcoholism: Experimental and Clinical Research*, June 2005; also: www.ama-assn.org/ama/pub/category/9416.html##).
(Adult Antisocial Syndromes Common Among Substance Abusers, http://Scipolicy.net)
(www.ama-assn.org/ama/pub/category/9416.html##).
(Adult Antisocial Syndromes Common Among Substance Abusers, http://Scipolicy.net)
*Alcoholism: Clinical and Experimental Research,* September 2004.
(*Alcoholism: Clinical & Experimental Research*, October 2003).
(www.oas.samhsa.gov.)
(*Alcoholism: Clinical & Experimental Research*, September 2003).
(http://www.jointogether.org/sa/news/summaries/reader/0,1854,555373,00.html).
*Human Molecular Genetics*, September 4, 2004.
(www.samsha.gov.)
(www.4woman.gov target =_new)
(*Journal of Studies on Alcohol*, January 2004).
(NSDUH report, http://www.DrugAbuseStatistics.samhsa.gov).

[15]"Wine Alcohol Content," Healthy Living with Carol Williams, updated July 21, 2005; available at http://wcpo.com/wcpo/localshows/healthyliving/36bc81d6.html.

[16]"College Students Overestimate Standard Drink Volumes; May Impact Their Reported Alcohol Use," CESAR, Center on Substance Abuse Research at the University of Maryland, July 1, 2005; available at www.jointogether.org/sa/news/summaries/reader/0%2C1854%2C577628%2C00.html.

[17]Steven Reinberg, "Malt Liquor Drinkers Consume More, and More Often," *HealthDay Reporter*, March 14, 2005; available at www.healthfinder.gov/news/newsstory.asp?docID=524475.

## CHAPTER 31

[1] Kate Zernike, "A 21st Birthday Drinking Game Can Be a Deadly Rite of Passage," *New York Times*, March 12, 2005.

[2] T. Trent Gegax, "An End to 'Power Hour,'" *Newsweek*, June 6, 2005, p. 28.

[3] Alcohol Poisoning, adapted from NIAAA; available at www.collegedrinkingprevention.gov/students/risky/alcoholpoisoning.aspx.

[4] List: nineteen people of college age who died of alcohol toxicity in 2004; available at http://lizditz.typepad.com/i_speak_of_dreams/2005/04/2005_alcohol_od.html, accessed October 8, 2005.

[5] B.R.A.D. 21—Be Responsible About Drinking. To educate young adults (high school and college age) and their parents as to the responsible use of alcohol, the effects of alcohol and how to deal with excess use by others; available at www.brad21.org/about_us.html.

[6] The Gordie Foundation; www.thegordiefoundation.org/home/default.asp. The Gordie Foundation is dedicated to the memory of Gordie Bailey, who was an eighteen-year-old freshman at the University of Colorado when he died of alcohol poisoning as a result of a fraternity initiation ceremony for pledges on September 17, 2004. The mission of the Gordie Foundation is to provide today's youth with the skills to navigate the dangers of alcohol, and through education and promotion of self-worth, to prevent alcohol poisoning, binge drinking, and hazing.

[7] The SAM [Student Alcohol Management] Spady Foundation. The mission of the SAM Spady Foundation is to educate all parents and students on the dan-

gers of alcohol, specifically high-risk consumption, and the signs and symptoms of alcohol poisoning; www.samspadyfoundation.org/.

[8] "Colo. State U. Death Details Released," *Daily Vidette*, September 21, 2004; available at www.dailyvidette.org/media/paper420/news/2004/09/21/News/Colo-State.U.Death.Details.Released-724920.shtml, accessed September 9, 2005.

[9] Alcohol Poisoning, adapted from NIAAA.

[10] Family Assessment, *From Binge to Blackout*; www.bingetoblackout.com.

## CHAPTER 35

[1] Raymond Carver, "Gravy," from *All of Us*.

[2] Robert Reynolds, "Beer Industry Needs to Follow Its Own Rules for Advertising"; available at www.jointogether.org/sa/news/features/reader/0%2C1854%2C576473%2C00.html, accessed August 23, 2005.

[3] "Alcohol Banned at USC Football Games," *Los Angeles Times*, September 14, 2005; available at www.jointogether.org/sa/news/summaries/reader/0%2C1854%2C578290%2C00.html, accessed October 15, 2005.

[4] "Bar Sued Over Binge Death," Join Together Online, June 14, 2005; available at www.jointogether.org/sa/news/summaries/reader/0%2C1854%2C577428%2C00.html, accessed August 17, 2005.

[5] Adapted from Peter E. Nathan, Ph.D., "Environmental Interventions to Modify Rates of Binge Drinking" and "Proposed Interventions for Students After Beginning College," University of Iowa, 2005.

## APPENDIX IV

[1] The Michigan Alcohol Screening Test; available at www.ncadd-sfv.org/symptoms/mast_test.html.

# TABLE OF BOX INSETS

# INDEX